ENFORCING the RULE of LAW

Cristián Doña Reveco

Lansing, 14 de Mayo de 2010.

C. DoñaR

PITT LATIN AMERICAN SERIES

George Reid Andrews, General Editor

Catherine M. Conaghan, Associate Editor

ENFORCING the RULE of LAW

Social Accountability in the New Latin American Democracies

Edited by Enrique Peruzzotti and Catalina Smulovitz

UNIVERSITY OF PITTSBURGH PRESS

Published by the University of Pittsburgh Press, Pittsburgh PA 15260

Manufactured in the United States of America
Printed on acid-free paper
10 9 8 7 6 5 4 3 2 1

Library of Congress Cataloging-in-Publication Data

Enforcing the rule of law : social accountability in the new Latin American democracies / edited by Enrique Peruzzotti and Catalina Smulovitz.
p. cm. — (Pitt Latin American series)
Includes bibliographical references and index.
ISBN 0-8229-5896-1 (pbk. : alk. paper)
1. Public administration—Latin America. 2. Rule of law—Latin America. 3. Government liability—Latin America. 4. Latin America—Politics and government—1980- 5. Democratization—Latin America. 6. Civil society—Latin America. 7. Political culture—Latin America. I. Peruzzotti, Enrique. II. Smulovitz, Catalina. III. Series.
JL960.E54 2006
320.6098—dc22
2005028747

CONTENTS

Part Two: Watchdog Journalism and Social Accountability

Part Three: Some Theoretical Issues

TABLES AND FIGURES

Tables

Figures

ACKNOWLEDGMENTS

Books have their own history, many parents, and sometimes enthusiastic mentors. Here we want to acknowledge and thank ours for their support and suggestions.

An ambivalent diagnosis about the state of the Latin American democracies motivated our initial questions. A political scenario in which institutional deficits made the exercise of accountability difficult coexisted with social movements and actors that demanded and monitored the lawfulness of governmental actions. Our concerns led to a conference and to a research project about the way in which the accountability of political authorities is being exercised in the region. The Tinker Foundation, and in particular Nancy Truitt, supported the conference, which allowed us to gather the expertise of the contributors to this book. The conference took place in Buenos Aires in May 2000, and as the chapters of this book show, our discussions there were lively and enriching. We want to thank the contributors for their insights and suggestions.

The Ford Foundation funded the research project that helped identify the questions and cases discussed at the conference. Its continuing support has enabled us to complete this volume and to pursue further research on this subject. In particular, we would like to thank Augusto Varas, who enthusiastically supported the project from its outset. At different stages of our research, Guillermo O'Donnell's and Adam Przeworski's comments and suggestions forced us to review and refine our concepts and arguments. We would also like to thank Alberto Fohrig, Osvaldo Iazzetta, Marcelo Leiras, Ana Maria Mustapic, and Hugo Quiroga for their continuous support and their valuable contributions at different stages of the project. Finally, we want to thank our colleagues at the Universidad Torcuato Di Tella in Buenos Aires, in particular José María Ghio, Natalio Botana, and Gerárdo Della Paolera, whose support greatly contributed to the success of this work.

ABBREVIATIONS

ABA	Asociación de Bancos de la Argentina (Argentine Association of Banks—Argentina)
ABAPPRA	Asociación de Bancos Públicos y Privados de la República Argentina (Argentine Association of Public and Private Banks—Argentina)
AFIP	Administración Federal de Ingresos Públicos (Federal Administration of Public Revenues—Argentina)
AMIA	Asociación Mutual Israelita de Argentina (Argentine Jewish Mutual Association—Argentina)
AMUPE	Associação Municipalista de Pernambuco (Association of Counties of Pernambuco—Brazil)
ARGRA	Asociación de Reporteros Gráficos de la República Argentina (Argentine Association of Photographers—Argentina)
ATE	Asociación de Trabajadores del Estado (State Workers' Association—Argentina)
BBVA	Banco Bilbao Vizcaya Argentaria
BCRA	Banco Central de la República Argentina (Central Bank of the Argentine Republic—Argentina)
CAJ	Comisión Andina de Juristas (Andean Commission of Jurists—Peru)
CAJ	Corporación de Asistencia Judicial (Corporation of Legal Assistance—Chile)
CAUSA	Comisión Argentina en USA (Argentine Commission in the United States—Argentina)
CCHR	Chilean Commission for Human Rights (Chile)
CED	Centro de Estudios para el Desarrollo (Center for Development Studies—Chile)
CEJIL	Center for Justice and International Law (Chile)
CELS	Centro de Estudios Legales y Sociales (Center for Legal and Social Studies—Argentina)

CENCOS	Centro Nacional de Comunicación Social (National Center for Social Communication—Mexico)
CENDHEC	Centro dom Hélder Câmara de Estudos e Acao Social (Dom Hélder Câmara Center for Social Study and Action—Brazil)
CLAD	Centro Latinoamericano de Administración para el Desarrollo (Latin American Center for Development Administration)
CODEJU	Comisión pre Derechos Juveniles (National Commission for the Rights of Young People—Chile)
CODEPU	Comité de Defensa de los Derechos del Pueblo (Committee for the Defense of the Rights of the People—Chile)
CONAMP	Associação Nacional dos Membros do Ministério Público (National Confederation of the Public Prosecution—Brazil)
CORREPI	Coordinadora contra la Represión Policial e Institucional (National Coordinator against Police and Institutional Repression—Argentina)
CPI	Comissão Parlamentar de Inquérito (Parliamentary Commission of Inquiry—Brazil)
CRS	Catholic Relief Services
CTERA	Confederación de Trabajadores de la Educación de la República Argentina (Confederation of Education Workers of the Republic of Argentina—Argentina)
EZLN	Ejército Zapatista de Liberación Nacional (Zapatista Army of National Liberation—Mexico)
FASIC	Fundación de Ayuda Social de Iglesias Cristianas (Social Help Foundation of the Christian Churches—Chile)
FETAPE	Federação dos Trabalhadores da Agricultura do Estado de Pernambuco (Federation of Agricultural Workers of Pernambuco—Brazil)
FLACSO	Facultad Latinoamericana de Ciencias Sociales (Latin American Faculty of the Social Sciences)
FORJA	Formación Jurídica para la Acción (Legal Training for Action—Chile)
FOSIS	Fondo de Solidaridade Inversión Social (Chile in Solidarity System)

FOSMO	Frente Opositor al Servicio Militar Obligatorio (Front of Opposition to the Compulsory Military Service—Argentina)
FUNAS	Fundación Acción Social (Foundation for Social Action—Chile)
FUNDEPUBLICO	Fundación para la Defensa del Interés Público (Foundation for the Defense of the Public Interest—Colombia)
GAJOP	Gabinete de Assessoria Jurídica às Organizações Populares (Legal Assistance Office for Popular Organizations—Brazil)
IDB	Inter-American Development Bank
IDELE	Instituto de Defensa Legal (Institute for Legal Defense—Peru)
IFE	Instituto Federal Electoral (Federal Electoral Institute—Mexico)
IMF	International Monetary Fund
INE	Instituto Nacional de Estadísticas (National Institute of Statistics—Chile)
INJ	Instituto Nacional de la Juventud (National Institute of Youth—Chile)
MID	Movimiento de Integración y Desarrollo (Integration and Development Movement—Argentina)
MNDH	Movimento Nacional de Direitos Humanos (National Movement for Human Rights—Brazil)
MP	Ministerio Público (Public Ministry)
MST	Movimento dos Sem-Terra (People without Land Movement—Brazil)
MST	Movimento dos Sem-Teto (People without Living Spaces Movement—Brazil)
ODEP	Organización de Defensa Popular (Organization for the Defense of the People—Chile)
OECD	Organization for Economic Cooperation and Development
PAMI	Plan de Asistencia Médica Integral (Comprehensive Medical Assistance Plan—Argentina)
PAN	Partido de Acción Nacional (National Action Party—Mexico)
PFL	Partido da Frente Liberal (Party of the Liberal Front—Brazil)
PMDB	Partido do Movimento Democrático Brasileiro (Brazilian Democratic Movement Party—Brazil)

PRD	Partido de la Revolución Democrática (Party of Democratic Revolution—Mexico)
PRI	Partido Revolucionario Institucional (Institutional Revolutionary Party—Mexico)
PRONASOL	Programa Nacional de Solidaridad (National Solidarity Program—Mexico)
PROVITA	Programa de Apoio e Proteção e Testemunhas, Vítimas e Familiares de Vítimas de Violencia (Support and Protection Program for Witnesses, Victims, and Relatives of Victims of Violence—Brazil)
PSDB	Partido da Social Democracia Brasileira (Social Democracy Party—Brazil)
PT	Partido dos Trabalhadores (Workers' Party—Brazil)
RMALC	Red Mexicana de Acción Frente al Libre Comercio (Mexican Network of Action against NAFTA—Mexico)
SCH	Santander Central Hispano
SERPAJ	Servicio de Paz y Justicia (Service for Peace and Justice—Chile)
SIAL	Sistema de Acompanhamento Legislativo (System of Legislative Accompaniment—Brazil)
SIDE	Secretaría de Inteligencia del Estadio (State Intelligence Agency—Argentina)
SIGEN	Sindicatura General de la Nación (General Syndicate of the Nation—Argentina)
SLA	System of Legislative Accompaniment
TCU	Tribunal de Contas da União (Union's Court of Accounts—Brazil)
UEJN	Unión de Empleados de la Justicia de la Nación (National Union of Judicial Employees—Argentina)
UTPBA	Unión de Trabajadores de Prensa de Buenos Aires (Buenos Aires Press Workers' Union—Argentina)

PART ONE

Civil Society and the Control of Political Power

1

Social Accountability

AN INTRODUCTION

Enrique Peruzzotti and Catalina Smulovitz

A SOMBER DIAGNOSIS has predominated in recent debates about and evaluations of the nature and quality of democracy in Latin America. Most authors seem to agree that the democratic regimes established in the last democratizing wave present serious institutional deficits, particularly in relation to the development of adequate and effective mechanisms of accountability. Most administrations, they argue, can effectively avoid the usual constraints posed by the various mechanisms of control of governmental decisions. Undoubtedly, these arguments call attention to the persistence of political practices and institutional deficits that prevent the consolidation of strong and accountable democratic institutions. However, the political stage has also been occupied by an array of social movements and a network of nongovernmental organizations (NGOs) demanding and monitoring the lawfulness of state actions, as well as by the outbreak of media scandals exposing numerous cases of corruption. This last phenomenon represents an innovative form of politicization in the region. The concept of social accountability places this disparate group of civil society– and media-based initiatives under a common analytical framework. Such politics, carried out by a diverse group of actors and through multiple strategies, constitutes an alternative mechanism for the exercise of accountability regarding governmental actions.

In spite of the scope of these phenomena, recent evaluations of the institutional performance of Latin American democracies have belittled the significance of social mechanisms of accountability. Current debates on the nature of existing regimes tend to view the weakness of traditional mechanisms of accountability as their defining characteristic. The absence of an effective intrastate system of checks and balances, the lack of truly autonomous judicial institutions, and the existence of corruption at different levels of the public administration are frequently cited as evidence of such weakness. There is no doubt that these are powerful indicators of the institutional deficits currently confronted by Latin American democracies. Yet by focusing on traditional mechanisms of accountability—elections, the separation of powers, and the existence of a system of checks and balances among the various branches of government—those analyses ignore the growth of alternative forms of political control that rely on citizens' actions and media organizations. Moreover, these alternative mechanisms address some of the intrinsic limitations of elections as tools of political accountability, and they are crucial in activating an often reluctant network of intrastate agencies of control.

Although the literature on democracy has been haunted by a basic suspicion of the relevance of autonomous civil society in molding the nature of the democratic relationship, traditional understandings of accountability, concerned mostly with the availability and nature of institutional tools for control, have largely ignored the contribution of civil society to the exercise of control.[1] The concept of social accountability attempts to specify how such relationships work and what specific consequences they may have in fostering more accountable governments. The introduction of the concept aims to highlight the relevance of an analytical space that has been largely ignored by debates on accountability, shedding new light on the complex relationships between social actors and politics. It must be emphasized, however, that acknowledgment of the role of civil society in the exercise of accountability says nothing about the ideological orientation of actions. Recognition of the role played by civil society only admits the existence of an empirical phenomenon that needs to be analyzed in order to understand the workings of present-day democracies. Its empirical and normative consequences are open to further empirical study and theoretical debate—study and debate that this book is intended to promote.

Legal and Political Forms of Accountability

One of the elements that distinguishes liberal representative democracies from other types of regimes is their combination of an institutional framework of authorization of political power with a framework oriented to ensure the responsiveness and accountability of authorized agents. Insofar as representative democracy implies the existence of a fundamental gap between political representatives and citizens, it requires the existence of institutional mechanisms to guarantee that such separation does not result in unresponsive or illegal governments. The central question addressed by the concept of accountability is precisely how to regulate and reduce the gap between representatives and the represented while simultaneously preserving the differentiation between political authorities and the citizenry that characterizes the relations of representation.

Accountability refers to the ability to ensure that public officials are answerable for their behavior—forced to justify and inform the citizenry about their decisions and possibly eventually be sanctioned for them.[2] The accountability of political power can be established on legal or political grounds. The notion of legal accountability refers to a set of institutional mechanisms aimed at ensuring that the actions of public officials are legally and constitutionally framed.[3] As James G. March and Johan P. Olsen argue, this form of accountability is guided by a logic of appropriateness: political actors are judged according to what is considered proper procedure.[4] Through separation of powers, the recognition of fundamental rights, and a system of checks and balances, modern constitutionalism establishes the institutions that enable it to curb the arbitrariness of state power. The constitutionalization of state institutions by public law parcels state power into judicial, legislative, and executive branches and delimits state activity into rigorously circumscribed competencies.[5] In addition, fundamental rights provide institutional safeguards against unlawful encroachments by state officials against citizens.

Constitutional norms, legal codes, administrative procedures, and fundamental rights provide a legal-constitutional frame that constrains the actions of elected and nonelected public officials. As Wolfgang Schluchter argues, modern constitutionalism establishes an institutional setting characterized by "regulated discretion within the sphere of abstract norms." In such a setting, public officials move within a defined realm of competencies and jurisdictions: between the legal norm and a particular decision, there is a limited realm of political discretion.[6] In sum, to hold a government legally accountable implies the ability to control governmental actions, to be certain that they do not infringe on the law or due process. For mechanisms of legal accountability to function effectively, a legal system capable of enforcing the law and making rulers obey it must exist. Without such a prerequisite, there cannot be enforcement of legal accountability.[7]

The concept of political accountability refers to the responsiveness of governmental policies to the preferences of the electorate. Political accountability is intimately intertwined with the concept of democratic representation. A government is politically accountable if citizens have the means to punish unresponsive or irresponsible administrations. It is usually assumed that elections are the central institution for this type of control.[8] They provide a regular mechanism for citizens to hold governments responsible for their actions, forcing out of office those incumbents who did not act in the best interests of voters and reelecting those who did.[9]

Citizens in representative democracies thus face an important challenge. Once they have delegated the task of governing to elected representatives, they need to ensure that their representatives' actions result in representative and legal governmental actions. Representative governments are both politically and legally accountable if citizens have the ability to make public officials answerable for their behavior, forcing them to justify their decisions and make them public, and if citizens can eventually sanction officials for their decisions or for unlawful acts.[10] How this is achieved, however, has proven to be problematic.

The literature on representation and accountability shows that since it is unclear what good representatives should do, it is uncertain what citizens need to control what they do and how they do it. Should citizens punish those representatives who, when acting in the best interests of others, promote policies that differ from those originally wanted or signaled by the electorate? Or should citizens punish those representatives whose actions, in respect for the signaled preferences of the electorate, lead to disastrous social outcomes? In other words, when "responsiveness" and "responsibility" are in conflict, how do citizens evaluate what is good representation, and how do they make representatives politically accountable?[11]

Other analyses have questioned the efficacy of the most privileged instrument of political control, thus casting doubt on the role of elections as mechanisms of accountability.[12] For authors such as Adam Przeworski, Susan Stokes, and Bernard Manin, electoral institutions have intrinsic limitations that make them inadequate as a mechanism for holding representatives accountable.

Elections, they argue, are ineffective as mechanisms of accountability, and consequently voters cannot induce governments to act responsibly. What factors prevent the efficacy of the vote as a mechanism of control? Przeworski, Stokes, and Manin provide three arguments. First, the nature of the vote is intrinsically limited, granting citizens only one chance to punish or reward numerous governmental decisions. Consequently, voters have very limited power in shaping the outcome of most governmental policies due to the inadequate nature of voting as a mechanism of control. Second, voting is a decentralized strategic action.[13] Since citizens cannot coordinate the orientation of their votes, there is no way of telling if a certain electoral result is prospectively or retrospectively guided. Third, the average citizen experiences a deficit of information that makes it difficult for her or him to adequately evaluate government performance and decisions.

Finally, the literature on legal accountability also shows that citizens face difficulties when they try to subject the actions of public officials to the rule of law. Citizens confront general difficulty when trying to make rulers obey the law. Some authors understand that citizens' problems coordinating the actions that will allow them to punish rulers who disobey the rule of law jeopardize the exercise of legal accountability.[14] Other authors stress that, in certain institutional contexts, such as those faced by newly established democracies, the main problem for the exercise of legal accountability rests on the absence of an independent judicial institution with the ability to enforce the law and make rulers obey it.[15]

In brief, the exercise of political and legal accountability faces two types of problems, the first intrinsic to the imperfect nature of the relationship of representation and the second deriving from the absence of certain institutional preconditions necessary for the effective functioning of controlling agencies. Both problems have generated a lively intellectual debate in Latin America. The institutional quality and performance of the newly established democracies has been a central axis of academic discussion and research, generating contrasting evaluations and interpretations of the quality and efficacy of accountability mechanisms in the region.

Democracy and Accountability in Latin America

Przeworski argues that the problem of accountability in Latin America does not differ from the problems of accountability faced by any democratic government. The difficulties confronted in the region, in his view, are generic to democracy rather than the product of local and idiosyncratic characteristics. A brief review of the literature, however, shows widespread consensus regarding the lack of governmental accountability in most of the region.[16]

Guillermo O'Donnell, for example, argues that Latin American polyarchies display a notorious deficit of legal accountability, to the extent that he questions the representative nature of these regimes. In his view, many existing Latin American regimes are not representative but rather *delegative* democracies.[17] In delegative democracies, the process of the electoral authorization of representatives (which O'Donnell terms *vertical electoral accountability*) is not complemented by an effective system of intrastate agencies "that are legally enabled and empowered" to check and sanction unlawful actions by state agencies or political representatives (*horizontal accountability*). Elections authorize representatives—the president, in the case of delegative democracies —yet there is no network of agencies capable of controlling the actions of the executive. Popularly elected presidents, O'Donnell argues, rule free of constitutional or legal constraints. Although power is formally divided by the separation of powers and there is a formal system of checks and balances, the operation of these countervailing mechanisms is blocked by an executive who perceives him- or herself as the embodiment of democracy and the nation and views horizontal mechanisms as obstacles to executive actions.

For Matthew Soberg Shuggart, Erika Moreno, and Brian F. Crisp, the apparent dearth of "horizontal accountability" in Latin America is a result of "the malfunctioning of vertical accountability." Following Madison, they assert that the checks and balances characteristic of horizontal accountability rest on the "principle of countervailing ambitions." Thus, unless different interests and opinions are properly represented in horizontal agencies—that is, unless the institutional design that translates vertical relationships between voters and legislators is the right one—horizontal accountability will not follow. In their view, Latin American horizontal accountability fails because vertical accountability, due to the nature of Latin American electoral institutions, fails. They call for reform of those aspects of the electoral process—the candidate selection process, the election of legislators, and the appointment of "autonomous agencies"—that in their opinion jeopardize the proper exercise of vertical accountability.[18]

Finally, as the large body of literature on political clientelism, vote buying, and electoral fraud shows, many of the region's democracies present areas where the free exercise of political rights is jeopardized by authoritarian actors who tamper with and manipulate electoral institutions.[19] Far from providing an effective mechanism of vertical accountability, elections in these areas contribute to the reproduction of authoritarian political structures.

In sum, there is generalized agreement that in Latin America, for generic or idiosyncratic reasons, both horizontal and vertical electoral mechanisms are weak. Some authors concentrate on specific cultural and institutional variables that conspire against the existence of accountable governments. It follows that if these obstacles are removed, more representative and accountable governments could be expected in the region. Other authors propose arguments of a different nature, highlighting the notion that deficits of accountability in Latin America are insolvable, deriving from the operative structure of the vertical mechanisms, which characterizes all democracies. The concept of social accountability addresses both kinds of arguments, drawing attention to the emergence of an alternative mechanism for rendering accountability that analyses of the last democratizing wave in Latin America tend to overlook.

Social Accountability as a Form of Control

O'Donnell's classification of accountability mechanisms as either horizontal or vertical follows a spatial metaphor. The words *horizontal* and *vertical* indicate the axis of operation of the controlling agencies. The concept of horizontal accountability thus refers to the operation of an intrastate system of controls, while the notion of vertical mechanisms implies the existence of external checks. Such a classification stresses the directionality of the system of control, as well as the arena(s) where exchanges take place. In the case of horizontal accountability, exchanges take place among a network of interacting state agencies that check and balance each other.[20] Vertical accountability instead implies the existence of an external social agent of control: mainly the electorate.[21] Elections represent a society-anchored agency of control, granting citizens the right to periodically punish or reward elected representatives with their vote.

Pursuing O'Donnell's metaphor, we would like to draw attention to another type of vertical mechanism that has been largely overlooked by current debates on accountability. Recent debates concerning the effectiveness of vertical mechanisms have focused exclusively on elections. While elections are the sole means for authorizing political representation, they do not represent the only vertical tool for holding politicians accountable. Elections need to be complemented by an active civil society and autonomous media institutions. The concept of social accountability thus aims to incorporate insights from the literature on civil society and the public sphere into the analysis of accountability.[22] The workings of civic associations, NGOs, social movements, and media organizations not only add new resources to the classic repertoire of electoral and constitutional institutions for controlling government but can also, on occasion, compensate for many of the built-in deficits of these mechanisms.

Social accountability is a nonelectoral yet vertical mechanism of control of political authorities that rests on the actions of an array of citizens' associations and movements and the media. The actions of these groups monitor public officials, expose governmental wrongdoing, and can activate the operation of horizontal agencies. Social accountability employs both institutional and noninstitutional tools. The activation of legal actions or claims before oversight agencies is an example of an institutionally channeled action; social mobilizations and media exposés are examples of noninstitutional ones.

Social accountability operates neither through the electoral aggregation of votes nor as part of an intrastate system of checks and balances. Rather, social accountability relies on interested, organized sectors of civil society and media institutions that are able to exert influence on the political system and public bureaucracies. The monitoring activities of many NGOs and the workings of a wide array of social movements, civic associations, and media organizations organized around demands for legality and due process expand the classic repertoire of electoral and constitutional institutions for controlling government and on many occasions might serve to improve and complement them or to compensate for many of their built-in limitations.

Unlike electoral mechanisms, social accountability can be exercised between elections and does not depend upon fixed calendars. It is activated "on demand" and can be directed toward the control of single issues, policies, or functionaries.[23] Like horizontal mechanisms, social ones can oversee the procedures followed by politicians and public officials while making policy.

Vertical, horizontal, and social accountability mechanisms also differ in the way they impose sanctions. The specific arena in which each of these mechanisms operates determines the resources available for their exercise of control. Unlike those exercising electoral and horizontal controls, actors using social mechanisms can perform watchdog functions without the need for special majorities or constitutional entitlements. Indeed, while actors operating in the electoral environment need to maximize the *extension* of their support in order to control the policies of representative bodies, those operating in the social environment can rely on the *intensity* of their claims and/or their impact on public opinion. Social mechanisms also differ from horizontal and vertical (electoral) mechanisms insofar as the sanctions they entail are, in most cases, not formal but symbolic.

The Aim of Social Control

What can be controlled? The mechanisms of social accountability are oriented toward making governments legally accountable. They entail a diverse group of civil society initiatives and media exposés organized around demands for the rule of law and due process. By exposing and denouncing cases of governmental wrongdoing, activating horizontal agencies of control, and monitoring the operation of those agencies, mechanisms of social accountability make a crucial contribution to the enforcement of the rule of law. Public exposure of issues and wrongdoing not only generates symbolic costs to the officials or agencies suspected of wrongdoing but also, by bringing cases of corruption or official misconduct into the public agenda, forces political institutions to address these cases and raises the actual costs of illegal or improper political behavior.

Given that social mechanisms do not depend on fixed calendars but operate in a decentralized and "piecemeal" way, they can avoid some of the structural problems of electoral mechanisms.[24] Each exercise of social control can have specific goals, and citizens do not need to use one instrument to achieve many purposes simultaneously. Such a piecemeal approach allows citizens to focus their attention on those policies and/or politicians they seek to control. Unlike electoral mechanisms, social ones are not blunt instruments used to evaluate all the actions and actors within an administration. Although they are more demanding in terms of participatory efforts, they allow for selective control, signaling, and the sanctioning of specific actors or behaviors.

Actors

Who are the actors that can exercise controls? Traditionally, the list was limited to individual citizens; political parties with parliamentary representation;

and the legislative, judicial, and executive branches of government. The concept of social accountability, on the other hand, draws attention to the control initiatives exercised by actors such as civic associations, NGOs, social movements, and the media that have been commonly neglected by the literature on accountability.[25] Important changes in civil society and the media have followed the last wave of democratization in Latin America. On the one hand, new civic associations and NGOs have sprouted throughout the region—human rights organizations, civic networks that monitor elections to prevent fraud, social movements against police abuse and violence, and citizens' organizations that demand clearance of public information. On the other hand, the region has witnessed the emergence of a more inquisitive type of journalism that is playing an important watchdog role in relation to public authorities. Both developments are vivid examples of the growth of an innovative type of politics in the region organized around demands for rights and accountability.

One of the forerunners of innovative civil society–based politics is the network of human rights organizations that emerged under authoritarian rule in several countries of the region, including Argentina, Brazil, Chile, Mexico, and Peru. The significance of such social actors for political life is that they inaugurated a new form of rights-oriented politics aimed at drawing clear institutional boundaries between state and civil society and restricting the discretionary use of state power.[26] A major legacy of the politics of human rights was the establishment of a permanent associative network composed of human rights groups, legal aid associations, movements and organizations against police violence, and so on, which plays a crucial watchdog role in the defense of social autonomy.

Human rights organizations are not the only civil society–based initiatives organized around demands for rights and accountability. In recent years, many civic associations, NGOs, and social movements organized around issues of accountability have flourished throughout Latin America. While their agendas have been broad, ranging from environmental issues to consumer rights, four main areas have been tackled by such groups: (1) citizen security, (2) judicial autonomy and access to justice, (3) electoral fraud, and (4) governmental corruption.

Security issues were prominent in the public agenda of the last decade, particularly acts of police violence against disadvantaged groups. Numerous episodes of state violence against sectors of poor and marginal populations have sparked a wave of social mobilizations demanding justice and police reforms. In Argentina and Brazil, a series of unrelated incidents of police violence led to the organization of local social movements and the establishment of permanent society-based monitoring associations. In addition, the death of two army privates serving in the Argentine and Chilean armies, as a result of abuses by their superiors, also generated popular responses and triggered scandals that, in the Argentinean case, led to the end of the military draft. In Peru, the Coordinadora Nacional de Derechos Humanos, a nationwide network of Peruvian human rights organizations, and the National Ombusdman Office repeatedly questioned the practice of the military's compulsory draft in rural areas, generating a broad debate and even a presidential acknowledgment of the need to reform or end the military draft.

Demands for *judicial autonomy* have also ranked high on the agenda of the media and civil society organizations. There are two different types of demands and initiatives: (1) movements organized around cases in which the provision of impartial justice seems to be jeopardized due to the control exerted by political authorities over the judiciary[27] and (2) initiatives by NGOs and civic organizations to reform the judiciary and promote the access of disadvantaged groups to justice. Initiatives of the first type have been advanced mostly by mobilizations of sectors of the population that find themselves in a disadvantaged position as a result of operating in geographical areas where legal guarantees are virtually absent or frequently violated.[28] Generally, these movements are organized around specific cases and a single claim: to a fair trial. In many cases, their efforts concentrate on monitoring police investigations and judicial proceedings to prevent political authorities from tampering with the evidence or influencing the proceedings. Argentina is perhaps the country that offers the most examples of this type of initiative (the María Soledad case, the Nahir case, the Cabezas case, the Carrasco case, etc.). In Peru, the Ombudsman Office (Defensoría del Pueblo) has also played an important role in monitoring and denouncing the actions of the judiciary under Alberto Fujimori.

Initiatives of the second variety have targeted the judiciary and the problem of judicial autonomy. Organizations such as Corporación para la Excelencia de la Justicia, in Colombia, and Poder Ciudadano, in Argentina, have organized campaigns for the legal education of the citizenry and established programs that deal with different aspects of judicial performance and reform. Problems of access to justice have occupied a prominent place on the agendas of many of organizations. In Colombia and Peru, Fundación para la Defensa del Interés Público (FUNDEPUBLICO), Viva la Ciudadanía, the Comisión Andina de Juristas, and the Instituto de Defensa Legal (IDELE) have played an important role in developing new legal instruments to improve defense of the rights of ordinary citizens and their access to justice. The incorporation in recent constitutional reforms of several of these instruments (e.g., Acciones de Tutela, Acción de Cumplimiento, Acción Popular, etc.) has resulted in an increase of legal mobilization. In addition, public interest law is being promoted by several organizations in the region, like Formación Jurídica para la Acción (FORJA) in Chile; FUNDEPUBLICO and Viva la Ciudadanía in Colombia; and Poder Ciudadano, Asociación por los Derechos Civiles, and Clínica Jurídica of the Universidad de Palermo in Argentina.[29]

Electoral observation is the third area in which social initiatives have been concentrated. Civic and media initiatives against electoral fraud have played a crucial democratizing role in Mexico and Peru. In both cases, a network of organizations oriented toward monitoring the electoral process to ensure fair elections has emerged and expanded. In Mexico, Alianza Cívica was formed in 1994 as the result of a coalition of civic groups interested in developing an autonomous network for electoral observation. The contribution of this movement to Mexico's democratization has been remarkable. Its actions have contributed greatly to electoral reform; the 1996 electoral code incorporated most of the demands of the movement and led to the establishment of an impartial electoral authority that made possible fair and competitive elections. In Peru, Foro Democrático and Transparencia were active in denouncing fraud and pushing for change of the electoral laws passed by President Fujimori. Foro Democrático organized a campaign calling for a referendum to block Fujimori's reelection, which, despite collecting two million signatures, was ignored by the legislature. Transparencia was created in 1994 with the goal of monitoring elections and was eventually able to establish a nationwide network of observers.[30]

Finally, the issue of *governmental corruption* has received wide attention from both the media and civil society. On this terrain, the media has played a central role in exposing governmental wrongdoing. The region has been shaken by numerous media scandals targeting governmental corruption at all levels of the public administration, from low-ranking civil servants to the presidential office. Civic initiatives have also been important in developing innovative tools for controlling governments. For instance, some civic organizations have developed programs to monitor the financial assets of public officials (Poder

Ciudadano in Argentina and Alianza Cívica in Mexico). The Colombian constitution established the Veedurías Ciudadanas, ad hoc civic committees to oversee governmental actions and procedures. Perhaps the most famous *veeduría* was the one established to monitor the impeachment of then-president Ernesto Samper on corruption charges. The *veeduría* was highly critical of the works of the parliamentary body in charge of the impeachment procedures and published a detailed document denouncing irregularities.[31] Other *veedurías* have been constituted with the aim of supervising public bids and the process of the privatization of Bogotá's public phone company.

Important developments in the postauthoritarian era brought new conditions for the operation of the media. First, the consolidation of democratic regimes has drastically redefined the environment in which the media operates. The reestablishment of constitutional guarantees and the end of state violence and censorship greatly contributed to the practice of critical reporting. Second, in many countries the media underwent a process of privatization, deregulation, and conglomeration that greatly changed the structure of media industries.[32] Such policies led to a transition from family-controlled media organizations to the emergence of large and diversified multimedia corporations. While media concentration conspires against the democratization of media access, the shift to a market system has nevertheless generated a more independent journalism. The decoupling of media industries from the state opened up the possibility of a critical journalism that has played a central role in exposing official wrongdoing and corruption and has also been an important actor in the politics of social accountability.[33] Many civic claims for equal treatment under the law, due process, or judicial independence began to exert considerable pressure on the political system only after they attained significant media coverage and visibility.

Press exposés have exerted a considerable toll on numerous public officials. In Brazil and Peru, disclosures of corruption brought down the Collor and Fujimori administrations. In Colombia, investigations of contributions made by the Cali cartel to the 1994 electoral campaign seriously weakened Ernesto Samper's presidency. A newspaper investigation of an illegal sale of weapons by the Argentine government to Ecuador during the Ecuador-Peru war led to the house arrest of former president Carlos Saúl Menem. The political crisis generated by the Senate scandal in Argentina severely damaged the governing coalition after Vice-President Carlos Alvarez resigned in disagreement with the way President Fernando de la Rúa handled the situation.

Sanctions

How do social actors sanction what politicians and bureaucrats do? The question is critical insofar as most definitions closely link the notion of accountability with the capacity to enforce decisions. We have already posited that the main resource available for social control is the intensity and visibility of "voice" and that most social controls expose wrongdoings but do not have mandatory effects.[34] For these reasons, some authors have regarded such mechanisms as window-dressing rather than as real checks on power.[35] It is our contention, however, that even when social mechanisms do not have mandatory effects, they can still have "material consequences." On the one hand, they impose reputation costs that may have damaging political consequences. In contexts where political survival rests on the extension of support, public officials cannot easily disregard threats to their reputations. Such threats could make a difference to their survival. On the other hand, in many cases social mechanisms are a necessary condition for the activation of those mechanisms that have "teeth." Social controls activate the operation of other agencies of accountability, such as judiciary or congressional investigative commissions. Indeed, in many cases, unless social mechanisms "turn on the alarm," vertical electoral and horizontal mechanisms do not start to work.[36]

If this is the case, we should ask how social mechanisms impose these sanctions and how they relate to other mechanisms of accountability. First, social mechanisms control by *exposing and denouncing wrongdoings.* Denunciations of specific cases provide vivid illustrations of shortcomings in the performance of horizontal agencies or wrongdoings of political representatives or bureaucratic agents. Exposition and denunciation of wrongdoings allow the identification of real victims and their victimizers, as well as determination of the scope of the damage done. Denunciations signal the existence of issues in a way the citizenry can relate to and, in doing so, place specific issues in a wider context. In signaling a problem, denunciations may produce changes in the social appreciation of a particular phenomenon, transforming it into an issue on the more general public agenda.[37]

When signaled problems become new issues on the public agenda, the number and scope of the topics under surveillance increase. Therefore, signaling and exposing behavior may have two different results. On the one hand, exposure can lead to the control of specific issues or claims. On the other hand, when the signaling and exposing of specific problems transform them into topics on the public agenda, the number of issues under surveillance increases. Indeed, by expanding the number of issues included on the public agenda, the signaling effect shows another way in which social mechanisms work. When signaling a problem results in the incorporation of a new topic on the public agenda, it enlarges the number of questions for which public officials can be held responsible and must answer. Therefore, social mechanisms also contribute to the exercise of horizontal and vertical controls, insofar as they may result in the extension of the scope of conflicts and issues public officials are obliged to inform the citizenry about.[38]

Second, social mechanisms control because they can *activate the operation of horizontal mechanisms.* The activation of horizontal mechanisms may result (1) when a social movement organizes and mobilizes around a particular demand or claim; (2) when the media gives coverage to actions or claims of a particular movement or when it develops its own investigation in regard to an issue;[39] or (3) when individuals or associations activate regular local judicial proceedings, international ones, or oversight agencies. These actions may result in the activation of horizontal and vertical mechanisms because they involve an increase in the reputation costs confronted by public officials and the threat of being taken to court.[40]

In democratic contexts, where the political life of elected officials depends on getting the greatest number of votes, the reputation costs that may result from these actions can become a dangerous threat to survival.[41] Therefore, it can be expected that elected officials will be willing to exchange the appeasement of negative reputation costs for the activation of control mechanisms or that they will avoid the commission of acts if the anticipated costs of disregarding social demands is considered high. This dynamic highlights, in turn, the fact that to assess the relationship among social, vertical, and horizontal mechanisms we need to understand how and when reputation costs achieve a threat level capable of activating the other mechanisms.

Social mechanisms can activate horizontal and vertical ones indirectly or directly. They indirectly activate them when they produce reputation costs, through social mobilization or media denunciation. In these cases, the efficiency of social mechanisms is mediated by public officials' evaluation of the anticipated costs of denunciation and by the assessment the electorate makes of specific denunciations. Therefore, although denunciation may be effective, it is not certain that public officials will necessarily evaluate the risks faced in a unique fashion or that they will act accordingly. Neither is there a guarantee that the electorate will consider denunciations when casting its vote. If public officials become convinced of the harmful effects of reputation costs, social mobilization, or press denunciations, they may attempt to minimize them by taking or reversing decisions to appear responsive to the public. Such decisions could entail the activation of judicial procedures, parliamentary investigative commissions, or policy changes.[42]

Indirect activation of horizontal mechanisms is possible because claimants organize and mobilize but also because they reach the media or the media reaches them. Regardless of the media's reasons for covering some of these events, one consequence of this new media role has been its simultaneous conversion into public prosecutor and judge.[43] Thus, once the media was revealed as an effective mechanism for controlling and accelerating public decisions, civil society organizations used this discovery to gain access to an alternative route to justice, to get attention from the public authorities, and to informally judge presumed illegal activities.[44] In some countries, this new press role has led to the emergence of a strong and sometimes threatening investigative journalism.

Social mechanisms can also result in the activation of horizontal ones without this type of mediation, when, for example, individual or social legal mobilization activates judicial proceedings or oversight agencies.[45] Since state authorities must respond to legal petitions, successful legal petitions advanced by individuals or associations allow the use of the state coactive powers to pursue desired interests. For these reasons, some authors have argued that legal mobilization can be considered the paradigmatic form of democratic participation.[46] Insofar as legal demands force the state to publicly and officially reply to advanced legal petitions, legal mobilization (individually or collectively engineered) could lead to the activation of horizontal mechanisms of control. It is worth noting that legal mobilization is the only form of social accountability that may end up having mandatory effects.

Before considering a third way in which social accountability produces control, one caveat: we have shown that social mechanisms can give visibility to and articulate the demands of actors who might be disregarded in the representative arena. While electoral mechanisms (and some horizontal mechanisms) can only be activated and justified on majoritarian grounds, social mechanisms derive their legitimacy from the right of citizens to petition for the enforcement of the rule of law, a right that does not require the demand to be widespread.[47] In both cases, electoral and social, "voice" is the mechanism available for control.[48] For electoral mechanisms to be effective, many people must voice the same claim; if they do, the effects can be mandatory. In the social arena, on the other hand, although the "voice" needs to be strong and intense, it does not need to be extensively represented. Presence rather than extension justifies the demands.

If those actors excluded from the representative arena are capable of making sufficient "noise" and are able to place issues on the agenda, it is possible that social mechanisms may force representative ones to consider topics that majoritarian requirements would convert into "nonissues."[49] However, since social mechanisms do not necessarily legitimize themselves on representative grounds, this may have ambiguous social consequences in terms of equal representation. This reveals one of the drawbacks of this type of control: the preferences of a loud and persistent minority may end up being "overrepresented."

Finally, social mechanisms control insofar as they sometimes result in the *establishment of parallel "social watchdog" organizations* that monitor the performance of specific public agents or offices. Experience provides examples of cases in which some particular issue has become the object of recurrent denunciations, resulting in the establishment of civic associations designed to continuously oversee the behavior of certain public officials in specific policy arenas. The institutionalization of some of these denunciation movements into more permanent organizations has resulted, in some cases, in the establishment of a parallel society-based structure of oversight actors.[50] Indeed, some of these social watchdogs have become guardians of the guardians attempting to enhance the performance of horizontal controls.

The Strategies of Social Accountability in Latin America

The exercise of social accountability in Latin America is taking place in three main areas: through the judiciary, through mobilization, and through the media. Although the strategies employed in these areas usually interact and feed each other, they can be distinguished by the main resources employed in demanding accountability.

Judicialization

The juridical or legal strategy entails submission by individuals or social actors of legal claims or legally framed petitions to the courts or other control agencies. This strategy has become an instrument that individual citizens and social actors use to force the state to intervene in political and social disputes public officials want to avoid or ignore.[51]

The transformation of social demands into legal claims serves two purposes: (1) it provides a legitimacy "seal" for the petitions, and (2) it forces the state to take a stand on the advanced claims. Civil society's use of the juridical strategy is part of the broader process of the judicialization of politics that is taking place globally.[52] This process is characterized by an increase in the number of regular legal claims, the appearance of new legal institutions that expand the ways citizens may petition for rights, and a greater number of actors authorized to make claims. Latin America has participated in all these developments.

In recent decades several countries in the region have experienced a sharp increase in litigiousness, encouraged by two distinctive forms of judicialization: on the one hand, litigation through regular judicial procedures and, on the other , petitions that use recently created institutional tools and those oriented toward recently established control agencies. Examples of the first type can be found in Argentina, Brazil, and to a lesser extent Chile.[53] The discovery of the courts is the result of the new place judicial institutions have started to occupy since the democratic transition. The revalorization of these institutions has placed them on the center stage of public life. The expansion of the use of traditional legal resources, however, is not necessarily linked to their effectiveness. It is worth mentioning that growth in legal petitioning parallels growth in skepticism about the performance of the judicial power. Therefore, it is possible to speculate that the increased use might be associated with the expressive needs of the actors involved rather than with a pragmatic search for solutions.

The last wave of constitutional reforms, which introduced many new institutional tools for demanding citizen rights, gave rise to the second form of judicialization. For example, the 1991 Colombian constitution established several institutional mechanisms for the protection of rights and for citizen participation. One of them, the so-called *acción de tutela,* allows any citizen to demand the immediate protection of fundamental rights in any court and without mandatory legal assistance. A study conducted by the Secretaría General del Consejo Superior de la Judicatura shows that between 1991 and 1999, the Colombian courts sent 213,404 *acciónes de tutela* to the constitutional courts.[54] In Brazil, two different institutions demonstrate the existence of a similar trend.

On the one hand, the inclusion in the 1988 constitution of the Açao Direta de Inconstitucionalidade expanded the number of actors authorized to initiate constitutional controls of rights.[55] A recent study by Luiz Werneck Vianna and others shows that the majority of the 1935 Açao Direta de Inconstitucionalidade presented between 1988 and 1998 were interposed by civil society organizations, public prosecutors, and left-wing parties.[56] On the other hand, as Rosangela Batista Calvancanti shows, the expansion of the responsibilities of the Public Prosecution Office has resulted in the emergence of an institution that, with regional variations, is acting as an agent of control and oversight of citizen rights and governmental actions. Its records show that at least 195 mayors and ex-mayors have been convicted for illegal acts while in office.

The creation of ombudsman offices has also contributed to the increase in the judicial oversight of rights and of administrative actions. In the last decade, national, regional, provincial, and municipal ombudsman offices have been created in Argentina, Bolivia, Brazil, Colombia, Costa Rica, Ecuador, El Salvador, Guatemala, Honduras, Mexico, Panama, Peru, and Venezuela. Official reports of the workings of these agencies in Argentina and Peru show a continous increase in the number of claims made by citizens. While 104,225 claims related to the actions of public administrators and agencies were presented in Argentina between 1994 and 1999, the Defensoría del Pueblo in Peru received 97,594 claims between 1996 and 2000.[57] Regardless of the actual achievements of all these new institutions, their proliferation and the increased use of petition mechanisms show the availabilty of new and alternative institutional tools for the exercise of control. Although their effectiveness still needs to be systematically studied, their recent explosion and potential control capacities cannot be ignored.

Another phenomenon that has fostered the significance of the legal strategy as a control mechanism has been the development of the "public interest law movement": a network of NGOs with a shared commitment to using the law to advance the protection of civil and human rights, as well as other social, cultural, and economic rights.[58] NGOs like FUNDEPUBLICO in Colombia; CELS (Centro de Estudios Legales y Sociales), Poder Ciudadano, and the Asociación por los Derechos Civiles in Argentina; IDELE and the Comisión Andina de Juristas in Peru; and FORJA and the Law School of the Universidad Diego Portales in Chile are prominent members of this network. Although their efforts cover a wide variety of topics, some have had a significant impact on controlling governmental actions. They attempt to control by filing actions demanding that governments or bureaucracies realize granted rights, taking advantage, in turn, of newly introduced constitutional reforms. They have focused, for example, on demanding that the police comply with their obligation to provide information about detained people (CELS); demanding that the Argentine national government make available a vaccine that, due to the fiscal crisis, it had discontinued, violating its obligation to protect the health rights of the population (CELS—Universidad de Palermo); demanding that the Colombian government take responsibility for the collective injury resulting from governmental corruption (FUNDEPUBLICO); and reprimanding privatized telephone companies for failing to follow required procedures in deciding to raise their rates.

Social Mobilization

Social mobilization is the second strategy employed in the exercise of social accountability. In this case, control is achieved when organized social actors are able to call attention to a particular problem or claims related to a perceived public wrongdoing. Traditionally, the study of social movements has concentrated on the impact that social mobilization may have on the satisfaction or defense of material needs or on the achievement of particular goals. Here, we concentrate on the use of social mobilization as a tool to demand legal accountability. This specific use is linked with the emergence of new forms of associative life in the region. One novelty of the last democratizing wave was the emergence of civil society organizations that demand due process and proper procedures. Their appearance implies a significant change in a political and social scenario that used to be mainly characterized by distributional conflicts and demands. Now public officials also have to deal with uncoordinated actors who demand not only public reasons for officials' actions but also that public acts follow proper procedures.

For social mobilization to be successful, a problem must become visible, must mobilize and aggregate public opinion, and must threaten or impose reputation costs to public agents who value and need to protect their reputations. If these factors coincide, that is, if the mobilization strategy calls attention to specific wrongdoings, aggregates important sectors of the population, and raises reputation costs, then other sanctioning mechanisms might be activated. The efficiency of the mobilization strategy is mediated by public officials' evaluation of the anticipated costs of denunciation. Therefore, although this strategy can be effective, it is not certain that public officials will necessarily evaluate the risks faced in a distinctive fashion or act accordingly. If public officials become convinced of reputation costs, they may attempt to minimize these costs by trying to appear responsive to the public.

As the following examples illustrate, although social mobilization can take place in conjunction with a legal strategy, this is not always the case. Indeed, many campaigns demanding information about the financial assets of public officials or denouncing electoral fraud or the extent of police violence are not intended to bring about legal claims. Police abuse, the corruption of public officials, and electoral fraud are now in the public eye because NGOs like Nucleo de Estudos da Violencia and Viva Rio in Brazil, CELS and CORREPI (Coordinadora contra la Represión Policial e Institucional) in Argentina, and Alianza Cívica in Mexico have been able to provide documentation and mobilize intense public support. As the experience of Alianza Cívica shows, not only have these organizations succeeded in placing such topics on the public agenda, but they have also become credible and authoritative advocates.

In contrast to those cases in which the social mobilization strategy has led to the formation of relatively permanent social watchdog organizations, the strategy has also been activated by circumstantially organized movements. In Argentina, for example, the "María Soledad," "Cabezas," and "Carrasco" cases illustrate such a use of the strategy by movements demanding application of the rule of law and investigation of the behavior of public officials.[59] In each of these three cases, a murder gave rise to a claim for justice and to social mobilization aimed at guaranteeing that public authorities did not obstruct the investigation and the judicial process. In each case, a local and circumstantially organized movement aggregated public opinion around demands for justice and due process. The press and the population followed the development of the investigations and the judicial process closely. The cases ended with trials and condemnations of the culprits. In each of the three cases, once the demand for due process had been fulfilled, the social movement that activated the case dissolved.

Mediatization

The mediatic strategy is the third available for the exercise of social accountability. Social accountability requires visibility, and the media is the most important instrument to achieve this goal. The strategy works because, as in the mobilization strategy, visibility imposes reputation costs on public agents who need to protect their reputations to hold public office. It can be activated either by individual journalists and media organizations or by citizens and civil society associations.

In recent years, two significant developments have taken place in this arena. On the one hand, a more aggressive investigative journalism has emerged. In several countries of the region, the media has played a central role in exposing abuses and keeping governments in check. In Argentina, for example, the social prestige of journalists has increased, along with the circulation of certain newspapers and magazines that specialize in denunciation. Newspapers such as *Página 12*, TV programs such as *Telenoche Investiga*, and magazines such as *Revista XXI* are all examples of this trend. In Brazil, press denunciations started the process that led to the impeachment of Fernando Collor de Melo in 1992. In Peru, the case of "La Cantuta," exposed by the newsweekly *Sí*, led to an investigation of the massacre of a group of college students by military squads.[60] More recently, a videotape aired by Peruvian television showing a high-ranking public official bribing an opposition legislator led to the scandal that initiated the end of the Fujimori government. Journalists have also uncovered, through the use of hidden cameras, evidence of the dubious behavior of low-level bureaucrats, such as the employees of a pension-fund agency and police agents soliciting or receiving bribes.[61]

On the other hand, citizens and civil society organizations seem to have discovered the power of the media to create public agendas, influence public officials, accelerate decisions, and condemn presumed or real violators of the law. Indeed, that is how the media functioned in the "María Soledad," "Carrasco," and "Cabezas" cases.[62] Citizens have also resorted to the media to demand "small claims." Indeed, in most countries, in addition to big scandals, newspapers and radio and TV programs are offering special, significant spaces dedicated to voicing citizens' discontent with public offices and policies. Examples can be found in the "Línea Directa" column in *El Mercurio* or in TV programs such as *El Ciudadano* in Argentina.

Although not all exposés have led to indictments, civic and social demands for legal accountability began exerting considerable pressure on governments only after significant media coverage. In spite of its effectiveness, this use of the media, characterized by some authors as the politics of shaming, has raised questions regarding the protection of individual rights.[63] Media accusations, even if unsubstantiated, create the perception of guilt. When the media is effective in drawing attention to a case, the rules of evidence are turned on their head: those accused of corruption are perceived as guilty until "proven innocent." Consequently, recognition of the media's new role as a mechanism of accountability cannot ignore the risks that this may pose for individual rights.

The other caveat to consider in regard to the performance of the media is related to the impact that the economic and political considerations of media firms have on the assertiveness and selection of their denunciations. As Silvio R. Waisbord has mentioned, the investigative capacity of the media and the selection of cases investigated depend on the economic interests of media firms: "when media enterprises had to court the state rather than the market to achieve commercial success, their willingness to sponsor investigative journalism decreased."[64] Therefore, although recent events show the emergence of an aggressive watchdog journalism, it should be remembered that the situation could be reversed if the economic needs of media firms changed and if the tactic of selling exposés became less attractive.

One final note: as in-depth analysis of particular cases demonstrates, social accountability has a greater chance of being effective when the three strategies interact.[65] That is, its goals are achieved when citizens not only initiate a legal action but also support that action with some kind of social mobilization and some sort of media exposure. There is no sequential relationship among these strategies. Their joint activation determines the ability to draw attention to a problem and make evident the costs that public authorities should appease or avoid. In contexts in which claims are backed with mobilization and media exposure, the likelihood of authorities' postponing or ignoring legal demands is less likely. In these cases, the exercise of social accountability has a greater chance of being successful because the task of control is distributed among different agencies with autonomous interests and because the number of external eyes overseeing the situation increases. Indeed, when the three strategies are simultaneously present, each one controls each other and prevents attempts to hide its consideration. The media observes and reports on the organization and mobilization of civil society; civil society organizations listen to and impel the media at the same time that they activate legal actions. This continuous observation forces state institutions to give preferential treatment to a problem.

Is social accountability an effective instrument of control? Ultimately, of course, this is an empirical question. On the one hand, given the penalties that social accountability may impose, public officials may conclude that it is more convenient to abandon certain practices that bring about reputation and/or judicial costs. On the other hand, since public officials can anticipate which activities or policies may bring about social penalties, this could lead to the development of more sophisticated and subtle procedures to "survive accountability," as José María Maravall has warned.[66] Indeed, the question is not whether such strategies can be effective, as in many cases they have proven they can be, but for how long and what type of issues can they control. Table 1.1. describes the different mechanisms and resources that each type of accountability strategy can use to its advantage.

The aim of this book is to analyze the implications of the operation of social mechanisms of accountability, examining from different angles the contribution of civil society and the media to accountable government in Latin America. The chapters provide theoretical reflections about the relation of civil society to the problem of accountability, as well as interesting debates about the current status of accountability mechanisms in Latin America, and analyze concrete cases drawn from the Latin American context.

The concept of social accountability has great potential for controlling governmental actions in representative democracies in general and in situations, such as the Latin American one, where the citizens' ability to control governmental actions has been questioned. Many roads can lead to the exercise of accountability. Some of them are different from those usually acknowledged by democratic theory. Although this book illustrates the fact that alternative social paths cannot be disregarded, numerous issues have been left open for further empirical research and debate. How, specifically, do social mechanisms impose controls? How may they be sustained? However, in spite of the remaining tasks, the discussion reveals that for democracies to achieve politically and legally accountable governments, the relationship between institutional mechanisms and specific social actions and actors should not be overlooked. Social mechanisms constitute an alternative mechanism for imposing costs on political actors and are a necessary condition for the operation of those institutional mechanisms that have mandatory sanctioning capacities. In other words, they show that the efficiency of horizontal and vertical controls depends on the ability of social actors to remind public agents that they can be sanctioned.

1.1 Types of Accountability

Who Controls	Actors	What Is Controlled: Politicians	What Is Controlled: Bureaucrats
HORIZONTAL ACCOUNTABILITY[a]			
Balancing	Executive power	Veto	Policy setting
			Regulation
			Administrative oversight
			Nomination and demotion of personnel
	Legislative power	Impeachment	Policy setting
			Regulation
			Administrative oversight
			Nomination and demotion of personnel
	Judicial power	Judicial review	
Mandated	Oversight agencies	Control of law abidance	Control of law abidance
		Investigative and denouncing faculties	Investigative and denouncing faculties
VERTICAL ACCOUNTABILITY			
Societal	Civic associations, NGOs, and social movements	Social mobilization and public denunciation	Social mobilization and public denunciation
		Denunciation by oversight agencies	Denunciation by oversight agencies
		Agenda setting	Agenda setting
			Litigation
	Media	Investigation and public denunciation	Investigation and public denunciation
		Agenda setting	Agenda setting
Electoral	Individual citizens	Voting	

[a] We are following Guillermo O'Donnell's classification of accountability mechanisms (see "Horizontal Accountability: The Legal Institutionalization of Mistrust," in Scott Mainwaring and Christopher Welna, eds., *Democratic Accountability in Latin America* [Oxford: Oxford University Press, 2003]).

NOTES

1. For some exceptions, see Víctor Pérez-Díaz, *Spain at the Crossroads: Civil Society, Politics and the Rule of Law* (Cambridge: Harvard University Press, 1999); Jonathan Fox, "Civil Society and Political Accountability: Propositions for Discussion," paper presented at the Conference on Institutions, Accountability and Democratic Governance in Latin America (Helen Kellogg Institute for International Studies, University of Notre Dame, May 8–9, 2000); Nuria Cunill Grau, *Repensando lo Público a Través de la Sociedad: Nuevas Formas de Gestión Ública y Representación Social* (Caracas: Nueva Sociedad, 1997).

2. Andreas Schedler, "Conceptualizing Accountability," in Andreas Schedler, Larry Diamond, and Marc F. Plattner, eds., *The Self-Restraining State: Power and Accountability in New Democracies* (Boulder and London: Lynne Rienner Publishers, 1999), 14.

3. In most constitutional democracies, there are various mechanisms available to guarantee that governments abide by the law and due procedures, e.g., courts, ombudsmen, inspectors, auditors, special appeals tribunals, complaint procedures, committees of parliament, etc. For a general overview of some of these institutions and mechanisms, see D. J. Galligan, "Making Government and Administration Accountable," paper presented at the Comprehensive Legal and Judicial Development Conference (Washington, D.C., June 6, 2000).

4. James G. March and Johan P. Olsen, *Democratic Governance* (New York: Free Press, 1995), 154.

5. Guillermo O'Donnell's concept of horizontal accountability centers on this aspect of the concept of accountability.

6. Wolfang Schluchter, *The Rise of Western Rationalism: Max Weber's Developmental History* (Berkeley: University of California Press, 1981), 111–12.

7. There seems to be widespread agreement among Latin American political analysts on the absence of such a prerequisite in most of the region. See Gabriel Negretto and Mark Ungar, "Judicial Independence, Rule of Law, and Democratization in Latin America" (mimeograph); Juan E. Méndez, Guillermo O'Donnell, and Paulo Sérgio Pinheiro, eds., *The (Un)Rule of Law and the Underprivileged in Latin America* (Notre Dame: University of Notre Dame Press, 1999); and Enrique Peruzzotti, "Modernization and Juridification in Latin America: A Reassessment of the Latin American Developmental Path," *Thesis Eleven,* no. 58 (Aug. 1999), and "Civil Society and the Modern Constitutional Complex: The Argentine Experience," *Constellations: An International Journal of Critical and Democratic Theory* 4, no. 1 (1997). For a more general discussion of problems related to the enforcement of the rule of law, see Russell Hardin, "Why a Constitution," in Bernard Grofman and Donald Wittman, eds., *The Federalist Papers and the New Institutionalism* (New York: Agathon Press, 1989); Barry Weingast, "The Political Foundations of Democracy and the Rule of Law," *American Political Science Review* 91, no. 2 (1997); and Catalina Smulovitz, "How Can the Rule of Law Rule? Cost Imposition through Decentralized Mechanisms," in Jose María Moravall and Adam Przeworski, eds., *Democracy and the Rule of Law* (Cambridge: Cambridge University Press, 2003).

8. Adam Przeworksi, Susan C. Stokes, and Bernard Manin, eds., *Democracy, Accountability, and Representation* (Cambridge: Cambridge University Press, 1999).

9. Bernard Manin, Adam Przeworski, and Susan Stokes, "Elections and Representation," in Przeworski, Stokes, and Manin, *Democracy, Accountability, and Representation,* 40.

10. Schedler, "Conceptualizing Accountability," 14.

11. For a discussion of these dilemmas, see Przeworski, Stokes, and Manin, *Democracy, Accountability and Representation.*

12. Manin, Przeworski, and Stokes, "Elections and Representation." In his contribution to this book, Przeworski extends his argument to most mechanisms of accountability. In his view, "the weakness of popular control over governments is generic to democracy."

13. Adam Przeworski, *Democracy and the Market* (Cambridge: Cambridge University Press, 1991), 12.

14. Weingast, "The Political Foundations of Democracy," 91, 92.

15. Guillermo O'Donnell, "Horizontal Accountability in New Democracies," in Schedler, Diamond, and Plattner, *The Self-Restraining State;* Matthew Soberg Shugart, Erika Moreno, and Brian F. Crisp, "The Accountability Deficit in Latin America," in Scott Mainwaring and Christopher Welna, eds., *Accountability, Democratic Governance, and Political Institutions in Latin America* (Oxford: Oxford University Press, 2003).

16. Giorgio Alberti, "Democracy by Default: Economic Crisis, 'Movimientismo,' and Social Anomie," paper presented at the Fifteenth World Congress of the International Political Science Association (Buenos Aires, July 1991). Also see the following works by Guillermo O'Donnell: "Horizontal Accountability in New Democracies"; "Accountability Horizontal," *Agora: Cuaderno de Estudios Políticos,* no. 8 (1998); "Illusions about Consolidation," *Journal of Democracy* 7, no. 2 (1995); "Delegative Democracy," *Journal of Democracy* 5, no. 1 (1994); and "On the State, Democratization and Some Conceptual Problems: A Latin American View with Glances at Some Postcommunist Countries," *World Development* 21, no. 8 (1993). See also Michael Shifter, "Tensions and Trade-Offs in Latin America," *Journal of Democracy* 8, no. 2 (1997); Francisco Weffort, "What Is a New Democracy?" *International Social Science Journal,* no. 136 (1993), and *Qual Democracia?* (Sao Paulo: Compania Das Letras, 1992); Laurence Whitehead, "The Alternative to 'Liberal Democracy': A Latin American Perspective," in David Held, ed., *Prospects for Democracy* (Cambridge: Polity Press, 1993); and Fareed Zakaria, "The Rise of Illiberal Democracy," *Foreign Affairs,* no. 76 (1997). For a critical overview of the delegative argument, see Enrique Peruzzotti, "The Nature of the New Argentine Democracy: The Delegative Democracy Argument Revisited," *Journal of Latin American Studies* 33, part 1 (Feb. 2001).

17. O'Donnell, "Delegative Democracy," 166, and "Illusions about Consolidation," 185.

18. Shugart, Moreno, and Crisp, "The Accountability Deficit," 108, 117.

19. See Fox, "Civil Society and Political Accountability," and "The Difficult Transition from Clientelism to Citizenship: Lessons from Mexico," *World Politics* 46, no. 2 (Jan. 1994); O'Donnell, "On the State"; Javier Auyero, ed., *Favores por Votos? Estudios sobre el Clientelismo Político Contemporáneo* (Buenos Aires: Losada Editorial, 1997).

20. It should be noted that O'Donnell's definition of horizontal accountability does not refer to any type of monitoring or controlling exchange among state agencies but exclusively to those actions oriented to controlling or punishing actions or omissions by agents or agencies of the state that may be qualified as unlawful. In his view, horizontal mechanisms are activated either when there is an "unlawful encroachment by one state agency over the proper authority of another" or in cases involving the corruption of public officials. In this way, O'Donnell narrows the concept of horizontal accountability to that set of intrastate controls and exchanges that are oriented toward enforcing legal accountability, leaving aside horizontal political controls. We will therefore adhere to O'Donnell's spatial metaphor and distinguish the direction in which these mechanisms

operate (horizontal or vertical) from the grounds on which control is exercised (legal or political). We want to acknowledge, however, that in a recent article O'Donnell has defended the narrow use of the concept. For a debate, see Guillermo O'Donnell, "Horizontal Accountability: The Legal Institutionalization of Mistrust," in Mainwaring and Welna, *Accountability, Democratic Governance, and Political Institutions in Latin America;* and Shugart, Moreno, and Crisp, "The Accountability Deficit in Latin America."

21. O'Donnell acknowledges the emergence of vertical mechanisms that are not necessarily related to elections. He refers to the workings of social demands and an independent media. See O'Donnell, "Horizontal Accountability in New Democracies," 30. Such a recognition weakens at least one of the central assumptions of the delegative-democracy argument: that the strength of a delegative political culture in civil society feeds presidential *discrecionalismo.*

22. The literature on civil society stresses the notion that the self-constitution and self-organization of citizens in civil society and the establishment of independent media institutions represent a crucial addition to traditional representative institutions, establishing autonomous spaces that play a crucial role in influencing the process of policy making and exposing the arbitrary use of political power. A theoretical synthesis of the concept of civil society can be found in Jean Cohen and Andrew Arato, *Civil Society and Political Theory* (Cambridge: MIT Press, 1992). For an analysis of the relevance of the concept to Latin America, see Sonia Alvarez, Evelina Dagnino, and Arturo Escobar, eds., *Cultures of Politics, Politics of Culture: Re-visioning Latin American Social Movements* (Boulder: Westview Press, 1988); Leonardo Avritzer, ed., *Sociedade Civil e Democratizacao* (Belo Horizonte: Del Rey, 1995); Larry Diamond, "Rethinking Civil Society," *Journal of Democracy* 5, no. 3 (1994), and *Developing Democracy toward Consolidation* (Baltimore: John Hopkins University Press, 1999), chap. 6; Guillermo O'Donnell, Philippe Schmitter, and Laurence Whitehead, *Transitions from Authoritarian Rule: Tentative Conclusions* (Baltimore: John Hopkins University Press, 1986); Philip Oxhorn, *Organizing Civil Society* (University Park: Pennsylvania State University Press, 1995); and Peruzzotti, "Civil Society and the Modern Constitutional Complex," and "Towards a New Politics: Citizenship and Rights in Contemporary Argentina," *Citizenship Studies* 6, no. 1 (2002). From another angle, the literature on social capital has also stressed the contribution of civic networks and associations to good governance. See Robert Putnam, *Bowling Alone: The Collapse and Revival of American Community* (New York: Simon and Schuster, 2000); and Bob Edwards, Michael W. Foley, and Mario Diani, eds., *Beyond Tocqueville: Civil Society and the Social Capital Debate in Comparative Perspective* (Lebanon, N.H.: University Press of New England, 2001).

23. This feature resembles the "fire alarm" mechanisms of control developed by Matthew McCubbins and Thomas Schwartz. See "Congressional Oversight Overlooked: Police Patrols versus Fire Alarms," *American Journal of Political Science* 28, no. 1 (1984): 168.

24. Since they can be addressed to *both* politicians *and* bureaucrats alike, social mechanisms can also overcome another important limitation stressed by Przeworski in his analysis of elections as mechanisms of accountability. See Adam Przeworski, "Democratization Revisited," *Item* 51, no. 1 (1997): 10–11.

25. Recent experience shows that international actors are also playing a role in the exercise of control. Not only transnational but also local NGOs and social movements have designed strategies to activate the oversight mechanisms of international agencies. See Margaret Keck and Kathryn Sikkink, *Activists beyond Borders: Advocacy Networks in*

International Politics (Ithaca: Cornell University Press, 1998); Jonathan Fox and L. David Brown, eds., *The Struggle for Accountability: The World Bank, NGOs, and Grassroots Movements* (Cambridge: MIT Press, 1998); and Diana Tussie, comp., *El BID, el Banco Mundial y la Sociedad Civil: Nuevas Formas de Financiamiento Internacional* (Buenos Aires: UBA-FLACSO, 1997).

26. This argument is developed in Peruzzotti, "Towards a New Politics," and "The Nature of the New Argentine Democracy."

27. See, e.g., Behrend's chapter in this volume.

28. See O'Donnell, "On the State."

29. For an overview of these initiatives, see Fundación Ford, *Rompiendo la Indiferencia: Acciones Ciudadanas de Interés Público* (Santiago: Fundación Ford, Oficina para la Región Andina y el Cono Sur, 2001).

30. For a general overview of different experiences of electoral observation, see Kevin J. Middlebrook, ed., *Electoral Observation and Democratic Transitions in Latin America* (San Diego: Center for U.S.-Mexican Studies, UCSD, 1998).

31. See Comision Ciudadana de Seguimiento, *Poder, Justicia e Indignidad: El Juicio al Presidente de la República Ernesto Samper Pizano* (Bogota: Utópica Ediciones, 1996).

32. See Guillermo Mastrini and César Bolaño, eds., *Globalización y Monopolios en la Comunicación en América Latina: Hacia una Economía Política de la Comunicación* (Buenos Aires: Editorial Biblos, 1999); Jesús Martín Barbero and Germán Rey, *Los Ejercicios del Ver: Hegemonía Audiovisual y Ficción Televisiva* (Barcelona: Gedisa, 1999).

33. Needless to say, the actual market structure of the media necessarily limits this watchdog role: the activities of Latin American watchdog journalists rarely expose private cases of wrongdoing that could affect an organization's commercial interests. Yet this observation should not diminish the watchdog role that the media is playing in relation to governmental wrongdoing. See Silvio Waisbord, *Watchdog Journalism in South America: News, Accountability, and Democracy* (New York: Columbia University Press, 2001).

34. Albert O. Hirschman, *Exit, Voice, and Loyalty: Responses to Decline in Firms, Organizations and States* (Cambridge: Harvard University Press, 1970).

35. Schedler, "Conceptualizing Accountability," 19–28.

36. McCubbins and Schwartz, "Congressional Oversight Overlooked."

37. If we were to use Keck and Sikkink's terminology, this phenomenon implies "framing" particular events with a wider cognitive context capable of linking and organizing specific experiences into a broader interpretative understanding. See Margaret Keck and Kathryn Sikkink, "Transnational Advocacy Networks in the Movement Society," in David Meyer and Sydney Tarrow, eds., *The Social Movement Society: Contentious Politics for a New Century* (Lanham: Rowman and Littlefield Publishers, 1998), 225.

38. Schedler has distinguished two main dimensions of the concept of accountability: answerability and enforcement. See "Conceptualizing Accountability," 14.

39. Silvio Waisbord, *Watchdog Journalism in South America,* and "Investigative Journalism and Political Accountability in South American Democracies," *Critical Studies in Mass Communication* 13 (1996); Germán Rey, *Balsas y Medusas: Visibilidad Comunicativa y Narrativas Políticas* (Bogota: Fescol-Fundación Social-Cerec, 1998); Heriberto Muraro, *Políticos, Periodistas y Ciudadanos* (Buenos Aires: Fondo de Cultura Económica, 1997).

40. John B. Thompson, "Scandals and Social Theory," in James Lull and Stephen Hineman, eds., *Media Scandals* (Cambridge: Polity Press, 1997); and *Political Scandal: Power and Visibility in the Media Age* (Cambridge: Polity Press, 2000).

41. Thompson, "Scandals and Social Theory."

42. Cases such as the "María Soledad" and "Budge" murders in Argentina, "La Cantuta" in Peru, or the constitution of the different Comissoes Parlamentares de Inquerito in Brazil illustrate the way in which "soft" types of social accountability result in the activation of horizontal mechanisms. See Catalina Smulovitz and Enrique Peruzzotti, "Societal and Horizontal Controls: Two Cases about a Fruitful Relationship," in Mainwaring and Welna, *Accountability, Democratic Governance and Political Institutions in Latin America*, 203; Flávia Schilling, *Corrupcao: Ilegalidade Intoleravel? Comissoes Parlamentares de Inquérito e a Luta contra a Corrupcao no Brasil (1980–1992)* (Sao Paulo: Instituto Brasileiro de Ciencias Criminais, 1999).

43. See Sibila Camps and Luis Pazos, *Justicia y Televisión: La Sociedad Dicta Sentencia* (Buenos Aries: Libros Perfil, 1999); Silvio Waisbord, "Investigative Journalism and Political Accountability."

44. Examples of this use of the media can be verified in cases such as the process that led to the impeachment of Collor or the legislative discussion about legal limitations of press freedom in Chile brought about by the Matus case.

45. Catalina Smulovitz, "Acciones Judiciales y Fiscalización de la Política Pública" (mimeograph); and "Ciudadanos, Derechos y Política," in Felipe González Morales, ed., *Las Acciones de Interés Público: Argentina, Chile, Colombia y Perú* (Santiago de Chile: Escuela de Derecho de la Universidad Diego Portales, 1997).

46. Frances Zemans, "Legal Mobilization: The Neglected Role of the Law in the Political System," *American Political Science Review* 77, no. 3 (1983).

47. For an analysis of the emergence of rights-oriented discourse and politics within civil society, see Isidoro Cheresky, *La Innovación Política* (Buenos Aires: EUDEBA, 1999), esp. part 2; Peruzzotti, "Towards a New Politics," and "La Democratización de la Democracia: Cultura Política, Esfera Pública y Aprendizaje Colectivo en la Argentina Postdictatorial," in Isidoro Cheresky and Inés Pousadela, eds., *Política e Instituciones en las Nuevas Democracias Latinoamericanas* (Buenos Aires: Paidós Editorial, 2001); and Smulovitz, "Ciudadanos, Derechos y Política."

48. Hirschman, *Exit, Voice, and Loyalty.*

49. Hirschman, *Exit, Voice, and Loyalty.* See also Steven Lukes, *El Poder: Una Perspectiva Radical* (Mexico: Siglo XXI Editores, 1985); and O'Donnell's contribution to this volume.

50. Examples include Ouvidorias Policiales in Sao Paulo, the Coordinadora contra la Represión Policial e Institucional, and Centro de Estudios Legales y Sociales in Argentina, Alianza Cívica in Mexico, and Transparencia in Peru.

51. Catalina Smulovitz, "The Discovery of Law: Political Consequences in the Argentine Case," in Garth Brian and Yves Dezalay, eds., *Global Prescriptions: The Production, Exportation, and Importation of a New Legal Orthodoxy* (Ann Arbor: University of Michigan Press, 2002).

52. Neal Tate and Torbjorn Vallinder, eds., *The Global Expansion of Judicial Power* (New York: New York University Press, 1995).

53. See Luiz Werneck Vianna, Maria Alice Rezende de Carvalho, Manuel Cunha Melo, and Marcelo Burgos, *A Judicializacao da Politica e das Relacoes Sociais no Brasil* (Rio de Janeiro: Editora Revan, 1999); Catalina Smulovitz, "Constitución y Poder Judicial en la Nueva Democracia Argentina: La Experiencia de las Instituciones," in Carlos Acuña, comp., *La Nueva Matriz Política Argentina* (Buenos Aires: Nueva Visión, 1995);

Jorge Correa, "Cenicienta se queda en la Fiesta: El Poder Judicial Chileno en la Década de los 90," in Paul Drake and Iván Jaksic, comps., *El Modelo Chileno: Democracia y Desarrollo en los Noventa* (Santiago: LOM Ediciones, 2000).

54. Corte Constitucional—Consejo Superior de la Judicatura, *Estadísticas sobre la Acción de Tutela* (Bogota: Imprenta Nacional de Colombia, 1999).

55. Rogerio Bastos Arantes, *Judiciario e Politica No Brasil* (Sao Paulo: Editora Sumaré, 1997). See also Calvancanti's contribution to this volume regarding the use of the Ministerio Público.

56. Werneck Vianna et al., *A Judicializacao da Politica*, 48–70.

57. Defensor del Pueblo de la Nación Argentina, Informe Anual 1999; Defensoría del Pueblo de Perú, *Resumen Ejecutivo del Segundo Informe del Defensor del Pueblo al Congreso de la República* (Lima: 2000).

58. Mary McClymont and Stephen Golub, eds., *Many Roads to Justice* (N.p.: Ford Foundation, 2000); Felipe Gonzalez and Felipe Viveros, *Ciudadanía e Interés Público* (Santiago: Cuadernos de Análisis Jurídico, Facultad de Derecho Universidad Diego Portales, 1998); Gonzalez Morales, *Las Acciones de Interes Público.*

59. The "María Soledad" case refers to the demand for justice in the case of a high school student who was found raped and murdered in the Argentine province of Catamarca. See Smulovitz and Peruzzotti, "Societal and Horizontal Controls." The "Carrasco" case involved the murder of a soldier who was fulfilling his mandatory military service. For an analysis of both cases, see the chapter by Behrend in this volume.

60. See Waisbord, "Investigative Journalism and Political Accountability," as well as his chapter in this volume.

61. See Camps and Pazos, *Justicia y Televisión.*

62. The "María Soledad" case was covered on practically a daily basis by most national newspapers. The televised event was dutifully followed by a massive audience; the trial aired across the country by approximately forty open TV and cable stations. Todo Noticias, a news-cable channel, transmitted the whole trial live without interruptions. Crónica TV, another nationwide cable channel, devoted 80 percent of its airspace, that is, an average of nineteen hours of transmission, to the trial. According to Camps and Pazos, the trial took an average of nine hours of programming. The estimated audience was between seven and ten million spectators. See Camps and Pazos, *Justicia y Televisión,* 244; *Revista Noticias*, Edición Especial 18, "Una Pasión de Multitudes," 70–72; and Aníbal Ford, "La Exasperación del Caso," in *La Marca de la Bestia: Identificación, Desigualdades e Infroentretenimiento en la Sociedad Contemporánea* (Buenos Aires: Grupo Editorial Norma, 1999), 267.

The "Cabezas case" refers to the demand for justice in the case of an Argentinean photojournalist who was savagely murdered while covering the activities of an entrepreneur suspected of money laundering.

63. Iris Marion Young, *Inclusion and Democracy* (Oxford: Oxford University Press, 2000), 174.

64. Waisbord, "Investigative Journalism and Political Accountability," 349.

65. See, e.g., Olvera's and Waisbord's contributions here, along with Smulovitz and Peruzzotti, "Societal and Horizontal Controls."

66. José María Maravall, "Accountability and Manipulation," in Przeworski, Stokes, and Manin, *Democracy, Accountability, and Representation.*

2

The Effectiveness of Law

CIVIL SOCIETY AND THE PUBLIC PROSECUTION IN BRAZIL

Rosangela Batista Calvancanti

In opposition to the obstacles to implementing participatory democracy processes in the context of the division between state and society, the Brazilian federal constitution currently in force, including the rules and regulations derived from it, seems to have been created with the understanding that representative democracy mechanisms used in combination with participatory democracy elements not only provide additional legitimacy to the decision-making process but also result in enhanced government performance.

In this context, where social actors are provided with new mechanisms to legitimize their active involvement in the public arena and their ability to pressure public authorities at different levels, formal judicial institutions have been faced with a diverse range of conflicts extrapolating the individualistic liberal model of judicial administration, becoming key elements for socially and politically based conflict resolution.

It is also in this context that civil society initiatives oriented toward a "real division of authority" have been provided with new and more efficient tools. As will be explained later, the most relevant of these tools are the regular associations between the Public Prosecution (MP) and civil society organizations, particularly those aimed at supervision of the public administration and the political arena.

Political Mechanisms of Social Participation and Control

In addition to describing Brazil's government as "democratic by law" and explicitly including other principles of current democratic governments, the Brazilian federal constitution currently in force provides for social participation mechanisms not only through voting but also through *direct control* over government organization and the existing branches of government. Contradicting arguments stating that participatory democracy elements may "obstruct" the decision-making processes of mass societies,[1] the 1988 Magna Carta includes several mechanisms promoting decisive citizen influence over public administration by expanding citizen participation, either individual or collective, in the public arena beyond the electoral process, including active involvement in the policy-making and policy-implementation process. In this spirit, additional laws were created, based on the constitution, aiming at a close supervision of government actions.

The principle of semidirect democracy is explicitly established in Section 1 of the current Brazilian constitution, which states that authority may be exercised by society through elected representatives or "directly." The democratic regime of Brazil is thus no longer exclusively representative but has become a hybrid, adopting three types of democracy: *direct democracy* (plebiscite, referendum, and popular initiative), *representative democracy* (congressional and presidential elections), and *participatory democracy* (councils).[2]

The first instrument of direct democracy that is made available to society is the plebiscite, which implies that citizens should give their opinions about a political or institutional issue prior to its elaboration by congress. Except for the "territorial plebiscites" incorporated in previous constitutions,[3] this mechanism has been used only once in Brazil, in 1993, when citizens were asked about the regime (republic or constitutional monarchy) and the government system (parliamentary or presidential) that was to be implemented. Needless to say, the choice was between the maintenance of the republican regime and a presidential system of government. The referendum, another mechanism of direct democracy stipulated in the 1988 federal constitution, is based on the presentation of bills approved by the legislative branch pursuant to the citizens' will.

Referendum and plebiscite decisions are binding, and government administrators may not prevent them from being enforced. The right to propose these initiatives falls within the scope of government institutions or a definite number of citizens (popular initiative). The popular initiative, also stipulated for the three levels of government—local, state, and federal—is the mechanism whereby citizens may submit bills for discussion by Congress.

In spite of their inclusion in the constitution, these three mechanisms of social participation have not been widely used: more regulations are still required, the mechanisms are restricted to certain issues, and they are delayed processes.

In any case, other procedures have been implemented in many Brazilian towns and cities based on the social participation principles set forth in the constitution for public administration and political/administrative decentralization, such as the creation of "tutelary" or representation councils, through which consumers and the society at large may participate in public-service planning, operation, and supervision. Local-level councils (regarding health, education, social welfare, minors, etc.) are deliberative and supervisory institutions with equal-participation policies, including members from both government and civil society.[4] For example, local-level councils are charged with the approval or rejection of government agencies' service programs.

On the other hand, the efficiency of these institutional participatory channels, which certainly enable increased participation by society in general-interest issues and significantly greater accountability, is linked to the practices of the administration in power. However, it is important to note that, despite the various limitations and conflicts, the new procedures still reflect greater in-depth control of government by society.[5]

Civil Society Organizations and Control over Public Administration

The Brazilian federal constitution currently in force, which is extremely detailed, and the legislation subsequently enacted based on its principles cannot be compared to any previous constitution in terms of the rights granted to citizens and their application to various social groups. Thus, the major challenge for Brazilian society has shifted from the law-making domain to the effective enforcement of laws already enacted. Also important is the fact that the government's relationship with citizens has been redefined, mainly through a reduction of activities directly performed by the state and an increase of public interest activities delegated to organized civil society groups.[6]

As mentioned above, this new government-society relationship provides for potential societal oversight of actions or omissions of the public administration, particularly at the local level. The transformation of such potential control into an effective oversight mechanism has not been easy, in spite of the numerous laws created for this purpose. Depending on the practices of the government in power, on many occasions social participation has not been encouraged or has even been made impossible. The redefinition of locally empowered institutions requires the introduction of democratization mechanisms to guarantee access to information reflecting local policy management, since there is neither autonomous decision making nor freedom of speech when information on conditions and contexts is missing. In other words, in order for citizens to get involved in the decision-making process, access to information should be made available so that they may decide with increased freedom and efficiency. Providing transparent information about administrative mechanisms, including participatory policy-making mechanisms in the domain of the legislature, is thus essential. Actions by citizens and their representative agencies are many times undermined because certain factors have not been addressed, such as the right to petition the branches of government for the protection of rights or against illegal practices; abuse of authority; or the approval of certificates from public organizations that, despite being enacted under the law, are not evidenced in many administrative practices.

In this context, judicial institutions have played a key role in seeking to guarantee legal efficiency. The judiciary, for example, which in the past was "a peripheral branch of government . . . has proven to be a core institution in the Brazilian democracy, both in terms of its particularly political expression and its intervention at the social level."[7] In addition, the MP, the major driving agent of the judiciary, with significant enforcement authority over other government agencies, has become a key element in the process of the conversion of formal rights into actual ones.

Civil society organizations or associations in Brazil have thus privileged strictly legal instruments, which, even if used for political purposes, have been powerful elements ensuring the enforcement of the law.[8] Indeed, the widespread use of legal instruments, both to incorporate wide sectors of society as citizens and to oversee the public administration, indicates that, in contrast to the past, organized civil society is getting increasingly closer to judicial institutions, to the detriment of the relationships traditionally established between the judiciary and political parties or other representative democracy institutions. This means that, in the case of Brazil, civil society groups have often sought not only to defend their interests within the judicial domain but also to control the public administration through legal channels.

Civil Society and the Public Prosecution Acting in Partnership

Within the newly established constitutional regime in Brazil, the judiciary has not only found solutions to intersubjective conflicts of interests based on the individualistic liberal model but has also acted as a balancing entity regarding social tensions, resolving social and political conflicts; implementing the promotional content encoded in constitutional laws and laws granting social rights; and protecting the environment, the consumer, and other diffuse and collective interests.[9] In this way, the judiciary has become a leading actor in the struggle for rights that originated within Brazilian society. However, for the judiciary to get involved in the realm of social relationships and in the political arena in particular, it must be provoked—that is, issues must be submitted for discussion and subsequent decision making. This does not occur in the case of the MP, which plays a more active role, even itself provoking the judiciary by submitting collective-interest issues for consideration.

The current federal constitution outlines a new Public Prosecution,[10] entrusting it with the protection of the judicial system, the democratic regime, and social and individual inalienable rights.[11] The MP's institutional functions have also been expanded, granting it legitimate authority to judge public criminal actions (exclusively); to suggest direct unconstitutional actions;[12] to oversee the public administration and public services; and to encourage public civil suits for the protection of the environment, consumers, disabled people, children and adolescents, workers, and other diffuse and collective interests.[13]

The Public Civil Action Act mentioned above has granted ample and legitimate authority to the MP to act as a party and as *custos legis* (prosecutor of the law) by carrying out arduous oversight activity, searching for uncertain and actual damages to an entire group. In addition to this ample and legitimate authority, the MP is also entrusted with investigative and preliminary activities in public civil suits. These activities, called *summary proceedings,* are equivalent to a police summary proceeding, although the MP's summary proceeding consists of peculiar features in terms of both procedure, which is considered administrative, and the activities' inquisitive nature, aimed at gathering sufficient evidence in order to advance a collective action.

Given its outstanding performance in overseeing various sectors of the public administration and enforcing laws protecting collective and diffuse interests, the significant expansion of its functions and, therefore, of its authority has made Brazil's Public Prosecution the major instrument of this two-way process, of the judicialization of politics and/or the politicization of justice. As stated by Luiz Werneck Vianna and others, "the new Public Prosecution has been conceived as an activist institution for advancing the defense of laws and of society . . . and with its inherent leadership prompting increased citizen involvement in public issues."[14] Thus, many civil society organizations have increasingly addressed their claims to the MP. In effect, the MP has granted space within the public sphere to an increased number of civil society organizations. Such associations point to a new path for current democratic practices, where mobilization and citizen representation occur not only through political means.

There is great potential for joint action by civil associations and the MP regarding the protection of children's and adolescents' rights. A member of the Council for the Protection of Children and Youth in a municipality of São Paulo, the most economically active state in the Brazilian federation, stated that his organization had chosen to work with the MP because its actions are intended to demand effective compliance with the laws: "In the past, government authorities had the prerogative of the so-called discretionary authority to determine the convenience of spending resources for works, services, and assistance to the community. But today government authorities have to observe the new constitutional principle whereby children are defined as an absolute priority. So compliance with such a principle should be guaranteed by the Public Prosecution."[15]

Actions brought to the MP in this domain, often by civil associations, have repeatedly questioned the discretionary power of political authorities: "Mayors can no longer hide behind the excuse of discretion because it would mean an infringement of the constitutional order of the absolute priority [of minors]. That is a completely false statement to avoid compliance with the service duty imposed on government authorities."[16]

Citizens or civil organizations address the MP for a variety of reasons, but in most cases their intention is to watch closely every step taken by public officials. In the midwestern Brazilian state of Goiás a suit was initiated against a mayor who had not provided adequate facilities for the operation of a tutelary council. As stated by the president of the council, its members tried to address the mayor on many occasions in order to find a solution, but he did nothing, so they addressed the MP: "The local government did not assume the role or responsibility expected by citizens, thus evidencing its contempt toward democratic participation in the public administration. The Public Prosecution thus brought an action to demand compliance with the law, stipulating that local governments will provide all the material conditions, officials, and facilities for the council." He continued arguing that "the imprudent should not take these new legal instruments for specific protection as a trespass on the public sphere by the judiciary. It is a different situation: such mechanisms are intended as a mere reminder for government authorities of the duties set forth under the law, under the rule and sovereignty of the law they pledged to comply with, and which everybody should observe, encouraging its enforcement for the benefit of all of us. Not for convenience or opportunity but as a legal and moral duty."[17]

Another case shows how the law invades the political arena. Some civil society organizations in Belo Horizonte (the capital city of the southeastern state of Minas Gerais), along with the MP, submitted a request to the judiciary to ensure the resumption of activities in the municipal network of schools because teachers had been on strike for over a month. As a result, they managed to get a decision passed to guarantee the resumption of school activities within five days; otherwise, a daily penalty would be imposed on the mayor, from the start date of the strike. The mayor was entitled to bring an action for payment against the teachers in case they did not go back to work, prescribing that they would also have to pay the daily penalty. Under the public civil suit brought by the civil organizations and the MP, responsibility for the strike was imposed on both local authorities and the teachers. The judge's unprecedented decision was based on the Statute for Children and Adolescents, under which the absence of regular schooling for children and adolescents ranging from zero to eighteen years of age is an "accountability crime."

In the state of Pernambuco, located in the northeastern region of Brazil, the Front of Nongovernmental Social Entities, including twenty-eight nonprofit civil associations, asked the MP to establish a public civil summary proceeding to investigate the irregular transfer of resources from the local-level executive branch to the Tutelary Council for Children.[18] In this case, before submitting the accusation to the MP, the council's president had tried to find a solution by addressing the mayor or his agent, but no positive results were attained. After investigating the accusation by means of a civil summary proceeding, the MP, with the civil organizations, filed a public civil suit: "In addition to the fact stated by the organizations, we also found that a regular policy for the care of the youth and the children was missing. Their rights are not being enforced, and they are being challenged, because the local government lacks programs to ensure integral protection, such as an official aid program for homeless children and adolescents, an inpatient/outpatient health care program, a psychological and psychiatric program, [or] treatment for alcoholic and drug addicted children and adolescents."[19]

As mentioned above, the issue of public authorities' discretionary power is a recurrent one in many public civil suits. This particular suit states: "Insisting on the argument that the new regime of political participation is an intrusion into the discretional sphere of the public administration, as is often stated, implies the risk of increasing social conflicts instead of finding a solution."[20] The text of the lawsuit follows, including over thirty pages. In fact, the content of a public civil suit is usually quite elaborate, since many aspects must be considered and the following items must be included in full detail: (1) legitimate authority (to file the lawsuit), (2) the facts, (3) legislation (a statement of the laws and decrees that reinforce the suit), and (4) the claims. This complexity is one explanation for the fact that civil associations, even if they are legitimately entitled to bring a public civil suit, prefer to address the Public Prosecution directly.[21]

MP members have been quite actively involved in the public health area, because civil society organizations have sought the institution to help find solutions to problems that have not been attended to by the public administration.[22] For example, among the increasing number of requests filed with this institution, one document, developed at a national conference of health professionals and representatives of health councils, states the following:

> SUS (Single Health System) managers and Health Councils must demand that the MP defend this system and other policies intended for the expansion and maintenance of the quality of life for the community. For this purpose, those who attended the tenth National Health Conference decided

> to: (1) defend the possibility that the MP may perform its constitutional and social role (as per Sections 129 and 197 of the Federal Constitution) through the democratization of access to that institution, the guarantee to information, and the commitment by the institution to protect the interests of citizens; (2) support the MP as guardian of the laws on health, social welfare, and the Statute for Children and Adolescents, by overseeing their implementation and execution in the public sector and taking the necessary steps in case of noncompliance with the contents of the law; (3) direct the Public Prosecution to create the Curadoría de Saúde [health council to specifically deal with health issues].[23]

Several representatives from the national health system thus demanded that the MP perform its constitutional functions—which are already quite expanded —and also claimed that it should be granted more authority to act, since they considered it a "guardian" of the laws safeguarding health and social welfare and the Statute for Children and Adolescents.

Obviously, the MP answered such claims promptly, since this institution, which is still building its new identity, has attempted to occupy all the domains of authority available to it. A document presented at a national meeting of attorneys general notes "the institution's commitment to protecting the single health system": "Whereas: (1) health is an essential and extremely relevant social right provided for under the Federal Constitution; (2) the Public Prosecution is charged with watching over public services; and (3) there are serious and endless problems in the health sector throughout the country, under this document it is resolved that: (1) a 'Permanent Committee for Health Protection' of prosecutors and attorneys general is established to ensure that the MP acts as a guardian of health relations."[24]

Regarding the fact that the MP is criticized for its overinterference in setting priorities for the public administration, one attorney general responded: "It is natural to find such criticism against the MP. Its members are not elected as in some other countries. However, many of those objections originate in areas with greater lobbying authority that are not pleased with the MP's performance. This nonelective nature is often found in social control instances, and that doesn't mean they are not legitimately entitled to exercise their competencies. But the MP's performance is not a monopoly. Duly organized citizen groups do not exclusively depend on the MP in order to protect their rights. The fact that the MP is flooded with requests originates because citizens have not found protection at other levels."[25]

In effect, the number of citizen requests made to the MP or other judicial institutions is equal, or even conversely proportional, to the claims submitted, for example, by political parties. The parties' inability to mobilize citizens results in a shift toward other interlocutory channels, such as the MP: "To put their inherently swaying vocation into practice, political parties in Brazil have traditionally addressed the state (with rare exceptions), restricting their search for civil society representation to elections and to mechanisms that are currently considered more effective—clientelism, patronage, personalism, etc. The gap between civil society and political parties, and the widespread dissatisfaction with party politics, show how precarious that mediation role is. The pursuit of more direct relationships with the state by civil society organizations is certainly linked to such precariousness."[26]

The MP's performance in the environmental arena is rated very highly, according to civil society organizations in the northeastern state of Paraíba: "The Environmental Protection Office [Curadoria do Meio-Ambiente] is one of our major interlocutors and is fairly devoted to environmental advocacy."[27] In the state of Bahía, also located in the Northeast, the relationship between the MP and environmental protection organizations is also positively rated: "At Bahía, environmental protection movements and the MP work together for furthering sustainable development in the pursuit of a sound environment."[28]

According to data from CONAMP (National Confederation of the Public Prosecution), the MP has been an actor in nearly 96 percent of all environment-related public civil suits that are under process in Brazilian courts. The great number of environment-related actions is a matter of concern for the public administration. A good example is found in the midwestern state of Mato Grosso. The discussion raised over the environmental impact of expansion and cost-reduction efforts for the distribution of agricultural products has mobilized NGOs and the MP. They have sponsored a series of judicial actions against the paving of routes or the building of bridges. The governor argues that these suits prevent the development of the state because high transport costs result in damages to agricultural producers. Under the shelter of environmental laws, environmentalists and the MP argue that such works would result in a negative environmental impact. The works at Mato Grosso are the most critical among the country's thousands of small works, which depend on licenses granted under environmental-impact regulations. Getting a license for the construction of a waterway, for example, may take two or three or even up to ten years when NGOs and the MP reject analysis results.

However, *improbidade administrativa* (administrative dishonesty or corruption) is what public officials fear the most, and it is precisely in this domain that the MP has focused most of its efforts. This is evidenced in the great number of committees created by state MPs in the past decade with the purpose of investigating accusations against public officials.[29] To further strict oversight control of the honesty of the public administration, many state MPs have introduced phone- or Internet-based mechanisms to channel claims against political authorities (mayors, town council officials, etc.), allowing citizens and associations to submit accusations directly to the institution. In Londrina, a city in the southern state of Paraná, during the 1999–2000 period, the MP initiated numerous investigations against the city's local government officials. According to statements made by officials, the prosecutors' work generated "inconveniences," so prosecutors became the target of pressure and witnesses were subject to different kinds of intimidation.[30] As a result, prosecutors requested help from the community and asked civil society leaders to take a look at the piles of accusations against the administration. The city's associations, more than eighty organizations from different sectors, organized the Movement for the Moralization of the Public Administration, which flooded the city's streets with continuous demonstrations, public meetings, and fund-raising events. The local press started to cover the issue, despite having initially rejected accusations against the mayor. As a result, the mayor's term in office was terminated. For that initiative, the MP and the Movement for the Moralization of the Public Administration were awarded the 2001 Transparency International Integrity Award, given for influential initiatives fostering the reduction of corruption in a particular city or region.

All this mobilization to increase oversight of the public administration is already producing changes in the profile of Brazil's political class. Mayors, town council officials, and other political actors are becoming aware that their disregard for public issues may be costly and may even result in termination of their period in office. Some administrators ironically argue that "the hunting season for mayors has opened." In fact, administering public assets with strict observance of the legislation in force has not been easy. A German foundation based in Brazil recently inaugurated a series of conferences targeted at "orienting" mayors for the struggle to enforce the new Fiscal Accountability Act, a federal law stipulating a new code of conduct for public officials at the federal, state, and local levels.[31] Under this act, civil society and the MP are granted increased authority, explicitly stipulating the direct participation of civil society in the public administration and defining in more detail the oversight role of the Public Prosecution. In effect, this two-way oversight role (by the MP and by civil society) has given rise to tensions in the political arena, making public officials more accountable and their behavior transparent.

In the current context, it is a mistake to believe that the "judicial route" is the mere formalization of a judge's decision. For public authorities, the MP, with all the power granted by the federal constitution in force, is often as feared as or even more feared than the judiciary. Public officials are conscious of the fact that the costs of an eventual investigation or civil summary proceeding for the purpose of bringing a public civil action may be quite significant. Similarly, as mentioned earlier, under the law, the MP plays a core role in the investigation of abuse of authority, using the instruments available to it.

In addition, to confront the problem of poor procedural efficiency in the area of administrative corruption, the MP has not only used the "state-of-the-art" tools available but also tools such as the civil summary proceeding and the public civil action. Furthermore, it "fights corruption" in its traditional area of operation, "the criminal arena": "In 1999, the fight against administrative corruption was finally declared a criminal action—particularly in the capital city of São Paulo—resulting in a more complicated situation for suspected politicians and public officials, some of whom were sent to prison."[32]

The Characteristics of the Public Prosecution–Civil Society Relationship

As mentioned above, to understand the relationship between the MP and civil society associations it is necessary to become aware of the changes that affected the relationship between government and society in the past few decades in Brazil. First, a change took place in civil society, which in the past had been significantly marked by an absence of autonomy with respect to the state.[33] Second, there was a change in the state, which currently allows increased participation by civil society in the public administration. One example of such change is the implementation of various councils, forums, sector chambers, participatory budgets, and so on, over the past decade, as well as the creation of the Public Prosecution. Due to the MP's additional functions, it stands to reason that it has collaborated in pointing its accusing finger at other institutions and government agencies.[34] Evelina Dagnino argues. "Transformations in the public sphere and civil society are evidenced in the new relationships established between them: the acknowledged rivalry, confrontation, and opposition that characterized those relationships in the period of struggle against the dictatorship have lost considerable relative space in favor of negotiation that bets on a potential joint action, which is paradigmatically expressed under the banner of 'civil society participation.'"[35]

This is the new viewpoint that should guide understanding of the relationship between the MP and civil society, implying association, a two-way path where the decision to investigate or accuse is often the result of a joint action. Such associations are reflected through meetings, conferences, and various contacts (regular or occasional): "Prosecutors participate in our conferences and other public events."[36] A civic association actor noted: "Public Prosecution staff have often attended our meetings. And together with them, individuals file cases regarding racism or discrimination. They provide much help to individuals in the judicial sector."[37]

However, it is obvious that this does not mean accepting the idea, certainly a naive one, that such associations imply a reduction in the gap between two opposite ends (state and society) in a game without losers or a conflict where the only objective is public welfare. On the contrary, the relationship between the MP and civil society should be understood as an uneven one combining progress, stagnation, and even regression.

Thus, civil society associations and organizations seem to be on guard, since the MP may be both a means to channel claims and an obstacle to civil suits, for instance, in situations where a conflict between opposing perspectives seems likely. Therefore, not all of civil society's experiences with the MP have been positive. Some exchanges with the institution are poor or even absent, depending on the domain of the association. For example, associations related to the homeless do not consider the MP a relevant means to channel their claims: "Concerning agricultural issues, the MP has only played its traditional role as accuser and has never challenged the citizenship rights of those who have trespassed on the land. That's why we ignore the side of citizenship protection that is so much discussed."[38] One explanation for this may be that the MP, in spite of defending the rights of citizens, especially the most underprivileged, cannot extrapolate positive regulations that curtail, under the legal property statute, claims that may violate this principle. In any case, some other statements also reveal the MP's reluctant performance in certain sectors: "The MP and every institution in the judiciary are unable to provide positive answers to social issues, mainly regarding homosexuals."[39]

Regarding these complaints, we may conclude, based on the statements gathered, that it is necessary to eliminate the great expectations—even if they are justified—certain actors have as to the institution's performance, for the response they expect may sometimes be out of the MP's scope. But there is another criticism that is often targeted at the MP—of political interference within the institution, particularly its leadership: "The Environmental Protection Office prosecutor currently in office is one of our main interlocutors and is fairly devoted to the environmental cause. She doesn't let things rest in a drawer. But the issue is when something gets to the attorney general and a rich person is involved."[40] Another member of a civic association notes: "Most MP members are independent and share the same human values, something that cannot be said of the leadership because they are closely linked with the governor."[41]

According to such criticism, the relationship between the MP and civil society may be, and usually is, both tight and permeated with conflicts of interests. In any case, while the conflicts that affect this relationship indicate that there are many factors at stake, they are by no means a sign of inefficiency: "The solution to problems cannot be outsourced by the MP, since that doesn't ensure success. On the contrary, there are challenges, but that doesn't undermine the importance of the association."[42]

When asked about how they deal with the issue of political interference within the institution or with other conflicts of interest, the people interviewed for this chapter argued that the path to follow was one of "permanent oversight": "Citizens must perform ongoing oversight; that is to say, they have to do it along with lawsuits. If they notice that the MP, for a rather nontransparent reason, takes too long in addressing their claims, they must strain their eyes. They may help, but they also know that there are some issues that affect certain interests and that it is therefore more complicated to deal with them."[43] Another source noted: "The issue is that prosecutors have been contributing a lot to further our cause, but citizens cannot just leave everything in their hands and forget about the issue. It doesn't work like that. Citizens should perform a continuous oversight control."

The use of other means to channel citizen claims illustrates the fact that the countless civil organizations that address the MP are aware that the defense of their interests does not end in their association with the institution: "The MP is not, and should not be, the single mediation instrument for social problems. The mobilization of society is usually the most effective way to solve the most serious cases that have been stopped because of overly bureaucratic investigations."[44] Another person interviewed stated: "When the situation becomes chaotic, that is when the community speaks out loud."[45]

Another example, from the state of Paraíba, shows how society may respond when confronted with the eventual inertia of the MP in finding a solution to certain issues that, some civil representatives say, "may affect interest groups." The issue arose with the construction of illegal barriers for the individual supply and use of water from rivers draining four state cities by powerful landowners of the region, including a member of the MP. Environmental groups and citizens noticed the inertia of some prosecutors in dealing with the case and mobilized the community and the media with the purpose of addressing the issue: "Once the community put it into the mouths of everybody, the MP confronted powerful people and pulled down private barriers, especially because at that stage the situation was chaotic. With the help of the community, tight boundaries were defined to ensure that prosecutors were investigating and doing their jobs to put an end to that harsh situation. The Public Prosecution and environmental organizations jointly filed a public civil action, the judiciary decided on a precautionary measure, and they came up with the court order."[46] Another member of an environmental association added: "This proves that association with the MP is essential to reinforce social control, though at the same time the MP itself, as well as the judiciary, may become the target of that social control."[47]

In an interview for a wide-circulation newspaper in the city of São Paulo, a member of that state's health council follows the same line of reasoning: "So the challenge is to develop a new citizenship. Citizens [should] . . . not only [be] conscious of the rights they have but . . . also discover it is their duty to protect their own interests and to act accordingly and responsibly in the instances of social control. . . . On the one hand, we should not wait until the last minute to address the MP, when the problem has already become quite serious, because nothing is done efficiently and independently until then. On the other hand, we cannot just take up the consequences without confronting the causes and without being bold enough to search for several legal instruments."[48]

It could obviously be argued that oversight control over the MP or any other judicial institution by civil associations and organizations is proportionate to their visibility and their recognized strength. That is, the stronger the association or organization, including its influence in the media, the more likely it will be respected or even feared, its claims thus accommodated more rapidly and with more efficient results. We could even venture the assumption that the MP's outstanding performance in the environmental domain, including the involvement of powerful advocacy organizations that are often supported by international organizations, is a result of this situation. Nevertheless, there are no investigations attesting such a direct relationship, and we cannot derive such an assertion from the data included in this chapter.

In any case, as mentioned before, various civil groups, organizations, and associations admit that their relationship with the MP is important. The successful results of many of their actions, they say, are due to their continuous association, to the extent that it contributes, along with other factors, to their overcoming obstacles originating in the requirement for technical qualifications (which civil society representatives lack), the absence of transparency (which makes access to information more difficult), and unfamiliarity with administrative machinery and procedures: "Civil society organizations address the MP mainly to open up 'secret boxes' with data about new colonels and also to investigate and support public civil suits."[49] Another source noted: "The MP is able to frighten government leaders who are most reluctant to deliver information and contribute to investigations that may turn against them. People address the MP because it will allow them to more easily demand the enforcement of their rights."[50] Therefore, the importance of the MP often lies in the compulsory and imperative nature of its actions, which, according to some people interviewed, supplements and reinforces civil society actions. Through their association, civil society and the MP set forth the duties of public authorities and require them to modify the inappropriate acts of politicians and public officials by provoking the judiciary or even delivering notices.

The Civil Society Dilemma

Based on the examples included in this chapter, the constant association between the MP and civil society has brought about undeniable benefits for the development of both individual and collective citizen participation. On the other hand, this has not eliminated a potential risk. Given that the MP is without doubt increasingly gaining strength to act on behalf of the community's interests, isn't civil society growing increasingly dependent on the MP, to the extent that its capacity to initiate actions may be compromised?

The MP's institutional characteristics reinforce this concern. Its decentralized organizational structure enables its members to have a great degree of autonomy, which leaves room for action, from the most progressive types to the most conservative. In addition, no explicit mechanisms of external control over the institution exist.

The joint action of the Public Prosecution and civil society may lead to two situations that are radically different. In the first instance, we have a civil society that acts and is strong and that knows how to use all the instruments available to enforce its rights and does not hesitate to partner with the MP in order to maximize its results. In the second instance, we have a civil society that may be delegating excessive authority to a government institution and thus rapidly becoming dependent and inefficient.

It stands to reason that civil society seeks the MP to better the performance of its oversight role regarding public assets, especially because its involvement in that domain is provided for under the constitution. But it is obvious that the MP cannot be a substitute for social control. On the other hand, that concern may be minimized: the number of civil society organizations has grown in the past few years, indicating the increased association capacity of Brazilian society. Therefore, civil society's continuous association with the MP may only reflect a widespread use of available resources, either political or judicial, by civil organizations, which does not imply dependency; in this context, civil society may be the only leading actor.

The responses of most of the people interviewed for this chapter also reflect the notion that social demands restrict the independence of the MP, whose role has developed based in large part on the community's demands. In effect, these statements perhaps suggest the misleading nature of arguments pointing to the absolute autonomy of the institution, whose actions are not merely the result of the intentional will of some of its members. In other words, the MP is not an "island" completely exempt from control or estranged from the sociohistorical context. The institution is defined by its relationship with civil society entities, which, as mentioned above, entails a combination of progress, stagnation, and even regression: "We are all required to get training—both society and government—in order to face up to the challenge of observing the constitution. Our culture is incorporating democratic ideas. Citizens, the MP, and various civil society organized sectors are learning day by day a little more about each other. It is not an easy process, but all those actors are assuming enhanced roles; they are getting to know each other and invited to make exchanges under the democratic rule of law."[51]

At present, we see a change in how claims are made and where social actors' demands are channeled because participatory democracy has allowed citizens to occupy a place within the state, generating all sorts of problems and challenges. This is a different stage of participation, where social actors engage in new kinds of relationships with each other and with actors from civil society or the state. Based on this new sociopolitical reality, in permanent evolution, these actors have a chance to invoke the law and, by means of other channels, seek to have their demands addressed within the formal justice system.

Access to the judiciary is curtailed by many obstacles, such as the monocratic nature of the system, which gives way to contrasting behavior. However, the expansion of access has produced fairly positive results. In contrast to the recent past, public authorities are now being increasingly monitored, thus restricting the likelihood of their acting against the public interest. Nevertheless, benefits in terms of effectiveness depend on public policies that are able to confront the sinister and inequitable distribution of income and social benefits in Brazil.

NOTES

1. Some authors state that participatory democracy mechanisms only operate properly in societies with a legacy of heavy participation and acknowledgment of citizens' rights. For instance, Loewenstein emphasizes that consistent civil participation is effective in Switzerland because it has "a politically developed and socially homogeneous society with a stable and moderate character" (Benevides 1990, 42).

2. Section 14 of the constitution states, "The people shall exercise its sovereign authority through universal suffrage and secret, direct, and equal vote as provided for under the law by means of I. Plebiscite, II. Referendum, and III. Popular Initiative."

3. The "territorial plebiscite" has remained a requirement for the creation of states and federal territories, as well as the creation, incorporation, merger, and division of local governments.

4. According to Carvallo 1995 (qtd. in Tatagiba 2002), over two thousand health councils were created throughout the country between 1991 and 1993, averaging nearly two new councils per day. In more recent research (1997), Carvallo again emphasizes this phenomenon of increasing councils: "In July 1996 it is estimated that nearly 65% of all Brazilian municipalities have councils . . . , which means that there are over ten thousand council members, a figure which is similar to the number of city council people" (qtd. in Tatagiba 2002, 48–49).

5. Those new procedures extrapolate the traditional arena of the control of political authority because the availability of these mechanisms enables social actors to exercise control in a more direct and forcible way. Thus, understanding the new situation using traditional concepts is increasingly more difficult, to the extent that new analytical concepts, such as the accountability concept, have been created: "The accountability-based mechanism is a vertical oversight control over political authorities in the electoral arena, based on the activities of a wide range of associations and citizen movements, as well as media action. The actions by these actors are intended to monitor public officials' performance and to report illegal acts which they may perform, and put horizontal over-

sight mechanisms into operation. These actions are channeled through institutional and non-institutional means. Legal actions or claims to supervisory organizations are examples of the first channel, while social mobilization and accusations by the media, usually targeting at symbolic sanctions, stand for non-institutional oversight mechanisms" (Smulovitz 2001, 2–3).

6. Falcão 1999.

7. Vianna et al. 1999, 35.

8. Since the 1980s, important laws relevant to this area have been enacted, including the Public Civil Action Act (1985), a major legal instrument for the defense of collective and diffuse interests; the Consumer Protection Code (1990); the Statute for Children and Adolescents (1990), etc.

9. Watanabe 1996.

10. The Brazilian Public Prosecution currently has a 10,000-member permanent staff, with 9,662 state-level prosecutors and 338 federal prosecutors.

11. See Section 127 of Brazil's 1988 federal constitution.

12. Under Section 103 of the 1988 federal constitution, those who may bring an action for unconstitutionality are the president, the federal Senate authorities, the members of the Chamber of Deputies, the Legislative Assembly authorities, state governors, the attorney general, the Federal Council of the Brazilian Attorney Association, any political party with representatives in the National Congress, a union confederation, or a national class entity.

13. Under Section 129 of the federal constitution currently in force in Brazil, additional institutional functions are established for the Public Prosecution: to defend the rights and interests of native groups through judicial means, exercise external oversight control over police performance, and request investigations and establish police summary proceedings.

14. Vianna et al. 1999, 49.

15. Interview, member of the Council for Protection of Children and Youth, São Paulo, Oct. 2000.

16. Interview, prosecutor of Minas Gerais, Belo Horozonte, June 2001.

17. Interview, prosecutor of Goiás, Gioania, June 1999.

18. The Local Government Budget Act provides for transfers of funds to be used for the maintenance of municipal councils.

19. Public civil suit 2000.81.00.034473-9.

20. Public civil suit 2000.81.00.034473-9.

21. The right to file a public civil suit is not exclusively granted to the Public Prosecution; civil society associations and other public organizations are also entitled to bring such suits.

22. MP members at the state level are prosecutors, while at the federal level they are attorneys general. This distinction refers to their different jurisdictions.

23. Tenth National Health Conference, Brasilia/DF, Sept. 2–6, 1996, <http://www.datasus.gov.br/cns/10CNS.htm>. *Curadorias* (promoting offices) are established according to the MP's different areas of action: the environment, minors and youth, consumers, etc.

24. See <http://www.pgr.mpf.gov.br>. The attorney general is the public prosecutor of the state.

25. Interview, attorney general of São Paulo, São Paulo, July 15, 1999.

26. Dagnino, 2002, 77.

27. Interview, member of the Friends of Nature Association, João Pessoa, Paraíba, Apr. 10, 1999. Also see Cavalcanti, qtd. in Sadek 2000, 60.

28. Interview, member of the Environmental Group of Bahía, Salvador, Oct. 10, 2000. Also see Sanches 1999.

29. The most common accusations against public officials are embezzlement or appropriation of assets as a result of holding a public office (49 percent); illegal contracting with public service providers (17 percent); bids—exemptions and fraud (12 percent); the diversion of funds for other purposes (8 percent); illegal, secret parcelling (4 percent); other unlawful administrative practices (6 percent); and other "common" administrative corruption crimes (4 percent) (Arantes 2000).

30. Interview, member of Transparency Brazil, São Paulo, Aug. 8, 2000.

31. The foundation is the Konrad Adenauer Foundation.

32. Arantes 2000, 15.

33. Avritzer, qtd. in Dagnino 2002a, 76.

34. In effect, many analysts and members of civil organizations agree that the MP's new role was not only a corporate gain but also the result of the decisive participation of organized sectors of civil society.

35. Avritzer, qtd. in Dagnino 2002a, 76.

36. Phone interview, member of the Studies Group of Enforcement Institutions, Feb. 2002.

37. Interview, member of the Black Movement, João Pessoa, Paraíba, Apr. 1999.

38. Interview, representative of the Pastoral Committee of the Land, João Pessoa, Paraíba, Feb. 8, 1999.

39. Interview, vice-president of Gay Group of Bahía, *CEAS Magazine,* Feb. 1999 (Sanches 1999, 80).

40. Interview, member of Paraiba's Friends of Nature Association, João Pessoa, Paraíba, Feb. 8, 1999.

41. Interview, member of the Studies Group of Enforcement Institutions.

42. Interview, member of Transparency Brazil.

43. Interview, member of Transparency Brazil.

44. Interview, member of the Environmental Group of Bahía.

45. Interview, member of the Friends of Nature Association, Apr. 10, 1999.

46. Interview, member of the Friends of Nature Association, Apr. 10, 1999.

47. Interview, member of the Friends of Nature Association, Apr. 10, 1999.

48. Interview, member of the Health Council of São Paulo, São Paulo, Feb. 2, 2002.

49. Phone interview, member of the Studies Group of Enforcement Institutions.

50. Interview, member of the Friends of Nature Association, Apr. 10, 1999.

51. Interview, member of the Health Council of São Paulo.

BIBLIOGRAPHY

Arantes, Rogério Bastos. 2000. "Ministério Público e Corrupção Política em São Paulo." In *Justiça e Cidadania no Brasil.* São Paulo: IDESP/Ed. Sumaré.

Benevides, Maria Victoria. 1990. *A Cidadania Ativa: Referendo, Plebiscito e Iniciativa Popular.* São Paulo: Ed. Ática.

Cavalcanti, Rosangela Batista. 2000. "Ministério Público na Paraíba." In *Justiça e Cidadania no Brasil.* São Paulo: IDESP/Ed. Sumaré.

Constitution of the Federal Republic of Brazil. 1988. In *Diário Oficial da União,* October 5.

Dagnino, Evelina, org. 2002a. *Sociedade Civil e Espaços Públicos no Brasil.* São Paulo: Paz e Terra.

———. 2002b. "Sociedade Civil, Espaços Públicos e a Construção Democrática no Brasil: Limites e Possibilidades." In Dagnino 2002a.

Falcão, Joaqui. 1999. *Mudança Social e Reforma Legal.* Rio de Janeiro: Comunidade Solidária.

Macedo, Ronaldo Porto, Jr. 1996. "A Evolução Institucional do Ministério Público Brasileiro." In Maria Tereza Sadek, org., *Uma Introdução ao Estudo da Justiça.* São Paulo: IDESP/Ed. Sumaré, Serie Justiça.

Sadek, Maria Tereza. 2000. *Justiça e Cidadania no Brasil.* São Paulo: IDESP/Sumaré.

Sanches, Alvino Oliveira. 1999. "Instituições, Cidadania e Movimentos Sociais: O Papel do Ministério Público da Bahía." In *Suplementos del CEAS.* São Paulo: Center for Studies of Social Analysis.

Smulovitz, Catalina. 2001. "Judicialización y Accountability Social en Argentina." Paper presented at the International Conference of the Latin American Studies Association, Washington, D.C., September.

Tatagiba, Luciana. 2002. "Os Conselhos Gestores e a Democratização das Políticas Públicas no Brasil." In Dagnino 2002a.

Vianna, Luiz Werneck, Maria Alice de Carvalho, Manuel Palácios Cunha Melo, and Marcelo Baumann Burgos. 1999. *A Judicialização da Política e das Relações Sociais no Brasil.* Rio de Janeiro: Ed. Revan.

Watanabe, Kazuo. 1996. "Novas Atribuições do Judiciário: Necessidade de sua Percepção e de Reformulação da Mentalidade." *Revista Escola Paulista da Magistratura* 1, no. 1.

3

Judicialization of Protest in Argentina

THE CASE OF *CORRALITO*

Catalina Smulovitz

> Today the area surrounding the Palacio de Tribunales became a chaotic scene. Hundreds of savers queued since daybreak, waiting to submit their appeals for legal protection against the *corralito.* Amid strong disputes and protests, the twelve-hundred-meter-long line made vehicular traffic practically impossible. . . . Savers arriving at the judiciary headquarters couldn't determine where the line ended.
>
> *La Nación,* February 20, 2002

> What? Have you closed banks to protect them against judges? You belong to another galaxy.
>
> Comment of an American official on hearing the news about a bank holiday to avoid judicial-mandated withdrawals, *La Nación,* April 24, 2002

HIGHLY MOBILIZATIONAL FORMS of protest are one of the trademarks of the current social, political, and economic crisis in Argentina.[1] Images of middle-class citizens pounding on bank doors, picketers' demonstrations, roadblocks, and supermarket lootings dominated public images of the recent explosion of protest. People were back in the streets, and social defiance appeared to challenge the ability of the state to impose political order. Institutions seemed to be withering away, and many social and political actors explicitly questioned the representative role and recent performance of political institutions. In this context, where massive, although fragmented, social and political protest regained the streets and reoccupied traditional protest spaces, a new resistance and protest movement appeared and organized around the use of legal tools to demand protection of property rights and to regain access to frozen and devaluated bank accounts.

Two policy decisions triggered this recent outburst of legal protest: the freeze and limitations placed on access to bank accounts, and the forced conversion to local currency at unfavorable rates of the dollar-based savings accounts that had been previously frozen. In the midst of intensive street mobilization, these two measures led to the emergence of a movement that also chose to use legal tools to frame its demands. What have the consequences of the legal mobilization process in the development of the crisis been? What has its effect been on economic policy and in controlling executive decisions? What have its results as a tool of social protest been? And what does this legal mobilization phenomenon indicate regarding the ways of doing politics in Argentina? These are some of the questions this chapter will address.

The Scenario of the Dispute

On December 1, 2001, Domingo Cavallo, then Argentina's economy minister, announced the establishment of restrictions on cash withdrawals from private and company bank accounts.[2] The decision took place in a context characterized by the continuous and persistent drainage of private-sector deposits. The outflow became particularly severe in the last quarter of 2001, building up to US$15.5 million in the year and amounting to US$1.5 million on November 30, 2001.[3] The government announced that the restrictions were temporary and that its intention was to protect deposits within the banking system without violating property rights.[4] However, only three days after these announcements were made, two pieces of information anticipated the legal framing of the coming conflict. On the one hand, Remes Lenicov, then House representative of the Partido Justicialista and later first economy minister of the Eduardo Duhalde administration, announced that his party intended to present an *amparo* (injunction) against restrictions of withdrawals from salary accounts.[5] On the other hand, the National Union of Judicial Employees (UEJN) initiated the first collective injunction claiming the unconstitutionality of the recent economic measures and their immediate rejection due to their "confiscatory" character.[6] A week after the announcement of the restrictions, a newspaper article mentioned the existence of 220 cases denouncing the unconstitutionality of the measure. In the following days, Judge Silva Garretón gave a favorable response to preliminary injunctions against the *corralito*.[7]

In the following days, popular anger, rioting in the provinces and in Buenos Aires, and the still unclear actions of the political opposition forced the resignation of the economy minister and of President Fernando de la Rúa. The crisis that led to de la Rúa's resignation had been in the making for some time. The events that should be considered to explain the crisis vary, but its history surely includes the resignation of Vice-President Carlos Alvarez in October 2000; the midterm defeat on October 14, 2001; key cabinet resignations; the International Monetary Fund (IMF) refusal to continue paying the bailout loan; and the still unclear role of some Buenos Aires province Peronist Party leaders in the lootings that marked the end of de la Rúa's government. When de la Rúa left power on December 20, 2001, around thirty people had died, mostly due to police brutality, and forty-five hundred had been arrested during the mobilizations that took place in those two final days of the Alliance government.[8]

On December 23, 2001, the legislative assembly elected Adolfo Rodriguez Saa, then governor of San Luis province, as president and called for general elections to choose a new president within three months. Rodriguez Saa immediately announced that Argentina would default on its international debt obligations but expressed his commitment to maintain the currency board and the peso's 1-to-1 peg to the dollar. Rodriguez Saa, however, was unable to rally support from within his own party for his administration, and this, combined with renewed violence in the federal capital, led to his resignation on December 30.

Another legislative assembly elected Peronist Eduardo Duhalde president on January 1, 2002. In the following two months, Duhalde abandoned the ten-year-old link of the peso with the dollar, establishing the total pesification of the economy and a dual exchange rate system—a 1.4-peso-per-dollar rate for official transactions and a floating rate for all other transactions.[9] It was also decided that debts in dollars would be converted to pesos at a 1-to-1 exchange rate, while deposits in dollars were pesified at a 1-to-1.4 exchange rate. In addition, the government imposed new restrictions on withdrawals from personal and corporate deposits, reprogramming their availability. These new restrictions, popularly known as *corralón,* expanded the previously established ones imposing up to three-year deadlines for withdrawals from safe deposits. In particular, these new measures established that (1) savers could take out 1,500 pesos as opposed to the previously authorized 1,000 pesos a month; (2) banks had to switch current accounts above $10,000 and savings accounts above $3,000 into fixed-term deposits; (3) deposits in dollars, depending on their size, were to be returned to savers in monthly allowances according to a preset long-term schedule (in some cases, returns were to start in January 2003, in others in September 2003); (4) smaller accounts in dollars had to be converted into pesos at the official exchange rate of 1.4 pesos to 1 dollar and could be withdrawn, but subject to the prevailing limits; (5) bank loans and mortgages of less than $100,000 had to be converted into pesos; and (6) banks had to renegotiate a cut in interest rates on all foreign currency loans. It should be noted that by December 2001, 70 percent of the deposits in the banking system were nominated in U.S. dollars[10] and that by July 2002, the floating exchange rate was over 3.5 per dollar. This set of measures favored those who had contracted debts in dollars and punished those who had their savings in pesos (which lost their buying power due to devaluation) and those who had their savings in dollars and had had them converted into pesos at an unfavorable exchange rate and frozen in the banking system.

Another feature that characterized this scenario was the initiation, soon after Duhalde took office, of the impeachment process against all the members of the Supreme Court. The Supreme Court, which had been packed at the outset of the Carlos Saúl Menem administration, enjoyed low prestige and from the beginning of the political and social crisis in December had been the target of street demonstrations demanding the resignation of its members. Three days after Eduardo Duhalde took office, there was news regarding the government's interest in "cleaning" the Supreme Court, given its low prestige and the intensity of the claims against its composition.[11] A month later, the Impeachment Commission of the House of Representatives decided to impeach all of its members.[12] The decision was based, among other reasons, on the behavior that ministers of the Court had shown in cases regarding the constitutionality of the restrictions of banking withdrawals; the illegal sale of arms to Croatia and Ecuador, which involved President Menem; the approval of telephone rate increases; and failures in the investigation of the 1992 terrorist attack on the Israeli embassy. On October 12, 2002, the House of Representatives voted against the initiation of impeachment procedures against the members of the Supreme Court.[13] However, during the ten-month period in which the conflict of powers remained unresolved, Supreme Court judicial decisions ostensibly became part of the political game. On the one hand, the government looked for favorable Court decisions, threatening its members with the activation or appeasement of the impeachment procedures. On the other hand, the Court threatened the government with decisions that would intentionally jeopardize the political sustainability of its emergency program and the fate of negotiations with the IMF. In September 2002, for example, the Court decided to strike down a 13 percent cut in government salaries and pensions made in 2001.[14] At the end of 2002, the Court indicated that it might give favorable treatment to an injunction that questioned the governmental decree that had converted dollar deposits into pesos.[15] By 2002's end, the Court was still deciding on a demand presented by the governor of San Luis province asking for the devolution of US$247 million that was frozen and converted into pesos at the outset of the crisis.[16]

It was in this scenario, characterized by a deep economic and social crisis, a crisis of representative linkages, the questioning of political authority, and an intense conflict of powers, that the process of legal mobilization and protest took place.

The Facts

The use of legal procedures as a tool for social protest and resistance is not new in the Argentinean context. There are some well-known cases of the use of such procedures, including the use of the habeas data during the dictatorship,[17] and some less notable cases, such as the demands initiated against the pension fund system.[18] Let's consider, then, some of the features that characterized the legal mobilization around the *corralito* claims. The historical reconstruction of the case is complex, reflecting the chaotic evolution and establishment of the policy. A first reading of this historical reconstruction shows that the *corralito* dispute can be read as an illustration of the "science of muddling through" by legal means, where actors attempt to impose a policy, to resist its imposition, and to redress its challenges through the use of legal tools backed with social mobilization.

3.1 Number of Injunctions and Amounts Paid (in %)

Amount of Money Paid by the *Amparos* (in pesos)	% of Cases	% of Money Returned
Up to $10,000	14.20	1.50
From $10,000 to 20,000	16.44	2.80
From $20,000 to 50,000	28.30	10.70
From $50,000 to 100,000	19.90	16.30
From $100,000 to 200,000	12.20	19.90
From $200,000 to 500,000	6.70	22.9
From $500,000 to 1 million	1.50	11.60
From $1 million to 2 million	0.50	7.70
From $2 million to 5 million	0.14	4.90
More than $5 million	0.03	1.90

The total number of injunctions considered in table 3.1 is 36,178.
Source: Clarín, June 8, 2002.

As has been mentioned, in December 2001, soon after the first restrictions were imposed, "injunctions" were presented questioning the constitutionality of the measures, and a federal judge sanctioned a preliminary measure against the imposed restrictions. Before the end of that chaotic December, newspapers were already reporting a wave of judicial cases against the *corralito* (at that time there were only 220 cases).[19] By April 2002, the office of the Procuración del Tesoro Nacional published the fact that 210,188 "*amparos* against the *corralito*" had been presented in the federal justice system.[20] The information explicitly specified that these numbers did not include injunctions presented in the provincial justice system, although several sources mentioned that the number of injunctions at the provincial level was similar to the number at the federal level.[21]

In April, the two banking associations (Asociación de Bancos de la Argentina [ABA] and Asociación de Bancos Públicos y Privados de la República Argentina [ABAPPRA]) submitted a written report to the Supreme Court. In their presentation, they warned the Court about the risks that favorable judicial treatment of *corralito* demands would bring about, given that the approximately 200,000 existing claims represented only a small number of the 9,000,000 savers in the financial system. The report also mentioned that returning the savings involved only in those 200,000 injunctions would imply a

3.2 Total Number of Injunctions and Amounts Paid in 2002

Month	Number of Cases	Money Paid (in million pesos)
Up to April	28,873	$2,695
May	11,407	$938
June	16,165	$1,207
July	17,974	$1,290
August	7,419	$573
September	13,367	$1,035
October	14,545	$1,055
November	12,920	$849
December	21,166	$1,786
Total	143,836	$11,428

Source: Banco Central de la República Argentina, Informe semanal 10, January 17, 2003.

142 percent increase in monetary circulation and that in such a case 75 percent of savers would be unable to get their savings back.[22] In April, newspapers reported the initiation of more than 20,000 additional injunctions and the presentation of two collective demands advanced by the National and Municipal Ombudsman Offices, demanding a halt in the application of the Reference Stabilization Coefficient (CER) that was to be applied to credits that were in dollars and had been converted into pesos, as had been established in Decree 214/02.[23] In May 2002, newspapers also reported possible wrongdoing in the way demands were being granted in certain provincial courts, noting that in these districts big claims were being favored over small ones.[24] However, information provided by the Central Bank showed that, until then, of the 36,178 *amparos* that had received favorable sentences, 58.9 percent were for claims under 50,000 pesos and 41.1 percent for claims between 50,000 and over 5 million pesos. The information also showed that claims between 50,000 and 1 million pesos received a bigger percentage of the frozen deposits than smaller or bigger claims. By January 2003, the weekly report of the Banco Central de la República Argentina (BCRA) on the status of the *corralito* demands indicated that from April 5, 2002, until December 2002, 143,835 *amparos* had received favorable responses. The average amount returned per injunction between April and December was US$22,930, and this amount decreased throughout the period (see fig. 3.1).[25]

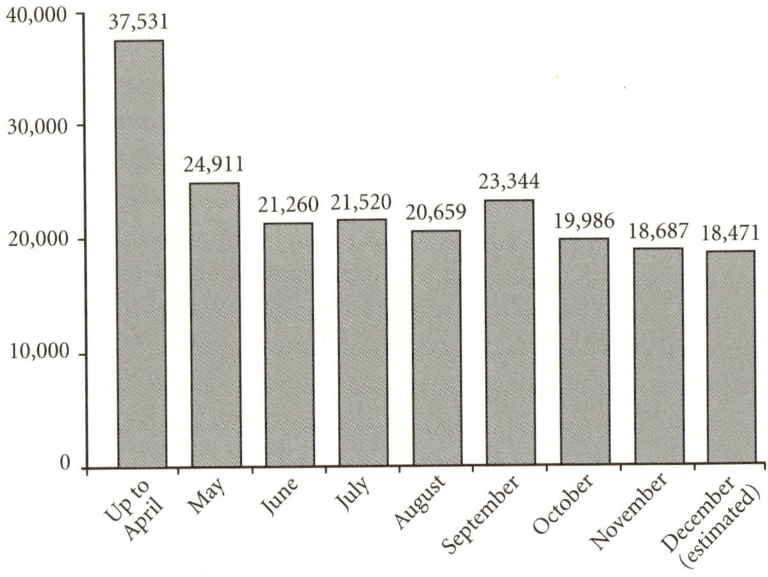

Fig. 3.1. Average Amount Returned per Injunction (in dollars)
Source: Banco Central de la República Argentina, Informe semanal 8, January 3, 2003.

Outcomes and Actors in the Legal Protest Process

What does the *corralito* legal mobilization show about the use of the law as a protest mechanism? What has it accomplished? And what does it show about the relationship between law and politics in the Argentinean context?

It should be noted that the label "*corralito* case" does not refer to one specific type of injunction but rather to a network of different judicial claims. Although the case started with a series of individual and collective *amparos* in December 2001 denouncing the unconstitutionality of governmental policy, due to violations of property rights, it rapidly grew into a loosely united social movement unified by a common action: advancement of literally thousands of *amparos*. The case also includes the presentation of another wave of *amparos* (more than twenty thousand) against the retroactive application of the CER, an actualization index to be applied to debts that were in dollars before the end of the convertibility plan. The political and judicial conflicts, interchanges, and responses that these legal disputes brought about resulted in the emergence of a series of subsequent legal disputes and claims. Indeed, the strength, effectiveness, and persistence of the *corralito* legal protest are highly associated with this continuous remaking and ramification of the first legal claims.

In the process, the government tried several responses to deal with the accumulation of claims and the risks favorable court decisions to these injunctions might have imposed on the financial system. Not all the attempted responses became actual policy. In some cases, when there were signs that proposed measures would face strong political and legal resistance, the government refrained from advancing them. In others the government had to try several institutional responses to achieve its goals. For example, in February 2002, in order to limit the execution of *corralito* court decisions ordering the devolution of deposits, the government sanctioned two decrees, Decree 214/02 and Decree 320/02, establishing a six-month suspension in the initiation of claims and the execution of court decisions ordering the return of deposits. These two decrees gave way to another wave of injunctions questioning their constitutionality insofar as they implied not only violations of property rights but also violation of the right to due process. Since these two decrees did not limit the drainage of deposits, at the end of April the government passed another law, popularly known as "Ley Tapón" (Law 25.587), which, instead of suspending the right to file demands, established additional procedural requirements for complying with favorable court decisions related to preliminary *corralito* injunctions.[26] Initially, and as a consequence of this new law, the number of injunctions decreased; however, after a while new *amparos* against the "Ley Tapón" were presented, jeopardizing the government's goals once more.[27]

Thus, the legal mobilization process developed as a succession of nested legal conflicts. The original conflict involved injunctions for violation of property rights; however, the government's response in confronting the original claims brought about "second-order" legal disputes that challenged governmental policy on different grounds. Historical reconstruction of the case shows, first, claims for violations of property rights and then claims for violations of the right to due process. In some cases, claims were motivated by governmental decisions, such as the ones that questioned the freeze and conversion into pesos of the deposits or the application of indexing formulas due to the pesification of debts. In others, claims were the result of the collapse of the judicial system due to the accumulation of claims; in still others, claims derived from the suspension and postponement of the execution of court decisions. The net result was that, a few months after the launching of the first restrictions, the government had to deal not only with political and social contenders but also with an array of legal ones less likely to be satisfied with political negotiations of the results.

The emergence and extensive use of injunctions to claim frozen deposits is perhaps the most notable manifestation of the process of the judicialization of politics that has been taking place in the Argentinean political context over the last twenty years.[28] In contrast to the European and North American cases, where the process of the judicialization of politics is mainly concerned with the increasing role of constitutional and supreme courts in policy making,[29] the Argentinean judicialization takes the form of an increased use of legal procedures for making political and social demands. It was in this context, characterized by the previous use of juridical instruments for strategic and extralegal goals, that the massive use of injunctions to make demands regarding the frozen and devaluated deposits should be understood.[30] In Argentina, previous experiences of legal mobilization revealed that social legitimacy derived from the use of legal arguments was a powerful instrument for resisting and redressing public policy and for ensuring participation of weak and nonorganized actors in policy debates. While claims and struggles around past human rights violations showed the potentiality of legal discourse to contest the legitimacy of a policy and to protect weak actors, the legal crusade of the pension fund movement established the potentiality of the legal strategy for organizing nonorganized actors and for resisting, delaying, and redressing unfavorable policy outcomes. Thus, the massive nature of the *corralito* legal claims should be understood in the context of the previous experience social actors had had with the use of the law.

How can the results of the legal mobilizational strategy be evaluated? Is the capacity to redress policy results the indicator of success? Does success depend on the number of claims that received favorable sentences? Or is the ability to determine the conflict agenda the indicator of success?

The reconstruction of the *corralito* case shows that neither the massive nor the successive waves of injunctions have been able to totally redress litigants' claims. *Corralito* claimants have not been able to achieve a clear-cut final Supreme Court decision regarding the unconstitutionality of the freezing of their deposits or of their conversion into pesos. In 2004, an ambiguous Court decision[31] established the constitutionality of the pesification of dollar deposits. However, a dissident opinion in that decision established that savers with claims under US$70,000 were entitled to the total devolution of their deposits. Given the ambiguity of the Supreme Court decision, some inferior tribunals have accepted the constitutionality of the pesification, giving no place to savers' claims; others have accepted the minority opinion, totally returning savings of claims under US$70,000; and still others have questioned the constitutionality of the distinction allowing the continuation of claims, demanding the restitution of savings over US$70,000.[32] Thus, although savers' claims have not been fully satisfied, achievements have not been irrelevant. A significant number of claims have received favorable juridical decisions,[33] and important extralegal results have been achieved. Although *corralito* claimants have not achieved a definitive victory, they have achieved "piecemeal" successes, such as individual court decisions ordering the total or partial return of the frozen deposits, which have eroded and complicated the scope and resilience of the governmental policy.

Reactions to these piecemeal successes give an idea of their significance. These piecemeal successes have motivated preemptive governmental interventions to protect the freeze, such as forced conversion of deposits into governmental bonds or the sanction of a law postponing compliance of preliminary injunctions. IMF interventions warning the government that "stand-by" agreements cannot be reached until the government has demonstrated its ability to curtail and control favorable court decisions regarding *corralito* injunctions are another sign of the potential threat implied by these piecemeal achievements.[34] The massive character of the injunctions and the juridical framing of the protest have forced the government to give official and public responses to the claims, restricting, in turn, its ability to impose imperative political decisions. Thus, from the claimants' point of view, the legal strategy has been an effective defensive approach insofar as it has been able to minimize initial losses.

Another consequence of the use of legal mobilization as a protest mechanism in the *corralito* case is related to the serial and apparently unending character of the dispute. Its unending dynamic and the succession of ad-hoc governmental measures developed to address it have brought about an unexpected effect. They have provided claimants and protesters with arguments and opportunities that prolong the intense life of the protest. The serial character of the legal conflict has prevented an early closure.

In a context characterized by the generalized outburst of social protest, legal procedures provided *corralito* protesters with an additional and powerful instrument. When massive attendance at demonstrations started to recede, and when the initial apparent unity of the protesters started to fragment, the tempo and ramifications of the legal process helped to keep *corralito* protests as a persistent and nonvanishing problem on the public agenda. Legal protest provided litigants with opportunities to maintain their contacts and networks. In a curious way, the legal architecture of the conflict provided unexpected "mechanical assistance" to the protest and allowed it to defy the mobilization fatigue that very often jeopardizes social mobilizations. This status of "perpetual process," which resulted from the serial and nested character of the legal disputes, also had additional consequences. It helped to establish the political legitimacy and relevance of the protest, contributing, in turn, to extending surveillance over the government's actions. In other words, the perpetual process and the nested character of the conflict not only prevented *corralito* cases from vanishing from the scene but also kept the savers' movement organized and focused.

Which actors promoted, participated, and used a legally framed strategy? The use of a legal strategy does not necessarily require the existence of preexisting socially organized actors. Legal protesters can act individually. In addition, since the Argentinean legislation does not include "class actions," private lawyers have low institutional incentives to represent protestors collectively, as a class. It should be noted, however, that the 1994 reformed constitution authorized the presentation of collective injunctions and that in the *corralito* case, both the National and Municipal Ombudsman Offices presented collective injunctions. Nevertheless, the enormous number of injunctions presented shows that most litigants opted to petition as nonorganized and nonunified actors.[35] In spite of this, links and bridges among this large and heterogeneous group of individuals began to be formed. After a few weeks of gatherings, pot banging on the banks' doorsteps, media visibility of the legal protesters, and favorable court decisions, some of these individual claimants began to get organized in loosely united associations and developed into a loose network of protesters.

In addition to social rage, the protesters had in common their inability to get free access to their savings and the fact that they were opting for a legal strategy. The Internet also provided a space that individuals and associations used to contact each other, to publicize letters to be sent to national and international organizations, and to communicate courses of actions and share experiences.[36] This unorganized movement also enjoyed the contribution of the media, which in those hectic days kept showing enraged, well-dressed, middle-class men and women pounding at the bank doors together with equally furious poor retirees. Gatherings and demonstrations and visibility in the media, as well as initial favorable court decisions, helped to disseminate and reproduce the use of injunctions as a common strategy.

Once the massive character of the legal actions became evident, other actors entered the scene. Their intervention was relevant insofar as they ended up acting as "de facto" organizers of the protest. Savers' associations, for example, started being organized in January 2001. Although they did not directly sponsor legal claims, they organized demonstrations and informed savers about their legal options. Savers organized associations in Buenos Aires (Asociación de Ahorristas de la República Argentina, Movimiento Independiente de Ahorristas Argentino, Ahorristas Bancarios Argentinos Estafados), in Córdoba (Asociación de Ahorristas Bancarios Estafados), in La Plata (Ahorristas Platenses, Asociación Argentina de Ahorristas), in Rosario (Ahorristas Rosarinos), in Mar del Plata (Red Nacional de Ahorristas Unidos), in Bahia Blanca (Asociación de Ahorristas Bahianos), and in Chubut (Ahorristas Valle del Chubut). In addition, a famous comic, Nito Artaza, a well-known lawyer, and a political party (Comisión Argentina en USA [CAUSA]) have become important advocates of the claim. In April 2002, an Asociación Hispanoamericana de Perjudicados por el Corralito was created in Spain.

One of the most salient characteristics of these associations has been their hyperactivity. Although they act independently, their actions reinforce each other's. They offer legal advice and information to savers, organize weekly marches in the principal cities of the country on Mondays, and have organized five national marches and two national conventions. They have also taken their case to and made presentations at the national and provincial legislatures, the Human Rights Interamerican Court, and an independent evaluation office of the IMF. As other social movements have recently done, savers' associations have also organized *escraches,* fasting, and massive meetings.[37] In June 2002, the comedian Nito Artaza organized a meeting that gathered three thousand people, and in July he organized another one attended by at least eight thousand. He also organized other massive meetings in the subsequent months.[38] Different parties have urged him, as the unlikely leader of a national movement, to run on their tickets in recent months.

As has been the case in other legally framed disputes, claimants in the *corralito* case have also resorted to foreign courts to readdress their rights.[39] In March 2002, an Argentinean lawyer presented a claim in the Spanish judicial system on behalf of one hundred Argentinean savers, and two Spanish ones, against two Spanish banks that had branches in Argentina (Banco Bilbao Vizcaya Argentaria [BBVA] and Santander Central Hispano [SCH]). A few months later, a Spanish court recognized the competence of the Spanish judiciary in the case and called for a conciliatory meeting among the parties.[40] The judge justified this decision given that legislation acknowledges Spanish courts' competence to intervene in civil claims when defendants are based in Spain.[41] In June 2002, a second Spanish judge accepted the competence of the Spanish courts to intervene in a claim presented against BBVA and SCH by 650 savers.[42] And in August, savers organized through CAUSA, and those who had their deposits frozen in branches of American banks, initiated a class action in a federal court in Miami.[43] Finally, in September 2002, the Asociación Hispanoamericana de Perjudicados por el Corralito, representing one thousand savers, advanced a new criminal claim against BBVA and SCH.[44] Regardless of the results, these actions merit a few comments. On the one hand, they show that the international card has become part of the strategic repertoire of the users of the legal strategy. For claimants, the benefits of this card are multiple. First, it expands the high visibility of the conflict. Second, insofar as foreign courts face fewer incentives and pressures to consider the political consequences of their decisions, the claimants' threatening capacity increases. And third, from the claimants' perspective, they are more likely to obtain beneficial extrajudicial agreements in foreign courts than in national ones because the former do not set an obligatory precedent for the latter.

The other actors who have had an impact on the diffusion and growth of the legal strategy are lawyers, in particular through some of their professional associations. In the first few months of the year, the ad pages of the newspapers were covered with announcements from legal firms offering their services to initiate injunctions and promising rapid recovery of the trapped savings. Between February and July 2002, the Colegio Público de Abogados de la Capital Federal organized at least twelve official events to train and update their associates about the use of injunctions, unconstitutionality claims, and the juridical aspects of the new economic measures.[45] Although information regarding attendance at each of these events is not available, newspaper articles noted that for the first time in its history the Colegio had used videoconferencing for these events. The Colegio also created a hotline to answer questions from its members. The Asociación de Abogados de Buenos Aires organized training activities to answer questions from its members. And law publishing firms such as

La Ley and El Derecho gave talks and issued special publications to meet increasing demand for updated literature on the topic.[46]

Regardless of the normative position lawyers may have had regarding the conflict, the massive presentations of injunctions were an important working and economic opportunity for law firms and lawyers. To initiate claims, individuals had to pay to the lawyer or firm taking the case between one hundred and one thousand pesos. Although claimants did not have to pay legal taxes, winning claimants had to pay 3 to 5 percent of the recovered savings to their lawyers, and losing claimants had to pay 3 percent of the claimed savings to the judiciary as a judicial tax.[47] Thus, the injunction avalanche provided an important opportunity for the profession and placed lawyers and their associations as an interested party in the development of the dispute. Given the particular and unexpected role lawyers and their professional associations played in the dispute, they facilitated potential savers' access to justice and, in the process, became "de facto" organizers of the legal protest. Thus, throughout the period, lawyers, law firms, and law associations played different roles. Not only did they offer lawyers "know-how" to cope with the demand, but they also gave claimants a ready-made "solution" to redress their damages. Thus, while they provided claimants with needed professional services and assistance, they also played an entrepreneurial role. On the one hand, their assistance and legal advice contributed to the diffusion of legal strategy. On the other, the benefits they could obtain helped to build the privileged position the legal strategy achieved among the options open to protesters.

A Final Note

What does the *corralito* legal mobilization show about the use of the law as a protest mechanism? And what has it accomplished?

Analysis of the *corralito* case illustrates that the use of the legal strategy can render legal protesters specific material benefits but can also radiate important symbolic and political ones. The historic reconstruction of the case shows that the legal strategy brought about significant material outcomes for protesters. Although legal protesters have not accomplished all their intended goals, have not completely redressed the policy, and have not recovered the totality of their frozen deposits, by December 2002, roughly 65 percent of the individuals who presented legal claims had received a favorable response. It should be noted that these benefits did not reach individuals affected by the economic measures who had not resorted to the legal strategy.

However, these results do not capture the political and social relevance of the *corralito* legal protest. Past experience has shown that legal strategies not only serve to redress policy outcomes but can also result in political and extra-legal benefits. Claimants in the *corralito* case have been able to reconfirm this observation. As has been the case in other legally framed conflicts, the intervention of judges resulted in some sort of satisfaction for claims and provided, in addition, legitimacy and public recognition to claimants. Legally framed social and political conflicts produce these results when rights are considered official promises and when judges are transformed into "guardians of past promises."[48] In such cases, judicial strategies may redress actual damages, and they may also create public empathy, social allies, and institutional custodians for the claimants' demands. The evolution of the *corralito* case illustrates all these dimensions. It enabled litigants to resist and redress the policy, it provided them with social legitimacy, it endowed a nonorganized and amorphous conglomerate of individuals with a social and collective entity, and it allowed them to find unexpected social and institutional allies.

As analyses of other legal mobilization cases illustrate, the achievement of these results depends on the existence of social mobilization.[49] The *corralito* case shows, as well, that throughout this period, social mobilization was an important companion of the protest. In this case, legal and social mobilization also received constant media attention. Media visibility illuminated the existence of an uncoordinated social phenomenon and disseminated the availability of a specific course of action and a "ready-made" solution for those affected by the economic measures. Although the life of a legal protest is associated with the presence of social mobilization, the impact the procedural architecture had on the permanence and vitality of the dispute cannot be underestimated. Legal procedures have certain rituals and tempos and are punctuated by specific events. Claims must be answered in certain ways, and there are external time limits to which protesters have to respond and adjust. In other words, external procedural requirements set the pace of the protest and present protestors with periodical procedural opportunities to re-create the mystique of the protest. The legal context provides events that force protestors to coordinate actions, preventing, in turn, the gradual erosion of the protest.

Two other reasons should be considered in examining how legal framing of disputes alters the development and resolution of conflicts. On the one hand, by legally framing disputes, protesters are able to incorporate other actors in the scene. They place judges and tribunals as legitimate and authorized parties and as observers of public behavior. Insofar as they expand the scope of conflict, they increase the number of parties with a voice in the conflict. Furthermore, this conversion allows protesters to introduce a permanent external surveillance actor to the process. On the other hand, the legal framing of disputes alters the resources involved in the decision-making process. Legal precedents, reasonable arguments, and preestablished rules must be considered in a decision. These requirements impose constraints on the possible outcomes of a dispute. If law becomes the new language of politics and procedures its grammar, the way conflicts can be solved confronts important restrictions.[50]

Finally, one comment should be made regarding the impact of the legal strategy on the collective organization of actors. The legal strategy allows individuals to overcome some of the difficulties they face in organizing collective actions. In contrast to other forms of protest, claimants can initiate protest actions even without coordinating with other actors. In this particular case, legal protest has become a social phenomenon due to the massive character it has achieved and to the social mobilization, media visibility, and public empathy the protest has been able to accomplish. However, when these conditions do not interact, legal protest can condemn citizens to a progressive atomization of their social and political resources.

NOTES

1. A study made by the Centro de Estudio Nueva Mayoría shows that, between Dec. 19, 2001, and Mar. 2002, 2,014 *cacerolazos* (pot poundings) took place in Argentina (*Nueva Mayoría,* Apr. 25, 2002). Further research registered 272 neighborhood assemblies in Mar. 2002 and 329 in Aug. 2002 (*Nueva Mayoría,* Sept. 6, 2002). Regarding roadblocks (*cortes de ruta*) the organization's last study indicates that there were 514 in 2000; 1,3838 in 2001; and 2,336 in 2002 (*Nueva Mayoría,* Feb. 10, 2003).

2. See Decree 1570/01. These restrictions are popularly known as *corralito* (enclosure).

3. Ministerio de Economía de la República Argentina, Report 39, "The Argentine Economy during the Third Quarter of 2001 and Recent Evolution" (2001).

4. *La Nación,* Dec. 1, 2001.

5. *La Nación,* Dec. 4, 2001. An *amparo* is a complaint regarding a violation of constitutional rights when such rights cannot be adequately and promptly protected by other means. See Guillermo Cabanellas de las Cuevas and Eleanor C. Hoague, *Diccionario Jurídico* [Law Dictionary] (Buenos Aires: Editorial Heliasta SRL, 1993).

6. *La Nación,* Dec. 4, 2001.

7. See *La Nación,* Dec. 5 and 7, 2001.

8. Centro de Estudios Legales y Sociales, *Derechos Humanos en Argentina: Informe 2002, Siglo XXI* (2002).

9. See Law 25.561, Decree 141/02, Decree 214/02.

10. Fundación de Investigaciones Económicas Latinoamericanas, Indicadores de Coyuntura, N 419 (Buenos Aires, Jan.–Feb. 2002).

11. *La Nación,* Jan. 3, 2002.

12. *La Nación,* Feb. 6, 2002.

13. *La Nación,* Oct. 12, 2002.

14. *La Nación,* Sept. 10, 2002.

15. *La Nación,* Dec. 3, 2002.

16. *La Nación,* Mar. 2, 2002. Since this chapter was written, several developments have taken place. On Mar. 5, 2003, the Supreme Court ruled unconstitutional the devaluation of a $247 million fixed-term deposit held by the province of San Luis and ordered the deposit to be changed back into dollars. On May 25, 2003, a new president, Nestor Kirchner, took office. During the first two years of his presidency, and with the support of the executive, the legislative power has impeached and threatened to impeach several members of the Supreme Court. Since June 2003, three of its member have resigned, and one was ousted after impeachment. Finally, on Oct. 26, 2004, the new Supreme Court ruled that the pesification of dollar deposits that took place in 2002 was constitutional. The decision established that savers were to receive, for each deposited dollar, 1.40 pesos, multiplied by the Reference Stablization Coefficient (CER). The decision also included a dissident vote that established that savers with deposits under US$70,000 were to receive in dollars the total amount of their deposits. See *La Nación,* Oct. 27, 2004.

17. See Carlos Acuña and Catalina Smulovitz, "Guarding the Guardians in Argentina: Some Lessons about the Risks and Benefits of Empowering the Courts," in James McAdams, ed., *Transitional Justice and the Rule of Law in New Democracies* (Notre Dame: University of Notre Dame Press, 1997).

18. The judicialization of the pension fund conflict began in 1960 when the state, unable to pay the expected pensions, established that pension debts would be paid in installments according to the fiscal availability of funds (see Law 17.583/67, Decree 1706/68, Law 18755/70). Since that initial wave of claims, retirees have made demands on the state on different grounds and at different times. Just to illustrate the magnitude of the problem, it should be mentioned that in 1999, the state faced 130,000 unfavorable sentences that represented 2,100 million in pesos, and another 90,000 unfavorable decisions were expected (*La Nación,* June 15, 1999). According to an Interamerican Development Bank report, in the year 2001, 20,000 claims were being initiated per year and 100,000 claims were still in process (Informe Final, Administración Nacional de la Seguridad Social, Préstamo BID 925 OC-AR [Mar. 2001], 55). For an analysis of the judicialization of the pension funds conflict, see Catalina Smulovitz, "Judicialization and Societal Accountability in Argentina," paper presented at the twenty-second International Conference of the Latin American Studies Association (Washington, D.C., Sept. 2001).

19. *La Nación,* Dec. 19, 2001.

20. *La Nación,* Mar. 23, 2002.

21. See Horacio Lynch, "Emergencia, Derecho, Justicia y Seguridad Jurídica (Reflexiones sobre la Crisis y las Libertades Económicas)," *La Ley,* May 29, 2002.

22. *La Nación,* Apr. 23, 2002.

23. *La Nación,* Apr. 17, 2002.

24. *La Nación,* May 5, 2002.

25. Banco Central de la República Argentina, Medidas Cautelares, Informe no. 10 (Jan. 17, 2003).

26. *La Nación,* Apr. 25, 2002. The new law was popularly labeled "Ley Tapón" as it was supposed to put a lid or a cork on the drainage of funds resulting from favorable sentences for *corralito amparos.*

27. See *La Nación,* June, 2, 2002: "After a pause imposed by the 'Tapon' Law, sentences have increased again."

28. As mentioned in previous studies, changes in litigiousness levels and in the composition of legal claims that have taken place since 1983 are important indicators of the emergence and consolidation of the phenomenon. See Catalina Smulovitz, "The Discovery of the Law: Political Consequences in the Argentine Experience," in Brian Barth and Yves Dezalay, eds., *Global Prescriptions: The Production, Exportation, and Importation of a New Legal Orthodoxy* (Ann Arbor: University of Michigan Press, 2002).

29. Neal Tate and Torbjorn Vallinder, eds., *The Global Expansion of Judicial Power* (New York: New York University Press, 1995).

30. Patricia Ewick and Susan Silbey, *The Common Place of Law* (Chicago: University of Chicago Press, 1998).

31. See *La Nación,* Oct. 27, 2004. Further details are provided in n. 18.

32. See *La Nación,* Nov. 10 and 23, 2004.

33. See table 3.2, which includes information from the BCRA regarding the total amount of *amparos* paid.

34. IMF intervention in the *corralito* case is paradoxical. On the one hand, the institution has severely criticized the Argentinean government for violation of the rule of law and the prevalence of a legally insecure context. On the other hand, it had demanded government intervention to curtail judicial decisions regarding *corralito* cases even when decisions had a legal ground. See, e.g., *La Nación,* July 22, 2002.

35. See Margin Bohmer and Ezequiel Nino, "La Justicia Acorralada y una Solución Procesal Posible," *Jurisprudencia Argentina* 1, no. 13 (2002).

36. See, e.g., <http://www.adapd.com.ar>, <http://www.aara.com.ar>, and <http://www.ahorristasplatenses.8m.net>.

37. *Escraches* are mobilizations that intend to denounce and to provoke public shaming. In Argentina the human rights movement originally used them, although lately they have been adopted by different social movements and organizations.

38. See *Clarín,* June 20, 2002, July 9, 2002, Aug. 8 and 21, 2002.

39. See Ellen Lutz and Kathryn Sikkink, "The Justice Cascade: The Evolution and Impact of Foreign Human Rights Trials in Latin America," *Chicago Journal of International Law* 2, no. 1 (2001).

40. See *Clarín,* June 10 and 11, 2002; *Página 12,* June 11, 2002.

41. See *Página 12,* June 11, 2002, for excerpts of the sentence.

42. *Clarín,* June 27, 2002.

43. *Clarín,* Aug. 10, 2002.

44. See *Clarín,* Sept. 13 and 14, 2002.

45. Information provided by the Colegio Público de Abogados de la Capital Federal. The information supplied also mentions that in 2001, it organized only two academic ac-

tivities related to injunctions and that no activities were organized in regard to this topic in the years 2000, 1997, 1996, 1995, or 1994. To understand the significance of this information in the analysis of the role of the lawyers' associations, it should be remembered that the 1994 constitutional reform introduced important changes regarding the use of injunctions, particularly regarding who is entitled to initiate them. Thus, regular activities on this particular topic could have been expected throughout the period.

46. "Furor por la Capacitación entre los Abogados," *La Nación*, Feb. 21, 2002.

47. *La Nación*, Feb. 21, 2002.

48. Stuart Scheingold, *The Politics of Rights: Lawyers, Public Policy and Political Change* (New Haven: Yale University Press, 1974); Antoine Garapon, *Juez y Democracia* (Spain: Flor del Viento Ediciones, 1997), 20.

49. Scheingold, *The Politics of Rights.*

50. Garapon, *Juez y Democracia,* 18.

4

Multiple Activation as a Strategy of Citizen Accountability and the Role of the Investigating Legislative Commissions

Ana Tereza Lemos-Nelson and Jorge Zaverucha

Challenges for Democratic Accountability in Pernambuco

THE DEEPENING of democracy in Latin America is happening in the context of a complex framework of previously dominant forms of authoritarianism, presenting to progressive reformers the challenge of destroying these sources of conservatism. One characteristic of this framework hangs in the axis of the opposition between five-century-old patrimonialism and aspiring republicanism. As Guillermo O'Donnell has pointed out, republicanism is one of the sources of contemporary democracy. In Latin America, however, patrimonialism, and its lack of separation between the public and the private realms, has had a negative impact on the democratic experience by obstructing the development of republican traits (1999, 31–33).

Patrimonialism also represents a serious obstacle to the development of the assumption or prerequisite of equality and the establishment of patterns of accountability. The forms of achievement and reproduction of power under patrimonialism place social, economic, and political power in the hands of the same elite, allowing this power to be reproduced by means of producing categorical inequality (Tilly 1998). A movement of constant expropriation of the means of social recognition and prestige (social and cultural discrimination), economic concentration (surplus value), and political domination (patronage and clientelism) creates dual societies characterized by first- and second-class citizenship.

Patrimonialism also presents overwhelming challenges to accountability because it commands informal arrangements that corrupt the formal separation of powers. Elitist executive dominance weakens the independence of the legislature and the judiciary, which are rendered highly ineffective in their oversight capacities. Patronage as a structural form of reproduction of the legislative branch harnesses its capacity to check the executive (Leal 1978; Faoro 2001; Pereira 2001; Graham 1997). As to the judiciary, politicization of decisions is one of the main obstacles to its effective operation. José de Souza Martins has observed that "patrimonial rule does not set itself up, in Brazilian tradition, as the rival of the rational-legal rule." On the contrary, it "feeds off it and contaminates it" (1996, 195). As a consequence, the lack of accountability not only of the executive but of all the powers is maintained through political tools created through highly questionable judicial decisions. Historically, and from the perspective of the rights of the disadvantaged, the legal system has been used as a system of rights exclusion, a "wholesale perversion of justice," a "tool for social control" (Barkan 1984, 554), as expressed in the often cited quotation of ex-president Getúlio Vargas: "For my friends, everything, for my enemies, the law."

On top of these processes, patrimonialism also has typical ways of dealing with violence. The essential form of command of seigneurial violence in patrimonialism is the paramilitary militia supported by the right to loot (Weber 1978). This arrangement has jeopardized the legitimate use of violence in at least two ways. First, executives see police forces as their private armies and do not allow their development under legal parameters, so as to keep them under control. Second, gray areas of informality are reproduced where paramilitary forces (death squads, *justiceiros*, etc.) increase the zones of armed power, and the public becomes indistinguishable from the private. Unaccountability, in the last instance, is maintained through the threat and the actual use of illegal violence by the state against private and political foes. We refer to patrimonialism as a wider sociopolitical structure of power that embeds and gives meaning to clientelist and patronage practices because we believe that this use of force, or its threat, characterizes the land-based social order.[1] Additionally, neopatrimonialism (Schwartzman 1988) pervades the sociopolitical relationships of the "modern" sectors.

In this context, the problem of establishing citizen accountability and deepening democracy becomes extremely complex: "Societal accountability involves actions carried out by actors with different degrees of organization that recognize themselves as legitimate claimants of rights. . . . They are critical for the activation of horizontal accountability" (Smulovitz and Peruzzotti 2000). Given the weakness of horizontal accountability (O'Donnell 1999), citizen accountability as a form of vertical accountability used to supplement electoral representation has the task of giving life to formal and informal institutions through which the popular will may be conveyed. Although these institutions are an assumption of democracy itself (Dahl 1971; Lijphart 1984), in transitional situations there may still be a great deal of work needed to create them or to make them operational.

This chapter analyzes the connection between horizontal and vertical accountability through focusing on the relationship among several recent CPIs (Parliamentary Commissions of Inquiry) in the state of Pernambuco, in northeastern Brazil, and their constituencies—social organizations and the media—and sometimes their clients: the political parties and the legislative branch itself. It will show that the CPIs, as investigative task forces, have the power and legitimacy to open up public spaces that would otherwise remain closed to public scrutiny. The actions of social accountability are in some cases important tools to bolster the investigative power of the legislature and produce change. CPIs have the potential to facilitate the oversight of government by the citizens in at least two significant ways: by reducing the costs of obtaining inside information and by increasing media visibility for a particular issue. This makes it more difficult for politicians to drop an issue from the political agenda. In this interpretive framework, the combination of citizen activation and CPI investigation forms a triangular dynamic aimed at opening up the executive branch and making it more responsive and accountable to societal needs and preferences.

The chapter argues that since citizens cannot trust the effectiveness of any of the formal powers in checking each other, they have to build strategies of *multiple activation* that will increase the contradictions among formal powers, making them function in ways that are convenient to democratic reform. We understand *multiple activation* as a strategy of resource mobilization simultaneously directed at several organizational networks, actors, and agencies, in both the state and the society, to maximize the effects of their actions. The objectives of citizen accountability go beyond short-term concerns or individual cases because it must target the system as a whole (patrimonialism) if enduring change is to be achieved. It could be said that in the context of dormant or paralyzed horizontal guardians, indirect or mediated accountability hits the executive through the activation of those actors entitled to horizontal oversight.

We propose that understanding the scope and possibilities of citizen accountability vis-à-vis CPIs has to be framed by explication of the limits of the accountability of the legislative branch itself, and of the legislative branch as the fiscal arm of the executive. Finally, the limits of the judiciary as the enforcer of the law also determine the degree of effectiveness that legislative investigative powers might have in generating punishment for wrongdoings. In other words, citizen accountability in the transition from patrimonialism/authoritarianism to democracy dwells in an extremely hostile environment where conservative forces undermine all the formal powers; make some representation limited and temporary; and frame the choice of strategies case by case, opportunity by opportunity. We therefore propose to study citizen accountability in the relationships between two different institutional frameworks of conflict—first, as vertical accountability in the activation of four formally (legally) established sets of actors: executive (including the police), legislative (in the different sets of suborganizations: committees, CPIs, coalitions), judiciary, and finally international (the principled networks of NGOs and the international commissions and courts); and second, as vertical accountability against the informal but deep institutional framework of patrimonialism, whose values and procedures contradict democratic values and expectations. We argue that in all cases the role of the media as a propeller of activation is central and crucial, both to the CPI process and to the effectiveness of citizen accountability. It has the potential to induce change in the formal structure by exposing and questioning undemocratic values and practices.

However, none of these factors is sufficient in itself. The articulation of the CPIs, supported by their striking legal powers of investigation, along with the media, creates a *free space* (Evans and Boyte 1992) where citizen action and demands can spur accountability. Free spaces are "settings between private lives and large-scale institutions . . . with a relatively open and participatory character. [They are] schools for democracy . . . that allow people simultaneously to draw upon and transform in democratic fashion their inherited identities and the ties of daily life" (Evans and Boyte 1992, ix). These free spaces, guaranteed by the presence of the CPIs and the media, are therefore the spaces of action where political identities are constructed through the very action of protesting and demanding. They are the spaces where individuals become citizens and organizations are given the opportunity to sharpen their tools of transformation.

We suggest that because CPIs are proactive but intermittent tools of accountability, societal actors tend to invest in short-term goals and to increase their pressure or maximize their resources by adopting inside-outside strategies. CPIs have enjoyed some success in terms of bringing corrupt politicians to justice but very little in reforming corruption in the long term. An agency permanently dedicated to combating corruption (Johnston 1999) has not even been considered.

The case of Pernambuco in northeastern Brazil is particularly interesting because the transition to democracy has set the stage for intense political competition. There are strong patrimonialist roots, given Pernambuco's agrarian structure, that are linked to the reproduction of family feuds and violence in the countryside. In contrast, Pernambuco has a libertarian tradition and a leftist history that has meant cultural and political resistance to conservative structures. The consequence of these contradictory inputs is a high level of conflict that has taken place in social and political, formal and informal institutions. Pernambuco is a showcase for the difficulties of democratization and change, as its political space is occupied by both the most conservative and the most progressive tendencies and actors. The metropolitan area of the capital, Recife, composed of fourteen different counties (with a population of over three million inhabitants), is the third most violent in the country, with a rising crime rate and an urban habitation structure always under pressure from migration from the interior, where the structures of patrimonialism seriously limit the economical survival of the most disadvantaged. These structures set the stage for politico-administrative corruption; economic stagnation; and belligerent political groups that, despite their influence in the federal arena, disregard compromise with the public good. Such major names of national politics have emerged from Pernambuco as Vice-President Marco Maciel, Inocencio de Oliveira, Minister Raul Jungman, Roberto Freire, Gustavo Krause, and Jose Jorge. Yet the state has appalling human-development indices.

In the Northeast, a good number of large cities already present some form of participatory administration, while most small counties are still strongholds of patrimonialism. The state of Pernambuco is an interesting example of these cases: the government of the state is run by a center-right coalition with some contradictory historical identification with the Left. The administration has paid lip service to the obvious attractiveness of the councils project, and some citizen councils have been activated. These councils differ a great deal in their representativeness. While some reflect wide participation of previously instituted social organizations, others have been recently directly nominated by the executive, who has attempted to co-opt power through them. In the metropolitan area of Recife, five of the twelve counties (Recife, Olinda, Camaragibe, Cabo de Santo Agostinho, and Moreno) are run by opposition mayors, and the experience of the councils is thus finding its first local interpretations. Recife, Olinda, and Camaragibe provide three examples of successful participatory administration experiences.

The three recent CPIs are diverse in both content and objectives. Interestingly enough, all three target different arms of the state and exist at different levels (state and county, although all are in the metropolitan area of Recife). They are (1) the CPI of the Narcotics Trade (the Narcotics CPI hereafter), developed at the state level by the Legislative Assembly of Pernambuco, based in Recife; (2) the CPI of the Construction Business (the Construction CPI hereafter), organized by the Chamber of Representatives of Olinda County; and (3) the Social Security CPI, developed by the Chamber of Representatives of Camaragibe County.

The Narcotics CPI was opened under public outcry when a similar federal CPI pointed to connections between the narcotics trade and several outstanding state politicians (mayors and legislators), police officers, and landowners. It caused a domino effect, eventually including under its spacious umbrella crimes involving other authorities: the robbery of truck cargo on the state roads, the extermination of children and the formation of paramilitary forces (*pistolagem*), illegal arms smuggling and sales, and finally corruption of political power and illegal financing of electoral campaigns. Underlying and connecting all the relationships uncovered, the patrimonialist structure emerged supreme. We could say that this CPI, with its wide reach, targeted patrimonialism itself. As to its objectives, this could thus be seen as a *systemic* CPI.

The CPI in Olinda was more similar to the *administrative* CPI model characterized by the traditional legislative role of oversight of the executive and the curbing of corruption. The Construction CPI was opened after heavy rain caused the collapse of several buildings in Olinda, with casualties and injuries resulting. It questioned the lack of executive supervision of construction patterns and the issuing of building licenses without control.

Finally, the Social Security CPI, in Camaragibe, aimed at tainting the reputation and prestige of a local mayor responsible for a highly successful project of participatory administration. It charged the mayor with appropriating Social Security funds for personal use, a move that, if successful, could have destroyed the credibility of a Workers' Party administration. This CPI targeted citizen accountability itself, the model of participatory budgeting, as detrimental to the interests of clientelistic members of the legislature, as it does not allow the development of the traditional schemes of patronage and clientelism and reduces corruption to something very close to zero (Santos 1998). As the population informally makes decisions on priorities, it becomes harder for the center-right legislative branch not to approve them. Consequently, the system affects the reproduction of the patrimonial legislative system as such and forces reform of political power. Or, as mayor Paulo Santana unpretentiously put it, it leads to "jealousy" from the legislative branch. This CPI could be classified as an *anti–citizen accountability* CPI.

As there are no studies of local CPIs, this chapter intends to shed some light on the local dynamics that push CPIs' investigative power by exploring their relationships to their closely connected constituencies. At another level, this can allow a tentative comparison with state and federal CPIs so as to evaluate their potential for producing democratic change.

The Organization of Social Movements and the Legislative Branch

If democracy is a "moving target" (Schedler, Diamond, and Plattner 1999a, 1), the relationship of social movements to CPIs should be evaluated in the broader context of the long-term relationship of organizations to the legislative branch as a constant refinement of representation. If, on the other hand, democracy is a process, "a journey, not a destination" (Evans and Boyte 1992, xix), this long-term relationship tells us more about the way democratic spaces are built.

Patrimonialism forms a kind of tight power structure that is in many respects comparable to the southern "power structure" (Ture and Hamilton 1992) faced by the U.S. civil rights movement in the fifties and sixties: the alliance of the executive, the legislative, and the judicial branches in ways that entirely eliminate horizontal accountability. The tightness of this structure is an obstacle to the progress of issues favorable to the minority interest. In such a context, the civil rights movement had to engage outside parties and use disruptive tactics to compel or elicit the irruption of the federal government on their behalf (McAdam 1982; Morris 1984). The availability of such third parties in the North, where the political and ethical systems were more progressive, strengthened the movement's claims (Lipsky 1968).

Unlike that correlation of forces, however, the social movement in northeastern Brazil cannot count on the intervention of such third parties, since corruption plagues most Brazilian states and there is no region where a functioning rule of law can provide a different model for confrontation. Aggregation of a pro-rule-of-law coalition faces the difficulties and costs of organizing and articulating local initiatives at a national level: "Subnational governments often lack their own checks and balances at the provincial or municipal level" (Fox 2000, 6). Moreover, the federal government is highly dependent on the support of the political Right in its congressional coalition, composed of a majority of politicians identified with conservatist landowning in the Northeast. This conjunction of parties makes any federal intervention in local matters extremely unlikely.

In the social movement's favor, however, is the fact that there is a significant national ethical rejection of the authoritarian/oligarchic model of politics and that the 1988 constitution reflects a progressive moment of national consensus in favor of change.[2] Despite its weaknesses, this constitution has provided a new institutional framework that is available to reformers. The thirteen-year period since its enactment has allowed some democratic institutional build-up that is supporting gradual change, despite frequent blatant violations that are facilitated by the lack of supporting legislation and enforcement. The major instruments for change outlined by the constitution in terms of accountability are the new prominent role of the Public Ministry regarding the protection of collective rights, Public Audiences within the Legislative Assembly, and the strong investigative powers granted to Parliamentary Commissions of Inquiry. These powers of fiscalization are meant to allow new practices to become institutionalized. Given its length, the constitution grants formal powers, but only the dynamics of constant claims and accountability can turn these formal powers into actual institutional frameworks.

Moreover, historically accumulated organizational resources have allowed access and limited penetration of traditional institutions by people based in social movements that facilitate the development of inside-outside strategies. The main channels of penetration are as follows. In the executive branch, progressive mayors have been elected to local governments and are implementing entirely new ways of doing politics, especially through the participatory administration discussed below. In the legislative branch, progressive representatives have been elected and are gearing some permanent committees toward new values and practices. Finally, the merit-based mechanisms of entry in the cadres of the Public Ministry have taken the institution from its previous defense of the state to defense of the citizenship (Sadek 2000; Sales de Albuquerque 2001; Santa Cruz 2001). The judicial branch, however, was least affected by the constitutional changes and, despite honorable exceptions, is still distant in its elitism and indifferent to the interests of the general public (Benvenuto 2001; Santa Cruz 2001).

Another relevant aspect of the constitution concerning accountability is the organization of citizen councils to participate in the decisions concerning public administration. These councils are meant to supplement representative democracy with some measure of direct democracy, increasing citizen accountability through the creation of a new blend of representation and participation. The democratic potential of participatory budgeting can only be understood if the primary unfairness of Brazilian society is taken as the starting point. The first experience of decentralization and popular administration began in 1989 in Porto Alegre when the first Workers' Party mayor was elected. The success of democratic urban management has won the status of an "urban innovation worldwide," granted by the United Nations (Santos 1998, 2). As a form of preempting patrimonialism, it resorts "to the direct participation of the population in the different phases of the budget preparation and implementation, with special concern for the definition of priorities for the distribution of budget resources." The impact on traditional structures is such that it has been evaluated as an "institutional mediation for the reinvention of democratic theory" (Santos 1998, 3).

If we consider that countries throwing off authoritarianism seriously lack those "institutions necessary for making the government policies depend on votes and other expressions of preference" (Lijphart 1984, 2), the contribution of this particular blend of representative and participatory democracy to strengthening democracy may be more thoroughly understood. Citizen councils allow "preventive accountability" since the direct participation of the citizenry in the decision process preempts the major and otherwise routine deviation of local budgets into politicians' pockets. Although participatory administration is growing steadily as a major tool against patrimonialism and its tools of patronage, assistentialism, and clientelism, it is still limited.

Pernambuco has a long tradition of social movement and resistance, dating back to the first century of Portuguese colonization, and much of its history may be understood as having its roots in the expulsion of the Dutch colonizers in the seventeenth century. As locals say, resistance "runs in the veins" (Pedrosa 2001). The imagery of the people is populated by the *caboclo* heroes who constructed a unique civilization in the tropics that resisted all attempts of domination.[3] Built on sugar cane plantations, Pernambuco was the state that suffered the most brutal repression during the military dictatorship: the strength of its peasant organization (Liga dos Camponeses) was identified as an instrument of "Cuban" subversion and received the heavy weight of the military arm.

In the beginning of the transition, new NGOs were founded that would consolidate the new structure of popular resistance. The Gabinete de Assessoria Jurídica às Organizações Populares (GAJOP) has been committed to the "democratization of the Brazilian State" since 1981.[4] Therefore, it is a sociopolitical actor that has participated in the transition from its beginning and sees the struggle against authoritarianism as a long-term battle against deep-seated cultural traits that are present both in the state and in society. The struggle is also seen as a fight against impunity. GAJOP currently coordinates several projects in the area of security and justice. It develops educational programs in human rights for police officers, along with other partnerships with the state and federal governments. It pioneered in the establishment of a witness protection program, PROVITA (Programa de Apoio e Proteção e Testemunhas, Vítimas e Familiares de Vítimas de Violencia), that has spread to other states.

Another important branch of popular organization dates back to the 1950s, based on the social work developed by the Catholic Church. Especially noteworthy is the work of Dom Hélder Câmara, who for many decades was an uncompromising supporter of the underprivileged. The ferocity of the dictatorship's anticommunism went to the extremes of labeling him a devil, but his clear advocacy for the poor survived dictators and left the legacy of an important network of church-related organizations. Among them, the Recife-based Centro Dom Hélder Câmara (CENDHEC), the Movimento Tortura Nunca Mais, and the Centro Luiz Freire should be mentioned.

A third but no less important root of popular organization concentrates efforts toward land issues, as is unavoidable in a state that still has sugar cane as its main source of income and powerful landowners in control of local politics. Particularly resistant has been the Federação dos Trabalhadores da Agricultura do Estado de Pernambuco (FETAPE), joined by the later Movimento dos Sem-Terra (MST); the Movimento dos Sem-Teto (MST); and Pastoral da Terra, connected to the Church.

These local organizations are nationally articulated through their common participation in the National Movement for Human Rights (Movimento Nacional de Direitos Humanos: MNDH). The MNDH is a civil organization founded in 1982, organized in eight regional branches, that currently includes 350 centers for the defense and promotion of human rights throughout the country. Since this organization sees that the necessary changes are structural, its long-term goal is to help build a new human rights culture in Brazil that will give priority to values built around life and human dignity. In the pursuit of this goal, it concentrates on strengthening public and private institutions that might contribute to the democratic rule of law, through which they expect to build fairness and solidarity in society. Among other principles directed toward this main goal, it specifically aims at building accountability through "(a) stimulating the organization of popular and civil society groups, so that they can build ways of achieving and enforcing their rights and defending themselves against violence and arbitrary power; and (b) struggling to guarantee the full enforcement of human rights, in any circumstance, fighting for the punishment of those responsible for violations and fair reparation for the victims" (GAJOP 2000, 1–2).

The regional northeastern branch of the MNDH is based in Recife, thus boosting the efforts of the local organizations. This branch includes sixty-three affiliated NGOs and acts through well-defined programs. The Database Program aims at giving agency researchers the capacity to collect data to fulfill the region's specific demands. The Monitoring Program for the National Program for Human Rights aims at creating state programs as a strategy to press for implementation of the national program.[5] Two other programs address institutional and leadership development, emphasizing specific training for juridical operators to increase access to information about the justice system and intervene in the legal field.

These organizations are also internationally articulated by the International DH Program, which is an initiative of GAJOP and MNDH, with support from Catholic Relief Services (CRS). This program was created to allow access to international jurisdiction both at the regional (Organization of American States) and global (UN) levels in cases of gross violations of human rights in the Northeast. They have presented cases of torture and summary execution before the Interamerican Commission of Human Rights and the Human

Rights Commission of the UN and have demanded and supported country inspections through the visits of special rapporteurs from the UN.

The relationship with the legislature during the democratization period was first established through GAJOP's monitoring and lobbying program, which represented for several years daily scrutiny of legislative agendas. Constant monitoring in the long term, however, is difficult to maintain because the agencies prefer to support activities that produce immediate results in terms of sociopolitical change. Consequently, permanent monitoring had to be dropped, with the substitution of close and constant relationships with the representatives who are more sensitive to human rights issues. The several human rights commissions of the legislative branch at the federal, state, and county levels became the channels through which the demands of social movements could be forwarded in search of accountability. This was facilitated by the election of representatives long identified with the cause of human rights who had previous ties to the social movement. Relationships with particular legislators thus substituted for a relationship with the legislative branch as a whole. The channeling of demands through the commissions has also meant specialization, since it favors the treatment of specific issues related to human rights. Even in this context, the commissions have allowed a broad range of human rights issues to be addressed. They represent the possibility of articulations from within the government and the development of inside strategies or lobbying that help frame more favorable visions and tactics that wouldn't be framed otherwise.

The Limits of Legislative Accountability and the Specificity of CPIs as Tools of Accountability

During the Brazilian parliamentary Empire (1822–89), the eligibility criteria of the voting system was based on patrimony: "the extent of the right to vote was measured by each man's patrimony, since only the richest voted in all elections (municipal, provincial, and national). Those who were not as rich voted in municipal and provincial elections, but not in national ones. People with modest wealth only voted in municipal elections. . . . In a certain sense, it was a scale of delegation of political rights and of indirect political action: those excluded from the right to vote were included under the tutelage of the rural bosses, as clients and protégés, even as far as properly political questions were concerned. Thus, the whole system was based on mechanisms of political mediation which had their basis in patrimony" (Martins 1996, 199).

This system, under executive command, was largely maintained through electoral fraud aimed at guaranteeing the reproduction of the conservative majority in a tightly knit pyramid of power from the local to the federal levels. There were several mechanisms of fraud that could affect all steps of the electoral process, from the eligibility phase up to the counting of votes. The processes of fraud required the participation of the judiciary and the police, creating bonds of illegality among the legislative, judicial, and executive branches that had links of patronage as their inevitable counterpart. As a consequence of the fluidity of criteria and the lack of law enforcement, electoral periods were the most violent ones in the life of communities, usually resulting in deaths and injuries. This power structure was maintained and even increased with the Republic (1889), as the state governors were solidly kept as political bosses and distributors of favors (Lemos-Nelson 2001):

> It is not at all surprising that the military, the heirs of monarchical absolutism, and historically opposed to the oligarchs, should have made a pact with them during the dictatorship that ended not long ago. Because what in fact happened, at Independence and with the Republic, was the preservation of a certain absolutism, which the Army represents; a certain verticalisation of power, with its basis, however, in the parallel, local power of the oligarchies, the bosses. The oligarchies ensured the stability of power. They are, in truth, the magistrates of the political process, as was seen in the election of Tancredo Neves as the first president after the extinction of the military regime, and was seen in the political agreements which defined the course of the presidential election of 1994. (Martins 1996, 199)

The evidence shows that, despite the strong ethical movement that supported the first moments of the transition to democracy, the system of patronage and clientelism did not abate, as the Collor case is inclined to show.[6] The procedures of conservative modernization also survived the Fernando Henrique Cardoso government and were in fact updated to increase the capacity of the executive to control the legislature:

> Strengthening the centralization of the budget process, an important institutional change, happened at the beginning of the Fernando Henrique Cardoso government, allowing even greater influence of the executive over representatives' behavior. It was the decision of the Cardoso government

> to centralize information about the representatives' behavior in the presidency of the Republic that was previously decentralized by the ministries; the centralization of the distribution of resources under the control of the executive; and the uniformization of the actions of the government toward the National Congress through the creation of a special system of legislative action, called the System of Legislative Accompaniment—SLA [Sistema de Acompanhamento Legislativo: SIAL], by Decree 1403 of February 21, 1995. (Pereira 2001, 6)

Pereira reports that

> according to Eduardo Graeff, consultant of the General Secretary of the Presidency of the Republic, "in the beginning of the government we noticed that there was no institutional mechanism able to control the demands of the legislators. It was not uncommon to see several representatives, many of them unfaithful to the government, demanding benefits to different agencies and ministries so as to help their electoral bases. We decided, therefore, to assume control of this situation by centralizing all the demands of the representatives in the SLA. This centralized system allowed us to have a perfect picture of what the legislators demanded, as well as to know up to what point the executive really responded to their demands." In other words, the SLA works by equilibrating the pressures of the parliamentary demands mediated by party leaders and the behavior of the vote inside the Congress. (2001, 6)

There is "strong evidence that the representatives' strategy of following presidential preferences and the indication of their party leaders with the expectation of obtaining access to political and financial benefits to be used in the electoral arena allows consistent electoral returns." In other words, "this is how the electoral connection really works in Brazil" (Pereira 2001, 12): "The greater the number of individual amendments of the legislator actually implemented by the president, the greater the probabilities for the election of the representative." The organization of a federal CPI to investigate corruption was demobilized through the selective distribution of funds to federal representatives (Pereira 2001, 12).

These mechanisms of the distribution of funds through party leadership, meant to generate legislative discipline, also severely curtail the capacity of the legislative branch to exercise oversight of the executive. They produce strong disincentives to representatives' initiative to expose the executive's wrongdoings.

The reproduction of these clientelist strategies among the governing center-right coalition has brought about a need for the opposition to create new possibilities for the exercise of political power: "Currently the success of the executive in getting its legislative agenda approved and its dominance in the enacted legislation increased drastically as compared to the 1946 democracy" (Figueiredo 2000, 4).

CPIs capitalize on the public's anger. Consequently, they also draw a great deal of media attention and present incentives in terms of exposure that might counterbalance the effects of the eventual loss of executive support. Moreover, they are nonmajoritarian tools that are available to the opposition, which wouldn't benefit from patronage anyway. High political gains in terms of media exposure might also be sufficient for some representatives of the governmental coalition to eventually defy party discipline and join the opposition. The calculus of cost/benefit is different from the calculus that guides decisions to vote with the party on the floor because the benefits might outweigh the costs. Federal CPIs are much more likely in democratic periods and seem "to be more closely related to periods of great political conflict" (Figueiredo 2000, 16).

In fact, CPIs might help legislative careers, since many leading politicians of the Left have participated in CPIs, often more than once, increasing their visibility and electoral gains (e.g., João Paulo, Romário Dias, Paulo Rubem, Pedro Eurico). This intimate relationship between CPIs and media exposure is both their strength and their weakness. It is their strength because it allows them to work as if enjoying a permanent public audience, with open channels of communication between representatives and the public. It doubles the perception of legislators' representativeness because they seem to receive their mandate both through the delegation of votes and through direct command of the population. In contrast, the gains of media exposure might motivate unnecessary CPIs developed only for electoral gain. The expression "CPI eleitoreira" (Sales 2001) describes this kind of investigation, aimed at tarnishing reputations. The damage done through the media with unfounded accusations is hard to completely remove, since the right to response is not necessarily granted, the public does not necessarily follow all the media shows, and the information is imperfect.

Some CPIs might be preemptive, initiated just to prevent other CPIs from being opened (Figueiredo 2000). CPIs are important in times of political transition because they increase accountability, expose contested values and behavior, and frame new desired attitudes. Transitions are characterized by conflicts framed by a model of state and society becoming obsolete and by the birth and eventual consolidation of a new model. The meaning of corruption in transitions rests in change as well as in values and institutions, concepts of legitimacy, and strategies of the legitimization of power (Johnston 1991).

The CPIs' main weakness remains their limited capacity to compel the judiciary to defend citizens' interests: "Lacking state action, some officials are thus spared the sanctions that would have probably resulted if the courts and/or other public agencies had intervened" (O'Donnell 1999, 30). If, on the other hand, we consider the breadth of systemic issues such as the destruction of patrimonialism, the CPI process in itself might go a long way toward exposing and counteracting the prestige of local bosses. As it challenges the very bases on which their power is built, it opens the way for further future change.

The CPI against the Patrimonial System

Federal and/or municipal CPIs vary in relation to their strategic goals, entailing different levels and forms of citizen participation for accountablity. The following section presents some case studies of contemporary CPIs in Pernambuco to analyze the relationship between the representatives' and the citizens' strategies. It shows the highest level of citizen participation and pressure for accountability, constituting a strategy we refer to as "multiple activation" (see earlier definition). The cases were chosen through two criteria: availability of sources and their ability to represent different strategic goals of the legislative branch so that their relationship to citizen initiatives would be more evident.

"Multiple Activation" and the "Movement" Strategy

Impunity and other consequences of the workings of the patrimonial system in Pernambuco provided fertile ground for the formation of an extensive area of marijuana farming in the Moxotó-Pajeú region, which came to be known as the "Poligone of the Marijuana," an area of around twenty-five thousand square kilometers. The consolidation of this area took root when the federal government extinguished lines of agricultural financing in the region in the wake of an episode of major corruption/violence known as "the scandal of the manioc." In substitution, marijuana cultivation spread rapidly. The symbiosis among landowners, political power, and armed power created spaces free from inspection where marijuana was farmed, commerce boomed, and new economic possibilities attracted both poor farmers and bankrupted landowners. A situation of gross human rights violations developed under the umbrella of corrupt police officers, judges, and politicians. Violations of the rights of peasants, including several summary executions, attracted the attention of the Church and human rights activists. Their complaints, however, could not overcome the tightness of the local power structure, and they therefore searched for national attention.

As the situation of the drug trade created many pockets of corruption and violations all over the country under executive omission, there was a national mood favorable to legislative investigation. A federal Narcotrafico CPI (Parliamentary Commission of Inquiry on the Narcotics Trade) was set up in April 1999 by the federal House of Representatives following a series of media scandals. The vice-president of the CPI was federal Pernambuco representative Fernando Ferro. The CPI visited Pernambuco to get firsthand reports on the "Poligone of the Marijuana," one of the main narcotics-producing regions of the country. The commission stated that one main reason for visiting Pernambuco was to find means to permanently eradicate the cultivation of the drug in the state.[7] Given the national visibility of the issue, the CPI was not met with resistance from the executive. The secretary of social defense attempted to preempt the investigation by presenting the representatives with a 150-page dossier outlining the conflicts in the region and suggesting that the alleged criminals, especially Mamédio dos Santos, or "Maninho da Pistola," serving in Canhotinho Penitentiary, and Osvino Cordeiro "Vinva" da Cruz, in the Aníbal Bruno Penitentiary, be interviewed. The commission also had a meeting with the governor, Jarbas Vasconcelos, Secretary of Justice Humberto Vieira de Melo, and State Attorney General Romero Andrade. The CPI staff was protected by 150 police officers (*Jornal do Commercio* [*JC* hereafter], April 4, 2000).

In its conclusion, the federal CPI suggested that another CPI be installed at the state level to investigate local problems, since it had indicted ten local individuals for having connections with drug dealers. Social movement organizations set out to convince local representatives to overcome their resistance and open a local CPI. Resistance was high because not just the executive would be investigated; evidence indicated that members of the Legislative Assembly itself were involved with organized crime.

A strategy of *multiple activation* of several possible forms of support was then developed by the organizations. They leaked information to the media and searched for support from their national allies, then joined efforts with the Public Ministry and the local public prosecutor, who produced a very critical report denouncing the inability of the justice system to act against the parallel system of (in)justice (MPP 2000a). They activated the judiciary by writing letters to local judges and pressured the executive with marches and street gatherings in the capital. The strategy was successful in building a general perception that either the crimes should be properly investigated or all public powers (legislative, executive, and judicial) could be seen as involved, with high political costs for those who could not distance themselves from accusations by revealing the names of those directly involved.

A major obstacle to both vertical and horizontal accountability was fear: given the known methods of operation of the accused, many parliamentarians feared for their lives in a context in which even the public prosecutor was threatened with death. But the costs of omission started to rise. Some issues uncovered by the federal CPI were extremely dear to public opinion. Specifically, the discovery that around one hundred street children who had disappeared had in fact been murdered and clandestinely buried over a period of four years by an extermination group in the Timbauba County area caused an enormous outcry. The issue of violence against children involves a historical struggle, initially supported by the Catholic Church, that branched out into various organizations that have been developing all sorts of outreach activities in the area over a long period of time. The social organizations, led by the MNDH, started a "real war" with public mobilization, manifesto writing, and lobbying to pressure representatives to open a state CPI (Pedrosa 2001). The scandal grew even greater as the groups evidenced the depth of executive involvement in the extermination group, its members acting as private security for local politicians and wearing T-shirts identifying them as "The Guardian Angels"; such was the sense of impunity shared by the violators.

The *multiple activation* and *inside-outside* strategies paid off as social organizations could count on the support of the representatives who had long been identified with the causes of the underprivileged and who had previously been social movement militants (Pedrosa 2001). The CPI of the Narcotics Trade and *Pistolagem* was installed in February 2000. It was set up to investigate the connection of the narcotics trade with killings by hired gunmen and frequent robberies of truck cargo on the state roads. It was initiated by state representative Pedro Eurico (PSB-PE), who justified it by stating that twenty-eight of the one hundred most violent cities in the country were located in the state of

Pernambuco. Its vice-president was Representative Lula Cabral (PFL-PE), and its other members included Henrique Queiroz (PPB), Marcantônio Dourado (PMDB-PE), Romário Dias (PFL-PE), and Sérgio Leite (PT-PE), some of them veterans of other CPIs or with a history of protecting human rights. The CPI also set up several debate cycles in the capital Recife, their themes including the progress of the narcotics trade and the strategies available to combat it and violence against and the extermination of children and adolescents. Visits to cities in the interior that were well-known for violence were also undertaken, including Palmares, Garanhuns, Caruaru, Serra Talhada, Limoeiro, Petrolina, Timbauba, Ipojuca, and Itambé.

The extensive paramilitary organization under politicians' protection in these localities created obstacles to citizen participation because of generalized fear. The members of the CPI decided to set up a toll-free number especially to collect information, and a large number of denunciations came through (CPI 2000, 36). Strengthened by the presence of authorities without local connections, organizations jumped in to offer information. The CPI received 180 written reports, letters, and memos from several organizations and state bureaus. In turn, the CPI sent out 647 memos requesting information.

The police immediately made seventeen arrests by request of the CPI for robbery, reception of stolen goods, narcotics trafficking, bank robbery, gun possession, extortion, murder, and participation in death squads. Some of the people arrested were police chiefs, attorneys, and even members of the legislature: Palmares County representative Teresa Josino Branes, for example, was the subject of an arrest warrant, her mandate cancelled for involvement in the murder of attorney Celia Maria (Resolution 001/00, June 20, 2000; CPI 2000, 134–39). Early in the process, the local Public Ministry issued an extremely powerful document called "Public (IN)Security in Timbauba." Reportedly, its investigation was prompted by the question of "why there are no criminal lawsuits in Timbauba." The answer was that an extermination group had been acting in the region for almost a decade as a "Court of Exception," controlling the police, the Public Ministry, and the judiciary (8).

No representative wanted to be responsible for writing the final report, since this document would carry the power of an indictment and could be used by the police and the public prosecutor to formally indict the accused. The CPI had to use a lottery to pick the official reporter, the responsibility falling on Representative José Queiroz (PDT-PE). The CPI concluded that the cultivation of marijuana is now controlled by several autonomous gangs that started to fight over economic and political control of the region: "There is not a unified command responsible for all the narcotics production in Pernambuco that could fit the international definitions of 'organized crime' (UN) since the activities lack money laundering, are not transnational, and do not use advanced technologies" (CPI 2000, 146–47). The CPI's report, however, also contradicts itself, discussing the ways drug dealers launder money in the region (158–60). This reluctance to clearly define the social situation of crime in the area was possibly due to the fact that if the illegal activities were defined as "organized crime," the federal police could claim jurisdiction over law enforcement in the area. The CPI thus protected the state interests of the parties in power against federal intervention.

Control over peasants is exerted through ruthless violence that is assimilated within family feuds. Such violent activities spread into other criminal behavior as bank robbery and the robbery of truck cargo, generating a steep increase in the violence index of the region (CPI 2000, 143). Extermination groups (death squads) grow under the protection and demand of these drug dealers turned politicians. The region of Mata Norte was believed to have developed under the "permanent action of extermination groups" (CPI 2000, 175).

The regional "capital" of the narcotics trade, the city of Carnaubeira da Penha, is located right in the middle of the area, with excellent natural irrigation from the Pajeú River and an outstanding climate with plenty of sunshine. Moreover, the topological formation of the area, with its protective thorny vegetation, provides a natural barrier against penetration by the police, while a network of roads allows for the easy export of the drug. State road PE 460, known as "Transmaconheira" (Transmarijuaner), has at its center the city of Salgueiro.

Governmental forces or agencies do not protect the state's frontier area with the state of Alagoas, which makes this frontier a likely escape route for bank robbers, assassins, drugs and arms dealers, and stolen vehicles. Besides these factors, taxes on the circulation of goods between these states cannot be collected. The states of Alagoas and Pernambuco used to be part of the same Hereditary Captaincy; "politically separated, the states of Alagoas and Pernambuco continue to be united by the seal of impunity" (CPI 2000, 176). There are many unofficial ways and several unchecked and clandestine passages through which it is possible to go from one state to the other. As a consequence, the CPI recommended that the presence of state institutions (police, judge, and state prosecutor) be strengthened. As to the police, it recommended that military police officers stationed in the region should be moved every twenty days so that local political influence would not be able to control them (CPI 2000, 177). This suggestion for solving the police problem "at home" preempts a possible increased presence of the federal police, over whom local authorities would have no power.

Local peasants produce marijuana under intense armed pressure from dealers; the associated criminal activities simultaneously finance the drug trade and political campaigns (CPI 2000, 147). Indeed, the CPI's report observed that the number of bank robberies increases enormously in the periods previous to elections (2000, 175). As a consequence, corruption spreads to the entire state machine, generating what the CPI called the "narcostate" in Colombia, although it denied its existence in Pernambuco. However, the CPI did conclude that:

(1) Police officers are involved in cargo robbery, filing false reports.

(2) Tax collectors participate in the information network of the criminals (CPI 2000, 181).

(3) Politicians (both legislative and executive) are financed with crime money, especially for their electoral campaigns.

(4) Corruption of state officers in charge of the prisons is so widespread that citizens can enter the prisons to buy drugs directly from the prisoners (CPI 2000, 183).

(5) "Extermination groups" (death squads) are generally formed by military police officers who become vigilantes in the service of politicians and businesspeople (CPI 2000, 186). These groups end up forming parallel militias that develop policies of terror that victimize all who oppose their deeds (CPI 2000, 187).

(6) Police corruption is also high in the different specialized precincts that deal with the crimes under scrutiny, and the criteria for assignment of police officers to these precincts are less than clear and attributed to political influence (CPI 2000, 188, 191). Besides, assignment to these precincts is known to be highly disputed among police officers, given the possibilities of extra gain through bribes and extortion (CPI 2000, 189).

(7) The pattern of police corruption had existed with impunity, as higher authorities did not address the obvious and quick enrichment of some police officers, ignoring it instead, leading to a low number of investigations (CPI 2000, 190).

The CPI found that "the level of involvement of the state apparatus with crime is a reason for concern; in all the police organizations (civil and military) involvement and connivance with criminals could be found" (2000, 186). The CPI's report continued: "The existence of military police officers developing activities of 'private security for authorities' is a practice to be reproached, given the promiscuous relationship established between the public and the private sectors; besides, the CPI found that military police officers who act as 'private security for authorities' end up getting involved in all kinds of illicit activities, especially because they lose sight of the limits between police activity and the activity of the hired gun [*jagunço*], and the latter prevails." The CPI demanded that such practices be repressed (2000, 186).

Moreover, the CPI found that the relative lack of articulation of the rule of law in the region is matched by an informal "policy" of agricultural financing developed by the main dealers that includes provision of seeds and other agricultural goods and a form of "insurance" provided by the guarantee of a minimum wage to the planter, regardless of the profits or losses that might strike agriculture, and the guarantee of a minimum price of sale, also protected from the fluctuations of the market (CPI 2000, 152). These measures allowed the consolidation of the region as a major producer of marijuana.

Faced with the extreme violence that exists in the *sertão* (backlands) of Pernambuco as a consequence of family feuds that have been unraveling for decades, and in which many people have lost their lives, including women, children, the aged, and even people entirely unrelated to the disputes, the CPI decided to attempt a peace accord among the families in conflict, in the hopes of obtaining a truce and a ceasefire so that the state would be able to reestablish its presence in the areas of conflict and put a stop to the absurd killings. The CPI organized a meeting of the Araquan, Benvindo, Gonçalves, Russo, Cláudio, and Nogueira families with CPI members and the judge of penal executions (CPI 2000, 139). Thirteen people who had already been arrested on murder charges were transferred from the Aníbal Bruno Penitentiary to the Salgueiro Penitentiary so as to facilitate their resocialization. The lawsuits against them were scheduled to be reviewed so as to grant them all the benefits allowed by the law. In order to address the clandestine nature of the activities in which several of the suspects were involved, the CPI promised to negotiate credit lines for those who wished to go back to legal activities. The main goal was to reactivate more than a hundred farms that had been abandoned during the conflict. The "Audience of Pacification" generated a peace accord in Salgueiro that was signed by the members of the families in the local courthouse in the presence of many important authorities of the legislative, judicial, and executive branches.

Although these conclusions seem extensive, they are not exhaustive. The fact is that the known involvement of many other powerful politicians, such as Inocencio Oliveira, with the drug planters who finance campaigns was not explicitly mentioned in the report. Moreover, Oliveira's local TV station entirely ignored the presence of the CPI in the area. The powerful were also easily "understood and forgiven." Families who were found to be deeply involved in the narcotics trade and its trail of violence ended up receiving pardons and agricultural credit so that they could substitute alternative crops for marijuana. The constructive side of the resolutions was emphasized, it is true, but critics will keep the suspicion that the traditional land/power structure was updated or even reinforced.

Most of the recommendations of the CPI addressed thirty-five items to the state executive, demanding changes in the police apparatus. Most suggestions involved reorganization of the agencies that handle narcotics crimes so as to increase their efficiency. Some proposed the replication of federal agencies and initiatives at the state level. Some involved information campaigns aimed at the general public. Five suggestions were made to the judiciary that proposed increased control over narcotics crimes and police behavior.

However, the nature of suggestions to the state legislature was dismal. No suggestions were made in relation to changes in existing laws, despite obvious problems involving the reproduction of local power. That is, the report did not address any of the assumptions of the patrimonial political reproduction that framed the investigated illegalities. There were only two propositions to the state legislature: one involved an increase in oversight of the penitentiaries by the Human Rights Commission, without any proposals of change to already existing activities, and the other suggested the creation of a permanent commission to oversee organized crime, something that the CPI said did not exist (2000, 200–201).

The question of why the commission targeted a member of its own house may be answered by two cumulative possibilities: there was a loud outcry for his downfall, and other representatives might have been interested in "inheriting" his electoral bases. In the spotlight, the Legislative Assembly reacted by taking the initiative to open the state CPI and deviating the problem to the issue of impunity in general and the poor performance of police work. A scapegoat was also found. The main public issue then became the suggested suspension of the mandate of Representative Eudo Magalhães, businessman and politician from the region of Mata Sul, who had already been singled out by the federal CPI as involved in organized crime. The fact was that Magalhães's brother was directly collaborating with the governor, and only after the accusations became public did the governor decide to relieve him of his functions. The state CPI confirmed his close relationships with known criminals and took the subject to the Assembly's floor for a vote. In the previous 165 years of the state's Legislative Assembly, only twenty-seven representatives had had their rights suspended, most of them in a six-year period between 1964 and 1970, during the military dictatorship. Some of those returned to politics in the transition and are still active, such as the county representative from Recife, Liberato Costa Júnior (PMDB), suspended in 1969; the current secretary of government, Dorany Sampaio (PMDB); the state attorney general, Sílvio Pessoa (today in PMDB, but a member of Arena at the time); and the mayor of Paulista, Geraldo Pinho Alves (PDT, a member of MDB at the time). Even without a tradition of suspending parliamentary prerogatives in democratic times, the Legislative Assembly received several requests to suspend parliamentary immunities in the last years but consistently denied the suspension (*JC*, April 6, 2000).

Under enormous popular pressure, competently enlarged by the media, the representatives started to concede that this was not a political problem and that therefore the parties should not force decisions on their members. Finally, with twenty-seven votes for and seventeen against, the Pernambuco Legislative Assembly suspended the mandate of the representative (PFL) for breaking the parliamentary code of ethics. The suspension would be effective for eight years. The main accusation was that he had lied before the CPI since none of the credible evidence supported his allegations. During all three hours of the secret voting process, the social organizations remained mobilized in front of the Assembly, shouting commands and accusations. The representative's supporters hired a little band to sustain a parallel event that paled in the face of popular anger.

In 2001, Eudo Magalhães filed a lawsuit through a request to return to the Assembly made to the Court of Justice, arguing that he had not had the right to ample defense when he was suspended. The court granted him the right to return. Once again, the judiciary disappointed the democratic citizenry. Several popular organizations noted that popular expectations for accountability were frustrated because the CPI does not have judicial powers. The population does not generally perceive that the CPI has only investigative powers and therefore lacks the ability to try the accused (Pedrosa 2001).

However, these organizations acknowledge that the CPI process was unique in identifying suspects and investigating and producing evidence, especially in the case of summary executions in Timbauba. Without its public visibility, patrimonial power would have remained locked to public scrutiny. Credible death threats did not discourage the commission, given the constant support it received from organizations and the population, which presented clues and demanded investigation. The CPI caused the indictment and arrest of the members of the extermination group that had killed the adolescents in Timbauba. It was found that the children and young men were involved with petty crime and were killed. However, the CPI failed to produce the accountability of the politicians, landowners, and businessmen who had hired the killers. As the popular saying goes, "It caught the small fish but left the sharks at large." This selective punishment frustrated popular sentiment especially because the connections of these politicians to the executioners were public knowledge. The members of the popular movement, however, did not restrain their activities to the CPI. They took the case to Amnesty International because they identified the need to circumvent the local limitations of a case that involved suspects related to the previous administration at all levels: the executive, the legislative, and the judicial (Pedrosa 2001).

The Narcotics CPI generated the follow-up of another "CPI of Violence." This initiative coincided with the visibility of the data produced by the Public Ministry—which showed that of murders committed in the state in the last three years, only 4 percent had been investigated, therefore conclusively blaming the police for the lack of punishment of violent crime. The police reacted by reorganizing the murder-investigation process through the establishment of a task force to deal with the backlog of cases, composed mainly of recent graduates from the police academy. The media closely followed all the strands of this chain reaction, and nongovernmental organizations that denounced cases of blatant impunity organized seminars and campaigns and added data to the investigations.

The Public Ministry, as the main "new institution" for the protection of citizen rights in the framework of the 1988 constitution, increased in strength and is currently in the process of consolidating its gains. It set foot more strongly in the Timbauba area, as well as in many other communities in the patrimonial interior, and has been able to disarticulate a second attempt of the extermination group to organize. It conducts, houses, and finances relentless campaigns against torture and corruption. The profile of its new acting capacities provides strong support to new citizen accountability demands that continuously emerge. It could be said that the Public Ministry's new strength was an important structural gain toward more progressive structures. Therefore, social accountability enjoyed both structural and conjunctural gains.

Community Relationships and Accountability in an Administrative CPI at the Municipal Level

Olinda (Oh Beautiful) is the former capital of the state of Pernambuco, a beautiful seventeenth-century city whose colonial buildings stretch out on a hill facing the sea. The architectural purity and homogeneity of the city put it under UNESCO protection as a "treasure of humanity." Recent occupation outside the limits of the primitive dwellings, however, has been almost chaotic, as the rhythm of urban growth has accelerated. Three years ago, tragedy struck the city as heavy rainfall caused the collapse of an apartment building, causing four casualties and several injuries. Shortly afterward, a second building collapsed. Popular anger grew as suspected construction irregularities were blamed for the tragedy. Street demonstrations demanded accountability.

Police investigations were slow and seemed not to get to the point, leaving victims unattended. Eventually, the *multiple activation* strategy was also used by this small community. Its members contacted the media; hired private attorneys; and banged at the doors of several state agencies related to urban planning, building licensing, and social security. Under popular clamor, county representatives were pressured to start their own CPI. The presidency was given to Representative Marcelo Santa Cruz, an attorney who had been identified with the opposition since the dictatorship expelled him from law school, arrested and tortured his sister, and kidnapped his brother and caused his disappearance. In the eighties, he was one of the founders of the Brazilian Committee for Amnesty (Comite Brasileiro pela Anistia) and of the Workers' Party (Partido dos Trabalhadores: PT). He also collaborated with Pastoral da Terra and was one of the founders of GAJOP and CENDHEC, becoming its first attorney. In 1992, he also participated in the constitution of the Network of the People's Attorneys of the State of Pernambuco and was pressured to present his candidacy for the county's legislature since there was a general perception that the time was ripe for someone with roots in the social movement to occupy a seat in the government. He believes this was the first time that someone involved with citizenship issues from a leftist perspective "introduced the practice of doing politics through compromise to strengthen social organization and combat clientelism and political assistentialism" (Santa Cruz 2001).

The victims and/or their next of kin could not pursue lawsuits because the evidence uncovered by the police was insufficient. The papers related to the construction of the buildings were under the control of the mayor's office

(Prefeitura), the Federal Savings Bank (Caixa Econômica Federal) that had financed sales, and the construction companies. Under direct pressure from the population, facilitated by the possibility of personal contacts in a small city, the CPI proved instrumental in obtaining the documents and releasing them to the victims' attorneys. In this way, citizen accountability was able to achieve some level of executive response through horizontal accountability enforced by the CPI. The press also contributed in raising public awareness of the issues involved, in a triangular feedback motion.

The CPI was also instrumental in garnering support from such executive agencies as the civil police, the forensics department, and the Public Ministry. Consequently, the several investigative authorities converged, each demanding the increase of the others' efficiency. By this time, the stakes had been raised: public opinion claimed that several other buildings could be in the same vulnerable situation, and the fear of future tragedies stirred a constant outcry. As a small county, Olinda still allows for close personal contacts, and mouth-to-mouth information spreads fast. In all public spaces, citizens commented on the case and expressed anger and anxiety. Direct contacts with representatives were an everyday pressure in every corner.

The more information was aggregated, the more the situation unfolded. The mayor's office was compelled to make a thorough evaluation of the condition of the city's buildings, and to the astonishment of most, 447 buildings, a colossal number, were found to be in a risky situation. The severity of the risk was rated on three levels, and 53 of the 447 presented an immediate risk of collapse. The evaluation determined that the dwellers of these buildings should be evacuated immediately, and the CPI demanded that the building companies provide new temporary lodgings for all the victims.

The technical evaluation concluded that the construction material that had been used was highly inadequate and of very poor quality. The projects were also found to be inadequate for the type of terrain, and unqualified professionals had signed off on some of them. Finally, it became evident that the mayor's office also exerted insufficient oversight of buildings in general. Bureaucratic examination without on-site investigation had, in most cases, been sufficient for the granting of licenses. The building regulations themselves were considered flawed.

These conclusions determined a new round of demands for the city to upgrade its control. Measures suggested to the mayor involved hiring a qualified technical staff to supervise construction and organizing a new city building code. The Federal Savings Bank was required to provide insurance to cover the damages. The Public Ministry demanded that the bank provide coverage to all buildings; otherwise, rent and sales contracts could not be accepted. The construction companies functioning without technical qualifications, it said, should be listed and controlled. The CPI's final report was approved on the Chamber's floor and sent to the Public Ministry for a civil public action against all responsible for the tragedy.

The Absent Citizenry and the CPI against Citizen Accountability

The positive role of the *multiple activation* strategy in dealing with citizen accountability issues that are raised by structurally weak horizontal accountability can best be understood by comparing the two previous cases, in which long-standing executive omission was addressed, with a case in which a CPI was opened without the presence of citizen accountability pressures. This case will demonstrate that CPIs at the local level are different from national ones and that this difference is due to *citizen awareness of the issues affecting their daily lives.* This awareness has an impact even on the eventual power of the media, which is, as we have seen, the main tool used to boost the power of the investigating legislative branch.

Camaragibe County is part of the great metropolitan area of Recife, with a population of 120,000 and a unique cultural heritage. Its population, once considered by the Recife population as "the Indians," in fact takes the nickname with pride. Camaragibe is a name of Indian origin that describes two local plants. Camaragibe was once the location of the biggest sugar mill in the area and, since the nineteenth century, of a successful textile mill set up under the supervision of liberal Catholic French entrepreneurs. The eventual construction of a "workers' village" gave rise to a particular organization of industrial workers with a special sense of self-esteem and pride.

Its mayor, in his first elective job, is Paulo Santana (PT). Santana, a doctor specializing in the health and sanitation of the poor, was a pioneer in the establishment of the participatory administration of the health secretariat in Camaragibe back in 1989. He gained this position as a reward for his excellent job as a leader of several campaigns to improve the basic health and training of community agents. A professor at the University of Paraiba, he asked for a leave of absence to put into practice his ideals for boosting the potentialities he saw in the social organization of Camaragibe. The 1988 constitution had just been enacted, and the first participatory budgeting was put into practice in the state of Rio Grande do Sul by the Workers' Party's mayor of the capital, Porto Alegre. In Camaragibe, the first *conselho municipal de saúde* (municipal council on health), under Santana's uncompromising leadership, assumed deliberative powers. His insistence on deliberation, not merely consultation, faced the opposition of the mayor, and he had to leave the government in January 1990. In 1992, the new mayor asked him to occupy the health secretariat, and he finally saw his dream of a deliberative health council come true. Municipal councils on health also acted as a mechanism of wide popular participation in framing priorities in health issues. In 1994, historically bad health indices in the region started to improve and reward Santana's efforts.

In 1996, Santana was elected as the first Workers' Party mayor in Camaragibe, earning 41 percent of the vote in a much divided city. The experience of citizens' councils spread to other areas as well. The idea was to enlarge the democratic space by increasing citizen participation so that budgeting would also be a tool of oversight. Participatory administration, Santana believed, should have three main goals: popular participation; improvement of the quality of life; and social control, so that citizenship can become effective as a force in public life (Santana 2001). The peculiar strategy of participatory administration developed in Camaragibe revealed an opportunity for territorially based redistributive policies that would shift priorities from the center to the peripheries. The Health in the Family program, for example, was the prototype of a strategy of mobilization/participation/intervention that would be adopted in the organization of the 1996 electoral campaign and later in the first Public Works Plan in 1997. It worked through a triple function of collecting information, defining articulations, and rendering public services. Over the years, the strategy generated a dense network (*malha fina*) of participation in the county's financial and urban management, health, education, and culture, revitalizing previously neglected peripheral areas (Bitoun 2001, 143–45).

Delegates were elected in popular assemblies in all microlocalities of the five county regions, one for every one thousand inhabitants, totaling 120 delegates. This territoriality contrasted with the other current formula of one delegate for every ten people participating in the assemblies. Santana's perception was that all governments, irrespective of their political leanings, dislocate power to a certain nucleus of decision making, be it an economic or a military power.

It was his belief that governments of the Left have a responsibility to dislocate this power to society and that it was his task to create channels for participation to remove citizens from their apathy or inertia. His function was to promote dialogue, maximizing the historical and cultural potential of the city (Santana 2001). He also had a strategy aimed at reducing and controlling the possibility of clientelistic intercourse among delegates and the population: a Commission of Ethics was formed to review the procedures of the Public Works Plan. Intense participation is also thought to limit clientelistic tendencies: the permanent agenda of public meetings held to discuss priorities and elaborate the Public Works Plan succeeded in involving some ten thousand people in the year 2000 alone. Moreover, raising the quality of urban services in the periphery was also intended to reduce the population's dependence on favors (Bitoun 2001, 154).

Since 1999, Camaragibe's administration has won several prizes for its successes. First, the Program of Participatory Administration was selected by the World Bank and the Getulio Vargas Foundation to participate in Project Partnerships, Poverty and Citizenship as one of the ten best programs for poverty reduction in the country. In the same year, it was named the country's best Health in the Family program by the Ministry of Health. In 2000, he received a prize for being the best mayor for children, granted by the Abrinq Foundation and UNICEF. Also in 2000, the Participatory Administration Program won fifth prize among 227 counties in Brazil in the Cycle of Public Administration and Citizenship, offered by the Getulio Vargas Foundation and the Ford Foundation. Camaragibe-born psychiatrist Jurandyr Freire Costa found the county outstanding in its "resistance to barbarism" (1999).

In the mayor's opinion, the legislative branch of government can hardly enjoy this cultural and political effervescence. As the relationship of the population with the mayor's office becomes more organic in a context of widened mobilization, the role of the legislature also has to be redefined. The traditional legislative function as manager of clientele through public works and sinecures has become obsolete. A new legislative role would emphasize law making and oversight, with public administration the primary function of the mayor. This new division of functions has been met with the jealousy and anger of conservative politicians who see their traditional reproduction threatened (Santana 2001). County representatives in the governing coalition have fewer restrictions on participatory budgeting because they speak with delegates (Bitoun 2001, 153).

Santana was elected for a second term as mayor with 61 percent of the vote of the 81,820 electors, representing a coalition of nine leftist parties, the Front of the Left. The coalition included the local Partido da Social Democracia Brasileira (PSDB), which in this state supports the governor in a center-right coalition with the Partido do Movimento Democrático Brasileiro (PMDB) and the Partido da Frente Liberal (PFL). He ran against the governor's candidate, the PFL's Luciano Andrade.

In August 2000, excessive rainfall in Camaragibe caused 118 families to lose their homes and left extensive damage to roads, hillsides, and access to poor areas. The initial estimate was that five million reais was necessary to repair the damage in Camaragibe (*JC*, August 4, 2000).The federal government came to the rescue of the thirty-eight affected counties with forty million reais, but the governor who received the money decided not to release the funds to the counties before the elections and to directly execute the public works instead (Santana 2001).

The counties were supposed to present reports of damage to the governor and wait for the work to be done. In order to avoid political exploitation of the funds, the region's mayors suggested that a commission be created to oversee the works. The counties, then, concentrated their action through the Association of Counties of Pernambuco (Associação Municipalista de Pernambuco: AMUPE) and the newly created Commission of the Oversight of County Recovery, formed by the mayors of Camaragibe (Paulo Santana), Água Preta (Eduardo Coutinho), Panelas (Sérgio Miranda), Moreno (Vavá Rufino), and Catende (Otacílio Cordeiro), who mobilized to inspect the works. The centralization of funds by the state government was strongly criticized by these regional mayors, who argued that the counties had the tools to execute the works if the funds were forwarded to them (*JC*, August 15, 2000).

The CPI opened in Camaragibe County in May 2001 charged Santana with manipulating and deviating Social Security funds for use in the emergency. The mayor was supposed to have opened a special fund to deposit the Social Security insurance paid by the county employees. Instead, he claims he used the funds to assist the people affected by the floods last year. Simultaneous with the opening of the CPI, the Tribunal de Contas da União (TCU) rejected Santana's accounting for 1997 and charged him with paying back R$44 thousand.

A few days after the charges were made, Santana said he had already dismissed sixty commissioned positions and cut extra hours in the office so as to develop a plan for replacement of the money. He argued that the money had not been used for his personal profit and that he had never stopped paying any of the workers' benefits that were to come out of the funds. In the County Assembly, four county representatives supported the mayor, and four supported the opposition. The remaining seven representatives were considered "independent," but Santana believed he would be backed by the majority of them if a vote was made on the floor. AMUPE supported Santana because reportedly his financial procedures were shared by all the mayors and the state governor himself. The association used the media to show its support of the mayor. The CPI used its powers to hear the testimony of a few members of the Camaragibe Workers' Union (Sindicato dos Servidores de Camaragibe). Forced under subpoena demands, the workers felt extremely uneasy about appearing before the commission to be interrogated in a perceived "betrayal" of the mayor.

Santana's county secretaries refused to appear for questioning, reportedly a set-up to publicly arrest them. The area police chief transferred the officer who had been paid to perform this "public job" by opposition representatives (Santana 2001). The CPI closed and presented its report in one month, requesting the suspension of Santana's political rights. The government and the opposition engaged in a legal battle: the mayor argued that the constitution of the CPI was illegal and that therefore his secretaries were not obliged to appear for the hearings, and the opposition opened a lawsuit to force the secretaries to appear for interrogation and maintain the right to approve the final report without a vote on the floor.

Santana argued that all the counties and the state governors, like himself, handled these funds in the same way so as to circumvent legal indefinition that would freeze the resources in the appointed account. Therefore, at the end of May, the Workers' Party, through representative Paulo Rubem, proposed a state CPI to investigate the situation of the funds in *all* 184 state counties. Santana argued that the accusations against him were a political scheme manufactured by the PFL with an eye on the next year's election: "If Representative Teresa Duere [leader of the Jarbas Vasconcellos government] wants an investigation, she should support this state CPI and start the investigation through Camaragibe. I am the victim of a circus set up by PFL that intends to tarnish the image of my administration, with the aim of next year's election" (*JC*, May 31, 2001). The PFL refused to support this new CPI on the grounds that municipal administration is not under the jurisdiction of the State Assembly.

Evidence, however, supports Santana's arguments. It seems that the opposition bet on the CPI's media visibility to cause damage to Santana's prestige. The legal weaknesses in the formal process of establishing the CPI would be secondary if media exposure could be guaranteed. Santana reports that the requested interrogation of his secretaries of administration and finances by the CPI was intended to be a media circus where the secretaries would be arrested and photographed, tainting his administration. As Santana was informed about this scheme in advance, he did not allow the secretaries to appear before the CPI.

The Camaragibe population followed these events with mixed emotions. There was a sense of confusion, since the arguments and accusations were never very clear. In administrative meetings, Santana was questioned, explaining over and over his version of what was going on. He reports that he was often stopped on the streets for questioning. At all the events he customarily attended, he was received with more questions and some manifestations of support. He ordered a survey made to best interpret the community's opinion, finding that all those who had voted for him still supported his position vis-à-vis the CPI. Two months later, the internal elections of the Workers' Party returned an amazing result: Santana had a sweeping victory and was elected state president of the party.

As of this writing, in October 2001, the legal battle between Santana and his accusers still continues in the courts. The lower court agreed with his accusers on the point of the legality of the CPI: although no county law defined the procedures, the court accepted that federal procedures could serve as guidelines. On the other hand, the TCU concluded that there had been no embezzlement and that no funds had been privately appropriated by the mayor. The CPI had to change its title from "CPI to Investigate the Deviation of Social Security Funds" to "CPI to Investigate the Undue Use of Social Security Funds." Santana's impeachment is now a distant goal of the opposition.

The Uneasy Association between Citizens and Their Representatives

Citizen accountability in the context of patrimonialist structures in Brazil is perceived as both a long-term and a short-term goal, and actions are taken and evaluated at both these levels: according to how much they contribute to cracking closed and unresponsive structures of abuse and to stopping short-term specific violations. The cases examined here allow us to think of citizen accountability as consisting not only of developing responsive strategies but also of building a network of citizens and principled public officials as an institutional front committed to change. Specific struggles identify allies, consolidate and institutionalize cooperation, open up new channels of participation, and push conservative power from some of its territories. Citizen accountability has proved the effectiveness of its role of establishing new ways for public officials to feel that they are obliged to report to the population, and some have certainly already started to voluntarily account for their mandates.

As nonmajoritarian tools of legislative accountability, CPIs are highly politically contingent. Their limited efficiency as tools of accountability is due to their wide investigative powers and the attention they draw from the media. Organized outside pressure is an important factor in preventing the premature death of the CPI and the unraveling of immediate policy change in favor of more accountable governance. However, immediate concessions are not necessarily related to long-term change in the form of building permanent institutions for increased accountability. Much to the contrary, although the trend toward strong checks and balances in the form of suspension of political rights and resignations might seem politically satisfactory in the heat of the struggle, these factors may preempt the final legislative outcome that CPIs are formally expected to produce. Sustained pressure is necessary to enable the permanent occupation of the public spaces freed by CPIs and to institutionalize channels of accountability.

The participation of the citizenry in CPIs has differed widely in terms of range of action and consequences, but the positive role of *multiple activation* is clear: such a strategy intensifies the struggle and keeps the issue in the media, ultimately producing some sort of horizontal accountability as well. The Narcotics CPI was pushed by constant participation at every level: unorganized citizens and victims offered clues and information through a toll-free number especially set up for the investigation, NGOs developed intense inside-outside strategies of mobilization and pressure, and the media followed with constant exposure of wrongdoings and channeling of citizen demands. The administrative CPIs examined here were fueled by victims' anger and intense community protests. Finally, the anti–citizen accountability CPI was met with citizen estrangement and received a popular veto: the mayor charged with appropriation in fact received a "promotion" as he was elected state president of the Workers' Party in the midst of the accusations. This outcome reveals that media exposure is not a sufficient condition for a CPI to achieve its goal. Although citizen participation is not decisive either, the sample of cases shows that the association of the media, CPIs, and citizen participation may achieve the best results.

The examination of this sample of CPIs allows us to conclude that CPIs differ enormously as tools of citizen accountability and that mobilization and support vary according to the issues involved. The Narcotics CPI touched the most unacceptable themes from the citizenship perspective. It involved issues of arbitrary life and death and the corruption of political power through the use of state violence for personal gain. The organizations supporting this CPI had a clear perception that they were fighting systemic problems that went well beyond the individuals involved. They acknowledged the power of the CPI to expose practices that they had been denouncing for a long time, with little success. For this reason, they backed it with the assumption that simple media exposure of these facts was a political gain. As they had accumulated knowledge on these issues, they were able to sustain a strategy of multiple interventions at multiple levels, aiming at unraveling a domino effect. The administrative CPIs examined here counted on different forms of support, confirming the fact that popular anger is strongest where issues of life and death are involved. Administrative CPIs sometimes have to keep "creating facts" to attract media attention and support.

Resource mobilization theory can still provide a useful interpretive framework for citizen action in terms of accountability vis-à-vis the legislative and executive branches of government. It is partially valid in explaining the dynamics of social accountability in activating CPIs. The organizational resources accumulated in the last decades allowed social movements to force the opening of both the state and the national Narcotics CPIs and to stretch the investigative activity of the legislature. However, these organizations alone were not sufficient. The organizations were there before the CPI and had not been successful in affecting the patrimonialist organization of power and violence. In this sense, they were sensitive to the opportunity of using the CPI to access information and provide visibility that would generate the dismantling of an extermination group and the arrest of some of those accused.

In this sense, the CPI was their shield and their weapon. Two factors have to be considered here. First, the federal CPI functioned as an outside party. Its lack of involvement with local power, its ability to avoid revenge by investigating and then leaving the area, and the power differential that it handled led to its ability to crack the resistant system of patrimonial authoritarian local power. In its investigation, the state CPI had a strong start. This point highlights the positive impact that different levels of accountability can have on each other. The different levels of CPIs make them able to activate local accountability. Second, this power differential allowed a frightened local population to come forward with information. The return of the federal CPI to Brasilia, on the other hand, allowed the local established powers to regain some of their space. Moreover, the judiciary was instrumental in the final lack of accountability.

CPIs are not the only tools of citizen accountability, but they have their role and work in a context of *multiple activation.* Multiple activation includes the citizenry's simultaneous mobilization of varied resources. Actors eligible for mobilization include principled networks; specialized professionals (attorneys, police officers, engineers, social workers); outside parties (international NGOs and multilateral organizations); other victims; and other state agencies at different levels. In multiple activation, visibility (the media) and legal powers open up agencies for scrutiny. With these two tools, CPIs create free spaces for citizen participation. The relationship is mutual: citizen participation boosts CPI investigation. The case of the Camaragibe CPI, without citizen participation, clearly shows the difference that results when an association is not organic.

The different levels of CPIs reveal different strategies of citizen participation. The capacity of creating "free spaces" is related to different experiences of democratic relationship: at the county level, for example, the direct participation of the population vis-à-vis representatives takes the form of a push-and-pull dialogue in which democratic actors constitute themselves through the demands for accountability. The wider the context, the greater the anxiety to command media attention. The democratic experience is "mediated," and inside-outside strategies are reconstructed and potentialized.

We have not defined what constitutes the "success" of a CPI. Instead, we find it more useful to highlight the complex processes of citizen accountability in times of political transition. The building of permanent institutions to hold public power accountable may demand sustainability in the long term. This is the challenge before the citizenry, and the short-term impact of CPIs can only be thought of as a temporary tool or facilitator. Deeper change requires that social movements intellectually construct democracy both as a "moving target" and as an everyday process.

NOTES

1. Jonathan Fox (1994) perceives this use of violence as intrinsic to clientelism, but we prefer to refer to Weber's ideal type as more encompassing.

2. In contrast, conservatism remained in the constitution's chapters referring to the land-ownership regime, civil-military relations, and the media, all three sectors heavily supported by the Right.

3. *Caboclo* often (but not always) describes the racial mix of Afro and Native descent. Culturally, it is also a magic entity that represents the Indian in the Afro cults: it is admired as an archetype of honor and pride, standing for all those who resisted enslavement.

4. Most of the information about GAJOP was obtained through an interview with attorney, political scientist, and journalist Jayme Benvenuto, current coordinator of the International Human Rights Programme of GAJOP, which is dedicated to increasing accountability by bringing cases of human rights violations in Brazil to international courts. Benvenuto recently published *Os Direitos Humanos Economicos, Sociais e Culturais* (Recife: Bagaço/Plataforma Interamericana de Direitos Humanos, 2005).

5. The National Program for Human Rights was created in 1994 by the federal government's initiative to promote deep changes in the country's appalling human rights practices. It solicited substantial inputs from civil society, a "partnership" that could not be accepted by NGOs without the proper construction of the monitoring activities that have since been developed. There has been an uneasy but constant dialogue between the federal government and NGOs since this time.

6. Collor was the first directly elected president after military rule. He ran on an anticorruption campaign, only to be found guilty of corruption, patronage, and clientelism, which led to his impeachment.

7. Representatives visiting Pernambuco included Magno Malta, Fernando Ferro (PT-PE), Laura Carneiro (PFL-RJ), Paulo Baltazar (PSB-RJ), Éber Silva (PDT-RJ), and Lino Rossi (PSDB-MT), who were also accompanied by Moroni Torgan (PFL-CE), Padre Roque (PT-PR), Robson Tuma (PFL-SP), and Reginaldo Germano (PFL-BA).

BIBLIOGRAPHY

Bailey, John, and Roy Godson. 2000. *Organized Crime and Democratic Governability.* Pittsburgh: University of Pittsburgh Press.

Barkan, Steven E. 1984. "Legal Control of the Civil Rights Movement." *American Sociological Review* 49, no. 4: 552–65.

Benvenuto, Jayme. 2001. Coordinator, GAJOP. Interview. Recife, May 10.

Bitoun, Jean. 2001. "Programa de Administração Participativa de Camaragibe-PE." In Ilka Camarotti and Peter Spink, orgs., *Redução da Pobreza e Dinâmicas Locais,* 127–59. Rio de Janeiro: FGV.

Brasil. Estado de Pernambuco. Poder Legislativo. 2000a. *Parecer n. 2482, Representação 1/2000, Relator João Braga.*

———. 2000b. *Resolução n. 430.* Recife, June 5.

Brasil. Estado de Pernambuco. Prefeitura de Camaragibe. 1997. *Programa de Administração Participativa.* Camaragibe. Mimeograph.

———. 1998. *Regimento do Conselho de Delegados(as).* Camaragibe, March 21. Mimeograph.

Camarotti, Ilka, and Peter Spink, orgs. 2001. *Redução da Pobreza e Dinâmicas Locais.* Rio de Janeiro: FGV.

Costa, Jurandyr Freire. 1999. "Brasil 500 d.c. Resistência à Barbárie." *Folha de São Paulo,* November 29.

CPI (Comissão Parlamentar de Inquérito). 2000. Brasil. Estado de Pernambuco. Poder Legislativo. *Relatório Final do Inquérito Parlamentar # 002/2000.* Recife. Mimeograph.

Dahl, Robert A. 1971. *Polyarchy: Participation and Opposition.* New Haven: Yale University Press.

"Deputados Sabatinam José Arlindo." 2001. *Jornal do Commercio,* June 26.

Evans, Sara M., and Harry C. Boyte. 1992. *Free Spaces: The Sources of Democratic Change in America.* Chicago and London: University of Chicago Press.

Faoro, Raymundo. 2001 [1957]. *Os Donos do Poder: Formação do Patronato Politico Brasileiro.* 3d ed. Sao Paulo: Olobo.

Ferro, Fernando. Federal Representative, Pernambuco State. Interview. Recife, October 9, 2001.

Figueiredo, Argelina. 2000. "Institutional Power and the Role of Congress as a Mechanism of Horizontal Accountability: Lessons from the Brazilian Experience." Paper presented at the Conference on Institutions, Accountability, and Democratic Governance in Latin America. Kellogg Institute, University of Notre Dame, May 8–9.

Fox, Jonathan. 1994. "The Difficult Transition from Clientelism to Citizenship: Lessons from Mexico." *World Politics* 46, no. 2: 151–84.

———. 2000. "Civil Society and Political Accountability: Propositions for Discussion." Paper presented at the Conference on Institutions, Accountability, and Democratic Governance in Latin America. Kellogg Institute, University of Notre Dame, May 8–9.

———. 2002. "La Relación Reciproca entre la Participación Ciudadana y la Rendición de Cuentas: La Experiencia de los Fondos Municipales en el México Rural." *Política y Gobierno* 9, no. 1: 95–123.

GAJOP (Gabinete de Assessoria Jurídica às Organizações Populares). 2000. *Relatório sobre Casos de Tortura no Nordeste do Brasil-2000.* Recife: GAJOP.

Geddes, Barbara, and Artur Ribeiro Neto. 1992. "Institutional Sources of Corruption in Brazil." *Third World Quarterly* 13, no. 4: 641–61.

Graham, Richard. 1997. *Clientelismo e Política no Brasil do Século XIX.* Rio de Janeiro: Ed. UFRJ.

Johnston, Michael. 1991. "Historical Conflict and the Rise of Standards." *Journal of Democracy* 2, no. 4: 48–60.

———. 1999. "A Brief History of Anti-Corruption Agencies." In Schedler, Diamond, and Plattner 1999b, 217–26.

Leal, Victor Nunes. 1978. *Coronelismo, Enxada e Voto: Municícipo e o Regime Representativo no Brasil.* Sao Paulo: Alfa-Omega.

Lemos-Nelson, Ana Tereza. 2001. "Judiciary Police Accountability for Gross Human Rights Violations: The Case of Bahia, Brazil." Ph.D. diss., University of Notre Dame.

Lijphart, Arend. 1984. *Democracies: Patterns of Majoritarian and Consensus Government in Twenty-one Countries.* New Haven and London: Yale University Press.

Lipsky, Michael. 1968. "Protest as a Political Resource." *American Political Science Review* 62:1144–58.

Manzetti, Luigi, and Scott Morgenstern. 2000. "Legislative Oversight: Interests and Institutions in the United States and Latin America." Paper presented at the Conference on Institutions, Accountability, and Democratic Governance in Latin America. Kellogg Institute, University of Notre Dame, May 8–9.

Martins, José de Souza. 1996. "Clientelism and Corruption in Contemporary Brazil." In Walter Little and Eduardo Posada-Carbó, eds., *Political Corruption in Europe and Latin America,* 195–218. New York: St. Martin's Press.

McAdam, Doug. 1982. *Political Process and the Development of Black Insurgency, 1930–1970.* Chicago: University of Chicago Press.

Méndez, Juan. 2000. "Legislatures, Judiciaries and Innovations in Horizontal Accountability." Paper presented at the Conference on Institutions, Accountability, and Democratic Governance in Latin America. Kellogg Institute, University of Notre Dame, May 8–9.

Morris, Aldon. 1984. *The Origins of the Civil Rights Movement: Black Communities Organizing for Change.* New York and Toronto: Free Press.

Movimento Nacional dos Direitos Humanos. 2000a. *Carta à Anistia Internacional.* Recife, November 21.

———. 2000b. *Carta ao Governador do Estado de Pernambuco.* Recife, November 21.

———. 2000c. *Ofício ao Procurador Geral da Justiça n. 91/2000/DCA.* Recife, November 21.

———. 2001. *Carta ao Presidente do Tribunal de Justiça de Pernambuco.* Recife, July 17.

MPP (Ministério Público de Pernambuco). 2000a. Brasil. Estado de Pernambuco. Procuradoria Geral da Justiça. *(IN)Segurança Pública em Timbaúba.* Timbaúba, March 30.

———. 2000b. Brasil. Estado de Pernambuco. Procuradoria Geral da Justiça. *Ofício GRJ n. 117/2000.* Timbaúba, October 18.

O'Donnell, Guillermo. 1999. "Horizontal Accountability in New Democracies." In Schedler, Diamond, and Plattner 1999b, 29–51.

Oliveira, Adriano. 2001. *Tiros na Democracia: De Que Lado Ficou a Imprensa Na Greve da Polícia Militar de Pernambuco no Ano de 1997?* Recife: Edições Bagaço.

Pedrosa, Maria Aparecida. 2001. Coordinator, Movimento Nacional dos Direitos Humanos-MNDH. Interview. Recife, October 9.

Pereira, Carlos. 2001. *A Conexão Eleitoral no Brasil: Existe Contradição na Coexistência de Partidos Fracos na Arena Eleitoral e Partidos Fortes na Arena Legislativa?* Oxford: Oxford University Press.

"Proceedings of the Workshop on Budgeting and Democracy." 1998. Sponsored by the Lyndon B. Johnson School of Public Affairs, University of Texas at Austin, and the Fundação Getúlio Vargas. Barra de Sahy, August 19–22.

Sadek, Maria Tereza, org. 2000. *Justiça e Cidadania no Brasil.* Sao Paulo: Ed. Sumaré.

Sales, Paulo J. G. 2001. "Espetáculos Eleitoreiros." *Jornal do Commercio,* June 27.

Sales de Albuquerque, Francisco. 2001. Secretary General, Public Ministry, Pernambuco State. Interview. Recife, October 3.

Santa Cruz, Marcelo. 2001. Representative, Olinda County, Pernambuco; Attorney, Centro Dom Hélder Câmara, CENDHEC. Interview. Recife, October 9.

Santana, Pedro Paulo. 2001. Mayor, Camaragibe, Pernambuco State. Interview. Camaragibe, September 28.

Santos, Boaventura de Sousa. 1998. "Participatory Budgeting in Porto Alegre: Toward a Redistributive Democracy." *Politics and Society,* December.

Schedler, Andreas, Larry Diamond, and Marc F. Plattner. 1999a. Introduction. In Schedler, Diamond, and Plattner 1999b, 1–2.

———, eds. 1999b. *The Self-Restraining State: Power and Accountability in New Democracies.* Boulder and London: Lynne Rienner Publishers.

Schwartzman, Simon. 1988. *Bases do Autoritarismo Brasileiro.* Rio de Janeiro: Campus.

Sen, Amartya. 1999. *Desenvolvimento como Liberdade.* Sao Paulo: Cia. das Letras

Silva, Francisco Rodrigues da. 2001. *CPIs Federais, Estaduais, Municipais: Poderes e Limitações.* Recife: Edições Bagaço.

Silva, Ivan Luiz da. 1998. *Crime Organizado.* Belo Horizonte: Edições Ciência Jurídica.

Smulovitz, Catalina, and Enrique Peruzzotti. 2000. "Societal and Horizontal Controls: Two Cases about a Fruitful Relationship." Paper presented at the Conference on Institutions, Accountability, and Democratic Governance in Latin America. Kellogg Institute, University of Notre Dame, May 8–9.

Tilly, Charles. 1978. *From Mobilization to Revolution.* Reading, Mass.: Addison-Wesley.

———. 1998. *Durable Inequality.* Berkeley: University of California Press.

Ture, Kwame, and Charles Hamilton. 1992 [1967]. *Black Power: The Politics of Liberation in America.* New York: Vintage Books.

Weber, Max. 1978. "Economy and Society: An Outline of Interpretive Sociology." In Guenther Roth and Claus Wittich, eds., E. Fischoff, trans., *Max Weber,* 2: 233–87. Berkeley: University of California Press.

Zaverucha, Jorge. 2000. *Frágil Democracia: Collor, Itamar, FHC e os Militares (1990–1998).* Rio de Janeiro: Ed. Civilização Brasileira.

5

Critical Junctures of Social Accountability

LESSONS FROM LATIN AMERICA

Nuria Cunill Grau

No one seems to doubt the importance of social accountability in optimizing the performance of the governmental apparatus. This lack of doubt is indicated in the recent increase in specialized literature on the subject. However, there still exists an excessive amount of ambiguity concerning this complex topic, which results in contradictions not only in terms of its intrinsic purposes but also for the strengthening of democratic governability.

An inconvenient homogeneity usually becomes apparent when there are failures to take into account the fact that the accountability of nonelected officials is not subsumed into the accountability of politicians. Our institutions do not provide mechanisms by which citizens can directly sanction the illegal actions of public officials. It must not be assumed, however, that people can only control their public officials indirectly, that is, through their politicians. This is the position of contemporary authors (see, e.g., Manin, Przeworski, and Stokes 1999) who endorse the traditional view that elections and a system of top-down commands and controls are the only mechanisms by which citizens can demand accountability from nonelected officials.

The realization that neither works well has recently led to the question of whether citizens should have direct control over public officials. In answering this question, the inconvenient homogeneity seems to become dangerously ambiguous in that beyond spurious attempts at transferring accountability to the market or direct consumer control,[1] solutions that view reinforcement of democracy and citizen building as the real goals usually fail to provide convincing answers about how this is possible.[2] Given the role played by public administration in crafting social life through its decisions, which are important both quantitatively and qualitatively, albeit to the detriment of decisions made by elected entities or their agents, it cannot be neglected as a specific target of social accountability. If lessons are to be learned, the weakness of the theory needs to be examined from a practical standpoint.

In this chapter, the task at hand will be approached from a macro- rather than a microsocial perspective, examining what Latin American governments have accomplished in recent years in trying to increase social control over public administration and the lessons that have been learned.

Some Insights into the Crucial Bottlenecks of Social Control

Several ideas come to mind when discussing social control. Among the more fundamental ideas is the question of what exactly to look for when referring to social control. If it is understood as any attempt at citizen involvement in the actions and decisions of public entities, with the purpose of voicing and defending social interests, no less a manifestation of such concerns would be participation by social actors on the boards of public organizations (and even nongovernmental organizations). An example is the denunciation function wielded by social organizations over the government apparatus. This has to do with phenomena that involve diverse types of relations with the government apparatus and that illustrate, in turn, two different models of civic participation: one that assumes a constituent relationship with government and policy and another that allows only for a regulatory relationship with the two.

The traditional model of citizen participation, which invokes pluralism, calls on social subjects in the adoption of public policies and decisions yet is based on the possibility of achieving mutual responsibility between them and/or a negotiated agreement that assures implementation. It involves the delegation of government responsibilities and, at the same time, a loss of political sovereignty over social representation. The result is functional collaboration in the exercise of policy, not influence or control over it.

Society's capacity to criticize and control the government apparatus, implicit in an alternative model of citizen participation, is conditioned on drawing a line between political authority incumbent on the state and social spheres demanding reciprocal recognition of political autonomy. If not a given, from at least a formal standpoint, it is impossible to evoke citizen intervention in controlling the government apparatus.

With this in mind, other problems remain to be solved. In fact, according to certain theories, developing a regulatory relationship solely with the government apparatus is not enough; indirect social influence is also needed. Jürgen Habermas (1990) argues that the only way to influence administrative power (affecting laws and representative entities) is to contribute, external to the government apparatus, a regulatory framework that will greatly reduce the value of the regulatory foundations it manifests. Administrative power should be compared to "communicative power"—the spontaneous formation of opinion in autonomous public arenas. Such arenas are occupied by volunteer organizations that create and publicize practical convictions, that is, topics for the whole of society, and categorize them convincingly and persuasively so they can be digested by the political system.

The majority of theories on deliberative democracy adhere to this position (see Warren 1999). But are civil society's associational structures the only spaces where communicative practice can translate into the formation of opinion and, in effect, be directed in an argumentative and autonomous fashion? Does there not also come into play society's direct influence over government, manifested through mediation found in government institutionality and exercised by a policy of inclusion of new political actors in decision making? The new political theory on civil society (see Cohen and Arato 1992) seems to support these possibilities by suggesting that the "contamination" that develops as a reason to manifest only indirect influence on government is not a given.[3] An interpretational understanding of social construction suggests that there is never only one solution to a political or social problem, imploring the need for a practical concept of the reasoning that prevails in the process of deliberating and providing "good reasons."

Restoration of a model of policy formation that is pervasive and democratic has important practical repercussions. It calls for common citizens and related interests to have the authority to make proposals about public policy. It is here that the role of policy design in an autonomous public sphere gains momentum. The need to create a structure for political opportunities in the different arenas of the government apparatus where public policies are designed and interpreted, so as to facilitate an empirical and regulatory dialogue between public-government and public-social actors, also becomes more clear. If, as is actually the case, administrative agencies are granted considerable legal discretion to interpret and implement policies and, as a consequence, formulate a contextual definition of public interest (Stivers 1990), there exists no theoretical or regulatory reason that can justify the unilateral configuration of public policies.

In this framework, improving public administration accountability demands an examination of decision making with the help of the society itself (March and Olsen 1995, 143). Hence, strategies are necessary that can facilitate deliberative democracy in the formation of actions by the government apparatus and that can maintain both the government's and society's autonomy (see Cunill Grau 1997, chap. 2). This has led to the opinion that criticism and control by the people can, in fact, affect processes and the formation of public policies and decisions.

It means, on the other hand, not only that the government apparatus can be influenced directly and indirectly but that this influence can occur both before and after an administrative action. Supporting this theory of social control, however, is a broad vision of accountability. If accountability is understood as satisfying legitimate expectations concerning the use of administrative discretion, that is, the legitimation of discretion (Stone 1995, 509), it would clearly not suffice to track and react to the results of administrative action; rather, the practices of accountability would influence decisions so that the consequences for society are taken into consideration. Accountability on the part of an actor exists when that actor is forced to reveal his or her actions or decisions, past as well as future; justify them; and be punished in the event of misconduct (Schedler 1999, 17).

Two other important matters must be addressed before reaching the point in the analysis of social control that will allow us to examine its implementation. One that has been addressed indirectly is related to those who are summoned as subjects when the topic of social control arises. The other is linked to the resources at the disposal of society that allow it to force government officials into modifying their actions or decisions, or to sanction them.

The issue of subjects allows for different approaches. While Habermas (1990) defines control subjects as volunteer organizations specializing in the generation and dissemination of practical convictions, Schmitter (1999) identifies them as exclusively permanent social organizations with enough power and information to confront government agencies and actors. Both groups' importance, as well as that of civil society organizations, whose job it is to demand accountability of government institutions and monitor their actions, is clear. Their visibility will be undeniable in the years to come. However, the question remains: until what point should they continue to receive all the attention?

To reiterate, the possibility of political interaction being communicatively rationalized in forming public decisions and policies demands that common citizens and related interests have preventative power. There is no reason to think that they cannot, or do not want to, exercise control over the outcome of government action. In order for deliberation to be joined with pluralism in social accountability, it is essential that citizen participation translate into the expression and defense of underrepresented social interests; be able to transcend the mere expression of determined interests; and above all make room for common citizens, who habitually lack organization. It is clear that focusing exclusively on the formal recognition of social organizations with the means to intervene in public matters will deepen social representation asymmetries in the political system. On the other hand, because the structure of socioeconomic inequalities is reflected in the structure of political opportunities, the mere opening of channels of citizen participation does not guarantee pluralism. Many institutional experiments have managed to minimize such risks, among them the lottery (see Cunill Grau 1997, 172–80). However, most have more to do with preventative control over the formation of policies and decisions than post-facto control over the outcome of a government apparatus or agency action, which leaves pending the problem of how to ensure due social pluralism by enabling this type of control. This leads us to the last important matter: the resources that social accountability needs to achieve the right reactions (and corrections) from public agents.

If it is agreed that any social subject, collective or individual, organized or unorganized, should have the right to control a public entity, resorting to symbolic resources, generally available only to actors who are organized or enjoy great social mobility, will not be enough. Nor will the election tool be enough: notwithstanding its availability to everyone, it only allows us to indirectly reward or punish (through politicians) an administration's conduct. One must, therefore, ask oneself if it is possible to appeal to other resources that can be used directly, not just indirectly, by society, and not merely by specialized agents, to sanction an administration and/or force it to react to a social control.

One might ask yet another question: can this type of resource be made available to society? The answer is no. Since citizens require resources with legal consequences, and require that conditions be made available for public deliberation and examination, granting resources would demand responsibility on the part of the government.

However, when the government participates in the institutionalization of social control, its answers to requests for resources and conditions for their exercise can be contradictory, and government could also apply restrictions on their use. To illustrate, the legal framework, as well as different types of institutional designs of post-facto social control, will be examined, with a focus on the subjects of social control, their resources, and the creation of the conditions for public deliberation and examination.

Resources and Conditions for Exercising Social Control

Empowering the Subjects of Social Control

Latin America is fertile ground for examining the different designs for institutionalizing social control. Furthermore, it is probably the only region in the world in the past decade where governments have made concerted efforts to create special entities. In countries such as Ecuador, certain forms of social control have been instituted but still need to be enacted. Such legal provisions have existed in other countries for years. In Colombia, Mexico, and Bolivia alone, there are several thousand agencies that were either created by law or enjoy ample government support. Although their scope and duties vary, all entities speak to the creation of government incentives for social accountability. However, when it is the government that institutionalizes social control, the subjects are prepackaged, with the risk of certain actors being privileged compared to others. When social control adopts a legal format, the preexisting social fabric can be undermined, depending on how the entities of social control have been established.

The Veedurías Ciudadanas, Comités de Vigilancia, and Contraloría Social models in Colombia, Bolivia, and Mexico, respectively, speak to the possibility of legalizing society's control correctly, although these models, too, can show evidence of the risks mentioned.[4] Only the Colombian model allows for the incorporation of individual common citizens as well as collective actors of any type (territorial- or functional-based social organizations) into the entities of social control that have been legalized (citizens' watches). Such bodies are elected by the community, and their mere existence is enough for them to be recognized by the government.

In the case of the Bolivian and Mexican models, however, actors who can damage the social fabric are excluded. The Comités de Vigilancia in Bolivia are made up of Territorial Base Organizations (a representative from each canton or district of the municipal jurisdiction), with legally authorized personnel. Not only is the legitimacy of such entities dependent on the government's legal recognition, but they do not include social organizations of a functional nature or ordinary citizens. The Contraloría Social in Mexico includes control and vigilance spokespeople elected by the community beneficiaries of different social programs (previously the Programa Nacional de Solidaridad, or PRONASOL). In contrast to the Comités de Vigilancia in Bolivia, such entities accept common citizens. They do not, however, specifically contemplate the incorporation of any type of social organization, whether territorial and/or functional. Knowing how committee members are directly elected, committees would appear to compete with preexisting social organizations. At least this was the case with PRONASOL, where the creation of thousands of solidarity committees was accompanied by the disintegration of part of the preexisting social fabric.

Assuming that individuals or groups of individuals have the right to claim social control, the last two designs clearly pose a problem. Bolivia is a case in point. One of the recommendations made while evaluating the Comités de Vigilancia was the need to expand control mechanisms to include people in general, civic, and community groups, and even city governments (see Guzmán Boutier 1998, 151). It is, therefore, clear that when trying to create specialized entities that will exercise social control exclusively, they cannot be only democratic, assuring their independence from the government. These entities must have enough flexibility so that private citizens and representatives from social, territorial, and functional organizations can become direct subjects of social control.

Yet why create entities of social control when legal authorization to use social controls might suffice? The answer might be found in the need to make specific resources for exercising social control official, leading us to the next topic.

The Availability of Sanctioning Resources in Exercising Social Control

When social control affects the outcome of administrative action, the problem of sanctions available to society in order to force the government apparatus to amend actions or decisions becomes crucial. When social controls are institutionalized through the adoption of a legal framework, it becomes more feasible to make such sanctions official and enforceable, making social controls, in turn, more viable.

The evidence does not, however, support this conclusion completely. First, and the Comités de Vigilancia in Bolivia are a good example of this, a poorly designed sanction can have an impact on the efficacy of a social control. Second, legally institutionalizing social control makes it extremely reliant on government control. Another important factor is the nature of the resources, given their influence on the empowerment of the subjects of social controls. This topic will be pursued in greater depth later.

The existence of specific sanctions, as well as the formal filing of complaints, seemingly would constitute a prerequisite for institutionalized social control to be efficient. A highly formal model, such as Bolivia's, would guarantee compliance on the part of the administration and call for a record to be maintained of denunciations and establishment of the type of sanctions that the public administration would have to accept. By law, denunciations by the Comités de Vigilancia begin in the executive branch (through the Ministry of Finance), which may issue a partial remedy or not answer at all, in which case the denunciations would be heard by the Senate, which might freeze the assets of the city government. The result, as has been demonstrated (see Rojas Ortuste and Thévoz 1998; Guzmán Boutier 1998), is to the detriment of the entities of social control. Because the whole of city government can be affected, the preferred method is one that is more individualized and can be implemented through other channels. Also, in the time it takes to freeze city resources, half a fiscal year could have elapsed. In sum, social control can include specific resources that help people's control over government agencies translate into actions on the latter's part. But when the design does not fit, the use of such resources exacts high social costs instead of punishing those accused.

An institutionalized social control underscores the significance of available resources. In fact, the potential efficacy of social controls will vary substantially when the entities of social control act as representatives of the administration's own agencies of internal control, having only those resources assigned (the case of the Contraloría Social in Mexico), as opposed to when they have at their disposal a wide array of resources that can be activated by either the administration's agencies of internal and external control or by a court (the case of the Veedurías Ciudadanas in Colombia).

In either case, although creating specialized entities of social control and equipping these entities with the tools to sanction would seem to add viability to the exercise of social controls, it still has its risks, especially in the case of Latin America. When resources are indirect only, they depend on the independence and authority of the controller and the courts. When they are weak, social control will, lacking any sense, not produce tangible results. This is one of the most important barriers in the effort to institutionalize social control by creating specific entities: while the flaws in the enforcement mechanisms at the disposal of social accountability would seem to be corrected, this could depend on how efficient government control is. Besides, the variety of control subjects would be limited unless the model happened to be absolutely open. It is for this reason that, more than merely creating entities of social control (even equipping them with appropriate sanctioning resources), the crucial matter would seem to be providing society with resources that it can use directly as a way to elicit a response from the government's controller institutionality.

Citizens can act as subjects of direct control, relatively independent of the efficiency of government control, if they at least have the following resources: the right to revoke a mandate or remove nonelected officials, administrative resources, and judiciary actions of interest to the public. I argue that, like elections, these are instruments of social accountability that, besides giving citizens greater autonomy, create the basic conditions for accountability to become a right not only of the civil society entities that specifically monitor government agencies (or any social entity, whether territorial or functional) but also of common citizens who may not qualify as an organization.

The Latin American picture is less encouraging as far as these resources are concerned. Peru's constitution (1993) is the only one that provides for the removal of nonelected officials (officials appointed by the federal or regional governments under regional, state, provincial, or district jurisdiction). However, it is difficult to satisfy the requirements.[5] Revoking the mandates of elected officials has been given more consideration and has even been sponsored in the past few years, with certain conditions.[6] The administrative resources available in Latin America usually are limited, and a record of them has not been accurately maintained, which has restricted knowledge of citizens' rights vis-à-vis their governments. Nor are there enough judiciary actions available to the people, individually or through social organizations, that allow them to take legal action to demand accountability from their officials. Only the right to petition has been expanded to a degree. In a few countries (Brazil, Colombia, and Argentina), *acciones populares* that constitute collective protection of their rights and interests are available. The right to protection, designed for those seeking protection from a judge when constitutional rights may have been violated or threatened by the action or omission of a public official, has been written into the constitutions of Guatemala, Mexico, Brazil, Bolivia, Peru, Costa Rica, Paraguay, Venezuela, Chile, and Colombia. In Chile, the measure can be used by any person or company, but it does not apply to social rights, with the exception of the right to live in an unpolluted environment. Colombia's is the only constitution in which the courts have the power to enforce such measures. In summary, serious gaps exist concerning the availability of resources. In the few cases where provision is made for resources, institutional barriers against their implementation stand in the way.[7] In the only other cases in which there are no corresponding regulations, their scope has not been defined.

The importance of these resources, appropriately designed from a societal perspective, is that they have the ability to make not only the actions of social control entities efficient but also those of common citizens or social organizations seeking to make government agencies or interests accountable. The actions of social movements do not have any legal consequences when resources have not been authorized and placed at their disposal without any institutional restriction.[8] Although there are social organizations (e.g., FORJA, in Chile) that have included the dissemination and promotion of such resources within the population itself, their efforts deserve more attention from civil society. Another, perhaps more urgent, task is creating the conditions for the public's examination and scrutiny.

Opportunities for Public Scrutiny and Deliberation

The possibility of public scrutiny and examination is embodied in the right to information and the legalizing of public forums. Legalizing resources, such as those mentioned, is essential when exercising social controls. Resources can even be strengthened when government control is weak. But there can be no progress as long as information on government actions is restricted or publication of information is subject to the discretion of the public apparatus.

In reality, the availability of information constitutes a basic condition of social accountability, for without it, the institutionalization of social control, as well as the legalization of resources for control, will be neutralized. However, social control can still work if public scrutiny is allowed. By creating opportunities for the democratic formation of public opinion, transparency of government actions will make it possible for society, whether by appealing to the press or resorting to mobilizations or protests, to at least exercise post-facto control over the government apparatus through social pressures. Making information available at the moment that decisions or policies are formed opens up opportunities for public deliberation and, therefore, preventative control by society.

Unfortunately, though such observations may appear to be obvious, the means necessary to make the needed changes are not so obvious. If information is readily accessible to individuals or social organizations, it needs to be available at all times (Osorio 1998)—hence the importance of information being constitutionally guaranteed, along with the disclosure of public information. Only by means of laws can the right to appeal be summoned each time the right to access information is obstructed. It is only through laws that the exercise of both rights will not be subjected to the discretion of public agents, as occurs with disclosure of the results of administrative action.

In the last six years, several countries (at least eleven) have passed laws allowing citizens free access to government information.[9] However, attention has been drawn to the fact that there is no expeditious way for the right to information to be legally claimed. The insufficiencies in this regard in Latin America are abundant. Faced with all the legal confusion concerning the right to information, a legal vacuum exists that is most likely not accidental. In fact, the main sources of governments' bureaucratic power lie in the disclosure of information. Purely administrative measures, in this context, can draw attention away from what is important, making the right to information a freedom/capacity. Laws and, ultimately, political means would logically be needed. But this is not the only area that is weak. Recognition of the reasons for an administrative action, even the possibility of public deliberation and the democratic formation of public opinion, also should be addressed.

The basic condition, as established, for exercising social control is the ability to revive a model of public policy and decision formation that is reflective. This premise, the possibility of a communicatively rationalized political interaction, together with pluralism in social representation, gives specific direction to the composition of public arenas for mediation between the government and society, while simultaneously making it possible for social control to concentrate not only on the results of administrative action but also on the formation of decisions (see Cunill Grau 1997, 165–80). Such a condition is at least unavoidable when the absence of transparency or conflict in the objectives makes it impossible to agree on what results should be obtained, making accountability according to results less viable, especially in the case of organizational networks (see the notion of "anarchic accountability": Deleon 1998). At minimum, publicity in the formation of political decisions can potentially link power to communicative justification (Warren 1999, following Habermas).

Certain events in Latin America have demonstrated the use of deliberative processes among those potentially affected by a public decision or policy, even attempts to incorporate the perspectives held by ordinary citizens. Some assume the organization of institutionalized forms of dialogue between legislatures and civil society, as is the case, for example, with events since the end of the 1980s by the Legislative Assembly of the state of Minas Gerais in Brazil (see Anastasia 1997). This sort of experience, in contrast to the exemplary one displayed by the "participatory budget," originally instituted in Brazil, shows how it is possible for citizen participation to facilitate parliamentary control over the public administration instead of weakening it, as the participatory budget would seem to do.[10]

At any rate, what prevails is the practice of the participatory budget, which has spread to other countries, thanks primarily to left-wing organizations. One particular instance is the Intendencia of Montevideo, Uruguay, begun in 1993, when the process of decentralizing the city was institutionalized. Some participatory budgets could serve as examples of preventative social control practices, which, in turn, could eventually benefit post-facto control, given that they are usually associated with accountability on the part of authorities and greater citizen obligation to monitor official actions. However, this has not always been the case. Referring to the El Salvador experience, Fadul and Muniz (1999) have stressed the fact that when a systematic control and evaluation process has not been institutionalized by the people, there is no guarantee that budget bills will be enacted. On the other hand, as far as social policy is concerned, deliberative councils have been set up in several countries, in some cases (as in Brazil) including the same number of members representing civil society and the government, responsible for making policy and controlling its execution. However, such councils are usually not at the local level and can even evolve into legitimators of government policies, as several studies have shown (see, e.g., Castro Kustner 1999).

To summarize, even though some examples of social control, promoted by government measures, constitute real opportunities for deliberation and public scrutiny, they are usually dependent on or connected with specific subjects or circumscribed arenas. With this in mind, it is necessary to address the importance of general institutional provisions that can contribute to deliberation and public scrutiny. In regard to decisions and policies made by the executive power, it is important to remember that public hearings and publication of drafts of general administrative measures can, at best, create institutional conditions that allow the influence of public spheres in society to be felt. These provisions act like "sensors" (see Habermas 1990; Cohen and Arato 1992) that can at least make the exercise of power more open, facilitating the democratic formation of public opinion. Demanding accountability with legal foundations can contribute to this end. Such provisions are not entirely new but are part of the republican democratic tradition. However, a review of the norm in this regard shows that little progress has been made in Latin America regarding the public administration, despite its obvious concentration of power.

Colombia has probably shown the most progress. Colombia's 1991 constitution requires administrative agencies to inform the public about decisions that can affect either the whole or specific groups and to listen to what the public has to say. In mid-1999, a decree was issued (no. 1122, of June 26) making it compulsory, in certain cases, for agencies to publicize, no less than two weeks before their release, all bills to be adopted through a general administrative act; to set a deadline for hearing observations, suggestions, or alternative proposals; and, once the deadline has been reached, to process the regulations in such a way that they reflect either acceptance or rejection.

A December 1998 law (no. 489) authorizes the holding of public hearings (Article 33) to discuss the formation, execution, and evaluation of government policies and programs. The law leaves to the discretion of the administration whether it is appropriate to hold such hearings. However, it also says that organizations can ask that public hearings be held even though the request for a hearing or its conclusions will not be binding on the administration. The law also requires that the administration explain the reasons for its decisions.

Public hearings have also been authorized in Argentina and have been called by senior officials of certain organizations to inform the public of their activities. The National Law of Administrative Procedures states that initiatives corresponding to administrative acts of a general nature "can be subjected to public information when its nature so justifies. Likewise, people or entities not part of the administration can be required to appear, even those who represent sectoral interests" (Title IX.107). A similar provision has been established in Costa Rica's General Public Administration Law. However, in both cases (in contrast to Colombia), the public announcement of general proposals remains at the discretion of administrative authorities. In Puerto Rico, the Uniform Administrative Procedure Law of August 12, 1988, states that as long as an agency intends to adopt, amend, or repeal a rule or regulation, it must publish a notice in a general-circulation newspaper. The agency concerned, the law says, must offer an opportunity for the submission of comments in writing within a given period of time, which would naturally curb any real chance for public debate.

As far as demanding accountability is concerned, other than the Bolivian case (in connection with the Comités de Vigilancia and the city sphere), generic provisions in Peru since 1994 and in the new Venezuelan constitution of 1999 ("it is the right of electors, male and female, that their representatives render a public, transparent and periodic accounting of their activities, in accordance with the program presented" [Article 66]) provide the only clear examples of countries where demands for accountability have a legal foundation and governance. Usually such provisions are circumscribed and difficult to carry out, as in Peru. That country's Law of the Rights of Citizen Participation and Control, passed in 1994, recognizes the requirement of accountability of anyone subject to dismissal because of their handling of a budget or resources. It also says that an official has sixty days to respond to a request and must publish it along with his or her reply. However, the law's Article 34 also says that at least 20 percent of the voting population in a particular zone must make the request. In Chile, mayors' legal obligation to provide a yearly public accounting was only recently established, in March 1999.[11]

In summary, an examination of the Latin American context allows us to conclude that demanding accountability, public hearings, and preannouncement of general administrative acts that create opportunities for the construction of public arenas of deliberation for the formation of public decisions and policies are practically nonexistent from a legal standpoint.

What Are the Priorities?

The context conveyed here would probably seem trivial and even formal in other settings. In most countries of Europe, and generally in all countries where democratic institutionality is strong, the basic conditions for social control are already guaranteed. Problems in such countries have more to do with where actions and means for exercising social accountability can be strengthened. In Latin America, in contrast, the use of social accountability vis-à-vis government demands actions on the part of the government, actions quite different from those that have thus far been witnessed.

With attention focused on what the government can offer to guarantee social controls in Latin America, the main problem is the effort, perhaps original, that will launch the institutionalization of practices of social control. In fact, as has been illustrated here, there have been many attempts to form organizations that will take charge of social control, even providing them with a scope of action and the resources they need to force the government to act. Institutional designs are varied, expressing different degrees of formalization, which, in turn, poses a series of risks. Thus, one would tend to assume that the state, in deciding who should exercise social control and providing them with a job description, may end up undermining not only pluralism but also social dynamics, for example, in terms of changes in the correlations of force, the content of problems that need addressing, and so on. But the situation would seem to be different for resources whose social control translates into actions (or corrections). Demanding specific sanctions, as well as putting on record the trail of denunciations and government perpetrators, seems to make social control efficient. However, depending on the design adopted, experience shows that there are still problems in these areas.

No one doubts that the power and independence of government institutions in the controller and jurisdictional areas are important for social accountability. Furthermore, regarding Latin America's weakness in this regard, attention has been drawn (see O'Donnell 1997) to the priority given to reform in the region and, hence, to the strengthening of "horizontal" accountability, that is, legally instituted government entities responsible for everything from routine investigations to criminal prosecution for acts or omissions by government institutions that could be considered illegal. But the question is whether social accountability must wait passively for the development of horizontal accountability.

If the problem were reproposed, would the likelihood of positive action be enhanced? A key factor is making social control so efficient that it will not rely exclusively on sanctions the government may decide to impose. Society, either the individual or a group acting on behalf of particular interests, must have the resources to be able to apply, directly or indirectly, sanctions on government agents and influence their decisions, with the understanding that public scrutiny is a real possibility.

What should come to mind at this juncture is the fact that elections are not the only direct resource that society has and accountability must not be limited only to politicians. Furthermore, it is possible to find other tools of social accountability. Veto power, voiced not just in the right to revoke a mandate but in the removal of particular officials, is a direct resource that can make social control work. Administrative resources allow society to gauge administrative effort and allow citizens to take action after an act has been committed, without recurring to a court of law. Further, people, individually or through social organizations, may bring a public matter before a jurisdictional entity, forcing it to participate in the control. All of these resources, made available to society, force officials or agencies to heed requests and denunciations. So that deliberation can be patented as a resource of social accountability, allowing its expression as a preventative measure, public forums for discussion must be recognized by the government.

But it is also clear that the real substance of public forums for weighing the reasons for particular policies, as well as the actual activation of resources at the disposal of social accountability, depends on the guarantee of public scrutiny. Key to this are plurality and the wealth of government information that independent "agencies of accountability" subjected to people's control supply (see Manin et al. 1999, 24). However, a more fundamental condition for making public scrutiny possible is the disclosure of government information as legal material, just as the right to access to information makes necessary a relevant law applicable when information is denied or obstructed. The weaknesses that exist in Latin America in this regard cloud regional efforts at institutionalizing social accountability. It is for this reason that the priority in the region is the enlargement of the rights clamored for by the legal system. This means pressuring the government into granting these rights instead of creating distractions. Social organizations and movements face a tough job ahead.

Of course, the path suggested here is hardly the only one that needs to be taken. It is important that citizen participation, with citizens acting as critics and controllers, be exercised over parliaments, political parties, and the media, as well as over diverse independent agencies created specifically for the purpose of exercising accountability. It is understood that all of these factors will constitute the institutional building blocks on which democratic accountability depends. Those institutions and movements that can contribute to public debate will play an important role, both by bringing before the "court" of public opinion matters that need addressing and by exercising scrutiny over the official auditors.

The way must be paved for all public matters to be the object of accountability, in part because of the recent importance given to the private allocation of public services and, in general, the proliferation of public activities developed through private means. Until there are laws that make available information on private entities that carry out public duties, the media, or whichever party is concerned, will not be able to develop some sort of scrutiny over such entities.

Building public accountability demands a democratic and practical ethos that entails paying attention to anything public as something of concern to all. But in the final analysis, nothing will be possible without a determined struggle on the part of society.

NOTES

1. Such attempts are clearly present in the hegemonic movement of "New Public Management," although there is ample literature that concludes, among other things, that public administration accountability is not increased by these mechanisms but, rather, weakened.

2. Cunill Grau (2000) includes a major review of recent literature on this subject, allowing such an observation.

3. It is important to remember that Cohen and Arato (1992, 555ff.) raise the possibility of instrumental actions operating simultaneously with expressive actions, but also of the "self-bureaucratization" of social movements not becoming an unavoidable consequence of policies that influence part of civil society.

4. A description of these models is provided in Cunill Grau (2000), calling attention to the fact that they reflect different degrees of how social controls are made official. The Comités de Vigilancia in Bolivia are an example of a case where social controls have been made official to an extremely large degree; Mexico's Contraloría Social is a case where they have been made official, but to a slightly lesser degree; and the Veedurías Ciudadanas in Colombia provide an example of a case where social controls have been made official to a much lesser degree. Their deficiencies are, therefore, different.

5. According to the particular legal guideline, an official is removed from office when the National Electoral Jury determines that more than 50 percent of the citizens from an electoral or judicial jurisdiction made the request.

6. In Colombia's case, its 1991 constitution provides for the possibility of revoking the mandate of an official, including if the individual has been charged with not carrying out a mandate. The request must have a motive; that is, the petition (signed by no fewer than 40 percent of the valid voters in the election in which the candidate was elected) must indicate the reasons for removal and whether it is related to nonfulfillment of a duty. The mandate will be understood to be revoked when it has been approved by no fewer than 60 percent of the citizens who voted, as long as the number of votes is no

fewer than 60 percent of the ballots cast the day the official was elected. The only ones who can vote are those who voted in the election in which the official was a candidate. In Peru, removal can encompass mayors and alderpersons, regional officials who were elected by the people, and magistrates elected by the people. Referendum takes place in an electoral district if 25 percent of an official's electors, with a maximum of four hundred thousand signatures, submit the request for removal to the appropriate electoral office. The official is removed by approval of half of the electors, plus one. Venezuela's constitution (1999) contemplates revoking the mandate for all officials and magistrates elected by the people. It requires that no fewer than 20 percent of the electors registered in a district request a referendum to remove the official. It also says that the same number of electors who elected the official, or more, must vote to remove him or her; as long as at least 25 percent or more of registered voters participate in the referendum, the mandate will be considered revoked (Article 72).

7. Referring to citizen measures to demand rights, Smulovitz (1997) calls attention to the fact that the possibility of citizens carrying out their rights depends not only on their existence, the knowledge citizens have of them, or their willingness to exercise them, but also on the institutional conditions in which they can be exercised, in the understanding that these can promote or discourage citizen practices.

8. An example of how these obstacles can be established is provided by Smulovitz (1997) in relation to Argentina's safe harbor bill (enacted in 1996), which makes it difficult, from a procedural standpoint, for associations to try to get protection in those cases of collective rights, even when recognized by law.

9. Updated information on this subject can be found at SIARE of the Latin American Center for Administrative Development (CLAD): <http://www.clad.org.ve/siare/innotend/control.html>.

10. Fadul and Muniz (1999) note that some attempts at incorporating a participative budget in Brazil, notwithstanding its democratizing character, have not been successful (at least in making the assignment of public resources more efficient) because they let the executive disregard the legislature or, at least, neutralize its decision-making power in public policy formation, deepening the tension that exists between the two. The authors analyze the case of the Municipal Prefecture in Salvador, Brazil.

11. The law in question (no. 19.602) establishes that a mayor's failure to provide accountability will be considered serious nonfulfillment of duties (Article 1, no. 3). Accountability must be rendered annually in front of a council, and even though the law says that citizens must have access to a given account in order to make their decision, only a portion has to be made available.

BIBLIOGRAPHY

Anastasia, Maria de Fátima Junho. 1997. "Mudança Institucional e Democracia: A Experiência da Assembléia Legislativa de Minas Gerais." Mimeograph.

Castro Kustner, Rocío. 1999. "Genero e Participação Cidadã para o Desenvolvimento Local: Os Conselhos Municipais de Salvador Bahía." Mimeograph.

Clark, David. 1996. "Open Government in Britain: Discourse and Practice." *Public Money and Management* 16, no. 1.

Cohen, Jean L., and Andrew Arato. 1992. *Civil Society and Political Theory.* Cambridge: MIT Press.

Cunill Grau, Nuria. 1997. *Repensando lo Público a Través de la Sociedad: Nuevas Formas de Gestión Pública y Representación Social.* Caracas: CLAD, Editorial Nueva Sociedad.

———. 2000. "La Responsabilización por el Control Social." In *La Responsabilización en la Nueva Gestión Pública Latinoamericana.* Consejo Científico del CLAD. Buenos Aires: CLAD, BID, EUDEBA.

Deleon, Linda. 1998. "Accountability in a 'Reinvented Government.'" *Public Administration* 76, no. 3.

Dryzek, John S. 1990. *Discursive Democracy: Politics, Policy, and Political Science.* Cambridge: Cambridge University Press.

Fadul, Elvia Maria Cavalcanti, and Reynaldo Maia Muniz. 1999. "Contradições Num Processo Democrático: A Prática do Orçamento Participativo nas Cidades Brasileiras." Mimeograph.

Fox, Charles J., and Hugh T. Miller. 1996. *Postmodern Public Administration: Toward Discourse.* Thousand Oaks: Sage Publicatons.

Guzmán Boutier, Omar. 1998. "Denuncias del Comité de Vigilancia o Cuán Efectivo Es el Control Social." In Viceministerio de Participación Ciudadana y Fortalecimiento Municipal 1998.

Habermas, Jürgen. 1990 [1989]. "Soberanía Popular como Procedimento: Um Conceito Normativo de Espaco Público." *Novos Estudos CEBRAP* 26.

Manin, Bernard, Adam Przeworski, and Susan C. Stokes. 1999. "Elections and Representation." In Adam Przeworski, Susan C. Stokes, and Bernard Manin, eds., *Democracy, Accountability and Representation.* Cambridge Studies in the Theory of Democracy. Cambridge: Cambridge University Press.

March, James G., and Johan P. Olsen. 1995. *Democratic Governance.* New York: Free Press.

O'Donnell, Guillermo. 1997. "Rendición de Cuentas Horizontal y Nuevas Poliarquías." *Nueva Sociedad,* no. 152.

Osorio, Hugo. 1998. "La Información: Un Derecho Individual de Bien Público." *Contribuciones* 15, no 2.

Rojas Ortuste, Gonzalo, and Laurent Thévos. 1998. "Presentación General." In Viceministerio de Participación Ciudadana y Fortalecimiento Municipal 1998.

Schedler, Andreas. 1999. "Conceptualizing Accountability." In Schedler, Diamond, and Plattner 1999.

Schedler, Andreas, Larry Diamond, and Marc F. Plattner. 1999. *The Self-Restraining State: Power and Accountability in New Democracies.* Boulder: Lynne Rienner.

Schmitter, Philippe C. 1999. "The Limits of Horizontal Accountability." In Schedler, Diamond, and Plattner 1999.

Smulovitz, Catalina. 1997. "Ciudadanos, Derechos y Política." In Felipe González Morales, ed., *Las Acciones de Interés Público: Argentina, Chile, Colombia y Perú.* Santiago: Universidad Diego Portales.

Stivers, Camilla. 1990. "The Public Agency as Polis: Active Citizens." *Administration and Society* 22, no. 1.

Stone, Bruce. 1995. "Administrative Accountability in the 'Westminster' Democracies: Towards a New Conceptual Framework." *Governance* 8, no. 4.

Viceministerio de Participación Ciudadana y Fortalecimiento Municipal. 1998. *Participación Popular: Una Evaluación-Aperndizaje de la Ley, 1994–1997.* La Paz: VPPFM.

Warren, Mark E. 1999. *Deliberative Democracy.* Mexico: FLACSO.

6

Violent Police, Passive Citizens

THE FAILURE OF SOCIAL ACCOUNTABILITY IN CHILE

Claudio A. Fuentes

THE REESTABLISHMENT of a democratic regime should imply an improvement of political and civil rights, but almost twenty years of democracy in Latin America have clearly shown that this is not the case regarding civil rights. While new democratic governments are theoretically protecting citizens' rights, the empirical record of human rights abuses shows that in many countries little real progress has been made. This is particularly true of a fundamental right: the protection of individuals' physical and psychological integrity. In many countries of Latin America today, citizens are subject to mistreatment and torture by the police, and most of the time, this misconduct goes unpunished.

As we may expect, given the lack of horizontal and vertical mechanisms of accountability in many developing countries, citizens have organized independent nongovernmental organizations to oversee state authorities and to publicly denounce their illegal behavior.[1] This mechanism has been called social accountability, a nonelectoral yet vertical mechanism of control that rests on the actions of an array of citizens' associations and movements and on the media. These "actions are exposing governmental wrongdoing, bringing new issues onto the public agenda, or activating the operation of horizontal agencies" (Smulovitz and Peruzzotti 2000, 150).

The emergence of social accountability is logical: as citizens realize that traditional institutions that should protect them from abuses are not doing their job, they take the initiative to control the state by themselves. However, not all citizens take an active part in this process, and those who do take part often do so for only short periods of time. The explanation for this behavior is simple: when common goods are in dispute, individuals face strong incentives to "free-ride" by passing the costs of protecting citizens' rights to others, while enjoying the benefits of others' achievements. However, societies have resolved this "free-riding" problem by relying on small but effective institutions that provide a given public good. Poder Ciudadano and the Centro de Estudios Legales y Sociales in Argentina, the Coordinadora in Peru, and Alianza Cívica in Mexico are some examples of small but effective organizations denouncing misbehavior by state officials, controlling police institutions, and overseeing electoral procedures.

In some cases, societies face especially serious roadblocks in responding to unjust and unfair government behavior. This chapter illustrates such a case. It shows how Chile, a country that is facing increasing problems of police violence, has experienced progressive deterioration in the role of organized groups in civil society demanding accountability over police institutions. While certain features of the social context provide strong incentives for human rights groups to control the state, what is observable is, in fact, a declining role of organized human rights groups controlling the state apparatus and, particularly, the police.

Why Do Groups Emerge and Survive?

Pluralists suggest that groups emerge to defend specific interests. The pluralist approach understands government policies as a reflection of interest group influence (Latham 1952; Truman 1951). Later, Mancur Olson (1971) challenged this pluralist notion that group formation is relatively easy and spontaneous by suggesting that while small groups have great advantages in organization and resources, other groups seeking collective benefits have considerably fewer advantages and are less likely to mobilize many potential members. Two reasons explain this phenomenon. First, for issues involving common goods, individuals have strong incentives to free-ride by allowing others to provide a collective benefit for them without paying a share of the costs. If individuals cannot be excluded from enjoying the benefits of a public good, then individuals' first inclination is not to spend resources and energy in the achievement of such a good.[2] Second, individuals are not willing to contribute to some organization if they perceive their contribution will not make a great difference in achieving its stated goal.

Thus, for issues that involve public goods such as the protection of civil rights or the environment, the economically disadvantaged, the jobless, and the poor, overcoming the obstacles to mobilization should be difficult (Baumgartner and Leech 1998, 67). In this sense, while all citizens want their rights protected from the abuse of power, few citizens engage in organizations that promote respect for their rights. According to Olson, these citizens perceive that the individual cost of participating in advocacy groups is greater than the benefit they may obtain from not doing so. These citizens free-ride by letting specific small voluntary organizations provide the public good of being protected from the abuse of power.

But Olson's claim regarding the difficulties of collective action was challenged by the emergence of "new" social movements in the developed world during the 1970s. Citizens in these groups had a broad commitment to making society better in terms of the environment, civil rights, and gender equality, among other issues (Berry 1977; Wilson 1995; Verba, Schlozman, and Brady 1995). For scholars, what was puzzling was the fact that collective action does occur, even though people have few resources and little permanent power (Tarrow 1994; Wilson 1995). How can we explain such an explosion of groups if incentives to free-ride are high?

To respond to this question, the literature on interest groups has addressed the need to understand group formation and maintenance by focusing on internal characteristics some groups have that enable them to advance their agendas and convince other people to mobilize. The *resource mobilization approach* considers groups' internal characteristics that make them more or less likely to succeed. For instance, this approach addresses issues such as organizational structure (whether groups are more or less hierarchical) and access to economic resources. More recently, this approach has addressed the importance of policy entrepreneurship as an important indicator of success. Entrepreneurs are individuals who pursue material or nonmaterial rewards and who take advantage of opportunities to make an issue noticeable, attract public attention, and engage citizens in the defense of certain principles and ideas (Salisbury 1969; Chong 1991; Sabatier 1992; Kollman 1998). In this regard, it is argued that some individuals are capable of visualizing and taking advantage of the opportunities that the social and political context provides, overcoming obstacles to group formation and, particularly, survival over time.

In contrast, other scholars have focused on contextual factors inhibiting/allowing social actors' action. A *political opportunity structure approach* observes how elements in the environment impose certain constraints on political activity or open avenues for it. According to this reasoning, social and political structures set a given equilibrium in a society that is difficult to change because of the self-enforcing nature of political institutions. However, at certain *critical junctures,* social actors can alter the existing status quo by taking advantage of opportunities for action. These opportunities are provided mainly within the context in which social interaction occurs. Certain stable and dynamic dimensions define the political opportunity structure. Among the former are state strength (Tarrow 1994), social and ethnic cleavages (Kriesi et al. 1995; Krain 1997), degree of openness of the political system (Kitschelt 1986), the institutional capacity to implement policies (Kitschelt 1986), state repressiveness (Schock 1996), and the existence of international social networks. More dynamic dimensions are major changes in the balance of power among political actors as a result of political realignments (Tarrow 1994), critical changes in rules allowing political participation to previously excluded groups, and critical and many times unforeseen events that may occur domestically or internationally triggering mobilization (wars, accidents, revolutions, extraconstitutional changes, etc.) (Krain 1997).

More recently, scholars have attempted to build bridges between resource mobilization and political opportunity structure arguments, integrating elements of both approaches in a single model (McAdam, Tilly, and Tarrow 2001). However, few works have tested these models empirically, and even fewer have considered developing countries. Moreover, few works have properly explained the causal mechanisms by which some contextual and individual factors cause specific outcomes. This work integrates the political opportunity structure and resource mobilization approaches in a single model in order to explain a particular issue: social actors' mobilization against police violence.

This chapter analyzes the puzzling experience of the human rights movement in Chile; while important contextual factors favor the survival of a traditionally strong movement network, the actual experience of the human rights movement in Chile after the transition shows a progressive decline in its ability to check and control the state. When democracy was reestablished in Chile in 1990, the human rights movement enjoyed national and international prestige, strong organizational capacities, and international contacts to pursue its objectives. Additionally, since the transition to democracy was particularly problematic, the armed forces and the police retaining important legal powers, human rights organizations had strong incentives to continue checking military and police behavior. Moreover, citizens' allegations of police brutality increased more than 100 percent during the first ten years of democracy. Furthermore, several independent sources documented continued police brutality against specific societal groups. Consequently, given this context, we should expect human rights organizations to monitor the police, but as this chapter demonstrates, human rights organizations in Chile show a progressive deterioration of their accountability role, particularly in relation to the protection of citizens from abuse of power by police forces.

I argue that a combination of certain contextual conditions and group characteristics determines whether these groups can influence the policy process. The context, or the "political opportunity structure," relates particularly to *the nature of political transition* and *access to the political system* measured in terms of state concentration of power, police autonomy, pluralism of mass media, and balance of power among parties. At the same time that the political opportunity structure either facilitates or inhibits effective action, *characteristics internal to the groups* are also important in that they allow groups to influence state policies at particular junctures. Thus, following recent developments in the literature on social movements, my research combines structural/contextual factors (the political opportunity structure) with an individual level of analysis (resource mobilization).

The Struggle for Human Rights in Chile since 1990

The protection of citizens' personal integrity from abuse by police forces, our dependent variable, is a widely accepted essential right in any democratic regime. However, history tells us that state agents at times violate individuals' rights even in the most advanced and stable democracies and that, therefore, the state and society develop institutions to control state behavior. As many citizens lack resources, time, and even willingness to publicly denounce such violations, human rights organizations, our independent variable, play an important social service in defending citizens and, more broadly, in checking and controlling state institutions.

In this case, "protection of citizens' rights" includes three mutually inclusive dimensions: (1) *Legal recognition:* This can be considered the first condition of individuals' guarantees. In this case, the focus is on the explicit legal recognition of the inviolability of an individual's physical integrity as a human right. (2) *Policy implementation:* This refers to the translation of recognized rights into specific procedures, including the creation and reform of organizations and the implementation of specific policies to protect citizens from abuse of power. (3) *Actual practices:* This refers to violation of the physical integrity of individuals in the form of extrajudicial killing, torture, and/or ill-treatment by police officers.

In countries that have experienced military regimes and serious violations of human rights, we may expect that the "protection of citizens' rights" constitutes a crucial aspect once democracy is reestablished. We should expect that new governments and/or organized societal groups would address the legal recognition of citizens' rights; the implementation of reforms within the police, particularly concerning respect for human rights; and actual police compliance with new rules. As Elizabeth Jelin suggests, transitions to democracy imply dismantling antidemocratic forms of exercising power, changing the rules governing the distribution of power, the recognition and legal sanction of rights, and the internalization of such new rules among citizens (1996, 102). Following is an examination of Chilean human rights organizations and an explanation of changes that have taken place in Chile in terms of citizens' rights since 1990.

The Dense Network of Chilean Human Rights Groups

Several studies have addressed the importance of the human rights (HR) movement during the Pinochet regime in Chile (Hutchison 1989; Lowden 1996; Loveman 1995; Ensalaco 2000). By the end of the military regime, the movement had a broad range of voluntary, academic, and professional human rights organizations (table 6.1), most of them linked to each other in a dense network of collaboration and reciprocity (Ropp and Sikkink 1999). Three types of organizations can be identified: (1) *Voluntary:* The main objective of these organiza-

6.1 Human Rights Organizations in Chile: 1990 and 2000

Organization	Type of Organization (1990)	Type of Organization (2000)
Vicariate of Solidarity	Voluntary/professional/political	
Chilean Commission for Human Rights	Voluntary/professional/political	Political
Committee for the Defense of the Rights of the People (CODEPU)	Voluntary/professional/political	Voluntary/professional/political
National Commission for the Rights of Young People (CODEJU)	Voluntary/political	Voluntary/professional/political
Social Help Foundation of the Christian Churches (FASIC)	Professional/political	Professional
Service for Peace and Justice—Chile (SERPAJ)	Professional	Professional
Chilean Chapter of the Ombudsman	Political	Political
RELATIVES		
Association of Relatives of the Detained-Disappeared	Voluntary	Voluntary
Youth Committee of Children of Political Prisoners and the Disappeared	Voluntary	Voluntary
Association of Relatives of Chileans Executed for Political Reasons	Voluntary	Voluntary
Association of Relatives of Political Prisoners	Voluntary	Voluntary
Committee for the Return of Exiles	Political	
National Commission against Torture	Voluntary	
Movement against Torture, "Sebastián Acevedo"	Voluntary	
Association of Relatives of Relegated and Formerly Relegated Persons	Voluntary	
FUNAS		Voluntary
ACADEMIC/PROFESSIONAL INSTITUTIONS		
Human Rights Program, Academy of Christian Humanism	Professional	
Chilean Association for Peace Research	Professional	
Quercum Center for Development and Social Studies	Professional	
Lawyers' Group for Political Prisoners	Professional	
Association of Pro–Human Rights Lawyers in Chile	Professional	
Foundation for the Protection of Minors Affected by States of Emergency	Professional	
INTERNATIONAL ORGANIZATIONS BASED IN CHILE		
Amnesty International, Chilean Section	Voluntary	Voluntary
CEJIL—Chile		Professional
PROMOTIONAL PROJECTS		
Derechos Chile		Professional
Organization for the Defense of the People (ODEP)		Professional/political

Sources: Hutchison 1989; Wiseberg, López, and Meselson 1990, 187–220; <http://www.derechoschile.cl>.

6.2 The Work of the Vicariate of Solidarity

Year	Number of Organizations	Number of Participants
1983	965	54,916
1984	1,448	44,994
1985	1,975	71,077
1986	2,524	81,245
1987	2,660	77,263
1988	1,373	58,361

Source: Lowden 1996.

tions is to denounce and mobilize citizens about specific claims (disappearance of persons, torture, political prisoners). In general, these organizations emerged as initiatives of victims' relatives. (2) *Professional:* The main objective of these organizations is to provide research on human rights and/or professional support (psychological, social) to the victims. (3) *Political/lobbying:* Although many organizations originally emerged with the clear objective of providing legal support for the victims and their relatives, some organizations adopted a more political role in trying to influence politicians and governments regarding the issue of human rights during and after Pinochet's regime.

During the military regime, the Catholic Church was particularly important in providing financial, institutional, and moral support to the victims of human rights violations through the creation of the Vicariate of Solidarity in 1976. To provide an idea of the social impact of this organization, table 6.2 summarizes its activity between 1983 and 1988 in terms of the number of organizations with which the Vicariate organized activities and the total number of participants. Its activities included support for human rights groups in medical, legal, psychological, and social matters, as well as workshops, nutritional support, committees for the homeless, and training classes.

During the transition, the Catholic Church closed the Vicariate of Solidarity based on the assumption that the new political authorities would take care of human rights problems in the future. Thus, the human rights movement was mainly reduced to two types of groups: voluntary organizations of relatives of victims and their friends and professional lobbying organizations such as the Chilean Commission for Human Rights (CCHR), the Committee for the Defense of the Rights of the People (CODEPU), and the Social Help Foundation of the Christian Churches (FASIC).

Implementing the Citizens' Rights Agenda

After the reestablishment of democracy in Chile, the human rights agenda was composed of three crucial issues: first, the search for truth, reparation, and justice regarding past human rights violations; second, the resolution of the problem of more than 350 political prisoners; and finally, legal and institutional changes to protect citizens' rights (Human Rights Watch 1991; Garretón 1996). This section analyzes the changes that have taken place in Chile since March 1990 in terms of legal reforms, institutional transformation within the police, and actual compliance by the police, tracing human rights groups' specific influence on such issues.

LEGAL REFORMS

Three main changes have been implemented in Chile since 1990: the ratification of international treaties concerning human rights (1990–92); legal reforms regarding prisoners' rights (1993); and the abolition of the "arrest on suspicion" clause and the establishment of a charter of rights for detainees (1998). In the first case, the executive played a key role in promoting these legal changes and lobbying Congress to pass such a bill. In the second and third cases, human rights groups played an important role in agenda setting, but an almost insignificant role in the actual discussion and approval of the final bills.

From the beginning of his administration, in 1990, President Patricio Aylwin had a strong commitment to ratifying international treaties that had been postponed by the previous regime. By 1992, the Chilean government had ratified several international treaties related to human rights, including the Covenant on Civil and Political Rights; the additional protocol of the Covenant allowing individuals to file petitions of grievance with the UN Human Rights Committee; and the American Convention, allowing the Inter-American Court of Human Rights to have compulsory jurisdiction over Chilean territory. In this context, there was no need for lobbying because of the compatibility of interests. Human rights groups had an indirect influence in this case through the presence in government of several lawyers with previous histories in the human rights network.[3]

The government also had to deal with the more than 350 political prisoners who were waiting for trial or who were already sentenced.[4] As one of his first acts, President Aylwin pardoned 47 political prisoners and sent a bill to Congress to improve the legal conditions of prisoners, particularly in cases in which terrorist crimes had been committed. The package sought to eliminate the death penalty, to amend the antiterrorist law, to reduce penalties, and to reexamine offenses set out in the various laws. Moreover, the proposal included some basic guarantees of decent treatment for detainees. In 1991, Congress approved some reforms regarding citizens' rights, including limiting detentions to a maximum of forty-eight hours, requiring judges ordering an extension of incommunicado detention to appoint a doctor to carry out a medical examination of the suspect, and guaranteeing detainees held incommunicado the right to see a lawyer to check on their physical condition.[5]

The government tried to solve the "political prisoners" problem for two reasons.[6] First, authorities had a strong commitment to reestablishing the rule of law in the country, and probably one of the most evident cases in which the principle of due process had been violated during the previous regime was concerning political prisoners.[7] In this sense, the government's electoral undertaking was to exempt from penal responsibility and pardon all prisoners except those who had committed homicide, serious assault, kidnapping, or the abduction of a minor. Following this commitment, in the first eighteen months of democratic rule, 250 political prisoners were released, the majority of whom left on bail, were paroled, or saw the charges against them dismissed, and 80 received pardons from president Aylwin (International Commission of Jurists 1992).

But a second reason for the government's concern was that human rights organizations were particularly active in lobbying the government, Congress, and international actors. In this case, human rights groups played three important roles. First, they made the issue noticeable by constant demonstrations of relatives and sympathizers outside Congress. The campaign was stimulated by hunger strikes, prison occupations, and demonstrations, some of which were violently repressed by the police (CODEPU 1994). Second, human rights groups played an important role in holding the government accountable to its agenda. For instance, after the government sent the bill package to Congress in 1990, the opposition tried to negotiate an agreement with the government that implied reduction of sentences for political prisoners against similar measures of clemency for military officers involved in human rights violations.[8] The government coalition agreed to begin conversations with the opposition in Congress. This attempt was strongly rejected by human rights organizations, which pressured allies in Congress not to accept such negotiations. After three weeks of pressure, the deputies of the government coalition abandoned these negotiations, going against even the president's will to achieve an agreement (International Commission of Jurists 1992, 179). Finally, human rights organizations actively denounced political prisoners' imprisonment and legal conditions before the international community. Local NGOs such as CODEPU and the CCHR provided information to the UN Committee against Torture and to several international nongovernmental organizations in order to obtain international support for their campaign. International organizations such as Human Rights Watch, Amnesty International, the International Commission of Jurists, and the Centre for the Independence of Judges and Lawyers published well-documented information regarding the status of political prisoners in Chile.[9] But probably the most important human rights group achievement was the fact that due to their constant reports, a special UN rapporteur visited Chile in 1995.[10]

The reform to the "arrest on suspicion" clause was the third legal instance in which human rights organizations partially influenced the government. The police had the power to arrest individuals based on their physical appearance; Article 260 of the Code of Penal Procedure states that police officers were authorized to detain "anyone who is present at an unusual time or at a place or in circumstances that give grounds to suspect malicious intent" (República de Chile 1996). After the reestablishment of democracy, organized groups coordinated by the National Commission for the Rights of Young People (CODEJU) initiated a campaign to eliminate this legal provision. Human rights organizations claimed that the "arrest on suspicion" clause allowed the police to arrest people, particularly youth, without justification, generating a propitious legal instance to violate citizens' rights. Given the increasing number of complaints received between 1991 and 1993, CODEJU decided to coordinate a national campaign to abolish this clause.

The campaign involved three strategies: first, the mobilization of activists in front of police buildings to denounce abuses by the police against youth; second, the formation of a "committee against 'arrest on suspicion,'" supported by secondary and university student unions, by three deputies sensitive to the issue, and by the National Institute of Youth (INJ), a governmental office in charge of dealing with youth issues; third, the support of lawyers in other human rights organizations who would initiate legal charges against police officers involved in such practices.[11] According to one leader of the movement, the most effective ways to influence the government were through public mobilizations to make the issue noticeable to authorities and the public and through the establishment of a strategic alliance with key actors within the government.[12]

The mobilizations were not massive, but constant. Generally, no more than twenty to fifty people peacefully protested in front of the police headquarters in Santiago's center. They were led by the director of CODEJU, José Sabat, who brought letters to the director of the police authenticating cases of police abuse. They received press attention thanks to the good public relations skills of CODEJU leaders, who recognized the importance of public relations and therefore established contacts with journalists before any public activity and provided reporters with pertinent information.[13]

At the same time, human rights organizations established key alliances with governmental actors. The INJ supported eliminating the "arrest on suspicion" clause and favored the 1992 creation of a committee against this clause.[14] Soon after the establishment of this alliance, a group of deputies led by Juan Pablo Letelier and Andrés Palma introduced a proposal in Congress to eliminate "arrest on suspicion." The project also included several clauses regarding the protection of detainees' rights.

Thus, CODEJU and other societal groups played an important role in setting the agenda for debate on this issue. As a culmination of this process, the president invited these organizations to participate in the principal act commemorating the third anniversary of the reestablishment of democracy, on March 11, 1993. As part of this event, the president promised executive support for the elimination of the "arrest on suspicion" clause.[15] Later on, CODEJU was invited by the director of the uniformed police, Rodolfo Stange, to talk about this issue, and a week later, the president of the Chamber of Deputies announced that he personally was asking the executive to give the bill urgent status after having received in his office the representative of the committee against arrest on suspicion.[16]

The pressure of human rights organizations partly explains the steady decline of arrests on suspicion since 1993 (table 6.3). As human rights organizations achieved notoriety and found allies within the government, the issue came to be considered an important priority by top-ranking authorities. Soon, the government pressured the police to stop such practices.[17]

Nevertheless, the constant decline cannot be solely explained by activist pressures. It is interesting to observe that while human rights organizations practically discontinued mobilizations and campaigns against arrests on suspicion after 1993, detentions still show a persistent declining trend. Conscious of the negative public impact of these arrests and the government's concern, the police used internal procedures to reduce the number of arrests on suspicion.[18] However, as figures of arrests on suspicion were drastically dropping,

6.3 Arrest on Suspicion in Chile: 1990–99

Year	Number of Arrests
1990	95,829
1991	127,012
1992	115,629
1993	35,408
1994	16,021
1995	11,566
1996	7,364
1997	5,465
1998	3,233
1999	0

Source: Carabineros de Chile and INE 1990–99.

from 127,012 in 1991 to 5,465 in 1997, the overall number of detainees was not diminishing proportionately. In fact, other causes of detention, such as misdemeanors, public disturbances, and drinking in public places, tended to increase between 1993 and 1995 (fig. 6.1). Thus, police forces simply shifted tactics by resorting to other legal tools to arrest people.[19] Interestingly, this was not an issue picked up on or publicized by either human rights organizations or the government.

Given the previous context, the 1998 approval of a bill eliminating "arrest on suspicion" seems odd. First, human rights groups, particularly CODEJU, stopped their public campaign against such arrests after Congress began to debate the issue in 1993. Second, the police had reduced the number of detainees on suspicion by a significant amount, making the issue less notorious. Third, the government did not accept Congress's petition to give urgent status to the project because it did not want to broaden the agenda of conflictive issues with the opposition. Finally, the right-wing opposition in Congress, with the strong support of the police, opposed any modification of this clause at least until 1996.

However, in July 1998, Congress approved the initiative with the support of moderate right-wing sectors, introducing some important changes. The new law established three innovations: for the first time in Chilean history the police had the obligation to read detainees their rights; the police could detain

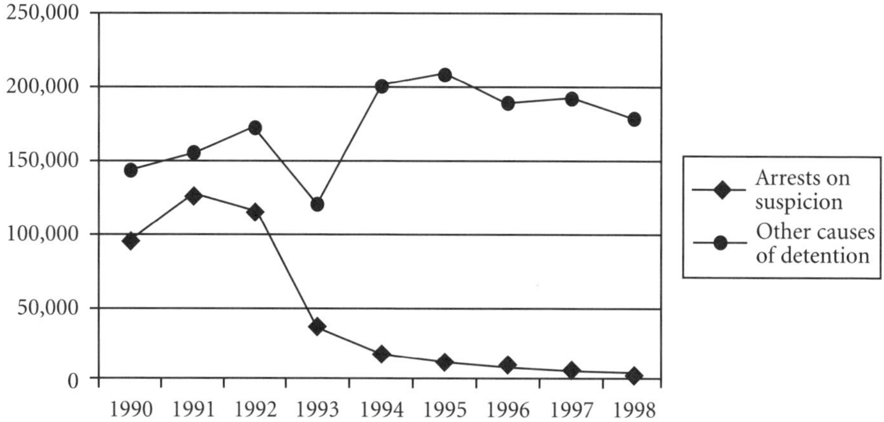

Fig. 6.1. Detentions in Chile: 1990–98

Note: The category "Other causes of detention" includes misdemeanors, drinking in public places, and street disorder.
Source: Carabineros de Chile and INE 1999.

persons only when they had a judicial notification to do so or when individuals were in the process of committing a crime, eliminating arrest on suspicion; and in cases in which individuals could not identify themselves with a legal document, the police could hold them for no more than four hours in order to establish their identity.

Human rights organizations recognize their insignificant role in lobbying Congress regarding this bill. As the director of CODEJU acknowledged, "The burden of following this topic in Congress was on the National Institute of Youth." In general, human rights organizations did not develop the technical capacity to systematically lobby in Congress. Moreover, the committee against "arrest on suspicion" confined its work to providing political support for the presentation of the 1993 motion in Congress but disbanded after the bill was presented in the Chamber of Deputies. According to CODEJU's director, "This committee provided nominal but not real support to specific leaders. No more than three or four people actually tried to convince the government to change the arrest on suspicion clause. And these people were in the National Institute of Youth."[20]

The fundamental reason for the approval of this bill can be found in a parallel process that was taking place in Chile: the reform of the judicial system. After 1994, the government gave high priority to a substantive revision of the

Penal Code, which in fact profoundly altered the structure of the penal system in Chile. The spirit of this reform sought to increase the efficiency of the overall penal system and provide individuals with certain basic guarantees of due process and compliance with the rule of law (Riego 1998; Vargas 1998). By 1997, the majority of congresspeople supported these two basic principles, paving the road for easy approval of the bill eliminating arrest on suspicion. The congressional debate between March and July 1998 was crucial for approval of the bill, and no human rights organization was invited to participate in it. At the time, most legislators agreed with the idea of eliminating arrest on suspicion based on the need to provide a coherent framework of principles for the new Penal Code and the actual reduction of arrests on suspicion by the police.[21] The final project that was approved followed most of the recommendations made by the government at the beginning of that year. Overall, human rights organizations played a moderate role in setting the agenda for some legal reforms, but they played no role during the political debate over the legal initiative.

POLICE REFORMS

A second sphere of potential influence is control over institutional transformations within the police. After seventeen years of military rule in which police institutions assumed repressive roles, human rights organizations should be expected to pressure the government in order to introduce reforms in police institutions' curricula regarding human rights, incorporate ethical codes within police institutions, and check whether these institutional reforms are actually being implemented.

However, the few changes observed within the police are the result of police and/or government initiatives rather than human rights organizations' influence. Chile has two police institutions: a uniformed police (Carabineros de Chile), a centralized and militarized institution in charge of Chile's public safety with more than thirty thousand officers distributed nationwide; and an Investigative Police (Investigaciones de Chile), a centralized civilian agency with approximately five thousand people in charge of the investigation of crimes nationwide.

Soon after the reestablishment of democracy, the government promoted an important transformation of Investigaciones that implied the removal of all officers involved in past human rights violations; the appointment of a director close to the government; a change in Investigaciones's academic curriculum, incorporating human rights as an important subject; and the appointment of a

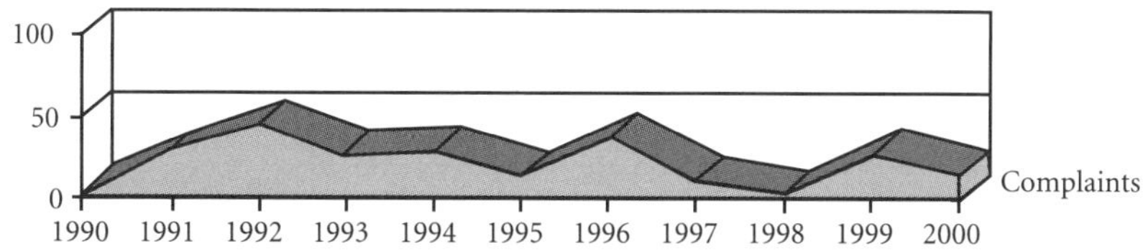

Fig. 6.2. Complaints of Police Violence Registered by CODEPU: 1990–2000

Note: The date indicates the date a case was presented in court. The data for 1999–2000 shows the total of complaints.

Source: CODEPU 1999.

lawyer with a background in human rights as an advisor of the director. Additionally, Investigaciones issued an ethical code, and several courses were implemented between 1994 and the year 2000. In contrast, the uniformed police introduced fewer significant institutional changes. First, they offered one compulsory course on human rights in the Police Academy. Second, after Congress approved a new penal code in 1998, the uniformed police offered training courses through private universities to update officers on new procedures. Although Carabineros was actively engaged in repression during the military regime, no major curriculum transformations were made. In all these changes, the participation of human rights groups was, at most, indirect. The presence of human rights lawyers in such institutions, particularly in the case of Investigaciones, was the most concrete way human rights activists could influence the development of police institutions.[22]

POLICE PRACTICES

One of the ultimate goals of human rights organizations is preempting police abuses, and the only way to do so is to collect information regarding police abuses, denounce such abuses publicly, and file suits against the police once a case is detected. According to CODEPU's statistics, between 1990 and 2000, the number of suits against the police declined (fig. 6.2). The overall trend shows an increase between 1990 and 1992, a constant decline between 1993 and 1995, and moderate increases followed by declines in 1996 and 1999. At first glance, this trend corresponds to legal and institutional changes already described. One may think that the decline of denunciations is in response to the police reduction of arrests on suspicion between 1993 and 1998, to institutional reforms within the police after 1992, and to the approval of legal provisions protecting citizens' rights in 1998.

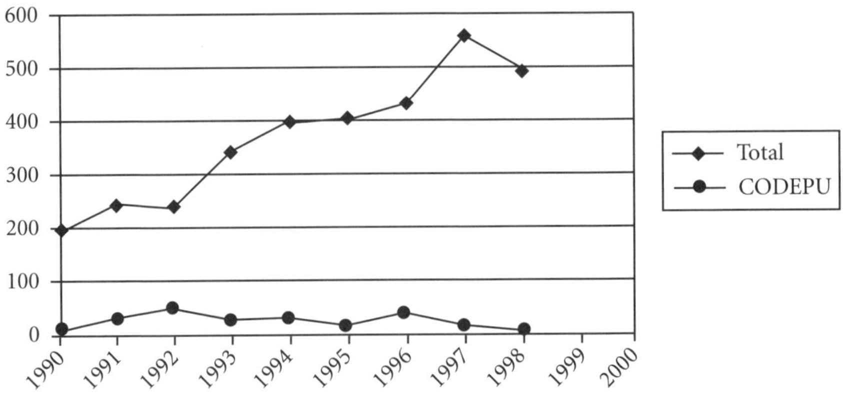

Fig. 6.3. Allegations of Police Violence Filed in Courts: 1990–2000
Note: The cases were presented in Santiago, the fourth, fifth, and sixth regions.
Source: Fuentes 2001.

However, if we consider the total number of allegations of police violence presented in the courts by civilians between 1990 and 2000, the picture is quite different (fig. 6.3). Here, we observe that while CODEPU's records show a declining trend after 1992, the actual number of cases claiming police violence presented in courts has increased abruptly and constantly since 1992. While citizens presented 194 legal complaints before courts in 1990, citizens presented 562 complaints in 1997.

Several reasons explain this increase in citizens' complaints against the uniformed police. First, the reestablishment of democracy made citizens more aware of their rights, generating a new environment for denouncing abuse of power by state officials. Although this is a plausible explanation, citizens did not have incentives to engage themselves in complicated and time-consuming legal procedures. In fact, no governmental or nongovernmental actors were promoting campaigns regarding citizens' rights until at least 1996.[23] Moreover, citizens had few incentives to present allegations, because the chances of obtaining a positive result are virtually zero: less than 3 percent of the cases filed in military courts have ended with the prosecution of a police officer.

A second explanation points to an actual increase in police violence during the last decade. Greater levels of socioeconomic problems, particularly after 1997, and greater levels of social protest have increased the opportunities for repression by police forces. Some qualitative sources confirm the continued police brutality in Chile after the transition. A private university study suggests that ill-treatment of detainees by the police in the interval between arrest and appearance before a judge or release was fairly common at the beginning of the democratic era (Jiménez 1994). In this study, based on interviews with prisoners in 1992, 22 percent said they had received good treatment, while 71 percent said they had received blows of various kinds, 49 percent said they had been subjected to electric shock, 20 percent said they had been undressed, 6 percent had been hung by their hands and feet, and 5 percent said plastic bags had been placed over their heads (Jiménez 1994, 193–206). A more recent study (1998–99) based on interviews with teenagers from Santiago's Center of Detention reveals that 81 percent received bad treatment from police officers at the moment of arrest. Of those who had received bad treatment, 93 percent said they had received blows of various kinds, 36 percent said they had been submerged in water containers, and 21 percent said plastic bags had been placed over their heads to produce asphyxiation (Jiménez 2000).

Overall, while citizens were presenting an increasing number of suits against the police and the social context was increasingly problematic, human rights organizations did not document this increase. The evidence suggests, first, that citizens were not channeling allegations through human rights organizations and, second, that the main human rights organizations were not aware of this increasing level of complaints and, if they were, did not spend time gathering the necessary information to make a more compelling argument before the government and the media.[24]

This lack of information led to misinformation on the international level. After 1994, the main way human rights organizations made their voice heard on police violence in Chile was through international reports on human rights, mainly those of Amnesty International and the UN Committee against Torture. Given the fact that these international reports based their information on local groups, they did not contain accurate information, and only a small number of cases were reported (table 6.4).

In sum, human rights groups have not played a crucial role in making police institutions accountable to the public after the reestablishment of democracy (table 6.5). Human rights organizations spent time and resources on defending issues of relevance in the past (i.e., political prisoners' rights), but they did not have a significant impact on the legal recognition of rights; the institutional transformation of police institutions; or, more important, controlling police practices in a democracy. What has happened in Chile is a progressive withdrawal of human rights groups controlling police institutions.

6.4 Chile: Alleged Cases of Police Abuse

Year	Torture	Extrajudicial Killing	Source
1990	25		AI 1991
1991 (Jan.–Sept.)	16		AI 1991 / UN 1996
1992	9	1	UN 1996 / IAAT / State 1996
1993	9	3	UN 1996 / Press / State 1994
1994	26	2	UN 1996 / Press / State / IAAT
1995	17	2	UN 1996 / Press / State 1996
1996	5	3	State 1997 / AI
1997	3	1	State 1998 / AI / Press
1998	13	2	State 1999 / AI / Press
1999		2	State 2000

This table includes mentions of specific cases considering several sources (including torture and other cruel, inhuman, or degrading treatment by the police).

Abbreviations: AI: Amnesty International; IAAT: International Association against Torture; Press: Chip News Service; State: State Department Report on Human Rights; UN: UN Committee on Human Rights.

6.5 Human Rights Groups Influencing State Policies and Practices

	Timing	Degree of Influence	Type of Influence
LEGAL			
Ratification of international agreements		Low	Indirect: HR network in government
Reforms (1991–92)	Agenda setting	High	Direct: campaigns
	Political debate	Medium	Indirect: issue linkage
	Implementation	High	Direct: international HR network
Reforms (1998)	Agenda setting	High	Direct: campaigns
	Political debate	None	
INSTITUTIONAL			
Police reforms	Agenda setting	Low	Indirect: campaigns
	Political debate	None	
	Implementation	Low	Indirect: international reports
BEHAVIORAL			
Arrest on suspicion	Implementation	Low	Indirect: campaigns
Police practices	Implementation	Low	Indirect: international reports

Explaining the Lack of Accountability

There are two explanations for this lack of accountability. First, while human rights groups faced an increasingly conflictive social context, certain features of the institutional context inhibited their actions. These constraining dimensions include the nature of the transition and access to the political system. However, the context does not fully explain the lack of activism. An additional element is groups' internal characteristics, which affected the way they adapted to a new context.

The Nature of the Transition

Chile's transition to democracy has correctly been depicted as a controlled or negotiated process from above. First, new authorities have to rule within a highly constrained set of rules defined by the 1980 constitution. Second, the armed forces were in a privileged position of power at the beginning of the transition, including a high level of professional autonomy and a high level of political involvement (Fuentes 2002). Third, the military regime established a decree in 1979 granting amnesty to those who had committed criminal actions between 1973 and 1978 or who had covered up or were accomplices in such activities. This included individuals who were not already involved in legal proceedings or who had not been sentenced before the law came into effect. Those found guilty by a military tribunal after 1973 also received amnesty (Comisión Verdad y Reconciliación 1993). Finally, new democratic authorities decided not to challenge the inherited legal framework, limiting their goals to achieving truth and justice "to the extent they were possible." Political authorities compromised themselves to search for those responsible for crimes committed during the military regime to the extent that this would not harm the stability of the transition process (Garretón 1996; Moulián 1997).

Given this context, the human rights groups' agenda was to exert pressure in areas where the state was unwilling to do so: solving the situation of political prisoners and searching for truth and justice in human rights violations committed between 1973 and 1990. Thus, most of the groups' material as well as human resources focused on the legal resolution of past human rights violations; establishment of pecuniary reparation for the victims; and, later on, denouncing torturers from the military regime. In this sense, the nature of the transition imposed a clear agenda related to the country's legacy rather than to new, emerging social conflicts.

Access to the Political System

Another factor is related to the chances of social groups getting their voice heard. In Chile, social actors have few options to access the policy process, because of four factors: concentration of state authority, police autonomy, the balance of power among political actors, and media ownership. The combination of these four elements has contributed to reducing civil society's options to influence the political process.

CONCENTRATION OF AUTHORITY

The 1980 constitution established a centralized presidential system in which the executive enjoys high powers vis-à-vis Congress.[25] For instance, the executive has *exclusive* authority to "introduce bills involving spending, change the duties and characteristics of public-sector administrative units, and modify the political or administrative configuration of the state" (Valenzuela 1999, 239). Moreover, the executive can define the political agenda by giving urgent status to bills during half of the legislative sessions and calling the legislature into special session to debate legislation proposed by the executive (Nogueira 1994, 43–54). In practical terms, this exaggerated presidentialism makes the executive the main actor in formulating new legislation and controlling the legislative agenda. Of all laws promulgated between 1990 and 1997, 83.5 percent had executive origin, while only 16.5 percent had legislative origin (Siavelis 2000, 24).

But this exaggerated presidentialism has other important implications. First, four agencies, the Ministries of the Presidency, the Interior, Foreign Affairs, and Communications, *concentrate* decisions within the executive, making it very difficult for subordinated agencies to express different opinions and disagreements. Second, these agencies are close to the president, *dominating* the executive's political agenda by defining what is relevant in legislative and political terms.

Hierarchical decisions affect the establishment of potential alliances human rights groups can make with low-ranking policy makers within the government, given the dependent relationship between the latter and top-ranking policy makers. When human rights groups look for political support within the executive, they have three alternatives: the Ministry of the Interior; the Ministry of Justice, specifically the Division of Human Rights of the Corporation of Legal Assistance; and the Division of Human Rights within the Ministry of Foreign

Affairs. But options to obtain political support in the Ministry of the Interior are small, given the fact that the ministry's agenda requires being on good terms with the police. Only in cases of extreme police violence has the Ministry of the Interior requested internal investigations of the uniformed police, but the legal impediments to reviewing internal police procedures seriously damage the ministry's option to exert more control over the uniformed police.

This leaves the Ministry of Justice and the Ministry of Foreign Affairs, but in both cases the specific Divisions of Human Rights have little ability to collect information in order to gain influence vis-à-vis other agencies, and, more important, they enjoy very low political leverage within the state apparatus.[26] The story of the Ministry of Justice's Human Rights Division at the Corporation of Legal Assistance (CAJ) is a good example of this. The CAJ depends on the Ministry of Justice and provides free legal counseling for people who cannot afford a lawyer. In 1992, the government created a Division of Human Rights in the CAJ to take care of cases concerning past and present violations of human rights, appointing lawyers linked to human rights organizations. Despite the fact that this division received an increasing number of allegations of police violence after 1995, it has not received the resources to do its job. Three part-time lawyers and one secretary, all sharing one computer, had to handle more than eight hundred citizens' consultations a year and more than five hundred lawsuits filed in the courts in the last five years.[27]

Other people more sympathetic to the human rights cause have had more room to maneuver, given their close relationship with the president and the specific leadership they have exerted. For instance, when the Division of Human Rights at the Ministry of Foreign Affairs was led by a well-known lawyer who had a personal relationship with President Aylwin (1990–94), the division enjoyed more autonomy than other agencies. This allowed it to promote the human rights agenda against other ministries' will.[28] However, as soon as these policy entrepreneurs left office in 1995–96, the division acquired a low profile and became less active.

Concentration of power allows the executive to exert tight control over what is relevant to public debate. Thus, if the executive's agenda conflicts with human rights groups' interests, the human rights groups' ability to influence the political process is seriously diminished. Indeed, the government has constantly faced a trade-off between promoting citizens' rights and defending the police from allegations of misbehavior. Interestingly, the analysis of policy makers' reactions to allegations of police misbehavior shows a *consistent* pattern of defense of police institutions, even though the government does not agree with the autonomous status of the police (table 6.6).[29]

The explanation for this pattern can be found in the way the political agenda on public safety issues has been designed and implemented. Since at least 1995, one of the top priorities of the government has been to control delinquency, given the increasing public perception of insecurity and the determination of the right-wing lobby to make this issue a priority even if there has been no actual increase. In this context, the government has developed specific programs to "tackle" delinquency by increasing the police budget, enhancing police coordination, and developing targeted programs to increase security in public spaces. While most of these measures have a direct impact on the relationship between the police and people in the streets, the protection of individuals' rights has not been part of the Ministry of the Interior's agenda.[30]

Given the fact that the government's agenda requires being on good terms with the institutions in charge of providing public safety, and given right-wing support for such an agenda, the government has adopted a *defensive strategy* in relation to allegations of police violence. This defensive strategy rejects accusations against the police by appealing to the effectiveness of national legal procedures, even though policy makers disagree with essential aspects of such a legal framework. Thus, the executive publicly protects police institutions, minimizing options for initiating a dialogue with human rights organizations.

A good example of how this government strategy has been developed can be found in the way human rights groups have attempted to influence the government's agenda on this issue. As human rights groups' activities have lost public notoriety, they have tried to overcome this problem through the use of international networks. CODEPU and Amnesty International (Chilean section) are the main human rights organizations producing yearly reports sent to international actors such as the headquarters of Amnesty International in London, the UN Committee against Torture, and Human Rights Watch. Moreover, the U.S. State Department uses CODEPU's report in its yearly report on the status of human rights in the world. Although these reports show only a fraction of the relevant cases, they have consistently included statements underlining police violence as a *continuing* problem in Chile. Thus, even though the topic of police violence has practically disappeared from the domestic agenda in recent years, it achieves public notoriety through international reactions.

The 1996 UN report on torture was a particularly relevant document for human rights organizations. After receiving reports of increasing levels of police violence, the UN special rapporteur on torture, Nigel Rodley, decided to visit Chile in August 1995 to gather firsthand information from governmental and nongovernmental organizations. Human rights activists inside and outside the government considered this visit an opportunity to address important issues such as police violence in a democracy, the lack of mechanisms of accountability, and the wide discretion of military courts.[31] However, once Rodley arrived in Chile, the government successfully restricted his public impact.[32] Indeed, the Ministry of Foreign Affairs provided a short press release stating that Rodley's visit was in response "to an invitation of the Chilean government" and that his activities "were part of his work as special rapporteur on human rights considering allegations of torture received all over the world."[33] In other words, Chilean authorities framed the visit as the government's initiative when, in fact, it was due to Rodley's interest in verifying increasing allegations of police violence. Moreover, this visit was framed as part of a global tour when, in fact, it was a visit only to Chile.

One year later, the special rapporteur made public a report asserting that although torture in Chile is not practiced either systematically or as a result of government policy, "the cases currently occurring are sufficiently numerous and serious for the authorities to continue looking into the problem and for the State's rejection of torture to be reflected in the adoption of specific measures" (United Nations 1996). The government adopted a defensive position, suggesting that "several cases in the report had not been verified" and that the report actually underscored the government's efforts to protect human rights.[34]

The government's defensive strategy was consistent with the director of the national TV channel's later decision not to transmit a special documentary on torture in democracy. After Rodley's report was released, journalists on the national TV program *Informe Especial* produced a special documentary called "Torture in Democracy," discussing the main conclusions of the report and interviewing individuals who had suffered police violence in recent years.[35] The channel's director suppressed this one-hour documentary for three consecutive years, arguing that the program could affect the Chilean police force's public image and its relationship with the government.[36] Although no government intervention in this decision has been proven, probable pressure by the government "is consistent with the government's frequent statements in de-

6.6 Government Reactions to International Reports

Report	Allegation	Government Reaction	Authority
U.S. State Department (Feb. 1994)	"Police forces were again responsible for human rights abuses in 1993."	"In Chile there is an absolute respect of human rights. Excesses are punished."	Undersecretary of foreign affairs
Human Rights Watch (May 1994)	"Military courts' powers should be restricted."	"The report recognizes recent progress made on human rights."	Undersecretary of foreign affairs
	"[There are] persistent abuses."	"We do not agree totally with this observation."	Undersecretary of justice
Amnesty International (July 1994)	"Persistent human rights violations."	"These cases have not been proven."	Carabineros
Association against Torture (Nov. 1994)	"Torture continues in Chile."	No reaction	
CODEPU (Jan. 1995)	"Torture continues in Chile."	"These accusations are false."	Carabineros
Amnesty International (July 1995)	"Recurring cases of torture [are] committed primarily by Carabineros."	No reaction	
U.S. State Department (Mar. 1996)	"Most serious cases of abuse involve police brutality."	No reaction	
UN Report on Torture (Apr. 1996)	"Cases are sufficiently numerous and serious for the authorities to continue looking into the problem."	"Cases should be verified." "The report recognizes government's efforts."	Chilean representative on UN Commission
U.S. State Department (Jan. 1997)	"Some problems remain. The most serious are complaints of torture, brutality and excessive use of force by police."	"The report is based on allegations that have not been proven." "The report recognizes government's efforts."	Undersecretary of the interior
UN Report on Torture (Mar. 1997)	"[The] government should accelerate approval of bills to protect citizens' rights." "[There is] concern regarding torture."	"The press distorts human rights reports. The report was positive." "The government is trying to reform the judicial system to improve citizens' rights."	Minister of foreign affairs
U.S. State Department (Jan. 1998)	"[There are] continuing allegations of police brutality."	"The government respects human rights." "In cases of abuse, officers are under judicial scrutiny." "In the U.S., immigrants are subjected to mistreatment as well."	Minister of the interior
U.S. State Department (Feb. 2000)	"Although the government respects citizens' rights, problems remained in some areas. The police committed a number of human rights abuses."	"Alleged cases are not sufficiently investigated."	Division of Human Rights, Ministry of Foreign Affairs
Amnesty International (Oct. 2000)	"We still receive reports of police violence."	No reaction	
U.S. State Department (Feb. 2001)	"Police abuse [is] the main problem of human rights in Chile."	"It is unacceptable that a state makes comments about other countries."	President
		"There is a country that has not reported on human rights: the U.S."	Minister of the interior

Sources: Press coverage in Chile.

fense of *Carabineros* when the police have been criticized for brutality. If the station were genuinely autonomous, it would not likely be concerned about the effect its program would have on the government's relation with the uniformed police" (Brett 1998, 128).

Analysis of the government's reactions toward international reports on police violence in the last eight years (table 6.6) provides probably the most compelling manifestation of this defensive strategy. The government's reactions have tended to be tightly controlled by top-ranking officials at the Ministry of the Interior and the Ministry of Foreign Affairs, showing a constant pattern of rejection of foreign intervention in domestic affairs and confirmation that all allegations have been channeled through "regular legal procedures." Interestingly, in no case did the government mention its programmatic rejection of the high level of police autonomy, and in only two cases did the government recognize the problems that regular legal procedures might face. Thus, the government has not taken advantage of these pressures to initiate reform within the police, adopting instead an extremely defensive position that affects human rights groups' options in influencing public policy.

POLICE AUTONOMY AND ACCOUNTABILITY

The uniformed police in Chile are probably one of the most autonomous police forces in the hemisphere.[37] This autonomy is evident in four ways. (1) The president cannot independently remove the chief of the uniformed police during his four-year tenure, but only with the approval of the National Council, in which the armed forces and the uniformed police hold half of the votes. Furthermore, the president cannot promote or remove any officer without the Carabineros director's approval. (2) Police officers can only be prosecuted by military courts for any crime, whether in service or not. (3) The military prosecutor in charge of an investigation is the only person who can request secret documents. Furthermore, lawyers involved in a judicial review conducted by a military prosecutor are not allowed access to any documents during the investigative part of the trial, even when they are relevant to their defense. According to the military judicial system, the investigative part of the trial (*sumario*) is secret. (4) The government can suggest an internal investigation in cases in which police officers are accused of violating citizens' rights. However, the police control internal investigations, and no independent institution within the state or outside the state, such as the Ministry of the Interior or congressional commissions, is allowed to verify the information provided by the police (Quintana 1998).[38]

The police take advantage of this institutional framework, which allows for a culture of secrecy, given the fact that no institution within the state or outside the state has the legal capacity to assess whether the information provided by the uniformed police is correct. As was stated, political authorities have few legal tools to punish abuse, and the punishment depends on a military court that tends to favor police officers and on the willingness of the director of the police to accept the government's requests.[39] As Augusto Quintana suggests, the main weaknesses of the Chilean institutional framework from the point of view of human rights are the independence of high-level officers, considerable judicial autonomy, and substantial discretionary power in operational terms (1998, 105).

The above factors seriously influence the effectiveness of human rights groups' legal and political strategies to check and control the police. From a legal point of view, lawyers in charge of investigations have three options. First, if the evidence in a given case is weak, lawyers generally send a formal letter to a competent police authority. Human rights activists know that these letters will have no effect because Carabineros is not willing to initiate legal actions against police officers. Carabineros would, at most, recognize administrative misdemeanors, but no legal action is likely.[40] However, activists still send these letters to informally warn police authorities that they may initiate legal actions in the future. Thus, the effect of these letters is preventive.

The second and most frequent option is to file a case in a civil court. Although lawyers know that cases in which officers are involved will end up in military courts sooner or later, they file cases in civil courts because it is likely the civil judge will collect important evidence such as medical examinations and witnesses' testimonies. When the judge establishes that the author of the offense is an officer, he or she has to transfer the case to the military court, which receives cases in which most of the evidence has been collected and in which the main issue is determining the responsibility and, sometimes, the identity of a police officer.

Finally, a third legal strategy is to file a case directly in military court. This happens when lawyers believe they have enough evidence to present in court. In cases of police violence, the prompt collection of evidence, that is, medical examinations, is essential. Another important aspect is the quick recognition of where the violence took place so that evidence may be collected before it is destroyed. The Chilean judicial system, however, establishes that information must be collected by the investigative and uniformed police.[41]

Lawyers know that the chances of succeeding in military courts are close to zero because (1) the defense is weak, given the prohibition against examining relevant evidence collected by the judge; (2) the investigative part of a trial (*sumario*) takes forty days, but the judge can extend this period indefinitely, weakening the defense's ability to promptly obtain additional evidence; (3) the collection of evidence depends on the investigative and uniformed police, inhibiting the chances for a transparent process; (4) even when the judge dictates a sentence against an officer, it tends to be short; and (5) when both the officer and the civilian claim to be the victim of the other's aggression, judges support officers' interpretation of the facts.[42]

Empirical evidence supports these claims. Considering all cases with a verdict (almost eight hundred) in which citizens alleged police violence between 1990 and 1997, the judge closed over 90 percent of them because no evidence of a crime was found or because it was impossible to identify the author of the offense. The judge condemned police officers in only 4.7 percent of these cases, and the penalty tended to be the shortest sentence the law allows.[43] In cases in which both the officer and the civilian were alleging the other's aggression (almost nine hundred cases), military judges tended to support the police officer's version of events rather than the civilian's. In these cases, while 11.7 percent of civilians were sentenced, only 0.2 percent of officers were sentenced (Fuentes 2001).

If taking legal action is difficult, human rights groups could expose cases to the scrutiny of public opinion in order to obtain public notoriety. However, when individuals make complaints through the press, Carabineros promptly responds by questioning the nature of the allegation by asserting that an internal investigation will be conducted or by indicating that administrative measures have already been taken.[44] As neither the government nor human rights organizations have access to internal investigations, cases are rarely subject to further examination by the media, the government, or human rights groups.

Furthermore, the legislation regarding freedom of the press also favors the police. The Code of Military Justice establishes "threats, offenses or defamation against the armed forces" and "incitement to sedition" as crimes (República de Chile 1999). Although prosecutions against journalists and social actors under these articles have become less frequent since the reestablishment of democracy, "there is no guarantee that a journalistic investigation into corruption in a branch of the armed forces [and the police] will not provoke litigation of military laws, [having] a chilling effect on the freedom to criticize" (Brett 1998,

78). Indeed, during the first six months of democracy, the armed forces and the police filed more than thirty lawsuits against journalists, some of them involving charges of sedition for having publicized alleged irregularities in Carabineros and charges of defamation against a newspaper for covering a death in police custody.

Finally, courts in Chile have given explicit precedence to the right to privacy and public esteem over the right to freedom of expression and information. In this sense, military judges can prohibit the publication of information, opinions, or images that can be considered "offensive" to the honor of individuals and their families. Preempting eventual court prohibitions, lawyers tend to be cautious in the information they provide to the press regarding a given case.

THE BALANCE OF POWER

As Timothy Scully suggests, parties in Chile "have almost always been the major mechanisms to channel and shape emerging interests" (1995, 100). This affects human rights groups in two ways. First, parties act as institutions that filter issues of public debate. Thus, human rights groups that do not receive party support have a hard time trying to access the political process and influence the government. Party intermediation is therefore a facilitating condition for human rights groups' success, while the lack of it is an inhibitor for groups' success. Some human rights groups have ties to the Concertación coalition, while others, particularly CODEPU, do not have ties to political parties with congressional representation. Second, accessing political parties implies broadening the audience for human rights groups, given the fact that the media generally listen to mainstream parties.

The question is why political parties, particularly on the Left, have not focused on issues of accountability over the police and police violence. The answer concerns the distribution of power among political actors. In the last six years, right-wing parties have monopolized the agenda and discourse on public safety, reducing the options for criticizing the police (Dávila Avendaño, 2000). In general, the agenda proposed by right-wing parties includes what has been labeled a "law-and-order" approach, considering increasing resources for the police to cope with higher levels of delinquency, improving efficiency in the use of such resources by reducing police bureaucracy and placing more officers in the streets, improving the relationship between the police and the community to prevent crimes, and providing a judicial system that promptly punishes those who have broken the law (Dávila Avendaño, 2000). This agenda leaves little room for issues related to the protection of individual guarantees and control over the police.

THE LACK OF A PLURALIST MEDIA

The monopolization of the public agenda by a "law-and-order" approach, however, is closely related to right-wing parties' privileged access to the media. In Chile, two powerful conglomerates connected to conservative parties own practically all newspapers with a national circulation.[45] The Concertación coalition has control of the state's newspaper and the national TV channel. Particularly relevant is the Edwards family's role, given the fact that they control three newspapers, one of them (*El Mercurio*) the most influential in Chile. In the early 1990s, after one of Agustín Edwards's sons was kidnapped by delinquents, the family decided to create a think tank (Paz Ciudadana) to study and propose policies regarding public safety. By 1994, Paz Ciudadana had taken a leading role in issues related to crime prevention, crime control, and public policy evaluation, developing an approach to public safety based on providing a more efficient police and judicial system, but without considering the causes of such social problems (Fundación Paz Ciudadana 1998). Its access to important financial resources and the media and its excellent public relations have made Paz Ciudadana the most influential think tank on this topic in Chile, developing projects in collaboration with several municipalities and even with the government.

In this context, the lack of alternative sources of information reduces the ability of human rights organizations and of "civil rights" views to gain leverage vis-à-vis other groups in society. As politicians close to human rights groups perceive that their ability to access the media will be seriously undermined if they pursue an agenda that contradicts what the media is advocating, they opt not to respond to human rights groups' demands.

As was stated, human rights groups have addressed the issue of police violence in recent years through their links with international actors. In general, politicians seem unreceptive to such allegations. For instance, after an international actor made public a report suggesting the continuation of practices of police brutality in Chile, very few politicians on the Left reacted by calling for police reforms or government action. In most cases, silence prevailed.[46]

However, there were two cases in which human rights groups were more successful in gaining politicians' attention: the demand for political prisoners' rights and the "arrest on suspicion" campaign. In both cases, deputies of the government coalition played a pivotal role by supporting human rights groups' demands and by pressuring the government to make the given issue part of its agenda. In both cases, the groups did not access the political process independently but did so through politicians who were willing to support their demands.

In order to obtain politicians' attention, human rights groups required some social support that did not necessarily imply high levels of participation in protests. For instance, most of the "arrest on suspicion" campaign included not massive demonstrations but press conferences and meetings with authorities that demonstrated the existence of a cohesive group of supporters behind the campaign.[47]

In sum, the few times human rights groups have tried to address the issue of police violence, they have faced an institutional environment that inhibits debate. The combination of exaggerated presidentialism, high police autonomy, uneven left-right distribution of power, and the lack of a pluralist media has seriously limited the debate, reducing it to a matter of whether the police are complying with formal procedures, but not whether those formal procedures are adequate. When human rights groups use legal strategies—presentations of lawsuits against police officers—they face a legal system that favors police officers. When human rights groups use political strategies, denouncing cases locally and internationally, they face a police force that promptly responds to such allegations and a strong executive that controls the debate and is not interested in bringing the topic to the public. As the government's agenda on public safety is controlled by a Ministry of the Interior with narrow objectives, the options for human rights organizations to influence the state are severely restricted. Additionally, even when human rights groups can find allies within the state, the politically and administratively dependent relationship of such "insiders" with top-ranking officials makes these alliances politically unproductive.

Blaming the Actors

A highly unfavorable context explains only part of this story. In fact, one could argue that an unfavorable institutional environment would promote rather than inhibit accountability. In other words, human rights groups may have more incentives to make this issue noticeable to the public in a context where the police enjoys high prerogatives, where cases of police violence have increased, and where the hope for justice is close to zero. For instance, one may wonder why no human rights group denounced the government's attempt to minimize the importance of Rodley's visit to Chile in 1995, why no human rights group has launched a campaign to reform the military judicial system, and why no human rights group has collected information to prove increasing levels of police violence.[48]

I argue that three elements internal to these groups have played an important role in defining agendas and priorities regarding the topic of police violence: leaders' early decisions, the way groups framed the human rights problem after the reestablishment of democracy, and human rights groups' organization and social composition.

LEADERSHIP AND EARLY DECISIONS

The reestablishment of democracy opened new dilemmas for human rights organizations. Many of the organizations were sympathetic toward the new center-leftist government, but at the same time, they wanted their demands to be addressed. Additionally, these organizations were aware of the institutional constraints the new government faced, particularly the high levels of military and police autonomy. Thus, the transition to democracy in Chile raised an important strategic question for these organizations: what was the best way to achieve their goals? By the end of 1989, two strategies were relatively well-defined. Those groups that were closer to the Concertación coalition assumed positions in the new administration, with the explicit intention of lobbying authorities from within. Activists from the Vicariate of Solidarity and the CCHR were politically connected to the Christian Democratic and Socialist Parties, and several of them actively participated first in the development of the new government's electoral program and then in the implementation of the program once the transition to democracy had taken place.[49]

Particularly relevant were the Catholic Church's decision to dissolve the Vicariate of Solidarity and CCHR's decision to dissolve a network of more than five thousand volunteers nationwide.[50] As the principal leaders of both organizations were assuming new positions within the state bureaucracy, it was impossible for them to maintain the same level of activity as before; from being an organization characterized by a dense network of grassroots organizations, the CCHR transformed itself into a bureaucratic entity with few people, fewer resources, and a lower level of interaction with social organizations.

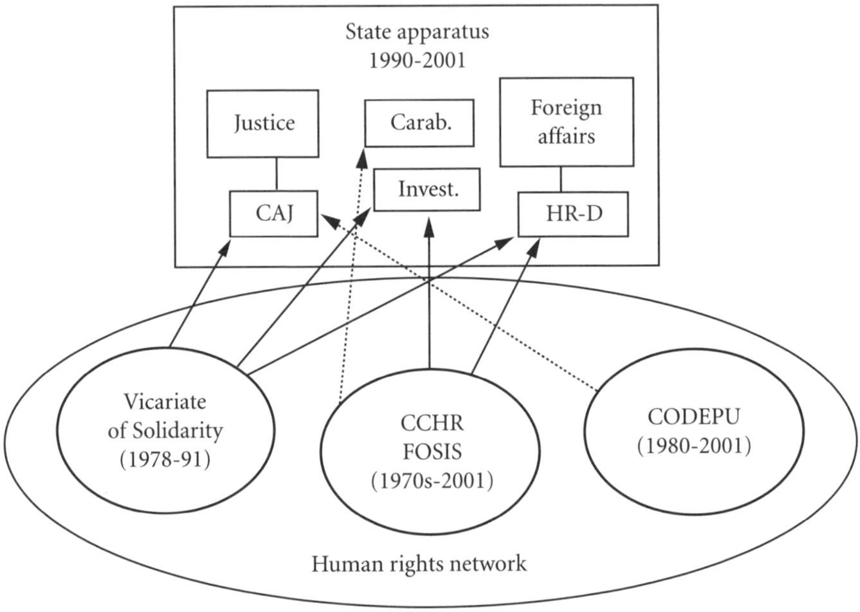

Fig. 6.4. Links between Human Rights Groups and the State

Abbreviations: CAJ: Corporation of Legal Assistance; CCHR: Chilean Commission of Human Rights; Carab: uniformed police (Carabineros); Invest.: investigative police (Investigaciones); HR-D: Human Rights Division, Ministry of Foreign Affairs.

Figure 6.4 summarizes the links between human rights groups and the state. While continuous arrows indicate direct links between actors working in NGOs and state repartitions, discontinuous arrows imply a more informal relationship. The *insiders* had a difficult time trying to influence the government agenda on human rights. First, insiders confronted a trade-off between their loyalty to the new government and their loyalty to the human rights cause. Second, insiders faced a government that was trying to balance the issue of preserving the stability of the country versus promoting the human rights agenda: the more the government pushed the human rights agenda, the more political instability the government had to confront, given the strong reaction of the right-wing opposition and the military. The insiders' ability to influence the government depended on specific individuals' leadership, the positions they occupied, and the personal ties they had with top officials in government. In practical terms, the insiders reduced their freedom to maneuver and seriously diminished their ability to incorporate a new agenda of social conflicts, as they did not maintain preexisting programs and lost contacts with old social networks.

Other groups, particularly CODEPU, assumed a more critical approach, distinguishing themselves from the government. Politically, CODEPU was closer to the leftist sectors that did not form part of the new government and opted to contest the government's policies from the realm of civil society. These *outsiders* faced the dilemma of whether to concentrate their scarce human and material resources to address the human rights agenda related to the past or to incorporate a broader definition of human rights and focus on current social problems such as police violence, the environment, and social and economic demands.[51] Early in the transition, CODEPU decided to concentrate most of its resources to address the problem of impunity for past human rights violations. This decision implied that, for instance, only one CODEPU lawyer, even today (twelve years after the transition), deals with allegations of police violence and that no campaign has been introduced to promote citizens' rights or CODEPU's counseling work. People are informed about CODEPU only through personal contacts with lawyers and through individuals who happen to know about CODEPU.[52] Thus, outsiders had more independence from state officials, but early decisions made by their leaders channeled these groups' focus toward a limited number of objectives, closing doors to observing emerging conflicts in society. Moreover, lack of material and human resources enhanced these groups' vulnerabilities, reducing their ability to obtain resources in a more competitive environment.

FRAMING HUMAN RIGHTS AS A "PAST PROBLEM"

This led to a second issue: framing the human rights problem. Most if not all human rights organizations concentrated on a very important but narrow segment of human rights issues (the legacy of the past), excluding from their main concerns other issues, such as police violence. As was stated, the political context encouraged human rights organizations to frame human rights problems in terms of the need to achieve truth and justice for crimes committed during the military regime. In this context, emerging problems such as police violence were, at best, considered part of a new agenda of "citizens' rights," but they were rarely considered as part of a more comprehensive human rights agenda. Indeed, issues of police violence were part of CODEPU's agenda during the first years of the democratic government as a problem political prisoners were facing, but not as a more general social problem. The current nature of the issue was not recognized until 1994–95, when CODEPU and other organizations started considering such issues as indigenous rights, police violence against the poor, and discrimination against immigrants as part of their main concerns.[53]

GROUPS' ORGANIZATION AND SOCIAL COMPOSITION

A final issue is groups' organization and social composition. Following the literature on social movements, I argue that groups built upon inclusive and extensive social networks are more likely to succeed. In Chile, both conditions, inclusiveness and extensiveness, do not hold.

First, human rights groups in Chile experienced several internal conflicts during the transition to democracy between the *insiders* who decided to promote the human rights agenda within the government and the *outsiders* who had a more critical view of government policies on human rights issues. With few exceptions, lawyers and activists inside and outside the government do not share information, cases, and strategies to deal with human rights issues. Moreover, conflicts among human rights groups regarding how to solve past human rights violations increased tensions among them.[54] As a general trend, lawyers deal with specific cases, without generating the space to share ideas and strategies with their colleagues.[55] For instance, studies that are initiated by private centers and universities are rarely considered by other nongovernmental institutions, thus increasing groups' isolation. This tension reduces chances to create a unified front within the human rights movement and to have a more coherent agenda regarding past and present violations of human rights.

Second, groups' social composition affects their capacity to reach other social sectors. Most human rights organizations are formed by middle-class professionals (lawyers, social workers) who mainly work on cases related to past human rights violations. Since victims of police violence tend to be lower-middle-class and lower-class (Fuentes 2001), human rights groups' early decisions to disconnect themselves from their social bases had an important impact on the quality of information they are able to obtain. This in part explains why citizens began to channel their complaints individually or through state lawyers and not through human rights organizations.[56]

Overall, leaders who decided not to maintain a social network early in the transition and who framed human rights as mainly a "legacy problem," and organizations that lack links to other social sectors, have helped to create "frozen" organizations that are not receptive to new and emerging social conflicts in society.

We know that disadvantaged and poor citizens face enormous difficulties in making their voices heard. While in some cases this problem has been resolved through the efficient action of policy entrepreneurs who "speak for the poor," in Chile this has not been the case. Chile's paradox is that while the social context provides strong incentives to develop mechanisms of social accountability, in practice these mechanisms have not been developed. There are two reasons for this paradox. First, the institutional and political context has inhibited the action of human rights groups in several ways. Particularly relevant are the high level of police autonomy, the difference in the left-right distribution of power, limited access to the press, and the high degree of concentration of power within the state. Even though the context does constrain social actors, this chapter suggests that social groups' organization and leadership also play a significant role, reducing their chance to have an impact on the policy process. Particularly relevant in this case are early decisions made by leaders to discontinue social mobilization and to frame human rights issues as a past but not a continuing problem in Chile. Thus, accumulated experience, networks, and economic and human resources were focused on solving the important, although not unique, problem of the human rights legacy, which reduced the options for coping with emerging social conflicts. As human rights groups have lost contact with their social bases, poor individuals have organized occasional protests against the police, remained silent, or looked to free state lawyers to solve their problems individually.[57] Moreover, human rights groups' social composition made them more distant from other social actors, inhibiting the chances of forming multiclass alliances.

The analysis of some successful and less successful human rights groups' actions in Chile underlines certain necessary conditions for success. First, in order to attract politicians' and the general public's attention, human rights groups require credible and significant information. The development of a social network that allows groups to collect information, and the adequate systematization of this information, are crucial aspects to building their reputation. The best way to convince people about your cause is by relying on credible information. Second, human rights groups would have more public impact if they were to look for the support of external groups to support their claims. The lack of local resources and restricted access to the press could be overcome by looking for allies abroad. In this sense, local and international actors together could have more public impact than local actors alone.[58] However, the Chilean experience shows that reporting and providing yearly information to international actors is not enough. In order to have an enduring impact, human rights groups need to develop a policy program in conjunction with international actors that considers the provision of updated information, policy recommendations, and follow-up mechanisms. Finally, human rights groups should frame human rights in Chile not as a legacy problem but as a continuing problem that requires a substantive transformation of the military judicial system and of the mechanisms of accountability over state institutions. In Chile, police brutality will not become a salient issue unless organized groups of civil society convince politicians that the problem exists (an information problem), that the problem is a human rights topic (a framing problem), and that the problem can be solved by introducing legal and institutional changes (a policy-implementation problem).

NOTES

1. Horizontal accountability refers to legal mechanisms that allow state agencies to take actions in relation to possibly unlawful behavior or omissions by other agents or agencies of the state. Vertical accountability refers to legal mechanisms that allow citizens to control and take actions regarding unlawful behavior by agents or agencies of the state. The latter includes aspects such as regular elections, a free press, the right to public scrutiny, and the right of association, among others (O'Donnell 1998).

2. A common collective or public good is defined as any good that, if consumed by any person in any group, cannot feasibly be withheld from the others in that group. In other words, those who do not purchase or pay for any of the public or collective good cannot be excluded or kept from sharing in the consumption of the good, as can occur where noncollective goods are concerned (Olson 1971, 14–15). A critical discussion of the concept may be found in Hardin 1982.

3. This could be particularly observed in the first four years of democratic government in the Division of Human Rights at the Ministry of Foreign Affairs, where former human rights advocacy leaders advanced the human rights agenda and kept in touch with NGOs (interview, Felipe Portales, former advisor of the Ministry of Foreign Affairs, Santiago, Sept. 14, 2000).

4. According to human rights organizations, there were 435 incarcerated political and security-related prisoners at the end of 1989. In January 1990, 47 escaped from the Santiago Penitentiary. By Mar. 1990 a total of 335 remained in prison.

5. Upon the request of the police, however, once the detainee has been brought before the judge, he or she may extend the detention period to up to five days. In case of terrorist offenses, judges may order detainees to be held incommunicado for ten days.

The original government proposal suggested abolishing the power of judges to extend police detentions (interview, Francisco Cumplido, former minister of justice, Santiago, Sept. 13, 2000).

6. This was clear in Concertación's program of government (Concertación 1989). Interviews with Cumplido and Carlos López, the representative of the National Commission of Human Rights (Santiago, Aug. 29, 2000) confirm this government concern.

7. In hundreds of cases, people were held in jail without specific charges, and several irregularities were detected in terms of the conditions of imprisonment and legal procedures in court (interview, Cumplido).

8. Chamber of Deputies, "Global Framework Agreed by the Members of the Commission of Constitution, Law, and Justice to be Considered by the Government and Political Parties" (June 5, 1990).

9. See, e.g., the Amnesty International report for 1990–94; Amnesty International 1991; Human Rights Watch 1991; and International Commission of Jurists 1992.

10. The special rapporteur received seventeen complaints between 1990 and 1992, forty-seven new cases between 1991 and 1993, and forty-six cases between 1992 and 1995. All these cases were reported by CODEPU (interview, CODEPU personnel, Santiago, Sept. 27, 2000).

11. Interview, José Sabat, former director of CODEJU, Santiago, Oct. 4, 2000.

12. Interview, Sabat.

13. The national press reported on these demonstrations extensively. One of the aspects the media always underlined was the high number of people arrested on suspicion. See *La Epoca* and *El Mercurio,* Feb. 8, 1993; *La Nación,* Feb. 11, 1993; *El Siglo,* June 21, 1993; *Las Ultimas Noticias,* Sept. 13, 1993; *La Nación,* May 16, 1994; *La Epoca,* May 20, 1994.

14. The INJ called the police several times to demand adequate procedures in the democratic rule of law. See *El Mercurio,* Oct. 21, 1992; *La Cuarta,* Oct. 31, 1992.

15. In his speech, President Aylwin noted that "the amount of arrest on suspicion is excessive and we need to regulate this system in a short term" (*La Tercera,* Mar. 12, 1993).

16. *La Nación,* Sept. 10, 1993; *Las Ultimas Noticias,* Sept. 21, 1993.

17. Personal communication, former advisor in the Ministry of the Interior, Oct. 2000. By 1993, the government was clearly concerned about the high number of arrests on suspicion. In Mar. the president mentioned the need to reform the system (see n. 15). In July the government announced a bill to eliminate arrest on suspicion (*La Tercera,* July 24, 1993).

18. Interview, Fernando Cordero, former director of the police, Sept. 29, 2000.

19. I thank Hugo Frühling for mentioning this point to me.

20. Interview, Sabat.

21. The Chamber of Deputies approved the bill unanimously (seventy votes in favor, with no votes against or abstentions). The mixed commission unanimously approved the bill, adding some changes. Finally, in the Senate the bill received a majority vote (Congress sessions, May 13 and 20, 1998).

22. In the case of Investigaciones, see Domínguez Vial 1996; and Investigaciones de Chile 1998 and 2000. In the case of Carabineros, see Quintana 1998; Peña 1998; and interview, Officer Harry Grunewaldt, Carabineros, Santiago, Oct. 5, 2000.

23. FORJA is developing a program on judicial assistance toward specific communities, but the subject of police violence has not been part of the program. CODEPU has

published some working papers regarding citizens' rights, but lack of funding has reduced the scope of such initiatives. Finally, the Corporation of Legal Assistance's Division of Human Rights distributed pamphlets in two shantytowns to let citizens know about this office's work. The government did not develop any specific programs to let citizens know about their rights at the moment of arrest after the bill was passed in July 1998.

24. I gained free access to the military courts' registration book of complaints after sending a formal letter to the person in charge. It took me one week to be allowed to see this documentation and no special "connection" with any public authority. The analysis of this documentation allowed me to quantify the number of cases in military courts since 1990, the status of each case (whether it was in a summary stage, close, or with sentence), the type of sentences applied by the judge, and the origin of the complaint (whether it was a case filed by an individual before a military or civil court or a case that originated in a police station). For details, see Fuentes 2001.

25. I thank Alberto Föhrig, who helped me to clarify the argument that follows.

26. Interestingly, this has not been the case in, e.g., Argentina, where the Ministry of Foreign Affairs and the Ministry of Justice have enjoyed more room to maneuver, forcing certain issues.

27. I spent two months in the Division of Human Rights of the CAJ organizing a database on allegations of police violence, interviewing several of its members.

28. Particularly problematic was this individual's relationship with the Ministry of the Interior (interview, Portales; interview, Roberto Garretón, Santiago, Dec. 12, 2000).

29. This can be observed in the programmatic goals of the three Concertación governments. See Concertación 1989, 1993, and 1999.

30. Ministry of the Interior programs between 1997 and 1999 show no mention of individual guarantees or control over police institutions (Ministerio del Interior 1997, 1998). Most of the public safety plan comes from the collaboration between the Ministry of the Interior and the nongovernmental organization Paz Ciudadana—a private foundation with ties to right-wing sectors. Paz Ciudadana has not considered the topic of police violence within its objectives and plans (interview, Javiera Blanco, Paz Ciudadana representative, Santiago, Dec. 12, 2000).

31. Interview, Portales.

32. Personal communication, former advisor at the Ministry of Foreign Affairs, Jan. 2001.

33. The only note regarding this visit appeared in the conservative newspaper *El Mercurio*'s "Visita Oficial a Chile de Relator sobre la Tortura," Aug. 24, 1995.

34. Jorge Berguño, chief of the Chilean delegation in Geneva, "Controvertido Informe sobre la Tortura en Chile Entregó Relator de la ONU," *La Epoca*, Apr. 5, 1996.

35. *Informe Especial,* the equivalent of the U.S. *60 Minutes,* is one of the most watched TV programs in Chile and includes in-depth analysis of social and political issues.

36. Interview, national TV journalists, Santiago, Dec. 15, 2000. The documentary received, first, an editorial objection because of its title, "Torture in Democracy," which was modified to "Police and Human Rights."

37. For a comparative study, see Frühling 1998. In practical terms, the institution that is most exposed to dealing with eventual violations of human rights is the uniformed police, Carabineros de Chile, given its role as protector of the public safety. Moreover, the members of Carabineros are proportionately more numerous than those of Investigaciones. For these reasons, I will mainly address the role of the uniformed police.

38. Congress can recommend to the executive an internal summary investigation when it believes there is evidence against a police officer. Congress can even call police authorities to testify before Congress regarding a case. However, Congress can only make recommendations, and no independent investigation to collect information regarding a case is allowed.

39. The only option is through the congressional requirement of an impeachment against the director of the police and through the president's request for the director's resignation to the National Security Council (in which the armed forces and the police hold half the votes).

40. Considering the whole universe of letters sent by human rights lawyers between Apr. 1997 and Oct. 2000 (112 responses), Carabineros responded to 78.7 percent of them. Of these letters, in 32.2 percent the police stated that an internal investigation would be initiated, in 43.5 percent the police defended the officer involved, and in 23.5 percent the police suggested that an "administrative misdemeanor" was detected but only in relation to formal aspects of the arrest. In no case did the police recognize that the officer's actions that had caused the alleged physical damage were unjustified or were a reason to submit the case to court.

41. Interview, Miriam Reyes, Santiago, Oct. 10, 2000; interview, Hugo Gutiérrez, Jan. 22, 2001; interview, Hiriam Villagra, Santiago, Oct 14, 2000; and interview, Nelson Caucoto, Santiago, Sept. 29, 2000. All these individuals are human rights lawyers.

42. Interviews, Reyes, Gutiérrez, and Caucoto.

43. Officers were condemned to prison for an average of 532 days. The law establishes that those officers who commit illegitimate violence must be condemned to jail for a period lasting from 541 days to a maximum of five years. In other words, military judges, on an average, apply minimum sentences.

44. Several cases illustrate this strategy. For recent cases see, e.g., "Abren Sumarios en Tres Comisarías por Denuncias de Golpes," *Las Ultimas Noticias,* Oct. 24, 2000; "Sumario en Carabineros por Supuesta Agresión a Joven," *La Tercera,* Nov. 3, 2000; "Joven Murió en Operativo Anti-drogas: Carabineros Investiga," *El Mercurio,* Nov. 19, 2000; "Documento Revela Mea Culpa de Carabineros en Maltrato a Mapuches," *La Tercera,* Nov. 24, 2000; "Denuncian Agresión Policial contra Joven en Curanilahue: Policía Uniformada Inició Sumario," *La Tercera,* Mar. 16, 2001.

45. Two conservative groups dominate newspaper ownership in Chile. The Edwards group owns the newspapers *El Mercurio, La Segunda,* and *Las Ultimas Noticias,* and the Copesa group owns *La Tercera, La Cuarta,* and *Qué Pasa.*

46. In this case, I am assuming that politicians fear being ostracized from the mainstream media when they defend a "civil rights" position. It may be the case that politicians actually made a shift from supporting "civil rights" views to promoting "law-and-order" views for personal as well as ideological reasons. In this case, they are willing to pay a reputation cost for this shift. In this chapter, I do not explore the reasons behind this "silence," but I thank Alberto Föhrig for clarifying this point to me.

47. In the arrest on suspicion campaign, the support provided by high school and university student leaders was determinant.

48. One may argue that access to information is a problem in terms of data collection. However, during my field research I had no access to military courts' archives.

49. To mention some of these activists, Alejandro González, Jorge Domínguez, Roberto Garretón, Carlos López, Felipe Portales, José Zalaquett, and several other pro-

fessionals who used to work in the Vicariate of Solidarity and in CCHR assumed new positions related to human rights in the government soon after the transition.

50. Interview, Carlos López, secretary of CCHR, Santiago, Jan. 19, 2001.

51. Interview, Gutiérrez.

52. Interview, Reyes.

53. Other human rights groups in Latin America have faced the same problem. In Argentina, the division between CORREPI, Madres de Plaza de Mayo, and CELS speaks in part for this difference.

54. An explicit division among human rights lawyers was evident in relation to determining the best strategies to deal with the Pinochet case in the year 2000. See "El Club de la Pelea: Las Querellas y Contraquerellas de los DD.HH.," *El Mercurio,* Oct. 22, 2000.

55. The Universidad Diego Portales, Centro de Estudios del Desarrollo, and FLACSO have developed academic programs to study reform of military justice and the police, but other nongovernmental centers are rarely aware of these efforts. Moreover, few academic institutions are aware of the work developed in the CAJ's Division of Human Rights.

56. See the gap between lawsuits channeled through CODEPU and the actual number of cases in courts (fig. 6.3).

57. The only massive protest against an act of police violence in the last ten years found by the author was in a poor neighborhood of Santiago (*La Tercera* and *El Mercurio,* July 18, 2000).

58. This is what Keck and Sikkink (1998) have called the "boomerang" effect, by which local groups rely on international groups to increase their chances of influencing the state.

BIBLIOGRAPHY

Amnesty International. 1991. "Chile. Reports of Torture since March 1990." London: Amnesty International.

Baumgartner, Frank, and Beth Leech. 1998. *Basic Interests: The Importance of Groups in Politics and in Political Science.* Princeton: Princeton University Press.

Berry, Jeffrey. 1977. *Lobbying for the People: The Political Behavior of Public Interest Groups.* Princeton: Princeton University Press.

Brett, Sebastian. 1998. *The Limits of Tolerance: Freedom of Expression and the Public Debate in Chile.* Washington, D.C.: Human Rights Watch.

Carabineros de Chile and INE (Instituto Nacional de Estadísticas). 1990–99. *Anuario de Estadísticas Policiales de Carabineros de Chile.* Santiago: Carabineros de Chile and INE.

Chong, Dennis. 1991. *Collective Action and the Civil Rights Movement.* Chicago: University of Chicago Press.

CODEPU (Corporación de Promoción y Defensa de los Derechos del Pueblo). 1994. *Informe Derechos Humanos 1990–1994.* Santiago: CODEPU.

———. 1999. *Informe Alternativo al Cuarto Informe Períodico de Chile sobre la Aplicación del Pacto Internacional de Derechos Civiles y Políticos.* Santiago: CODEPU.

Comisión Verdad y Reconciliación. 1993. *Informe sobre la Situación de los Derechos Humanos en Chile entre 1973 y 1990.* Santiago: Ministerio Secretaría General de Gobierno.

Concertación. 1989. *Programa de Gobierno de la Concertación de Partidos por la Democracia.* Santiago: Ministerio Secretaría General de Gobierno.
Concertación de Partidos por la Democracía. 1993. Programa de Gobierno, Santiago. Mimeograph.
———. 1999. Programa de Gobierno, Santiago. Mimeograph.
Dávila Avendaño, Mireya. 2000. *Seguridad Ciudadana: Actores y Discusión.* Nueva Serie FLACSO. Santiago: FLACSO-Chile.
Domínguez Vial, Andrés. 1996. *Policía y Derechos Humanos.* Santiago: Policía de Investigaciones de Chile, Instituto Interamericano de Derechos Humanos.
Ensalaco, Mark. 2000. *Chile under Pinochet.* Philadelphia: University of Pennsylvania Press.
Frühling, Hugo, ed. 1998. *Control Democrático en el Mantenimiento de la Seguridad Interior.* Santiago: CED (Centro de Estudios del Desarrollo).
Fuentes, Claudio. 2001. *Denuncias por Violencia Policial.* Santiago: FLACSO-Chile.
———. 2002. "Resisting Change: Security-Sector Reforms in Chile." *Journal of Conflict, Security, and Development* 2, no. 1: 121–31.
Fundación Paz Ciudadana. 1998. *Propuestas para la Prevención del Delito.* Santiago: Fundación Paz Ciudadana.
Garretón, Manuel Antonio. 1996. "Human Rights in Democratization Processes." In Jelin and Hershberg 1996.
Hardin, Russell. 1993. *Collective Action.* Baltimore: John Hopkins University Press.
Human Rights Watch. 1991. *Human Rights and the "Politics of Agreements."* Washington, D.C.: Human Rights Watch.
Hutchison, Elizabeth. 1989. "El Movimiento de Derechos Humanos en Chile bajo el Rég imen Autoritario, 1973–1988." In P. Orellana and Elizabeth Hutchison, eds., *El Movimiento de Derechos Humanos en Chile, 1973–1988.* Santiago: CEPLA.
International Commission of Jurists and Centre for the Independence of Judges and Lawyers. 1992. *Chile: A Time of Reckoning.* Geneva: International Commission of Jurists.
Investigaciones de Chile. 1998. *Gestión 1992–1998.* Santiago: Policía de Investigaciones de Chile.
———. 2000. *Planes de Estudio. Año Académico 2000.* Santiago: Policía de Investigaciones de Chile.
Jelin, Elizabeth. 1996. "Citizenship Revisited: Solidarity, Responsibility, and Rights." In Jelin and Hershberg 1996.
Jelin, Elizabeth, and E. Hershberg, eds. *Constructing Democracy: Human Rights, Citizenship, and Society in Latin America.* Boulder: Westview Press.
Jiménez, María Angélica. 1994. "El Proceso Penal Chileno y los Derechos Humanos." *Cuadernos de Análisis Jurídico* 4:1–275.
———. 2000. *Adolescentes Privados de Libertad y Justicia de Menores, Informe de Investigación.* Santiago: Universidad Diego Portales.
Keck, Margaret E., and Kathryn Sikkink. 1998. *Activists beyond Borders: Advocacy Networks in International Politics.* Ithaca: Cornell University Press.
Kitschelt, Herbert. 1986. "Political Opportunity Structures and Political Protest: Anti-Nuclear Movements in Four Democracies." *British Journal of Political Science* 16:57–85.
Kollman, Ken. 1998. *Outside Lobbying: Public Opinion and Interest Group Strategies.* Princeton: Princeton University Press.

Krain, Matthew. 1997. "State-Sponsored Mass Murder." *Journal of Conflict Resolution* 41, no. 3: 331–60.

Kriesi, Hanspeter, Ruud Koopmans, Jan Willem Duyvendak, and Marco Giugni. 1995. *New Social Movements in Western Europe: A Comparative Analysis.* Ed. B. Klandermans. 5 vols. Vol. 5, *Social Movements, Protests, and Contention.* Minneapolis: University of Minnesota Press.

Latham, Earl. 1952. *The Group Bias of Politics: A Study in Busing Point Legislation.* Ithaca: Cornell University Press.

Loveman, Brian. 1995. "Chilean NGOs: Forging a Role in the Transition to Democracy." In C. Reilly, ed., *New Paths to Democratic Development in Latin America.* Boulder: Lynne Rienner Publishers.

Lowden, Pamela. 1996. *Moral Opposition to Authoritarian Rule in Chile, 1973–1990.* London: MacMillan Press and St. Martin's Press.

McAdam, Doug, Charles Tilly, and Sidney Tarrow. 2001. *Dynamic of Contention.* Cambridge: Cambridge University Press.

Ministerio del Interior. 1997. Plan Nacional de Seguridad Ciudadana. Santiago: Ministerio del Interior.

———. 1998. Plan Nacional de Seguridad Ciudadana. Memoria 1998. Santiago: Ministerio del Interior.

Moulián, Tomás. 1997. *Chile: Anatomía de un Mito.* Santiago: LOM Ediciones.

Nogueira, Humberto. 1994. "Formas de Gobierno, Distribución de Funciones y Controles Interórganos en el Régimen Político Chileno." In C. Jackisch, ed., *División de Poderes.* Buenos Aires: Konrad Adenauer-Stiftung A.C. and CIEDLA.

O'Donnell, Guillermo. 1998. "Horizontal Accountability in New Democracies." *Journal of Democracy* 9:112–26.

Olson, Mancur. 1971. *The Logic of Collective Action.* 2d ed. Cambridge: Harvard University Press.

Peña González, Carlos. 1998. "La Policía y el Sistema Democrático." In Frühling 1998.

Quintana, Augusto. 1998. "Informe Nacional: Control Democrático de los Organismos de Seguridad Interior en Chile." In Frühling 1998.

República de Chile. 1996. *Código de Procedimiento Penal.* Santiago: Editorial Jurídica de Chile.

———. 1999. *Código de Justicia Militar.* Santiago: Ediciones Publiley.

Reyes, Myriam, Federico Aguirre, and Oliver Bauer. 1999. "Tortura durante la Transición a la Democracia: El Trabajo de CODEPU en el Período." *Serie Retrospectiva y Reflexión* 4:1–62.

Riego Ramírez, Cristián. 1998. "La Reforma Procesal Penal Chilena." *Cuadernos de Análisis Jurídico* 38:15–54.

Ropp, Stephen, and Kathryn Sikkink. 1999. "International Norms and Domestic Politics in Chile and Guatemala." In T. Risse, Stephen Ropp, and Kathryn Sikkink, eds., *The Power of Human Rights: International Norms and Domestic Change.* Cambridge: Cambridge University Press.

Sabatier, Paul. 1992. "Interest Groups' Membership and Organization: Multiple Theories." In M. Petracca, ed., *The Politics of Interests: Interest Groups Transformed.* Boulder: Westview Press.

Salisbury, Robert. 1969. "An Exchange Theory of Interest Groups." *Midwest Journal of Political Science* 13:1–32.

Schock, Kurt. 1996. "A Conjunctural Model of Political Conflict." *Journal of Conflict Resolution* 40, no. 1: 98–133.

Scully, Timothy. 1995. "Reconstituting Party Politics in Chile." In Scott Mainwaring and Timothy Scully, eds., *Building Democratic Institutions: Party Systems in Latin America.* Stanford: Stanford University Press.

Siavelis, Peter. 2000. *The President and Congress in Postauthoritarian Chile: Institutional Constraints to Democratic Consolidation.* University Park: Pennsylvania State University Press.

Smulovitz, Catalina, and Enrique Peruzzotti. 2000. "Societal Accountability in Latin America." *Journal of Democracy* 11, no. 4: 147–58.

Tarrow, Sidney. 1994. *Power in Movement: Social Movement, Collective Action and Politics.* Cambridge: Cambridge University Press.

Truman, David. 1951. *The Governmental Process: Political Interests and Public Opinion.* New York: Alfred A. Knopf.

United Nations. 1996. "Report of the Special Rapporteur, Mr. Nigel S. Rodley, submitted pursuant to the Commission on Human Rights." Resolution 1995/37. E/CN.4/1996/35/Add.2. Geneva: United Nations.

Valenzuela, Arturo. 1999. "Chile: Origins and Consolidation of a Latin American Democracy." In L. Diamond, J. Linz, J. Hartlyn, and S. M. Lipset, eds., *Democracy in Developing Countries: Latin America.* Boulder: Lynne Rienner.

Vargas, Juan Enrique. 1998. "La Reforma a la Justicia Criminal en Chile: El Cambio del Rol Estatal." *Cuadernos de Análisis Jurídico* 38:55–169.

Verba, Sidney, Kay Lehman Schlozman, and Henry Brady. 1995. *Voice and Equality: Civic Voluntarism in American Politics.* Cambridge: Harvard University Press.

Walker, Jack. 1991. *Mobilizing Interest Groups in America.* Ann Arbor: University of Michigan Press.

Wilson, James. 1995. *Political Organizations.* Princeton: Princeton University Press.

Wiseberg, Laurie, Guadalupe López, and Sarah Meselson. 1990. *Human Rights Internet Reporter,* vol. 13. Cambridge, Mass.: Human Rights Internet.

7

Social Accountability in Mexico

THE CIVIC ALLIANCE EXPERIENCE

Alberto J. Olvera Rivera

In Mexico, the study of social actions, procedures, and institutions referring to the diverse forms of accountability is yet to be accomplished. The fact that the country rid itself of the octogenarian authoritarian regime only recently explains the lack of political as well as intellectual traditions in this area.[1] Nevertheless, this does not imply that civil society did not develop means of accountability in the past or, much less, that this is not done in the present. As we will see in this chapter, the experiences that Catalina Smulovitz and Enrique Peruzzotti (2000) call "societal accountability" are numerous and varied, though their practical impact has been limited in institutional and political terms. It goes without saying that the nature of these practices is to a great extent determined by the type of political system in which they are produced, since the extent of liberties and democratic institutions is what defines the spaces of societal action and the intensity of influence of the public sphere on the political system.[2]

Smulovitz and Peruzzotti define *social accountability* as "a non-electoral, yet vertical, mechanism of control that rests on the actions of a multiple array of citizens associations, movements, or the media aimed at exposing governmental wrongdoing, bringing new issues to the public agenda or influencing or reversing policy decisions being implemented by public officials. It employs institutional and non-institutional tools. The activation of legal actions, claims in oversight agencies or the participation in arenas for monitoring and policy making are examples of some of the available institutional resources; social mobilizations and media denunciations illustrate some of the non-institutional ones" (2000, 150).

As we can see, this definition may have a counterfactual dimension and a propositive and constructive one. The former refers to a criticism, which compares discourses, policies, and legal commitments to real efforts and measurable results. It deals with the problem of the non–carrying out of duties, violation of statutory rights, and operational inefficiency and is therefore mainly a negative critique based on an ideal-type criterion emanating from law, public morality, and the prevailing concept of justice. The second dimension is concerned with how things are done, with anticipating effects and implications of government actions, even while accepting their supposed legitimacy. This dimension is grounded on rights of information and participation and may be of a positive nature in the sense that it generates societal input in the process of defining public policy.

Such a vast area of application of the notion of accountability brings with it the risk of conceptual vagueness. At the level of actors, a more precise concept of accountability demands a restricted notion of civil society, confined to actions and actors who do not claim particular interests or who, during the process of claiming such interests, appeal to recognized and generally applicable rights. Otherwise, almost all defensive and/or particularistic collective action could be interpreted as a demand for accountability. Collective resistance is not necessarily a form of claiming accountability, although in a general sense it places some sort of control on government. Moreover, not all forums, which constitute interfaces between government and society, are of a controlling nature. They may be constructive and determinant, consultative or debate oriented, and only in a general sense are they "spaces of control." It is important to bear in mind that the public sphere constitutes a series of concrete public spaces of a more specific nature, though interconnected.[3] The spaces of social control over government actions are expressions of resistance, which frequently substitute institutional gaps within the political system and urge it to restrict itself to legality. These are bottom-up forms of control, and in this sense vertical, and in themselves have no capacity of execution. In the following chapter the concept of "social accountability" will be limited to actors and public spaces having the capacity to appeal to rights and general principles and to exert pressure on the political system, thus avoiding risks of clientelistic or corporatist involvement.

This limiting is pertinent to avoiding confusing different types of collective action. We are mainly interested in those actions that are produced in and relate to public spaces and that confine their field of action to: (1) disputes over observance of laws and regulations of universal character; (2) evaluation of government performance in whole areas of public policy; and (3) campaigns of denunciations of corruption, inadequate selection or appointing of public officials, and systematic governmental violation of rules.

Thus, we avoid including in the concept of social accountability the multiple, constant, and omnipresent ad hoc negotiations that social actors carry out with public agencies in order to influence, modify, adjust, or alter government policies. The traditional practice of lobbying is excluded from this concept, as is any form of private and/or particularistic negotiation. Publicity and generality here are defining criteria.

Also excluded from this concept are the campaigns that civil society wages in favor of new public policies, unless they imply analysis, criticism, and public debate of existing concrete policies. If not, many of the so-called new social movements would find themselves assimilated within the concept of accountability. Even though it is true that cultural criticism of developmental models, sexism, and violence is a form of accountability, this is true only on a more general level, which targets the entire society and not specifically government practices.

The mass media also carries out this function in two ways: through making public criticisms of government, its agents, and its policies by civil society actors; and by itself investigating governmental mistakes and shortcomings inasmuch as its denunciation is a sellable product reclaimed by society. The media, for commercial rather than ethical principles, creates a critical space in the public sphere when electoral democracy has attained a certain degree of consolidation. If this condition does not exist, the media is subject to various forms of government control, as has been the case with Mexico throughout its history.[4]

From all this we can assume that, strictly speaking, social accountability unfolds during the phase of liberalization and spreads out in the phase of democratization. Electoral democracy is at the same time a product and a result of certain forms of social accountability and its condition of being generalized, inasmuch as democracy offers legal and political protection of public spaces. It is not strange, then, that emerging Latin American democracies are today a laboratory, still somewhat precarious, of these civil practices, whereas in the earlier stage only symbolic resistance to power was seen as a form of social accountability.

Social accountability, strictly speaking, implies a superior level of organization of civil society. Reclaiming the application of rights in relevant instances involves an organizational and legal capacity, which has to be developed. Criticizing public policies demands theoretical knowledge, which is not within reach of the majority of the population. Investigating corrupt practices means having financial, technical, and human resources. Media access demands having contacts, belonging to networks, and having the capacity to construct messages. These capacities are developed throughout the years, since they demand organizational and technical apprenticeship, as well as a level of professionalism that is not characteristic of all civil society actors.

The following pages will examine one of the few relatively successful examples of social accountability in Mexico. Civic Alliance was the chief social prodemocratic movement in the country, which, throughout the 1990s, organized great mobilizations demanding fair, equitable, and legitimate elections. Electoral observation, the form of citizen monitoring of the electoral process developed by Civic Alliance, achieved national coverage and signified considerable pressure on the political system. Increasing electoral competition, and acceptance of such general principles as equity in campaign coverage by the media, regulated access to public financing, restrictions placed on private financing, and citizen control of electoral organization, are all achievements of this movement, along with opposition parties' efforts.

Civic Alliance's success is relative, however, since transition toward electoral democracy in Mexico is still an unfinished process, insofar as some local electoral processes are still unfair.[5] Similarly, attempts by Civic Alliance to encompass other areas of social accountability, such as "control of government practices" and the carrying out of agenda-setting campaigns such as "public consultations," have been less successful.[6] The causes of this difficulty in taking up new areas of action will be analyzed in order to evaluate the extent and limits of the politics of social accountability in semiauthoritarian and transitional contexts.

Social Accountability in the Historical Context of Mexican Democratization

The concept of accountability is just being introduced in Mexican political culture. The prolonged duration and notable stability of the authoritarian regime helped to create a political culture in which politicians had a sort of accepted patrimonial right over public goods (Olvera 2003). The patrimonial character of political bureaucracy reached its highest point during President Carlos Salinas's term (1988–94). The so-called secret account (the president's right to spend at his or her discretion a part of the public budget) represented 25 percent of the total budget. Certainly, in Mexican history presidents had decided with ample discretion the forms of management of state resources. However, formally there was an active Congress, which supposedly watched over the executive's expending. Obviously, with a single-party, centralized presidential regime, the forms of horizontal accountability prescribed in the law were simply ignored, bypassed, or faked. This order of things was repeated at the levels of state and municipal government.

Under such historical circumstances, the only way through which Mexican society could exert some influence over public policies and limit somewhat the regime's excesses was collective action, especially social movements. Before the beginning of liberalization (1972), there were no free public spaces, and limited, single-issue, and usually local massive mobilizations were virtually the only way to oppose, resist, ask for, or negotiate public policies.[7] In the phase of liberalization, denunciations in a relatively more open press and regional and national massive mobilizations turned into possible forms of post-facto reactions to public policies. However, none of these forms of action turned into processes of rational and public critique of state policies.[8] Indeed, due to the limitations imposed by the regime, most mobilizations ended up in more or less private negotiations and/or particularistic agreements, and not in general changes and public compromises. Even denunciations in the press worked as a form of political protection, not as a way of promoting public dialogue, which the regime abhorred.

In the late seventies, the regime created several forms of "evaluation" of public policies, by means of which spaces of critique were supposedly opened. For example, the so-called National System of Evaluation (1979) was one of the first institutional mechanisms through which the government would become accountable. There would be public forums in which the government would receive critiques and proposals. However, such forums were completely controlled by the government itself and ended up as celebrations of the regime's "successes." During President Miguel de la Madrid's term (1982–88), development planning was introduced at a constitutional level as one of the duties of the government. A vast number of formally open forums, consultative councils, and evaluation instances, most of them with formal citizen participation, were created in the three levels of government (federal, state, and municipal). However, the Mexican tradition of legal fictions continued. No critique, no discussion, but only legitimization of state actions characterized such spaces. Some of these spaces still exist today, and some have become, in the period of democratization, useful instances for the development of healthy exchanges between state and society at the municipal level.[9]

In recent times, there have been some experiences that can be assimilated within the notion of *social accountability*. Among them are:

1. The experiences of peasant movements with public policy. Within the government of President Carlos Salinas (1988–94), there were several cases of negotiation of rural development policies for specific agricultural branches. One of these, that of the National Coordinating Body of Coffee Growers' Organizations (Coordinadora Nacional de Organizaciones Cafetaleras), went well beyond the normal limits and led to the development of one of the rare positive experiences of constructive collaboration between government and social actors, as well as promoting a certain degree of accountability.[10]
2. The experiences of social movements and pressure groups with economic policy. The Mexican Network of Action against NAFTA (RMALC), established in 1991 as an alliance of intellectuals, some peasant and union organizations, and even a small association of entrepreneurs, monitored the North American Free Trade Agreement's (NAFTA) negotiation process. After the crisis of late 1994, the group developed close monitoring of the government's economic policy and a constant critique of neoliberalism. However, the RMALC could not become an authentic social movement and was unable to move beyond denunciations in the press.
3. The experiences of environmental groups with public policy. Good at monitoring in general, some of these groups have been active in lobbying for and proposing interesting laws and programs. However, reduced mobilizing capacity and a lack of articulation with local social movements have made environmental groups' strengths ineffective, especially since the government easily breaks compromises and is unable to enforce environmental laws.

4. The experiences of feminist movements with social policy and public opinion. Feminist groups have been very active in lobbying and agenda setting. As a whole, the contribution of the movement in terms of cultural change and legislative innovation has been extremely important.
5. The experiences of the solidarity movement with Indian peoples, especially from Chiapas, with the politics of recognition. This was Mexico's main social movement in the second half of the nineties. Its main success was stopping the extermination of Indian insurrectionists in 1994, forcing the government and the Zapatista army to negotiate. At the same time, in terms of agenda setting, the movement put in the center of the national agenda the issue of Indian rights, neglected throughout Mexican history. Notwithstanding the national character of this movement, so far Indian rights have not been approved, nor has violence been controlled in Chiapas.

Several other examples can be offered. A civil society with a long tradition of mobilization, but with a historical lack of rights, continuously creates acts of resistance against state abuses. Among these, the case of Civic Alliance stands as one of the most relevant in contemporary times.

Political and Cultural Processes That Facilitate the Formation of a Civil Arena and Prodemocratic Social Movements

Three main political and cultural processes define the origin of prodemocratic movements in Mexico: first, the evolution of the social discourse of the Catholic Church, given that the origins of nongovernmental organizations in Mexico can be found in the institutions and processes promoted by the Second Vatican Council;[11] second, the process of political radicalization of part of the Mexican youth as a result of the repression of the 1968 student movement, which led to a wave of radical activism in popular social movements;[12] and finally, the slow but steady political liberalization during the seventies and the eighties, which helped in the formation of a party system and also in channeling part of the social unrest generated during the period of neoliberal adjustment toward the electoral ground.

The politics of political liberalization was carried out in the context of a prolonged economic crisis. From 1982 to 1988, the country experienced no growth, high inflation, and the free fall of real wages. The objective separation of state and society brought about by the crisis of the development model led to the emergence of a small, weak, and fragmented civil society based on associative class-type models that lacked stability and juridical security. The popular sectors did not propose criticisms of the rupture between legitimacy and legality through their collective actions but rather symbolized popular complaints against the practical rupture of the morality of the populist-authoritarian regime (the promise of substantive justice).

On the other hand, the urban conservative movements produced an undoubtedly important cultural mutation by questioning the monopoly of politics by the official party and by accepting the possibility of leaders directly governing their local areas through participation in the electoral system (Tarrés 1992). The influence of this movement is yet unfinished due to the fact that middle-class and business sectors from other parts of the country have only recently become involved with it.[13] The middle classes of the North initiated an associate practice, which meant a break with the old tradition of privatism. This should be considered an important cultural change even though it has been produced in very conservative sectors and takes as its departing point the rescue of traditional norms and values.

The crisis of the eighties thus activated all sectors of society. For the business and middle classes of the North, it meant the necessity of openly acting in the political arena, and they saw in the historically marginal right-wing party, the National Action Party (PAN), a way to compete for municipal and state governments (Chihuahua, Sonora, Baja California, Guanajuato, Sinaloa, San Luis Potosí). The radical-leftist actors also tried to enter the electoral field, although with very little success. The remaining civil organizations continued to be on the outside of the political electoral arena. Human rights groups, for example, were concerned about solidarity with Central American immigrants.

One more factor of change was the internal division in the official party in 1987, caused by the withdrawal of the Corriente Democrática of Cuauhtémoc Cárdenas and Porfirio Muñoz Ledo, which led Mexican citizens to turn to elections as a possible outlet for the democratic transformation of the system.[14] Indeed, in 1988 popular desperation was expressed massively in the ballots, leading to the very likely victory of Cuauhtémoc Cárdenas (massive fraud was denounced) and to an increased presence, countrywide, of the PAN.

From then on, gradually, and at a high social cost in terms of social and political mobilization, political liberalization was extended to the electoral arena, and an authentic electoral competition began to take place. A party system on a national scale was created, in which the PAN was placed as a democratic right-wing party and the newly formed Party of Democratic Revolution

(PRD) was the left-wing party. The PRD (1989) absorbed the populist currents of the PRI (Partido Revolucionario Insticional); the majority of the organized leftist party groups; and the leaders of numerous social movements, especially popular urban movements, peasant organizations, and student movements. The civil society represented by nongovernmental organizations chose not to join this process, instead maintaining political and organizational autonomy.

The period between 1988 and 1994 was characterized by the development of an ambitious but failed project of self-transformation of the ruling political system. In the economic arena, an accelerated process of economic opening culminated in the signing of the North American Free Trade Agreement in 1993. The nationalized banks were privatized. The agrarian reform ended. The state-owned companies connected to agriculture were closed. The government attempted to administer the advance of opposition parties in different regions by means of electoral fraud, increasing political instability in the country.

In this context, nongovernmental organizations flourished throughout the country. Their numbers increased; their actions were diversified; and their visibility was amplified to such a level as to elevate the quality of their actions and create networks of national coordination, which allowed them to articulate actions and gain public presence and recognition. This growth is explained partly by the despair felt in the educated middle classes in the face of limited possibilities of independent electoral participation within the opposition parties. Two other factors intervened in this process: increasing access of NGOs to international financing in the eighties and the gradual replacement of the old concept of service to popular movements with a growing professionalism and orientation toward the definition of alternative social policies in the nineties. This conjunction of factors led to the multiplication of the number of nongovernmental organizations and the formation of thematic networks of civil organizations, as well as the birth of national networks such as Forum for Mutual Support (Foro de Apoyo Mutuo [1992]) and Convergence of Civic Organizations for Democracy (Convergencia de Organismos Civiles por la Democracia [1991]).[15]

Meanwhile, popular movements for democracy expressed themselves basically in postelectoral battles against fraud, headed by the political parties. Nevertheless, the idea of exerting social pressure against the government to stop fraud before and during the electoral process began to take form through the experiences of different regional civic movements. Among these we can include the Family Civic Front (Frente Cívico Familiar de Yucatán [1989]) and the Citizen Movement for Democracy (Movimiento Ciudadano por la Democracia [1992]), formed during the 1991 struggle for democracy and against fraud in San Luis Potosí in 1991. The latter organization is itself a front for NGOs and regional civil movements. Other civil groups (formed by intellectuals and journalists) were also created to promote the cause of democracy, such as the National Accord for Democracy (Acuerdo Nacional por la Democracia [1990]) and such research organizations as the Fundación Arturo Rosenbluth, which helped bring methodological consistency to the effort at electoral observation.

Among NGOs, an important symbolic change occurred when human rights organizations extended their interest to the area of political rights (Concha Malo 1995). This recognition justified the increased activism of the Academia de Derechos Humanos in this field and of numerous NGOs in general. This slant toward democratic liberal imagery was a recognition of the end of revolutionary utopias, an adaptation to people's aspirations, and an expression of collective learning in the normative terrain. This imagery also incorporated a republican perspective as a constitutive element: only the collective action of organized citizens would force the government to accept the democratization of public life. The increasing adoption by this sector of a collective identity as "civil society" reflected in a precise way a new conviction: the defense of individual political rights demands collective action and the presence of actors more or less permanently organized.

The emergence of the Zapatista Army of National Liberation (EZLN) in January 1994 dramatically modified the panorama of the political transition. The indigenous uprising constituted a moral shock for society and led to the formation of a national movement in support of indigenous causes. Great spontaneous massive mobilizations of the urban middle and popular classes were staged in 1994 and 1995. This process increased the urgency of a peaceful solution to the country's political crisis, accentuated by the assassination of the PRI's presidential candidate in March 1994.

One of the emergent measures the government implemented to avoid a total lack of credibility in the 1994 electoral process was acceding to an old demand of the opposition parties and prodemocratic civil movements: the autonomy of the electoral agency, the Federal Electoral Institute (IFE), which in Mexico depended directly on the government. This process was known as "citizenization." This process was more symbolic than real, due to the fact that the six new "citizen counselors" named in 1994 found that everything had been prepared for the August federal elections. There was little they could do to avoid the manipulation of presidential elections by the government.

It was in this context that Civic Alliance was born.

Citizens' Power and Its Limits

The Power of Electoral Observation

In April 1994, Civic Alliance was created as a coalition of civil groups: Convergencia de Organismos Civiles por la Democracia (a network of NGOs); Movimiento Ciudadano por la Democracia (a network of prodemocratic regional groups); Academia Mexicana de Derechos Humanos (a professional and stable NGO); Acuerdo Nacional por la Democracia, Instituto Superior de Cultura Democratica, and Asamblea por el Sufragio Efectivo (small groups including members of Mexico City's political and cultural elite); and Fundación Arturo Rosenbluth (a professional research NGO). Civic Alliance's specific aim was to observe the presidential elections of 1994 as a means of giving citizens the ability to force the government to abide by electoral laws. Through the network of existing NGOs and through connections with local established democratic movements, a national social movement was quickly established.

The very notion of electoral observation had a ten-year history in 1994. The movement for observation had originally been an international effort to stop the violation of political rights in small countries around the world. The most relevant examples in Latin America were the observation of the 1988 Pinochet referendum in Chile; the 1990 presidential elections in Nicaragua; and several elections in Haiti, the Dominican Republic, and Panama (Middlebrook 1998). In a country as big as Mexico, which has a strong nationalist culture, foreign-led observation had no viability. Besides, both the United States and the international community had been comfortable with the PRI authoritarian regime, as it had guaranteed the political stability of the country (Aguayo 1998). Only an internally led, civil prodemocratic process could succeed in Mexico.

Civic Alliance was legally registered as a "civil association," which was necessary in order to receive national and international financing. On May 24, 1994, Civic Alliance presented its first report on the media, in which it denounced the enormous bias of the chief television news programs in favor of the official party. The monitoring of the media was introduced by the Mexican Academy of Human Rights, which deserves credit for having created the principle that citizens should press the media to comply with its public responsibilities. This endeavor was successful in the sense that the Federal Electoral Institute immediately exhorted the media to act with objectivity and equity.

On June 29, the results of an opinion poll were publicized, analyzing the degree of citizen confidence in the electoral institutions. This form of the politics of influence, by means of representative surveys, was a technical innovation introduced by the Fundación Arturo Rosenbluth, which offered technical support in almost all the electoral observations that followed, as well as in the design of the majority of the public surveys that would be carried out in the future. The foundation also introduced the then-innovative practice of the "quick count" in the federal elections of 1994.

The viability of Civic Alliance was strengthened by the economic resources that the government was forced to give to the Unit of Electoral Affairs of the United Nations, to be distributed in turn to observers' organizations.[16] In this way, an attempt was made to legitimize an election that was at risk of leading to results unacceptable to the population. Civic Alliance accepted about two million dollars under the hypothesis that a good national observation effort, duly financed, would demonstrate the existence of fraud or legitimize a likely victory of the opposition. This expectation, as will be demonstrated, was completely misled.

On July 23, 1994, Civic Alliance began a process of verification of voter lists in five major cities using a method of the Fundación Rosenbluth. At the same time, it proceeded to legally register more than 12,000 observers countrywide. Civic Alliance designed a special program for rural areas, called "Ponte Vivo," through which 4,500 observers were sent to critical rural zones. At the same time, it coordinated the visits of 420 international observers from twenty-four countries.

On August 19, Civic Alliance presented a report on the conditions prior to voting day, in which it listed 398 denunciations of inducement and coercion of votes. This was the result of an investigation carried out between July 18 and August 18 in ten areas of the country.

The observation on voting day was an enormously complicated operation. The Fundación Rosenbluth defined a representative sample of all the polling sites countrywide, rigorously covered by an army of voluntary activists. Though the logistical aspects were centrally designed and applied, the operation was decentralized and depended on the initiative and capacity of local groups. The observation was of a qualitative nature. Indeed, observers considered the whole set of possible incidents that could affect the election at the level of the polls: the presence of selected and trained officials in charge of the polls, procedures surrounding the opening and closing of the polls, the presence or absence of party agents at the polls, the processing of nonregistered voters, the coercion of votes, and so on.

The sample of almost ten thousand polling sites was covered to about 93 percent, a notable achievement considering the lack of a precedent for this kind of civic effort. Citizens from all the states (provinces) of the country, up to twenty thousand individuals, participated in the observation of the elections of August 2, 1994. The secret to the success of the movement lay in the combination of almost professional leadership, experienced in electoral observation, with a mass of spontaneous participants whose education and resources allowed them to carry out the instructions and methodologies provided by the leaders.[17] This enormous capacity for collective action showed that there was a great expectation among citizens that fair elections would mean the automatic defeat of the PRI.

The 1994 electoral observation was a success in terms of carrying out its objectives, but it was unable to demonstrate the existence of generalized fraud on election day, simply because this did not exist, except on a local scale. The report of Civic Alliance pointed out that the election had been legal but illegitimate, since it had been based on a profound iniquity in regards to electoral competition. The ruling party could draw on endless resources, overwhelming media coverage, and discretionary and clientelistic managing of social policy. In rural areas, there was generalized and outright buying and coercing of votes.[18]

It was clear that for a high percentage of the population, political rights were more fictional than real. The buying and coercing of votes were overwhelming. In addition, the enormous advantage the PRI held over the opposition in terms of economic resources and media access meant that elections were unequal and biased. The opposition parties had not managed to obtain sufficient credibility to cause massive change in the electoral preferences of the population. Moreover, the division of the opposition into two big national parties split the protest vote. However, neither the PAN nor the PRD envisioned the need for a broad alliance in order to first defeat the official party. Both of them miscalculated the strength of the authoritarian regime.

The fact that in a way Civic Alliance was recognizing the PRI victory was not seen in a good light by political leftist groups, whose members had expected incensed denunciation of electoral fraud. But Civic Alliance did not bow to this pressure, demonstrating that it was a movement with professional seriousness and autonomy. From then on, Civic Alliance enjoyed the prestige of impartiality and professionalism, highly valued by the organizations and citizen groups that were its mainstay, as well as by the national and local media.

The electoral result was surprising and dismaying for the active citizens, who expected a quick transition to electoral democracy. However, far from becoming paralyzed, participants in the prodemocratic movement decided to keep working together, accepting that they needed to engage in a long-term, sustained effort.

On September 30, the first National Assembly of Civic Alliance took place. Representatives from all over the country decided to continue observing electoral processes and to intensify the new lines of action that had been developed during the previous months. These included:

1. Democratization of the media through citizen monitoring;
2. Promotion of the autonomy and independence of the electoral institutions at federal, state, and municipal levels;
3. Promotion of campaigns on civic education for the general public as the only antidote against the buying and coercion of votes;
4. New "consultations" with citizens about issues of national interest as a way of establishing a national civic agenda.

This decision transformed a social movement that had considered itself temporary into a civil organization with permanence and a minimum of institutionalization. The original national coordinating body (including six persons, one per constituting organization) and the executive secretary, Martha Pérez, were ratified. Financially the project was viable, because several international agencies offered to support the continuity of Civic Alliance. At least two, the National Democratic Institute (U.S.) and Development and Peace (Canada), were quite committed to this idea. In the following years, these and other international agencies and NGOs financed Civic Alliance. However, the amounts were modest, only enough to keep a national office in Mexico City with a staff of five paid personnel and to cover the expenses of the coordinating body's meetings and the national congresses.

A structural problem emerged, given that there was a contradiction between the national dimension of the movement and the centralized direction composed only of Mexico City civic leaders. There was also another contradiction, this one between the political and social plurality of the movement and the political homogeneity of the governing board. The latter, as we have seen, was made up of NGO representatives whose trajectories were relatively compatible. These individuals had great experience in the field of NGOs, and most of them came from progressive groups within the Catholic Church. The groups that made up Civic Alliance itself, on the other hand, exhibited a variety of social and political profiles.

In the federal district, the majority of the mobilized groups were based in the movement of solidarity with the Chiapas indigenous people. Other groups developed from informal networks of citizens who could identify themselves with the existing NGOs only in exceptional cases. This was also true for the state of Mexico, which, due to its population dispersion, had to have a decentralized organization. In various states, Civic Alliance was an aggregation of ecclesial base communities, NGOs, and groups of professors and students from local universities (Veracruz, Morelos, Oaxaca, Chiapas, Guerrero, Guanajuato, Queretaro, Michoacan, Chihuahua–Juarez City, Jalisco). In others, Civic Alliance was more an expression of academics and students and some preexisting citizen groups (Sonora, Baja California Sur, Tamaulipas, Quintana Roo, Nayarit). In still others, Civic Alliance was a curious mixture of conservative citizen groups, academic staff, and social activists (Sinaloa, Nuevo Leon, Chihuahua [the capital city], Yucatan, San Luis Potosi, Durango). In other states, Civic Alliance included groups closer to the political Left (Coahuila, Guerrero). There were also groups that did not accept participation in state organizations (Chihuahua, Sonora, Guanajuato, Chiapas).

In part, this diversity suggests the inadvisability of a national representative board, since it was not really clear who would remain in the movement or who would not. On the other hand, the short campaign of 1994 had not been able to eliminate the imbalance in experience and know-how. Finally, in the face of the lack of economic resources, and given the voluntary nature of the organization, there was not much interest among the participants in occupying management positions.

THE DEVELOPMENT, EFFECTS, AND LIMITS OF ELECTORAL OBSERVATION

On November 20, 1994, the observation of state elections began in Tabasco, where a thorough job was done. The observation was integral, involving analysis of practices of buying and coercion of votes and of the State Electoral Law and scrutiny of campaign spending and of the quality of the election. The Tabasco Civic Alliance denounced an outrageous clientelistic operation ori-

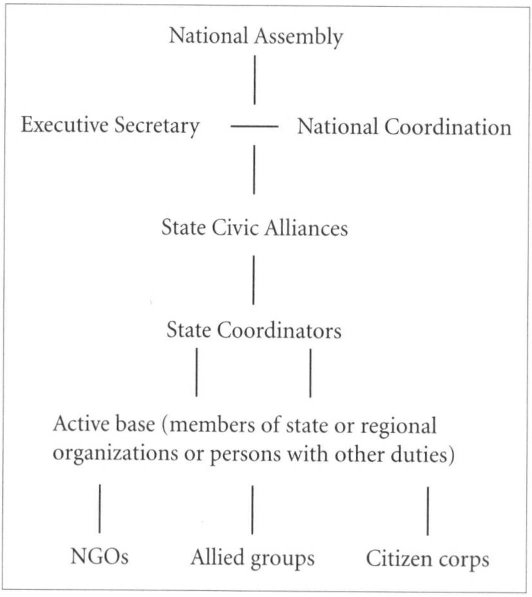

Figure 7.1. The Structure of Civic Alliance: 1994–96

ented toward a massive buying of votes, as well as the iniquity of the contest and bias in media coverage. But the PRI won.

In 1995, the extraordinary energy of the prodemocratic movement allowed Civic Alliance to organize the observation of twelve state elections: Jalisco (February); Yucatan and Guanajuato (May); Veracruz, Baja California Norte, and Aguascalientes (August); Chiapas (October); and Michoacan, Oaxaca, Puebla, and Tlaxcala (November). In all these cases, an attempt was made to conduct integral observations. The best experience was in Yucatan, where the studies and reports were of excellent quality due to the experience accumulated by the Civic Family Front, the local civic organization. Generally speaking, all these observations were characterized by great citizen participation. An average of two hundred observers participated in each process and covered all the areas of observation mentioned in the case of Tabasco. Civil activism proved to be important in almost all these cases to guarantee that the opposition parties' victories were acknowledged. That year the PAN won the elections for governor in Jalisco, Guanajuato, and Baja California Norte, as well as for numerous town councils in other states. The PRD won many municipalities in Veracruz, Michoacan, and Oaxaca. Yet the visibility of Civic Alliance began to wane due to the fact that elections were becoming very competitive and that opposition victories were generally respected.

In 1996, Civic Alliance was still enthusiastic in the area of electoral observation. The following local and state elections were observed: Quintana Roo (February); Guerrero (October); and Coahuila, State of Mexico, and Hidalgo (November). The most successful experience was in Coahuila, where Civic Alliance succeeded in banning a slogan used by the PRI because of its similarity to others used in announcing public works done by the state government. In addition, the electoral law was changed, and some of Civic Alliance's suggestions were incorporated. Moreover, the local Civic Alliance attempted to monitor campaign expenses by means of an elaborate instrument, which was also applied in other states. This experience demonstrated that it was almost impossible, without an army of volunteers, to keep track of campaign expenses. Some criticisms and denunciations were made, but a complete investigation was not done.

This time the opposition parties were unable to win more state governments, although they still won hundreds of municipal governments. However, in most elections the iniquity in competition was as marked as before, along with the buying and coercion of votes. A sense of relative impotence developed. Moreover, Civic Alliance was unable to turn the problems of local elections into a national issue.

In October 1996, the Federal Elections Code was modified to include a majority of the changes proposed by the opposition parties and Civic Alliance. The appointment of nine new "citizen electoral counselors" was also a central issue. The prodemocratic groups played no role in this process, as the parties decided to monopolize selection, assigning to themselves a share of the counselors, namely, two for each of the three major parties and two for the rest of the small parties. The last counselor, and president of the Federal Electoral Institute, was selected by agreement of all the parties.

However, the new group of counselors represented a great breakthrough because they were truly independent personages. The long-desired autonomy of the Federal Electoral Institute, in charge of organizing elections and distributing public funds to the parties, seemed at last within reach. The new law underlined equitable criteria for party financing.[19] It indicated with greater precision the nature of electoral misdemeanors and created a court in charge of dealing with these accusations. It established a mechanism for the "cascade" appointing of citizen electoral officials at district and state levels, removing real control of the electoral process from bureaucracy. Finally, the new law gave the Federal Electoral Institute the capacity to monitor both media coverage of electoral matters and some federal social programs with clientelistic potential. Civic Alliance and opposition parties had promoted these dispositions since 1994. Nevertheless, during the process of negotiation in the Chamber of Deputies, Civic Alliance was neither consulted nor mentioned. The political class decided not to grant the movement greater public prestige.

In 1997, Civic Alliance decided to pursue several goals: first, investigating the actual operation of electoral institutions; second, investigating the mechanisms for buying and coercing votes; third, investigating media coverage of political campaigns in as many states as possible; and finally, intervening in zones of high risk to avoid fraud perpetrated through the buying of votes and forced voting. These objectives would be achieved through citizen action, but also by means of a permanent dialogue with electoral counselors, who were considered persons committed to democracy.

At the same time, observation of the federal elections of July 1997 was prepared. This was a decisive election, insofar as important offices were in dispute, of federal deputies (five hundred), half the entire number of senators, and the head of government in Mexico City (for the first time in history). There would also be elections for governor in several states, including Queretaro, Chiapas, Sonora, Yucatan, and Nuevo Leon.

Comparative study of the behavior of the media in fourteen states of the republic was vital, demonstrating that the media tended to be less biased than before and was highly sensitive to citizen monitoring. The study of vote buying and coercion showed that there were systematic patterns of pressure on voters, but no specific programs of a federal nature, used for clientelistic purposes, were found. Actually, vote buying had become decentralized and disguised through multiple mechanisms. State governors played a predominant role in the administration of these processes. This study, which was presented to the national electoral counselors on May 29, 1997, convinced them of the necessity of devising measures and strategies that would avoid this form of the violation of political rights. Unfortunately, the Federal Electoral Court considered that IFE's program, designed to monitor the application of social policies in a sample of electoral districts, was illegal.

The elections of July 1997 were historic because, for the first time, the opposition parties obtained the majority in the lower chamber of Congress, the Chamber of Deputies (257 versus 243). The PRD swept to victory in Mexico City, and the PAN won the governments of Queretaro and Nuevo Leon. At the municipal level, the opposition parties' victories were also significant, includ ing states traditionally inclined toward the PRI, such as Veracruz, where, for the first time in history, the PRI lost half the municipal governments in the elections of October 1997.

This historic advance of the opposition parties made people forget that the elections continued to be inequitable and stained by the buying and coercion of votes. Some leaders of Civic Alliance believed that because the IFE was now in the hands of trustworthy citizens and had achieved true autonomy, because the opposition was obtaining more and more electoral wins, and because the media was becoming increasingly impartial, the main aim of the organization could be considered accomplished, thereby allowing it to give way to organizations more specialized in other fields of civic action. Besides, the level of citizen participation in electoral observation had diminished considerably.

In December 1997, a Civic Alliance workshop was held in Cuernavaca, Morelos, in which the National Coordination, along with invitees from other civil organizations, considered its activities and decided whether to continue as an organization, whether its mission was still valid, and whether there was still the collective will to maintain the organization. Prior to this, all branches had been asked to fill out a questionnaire related to evaluation of Civic Alliance's activities and its political future.

The general opinion was that Civic Alliance had gained great strength through its accumulated prestige, public stand, national character and credibility, access to the media, experience and knowledge, and ability to innovate in terms of citizen participation in the public arena. It was noted, however, that the organization also had substantial weaknesses: a lack of financial and material resources and an insufficient capacity to obtain them; an insufficient presence in some states, to the extent in some locations of having disappeared; internal conflicts in a few local and state sections; lack of confidence in the national coordination; the ineffectiveness of the "consultations," seen in the insufficient clarity of results; the low quality of the observation of the recent elections; and, finally, incoherence between local and national agendas.[20]

Only a few persons spoke about the reasons for breaking up the organization. The rest insisted on the validity of its mission. This perspective seemed to be charged with high doses of willingness and little objectivity. As a matter of fact, some insisted that the electoral agenda was incomplete in two ways: on the one hand, the "civilianizing" of the electoral institutions was an unfinished process in the sense that the majority of state electoral commissions were still manipulated by governors, and local boards and district commissions were still unable to guarantee their own autonomy and keep real control over the electoral process; on the other hand, the buying of votes and forced voting still continued on a large scale, creating the risk of involution in the present and the future. But this meant that Civic Alliance would have to develop the capacity to make local problems part of a national agenda, which it had so far been unable to do.

The meeting ended with a new internal pact, both national and local leaders ratifying their willingness to continue with the movement, trying to overcome the problems that had been detected, and seeking new forms of civic participation in public life. To achieve these aims, several steps were necessary:

1. Restructuring the national committee to include leaders of civil society who would contribute to giving a political orientation to Civic Alliance;
2. Restructuring and strengthening the state Alliances, nine of which had disappeared, with twelve intermittent and only eleven still maintaining some capacity for action;
3. Elaborating new programs in sensitive areas of civil action, like control of the government (especially vigilance over public spending), the struggle against vote buying and coercion, and setting up a citizens' agenda.

In 1998, Civic Alliance faced the harsh reality that, instead of improving the quality of its action, it had fallen into a period of extreme lethargy.

The "Public Consultations" as Agenda-Setting Actions

On December 12, 1994, Civic Alliance created the National Consultation System, an original idea of Enrique Calderon, from the Fundación Arturo Rosenbluth, which would act as the source of a new form of citizen participation in public life. The idea was to generate a current of public opinion on topics of national interest with the aim of influencing the political system, making public opinion felt through a symbolic medium, such as a public opinion poll, called a "consultation."

The economic collapse of December 1994, the confrontation between incumbent President Zedillo and former President Carlos Salinas de Gortari, and the military attack against the Zapatista Indian forces on February 15, 1995, were all factors that created the urgency and the opportunity to carry out the first consultation poll. On February 26, 1995, around 16,000 citizens cooperated in installing 3,491 consultation tables at which 626,525 citizens gave their opinion on the need to bring former President Carlos Salinas to trial; to reject the credit package offered by the United States, which would jeopardize the country's sovereignty; and to resort to dialogue (instead of military action) in order to solve the Indian problem in Chiapas. This consultation was symbolically important, but politically ineffective. However, it consolidated a practice that had begun in March 1993, when the first independent citizen consultation ever carried out in Mexico was organized. The aim was to promote the political rights of Mexico City's inhabitants, up to then deprived of their right to elect a governor. Thus, a new area of citizen participation had been created, one to which civil society would continue appealing with relative frequency during the following years.

In June 1995, the Zapatista army asked Civic Alliance and the National Democratic Convention (Convención Nacional Democrática) to organize a vast national survey (consultation) on which direction the EZLN should take in the future.[21] On August 27, 1995, the National Consultation for Peace and Democracy, solicited by the EZLN, was carried out. Twelve thousand persons took part voluntarily at 8,652 consultation tables, with over fifteen hundred indigenous communities also giving their opinions. A total of 1,088,094 citizens took part in the national survey, the most significant aspect of which was that a vast majority asked the EZLN to change and become an independent political force. The necessity of adding a chapter on indigenous rights to the constitution was fully approved as well. This time the political effect was greater, because the federal government decided to start formal and open negotiations with the EZLN.

In the month of June 1995, a wide coordination of social and civil organizations was instituted to carry out the so-called Referendum for Freedom, which was expected to press the government into changing its economic policy. The organizers were the National Coordinating Body of Coffee Producers' Organizations (Coordinadora Nacional de Organizaciones Cafetaleras), the National Association of Industry (Asociación Nacional de Industrias de la Transformación), the Mexican Network of Action against NAFTA (Red Mexicana de Acción Frente al Libre Comercio), El Barzón (a set of organizations of indebted small entrepreneurs), and the Peasant Regional Independent Organizations Union (Unión de Organizaciones Regionales Campesinas Autónomas). These were social organizations with significant regional and sectoral representation. Compared with these, Civic Alliance was just a kind of support group, since, as an organization, it did not represent any social group. The aim of this front (to promote an alternate economic strategy) was way beyond the scope of Civic Alliance. This situation generated tensions in its midst, since some of Civic Alliance's local groups did not share the leftist ideology of this social front. The position of Civic Alliance was ambiguous and difficult.

Between September and November 1995, a national campaign to encourage people to endorse the alternative economic strategy took place in the context of the Referendum for Freedom, which sought to support (by getting citizens' signatures) the Alternative Economic Strategy for National Development. A total of 428,345 signatures were obtained. The low number of supporters in the first prolonged campaign in which Civic Alliance participated proved that the great majority of organizations in favor of the consultation lacked the organizational capacity to implement the inquiry.

In September 1996, the same group of organizations that had promoted the Referendum for Freedom held the First National Campaign of Denunciation of the Government's Economic Policy. One thousand nine hundred and fifty tables were set up in twenty states, with 182,366 citizens presenting their testimony on the damage caused by this economic policy. This was merely a symbolic act designed to gain public attention for the social disaster caused by the economic crisis and for the need to change the nation's economic policy. The poor success of this initiative proved that economic issues were not Civic Alliance's area and that the participating social organizations lacked true mobilizing power. Even so, as part of this process, Civic Alliance presented a legal motion in the House of Representatives to diminish the added value tax (IVA) from 15 to 10 percent.

Toward the end of 1996, there was increasing dissatisfaction in some states over the excessive centralism in the political leadership of Civic Alliance. All consultations had been designed, defined, and publicized from above by the national coordination. Frequently the state Alliances were called to participate in the "consultations" only a few weeks in advance. In addition, many local initiatives had not received the support of the main office or sufficient national media diffusion.

At the beginning of 1997, there was a feeling that the consultations had reached saturation point. Citizens were not seeing the practical effect of these symbolic mobilizations, which, moreover, lacked continuity; that is, they were not part of a long-term strategy. The National Zapatista Liberation Army had taken no notice of public opinion, and the government had taken even less. The call for a new economic policy had not led to the formation of a truly national front, and this lack of social power had allowed the government to enforce its neoliberal economic policy. In the light of these factors, the national coordination came to the conclusion that its work in favor of the democratization of public life should be more professional and oriented toward putting forward new ideas, programs, and principles.

In order to carry such a plan out, it was decided that Civic Alliance should insist on a new relationship between Congress and society, which would be achieved by means of a public proposal to "give a mandate" to future legislators. The idea was that, by means of a citizens' consultation to be held in June 1997, a series of legislative motions would be agreed on that future representatives would be obliged to promote. This obligation would be merely symbolic, obtained by means of public encounters and specific compromises.

This new orientation of action meant a clear shift in Civic Alliance from a civil movement to a nongovernmental organization. Indeed, in the electoral field a series of investigations were proposed that the state Alliances evidently could not carry out without resources, qualified personnel, and time. The "Citizens' Agenda" implied a previous systematization of the proposals that should be made to citizens, and this was far beyond the internal capacity of the state groups. In the end, it was agreed that the proposal would consist of a series of eight sets of questions. The questions concerned:

1. Improvement of the economic situation of the working poor;
2. Revision of the public budget to attend to social demands;
3. New measures to end corruption;
4. The design of new forms of public participation in public decisions;
5. The effective application of the right to free association;
6. New policies to achieve gender equality and defend women's rights;
7. New policies to strengthen municipal and state finances; and
8. Respect for and application of the agreements signed by the government and the EZLN on matters of indigenous rights.

On June 6, 7, and 8, 1997, the "National Consultation in Support of the Civil Proposals" was held. Eleven thousand three hundred volunteers participated in its organization and assisted in the installation of 2,061 tables in the thirty-two states of the country. In at least twelve of them, there was merely a symbolic presence. Only 156,000 citizens emitted their opinion. The questionnaire concerned an obvious resolution and was of a symbolic nature, supporting broad demands that did not really constitute a legislative agenda, but only a thematic one from which future laws could be derived. Because of low participation and scarce media coverage, the survey was not very practical and confirmed the weakening of this form of citizen intervention in the public sphere.

Monitoring Government Performance

In 1994, the Mexican Academy of Human Rights proposed a new program to be carried out by civil organizations: "Adopt a Government Official." The program was more like a good intention: groups of citizens in different cities should learn to carry out monitoring of the activities of important government and public figures. Actually, there was no precise methodology, only a vague set of recommendations: keep track of denunciations of corruption in the media, ask for official information about public works, compare promises against realities, construct a database on the career of politicians, and so on.

Civic Alliance "adopted" the program and helped to launch it in 1995. The first and perhaps most relevant case was that of the "adoption" of the incumbent president, Ernesto Zedillo. The objective was to force the president to inform the public about the real amount of the public budget at his discretionary disposal, given that almost 25 percent of the 1995 federal budget was labeled as a "secret fund" at the president's disposal. Moreover, he was asked about the personnel who assisted him in performing his tasks and the total amount of salaries paid (to himself and to his personnel). None of this information was public. Toward this end, a written petition was prepared and handed over in March 1995 in which Civic Alliance, basing its demand on the constitutional right to information (Article 8), urged the president to make available information about the organization and personnel of his office and how the "secret fund" was managed and to publish his assets.

A year later, in the face of an absolute lack of response from the president, the national coordination of Civic Alliance decided to undertake legal proceedings so as to defend the constitutional rights of petition and information, establishing a precedent in national jurisprudence. Civic Alliance asked the judge to order the president to comply by providing the required information, since failure to do so represented a violation of the right to information, whereas the absence of a reply meant the trampling of the right to petition. The Fifth District judge unexpectedly ruled in favor of Civic Alliance. Nonetheless, the president's defense lawyers presented several recourses of revision until finally a collegiate court backed the decision of the judge, who in turn threatened the president with taking the case to the Supreme Court of Justice. Unfortunately, in June 1997, the judge revoked her decision, thus blocking the juridical recourses available to Civic Alliance. This case demonstrated that the autonomy of the judiciary, one of President Zedillo's main promises, was as fictional as ever, especially when the president was involved in a case.

In 1996, the program was extended countrywide. In July 1996, the Tabasco branch of Civic Alliance "adopted" the governor, Roberto Madrazo, national champion of electoral fraud and authoritarianism. He was legally requested to make available information about his salary and clarify specific doubts about the use of the 1995 public budget. Moreover, he was asked about the criteria for defining the 1996 budget. The governor did not respond, and Civic Alliance then presented a legal petition of *amparo,* a legal figure in the Mexican system through which citizens can ask a judge for the protection of a right. In this case, Civic Alliance alleged a breach of the constitutional rights of petition and information. The Second District judge rejected the petition, allegedly because the governor had already responded. Indeed, the state chief accountant had sent a letter recommending that Civic Alliance consult the "Official Journal of the State of Tabasco," the publication in which the state government announces its legal decisions. Of course, such a "journal" contained no information whatsoever about the matters under discussion.

Civic Alliance of Celaya "adopted" the city mayor, Leopoldo Almanza, in June 1996, requesting information about his salary, personnel in his service, and some city programs. The mayor did not respond, so one more *amparo* was presented to a judge. The Fifth District judge granted the *amparo* and asked the mayor to respond within ten working days. However, the mayor never responded, and the judge did not enforce his decision.

Given that the national courts were unable to enforce the law, in mid-1997 Civic Alliance and the Mexican Academy of Human Rights presented a lawsuit against the Mexican government in the Interamerican Commission of Human Rights. The accusation was of the breach of fundamental political rights (to petition and information) at all three levels of executive power: federal (the president), state (the governor of Tabasco), and municipal (the mayor of Celaya). The aim was to establish a juridical precedent at the international level: for the first time political rights would be considered fundamental human rights. Moreover, Civic Alliance was trying to demonstrate, in the international public arena, that the rule of law was not operative in Mexico. Nonetheless, the commission's verdict was unfavorable. The legal space for monitoring government officials was closed.

The Crisis of Civic Alliance and the Paradox of Success

The great expectations arising from Cuauhtemoc Cardenas's victory in the federal capital, and from the existence of majority opposition in Congress, caused public attention to be concentrated on the political system. The majority of NGOs and national networks dedicated a great deal of their energy to negotiating with Mexico City's government, attempting to participate in the design and implementation of public policy, an area in which they were not trained to act. Many NGO cadres began taking up administrative positions and carrying out assessment duties. Generally speaking, civil society in Mexico City entered into a phase of symbolic interaction with the local government and flagrantly neglected its function of criticism of those in power, as well as its national responsibilities.

The political framework opened by the 1997 elections can be defined as a sort of "halfway transition to democracy." The marked increase in positions of power for the opposition led to the dispersion of the NGOs and the absorption of many of their cadres into public service. The most dramatic case was south of Sonora, where most Civic Alliance leaders became municipal officials.

The crisis of Civic Alliance in 1998 and 1999 is related to the beginning of this new phase of the political transition and the consequent exhaustion of a form of collective action and public identity that had been very significant during the authoritarian phase. The avenues for civic action that had been clearly detected by the movement as the most important in the new phase—control of government actions, construction of a public citizen agenda, legal recognition of citizen political involvement—could not be covered by a massive social movement, but by organizations that specialized in actions that, by their very nature, require a greater degree of professionalism, institutionalization, and permanence. In these circumstances, citizen-type social movements can only develop in very specific situations and around new causes.

Nonetheless, Civic Alliance's ruling body did not accept this conclusion in practice and insisted on trying to fill all spaces at the same time. Their program for reviving the social movement was to design mechanisms that would allow the creation of a public agenda, such as the one attempted in 1997. This would represent a sort of common civil forum from which to negotiate with political parties.

This is the idea behind the campaign called "Citizen Power," carried out in its first phase in September and October 1999. The specific aim was to reactivate NGOs and social organizations throughout the country around the definition of a common political agenda. With this in mind, seven regional meetings were held based on a series of vital questions, at their center the government's failure to implement basic rights (political, social, and economic). In addition, there was an attempt to define the human and collective rights of the new generation (ecological rights and those of minority and ethnic groups and women). The process was finalized in a national assembly in late 1999 during which a national agenda was formulated as a synthesis of all the regional agendas, together with an action plan.

This proposal came from a promotional group close to the government of the federal district and to the PRD, which, as a matter of fact, was the historical governing body of Civic Alliance. This was a politically homogeneous group whose members decided not to open the process to other civil organization networks. Consequently, the sectional representation of "Citizen Power" was narrow, and its political effects may not have been very meaningful, since its defined agenda was basically leftist and strikingly similar to that of the PRD. This was not bad per se; the problem was that under such circumstances, "Citizen Power" could not claim to represent *the* civil society, but only of a part of it.

The aspiration of many—pushing an alliance of opposition parties in order to defeat the PRI, sought in September and the beginning of October 1999—was not taken up by the leaders of Civic Alliance and "Citizen Power." This fact demonstrates their fear of decisively intervening by putting pressure on the political parties. In this way, a singular opportunity to oblige the opposition parties to assume their historic responsibility and abandon dependence on personalistic leaders was lost.

For Civic Alliance, this circumstance was a very risky one, since the likelihood of the organization's ever again exerting public pressure on the political system, so that elections are held in conditions of equality and legality, depends on it continuing to regard itself as independent and autonomous.

In the meantime, the state Alliances continued to carry out multiple civic labors in consolidated areas or in places where they had won political space. In Chiapas, a strange coalition of NGO activists took up the name of Civic Alliance to carry out joint actions in defense of the rights of ethnic groups and of political rights generally. In Tlaxcala, the name Civic Alliance was taken up by a group of intellectuals who work along with parties, playing a very visible and decisive role in local politics from 1997 on. In Oaxaca and Guerrero, Civic Alliance's identity is used by groups of NGO activists when they need to protect themselves from state government action and to defend political rights. Only in Yucatan and in Coahuila does Civic Alliance continue to be the center of articulation for various civil battles. In other parts of the country, it is in a latent stage, waiting for better times.

Final Remarks

The contribution of the prodemocracy movement to democratic governance has been remarkable, although limited to the electoral field. In several ways, the contribution can be understood in terms of the concept of social accountability. Indeed, this social movement struggled for the generalization and application of fundamental rights, without concern for specific and particularistic purposes. The case study of Civic Alliance demonstrates that in the other areas of activity that this movement assumed, for example, the creation of civic agendas through public referendums and the surveillance of government business through civic monitoring, it has enjoyed very few transcendent and durable results. Nevertheless, these efforts are clear examples of social accountability.

The public referendums of 1995, 1996, and 1997 were symbolic mobilizations about serious problems of national importance. Although they were effective in attracting public attention to problems such as the rights of indigenous people, the need to change neoliberal economic policies, and the advantages of widening the range of social rights for Mexicans, their effect was limited to a specific moment in time and unconnected with any committed effort by the parties or the government. The referendums showed that no communication bridges existed between the most active sectors of civil society and political actors and that the national social movements were not strong enough to force the government to concede to civil demands. This lack of effectiveness proved that the construction of a civic agenda in the absence of substantial social mobilizations is not politically viable.

The case involving projects to monitor government activity, particularly the "Adopt an Official" program, demonstrates that in the absence of laws and institutions that force governments to offer information to the citizens who demand it, the symbolic resources and basic investigation techniques used by Civic Alliance are insufficient. Despite appealing to the constitutional right to petition and obtain information, Civic Alliance was unable to force the president of the republic, the governor of Tabasco, or the municipal president of Celaya to provide the basic information it was requesting. So even this direct form of social accountability lacks power and effectiveness in the absence of the rule of law.

The lack of knowledge on the part of civil activists of the legal, financial, and technical aspects of this issue was in clear evidence, as was the absence of laws and regulations that would oblige the government to carry out its business in a transparent way. Civic Alliance did not have the capacity to propose legal reforms in this field, thus demonstrating that the legal vacuum affects not only the hermetic nature of the authoritarian régime but the lack of proposals from civil society. The contribution of the prodemocracy movement to this central issue of social accountability has therefore been smaller.

The tasks of social accountability demand a much greater degree of professionalism and technical sophistication than a social movement can provide. The continuity of Civic Alliance as an organization cannot be an end in itself, and the most likely outcome is that the movement will give way to a series of new, more specialized groups involved in different forms of civil intervention in public life once the electoral phase of Mexico's democratic transition has run its course.

Civic Alliance's case demonstrates in this way the achievements and limitations of prodemocracy movements in the field of social accountability. In decisive moments of the democratic transition process, such movements are very important for promoting defining events such as foundational elections. They contribute greatly to changes in political culture by criticizing violations of the law, client-patron dynamics, and corruption. They also help to define a new culture based on respect for the law, the effective application of rights, and recognition of civil dignity. They encourage the media to act with greater honesty and objectivity and criticize the political parties when they are unable to defend democratic norms. However, they lack sufficient power in themselves to force the political system to change, and their capacity to make proposals in legal and institutional terms is relatively limited. Within themselves, they reflect the organizational, economic, and cultural limitations of their members. They frequently compete with similar groups or movements, the tolerance they demand from the political system not always practiced in their own relation with civil organizations with different political orientations. On the whole, however, the contribution of the civil prodemocracy movement to the building of electoral democracy and a tolerant and pluralistic political culture has been fundamental in guaranteeing the alternation of power that Mexico today is living, as well as in launching a new tradition of social accountability.

NOTES

1. Mexico had until December 2000 the doubtful honor of bearing the burden of the oldest authoritarian political system in the world, the origins of which go back to the consolidation of the Mexican Revolution (1920–29).

2. On this point, consult *Metapolitica* 4, no. 14 (2000), particularly the articles by Faria and Avritzer.

3. See Olvera 1999.

4. See Sánchez Ruiz 1981.

5. The 2000 presidential election was the prodemocratic movement's greatest success. However, the election of the governor in the state of Tabasco was considered illegal by the Federal Electoral Court, and problems still remain in southeastern Mexico.

6. "Control of government practices" defines a vague consort of actions aimed at keeping a vigil on a specific public policy. "Public consultations" consist of the public's responding to a questionnaire on specific topics on behalf of great social thematic movements. See further discussion later in the chapter.

7. Massive mobilizations were always innumerable in Mexican public life. Repression was selective, a last-instance form of dealing with conflict.

8. For a critique of the particularism embedded in most collective actions, see Olvera and Millán 1994.

9. On this issue, see Rivera 1998.

10. See Olvera, Millán, and Hoffmann 1997.

11. A new interest in the civil organization of society characterized a portion of the Catholic hierarchy from the mid-sixties, especially that part most sensitive to problems within the popular sector. The Social Secretariat of the Church contributed to the formation of the first NGOs concerned with development, including Popular Promotion and Development (Promoción del Desarrollo Popular), the Operational Housing Center (Centro Operacional de Vivienda), and Foundation for Rural Development (Fundación para el Desarrollo Rural), among others (1964–66). Other class-type social organizations were also created, such as the Authentic Labor Front (Frente Auténtico del Trabajo) and the Mexican Businessmen's Social Union (Unión Social de Empresarios Mexicanos) (1965). Later, other civil organizations were formed, such as the Centro de Comunicación Social (CENCOS), which denoted the Church's interest in active intervention in the public sphere, as could also be seen in Fomento Cultural y Educativo (cultural rural radio programs for peasant farmers). This activism meant that the Church was becoming an actor in the symbolic field of social justice, monopolized until then by the ruling government party.

12. The collective response to this affront was the massive recruitment of young university students to political activism and the forming of dozens of leftist organizations, some of which became guerrilla groups. The latter were completely defeated by the government around 1976.

13. The nature of the cultural changes implicit in a pattern of collective responses articulated around a new vocation for politics and public protest has not been analyzed.

14. The Corriente Democrática represented the radical nationalist-populist wing of the official party. Cárdenas is the son the of the creator of the modern Mexican state, Gen. Lázaro Cárdenas.

15. According to data from the Centro Mexicano para la Filantropia, there were more than 3,000 NGOs in Mexico in 1993. Sergio García (1997) believes that there are more, since about 40 percent of them are not legally registered. Of these, 271 are working with indigenous groups and over 300 with rural farm workers on projects of sustained development and of protection of human rights. There are about 340 associations dedicated exclusively to the defense of human rights, but another 570 see this as part of their daily work. There are over 1,000 environmental associations, and about 500 are exclusively concerned with gender issues. There are around 100 associations involved in education and over 200 in public health. Institutions devoted to the handicapped number about 700, to children 550, to women's health 450. About 150 groups work with youth and a similar number with the elderly. There are many associations dedicated to more specific affairs.

16. President Carlos Salinas gave five million dollars to the Unit of Electoral Affairs in May 1994. The government was attempting to give international credibility to the 1994 electoral process.

17. The indigenous uprising, and the assassination of the ruling party's presidential candidate in March of that year, had cast doubts over the legitimacy of the electoral process. The antecedent of the great fraud of 1988 complicated the situation even more. The promotion of observation was one of the mechanisms through which the government hoped to give credibility to the process. The strategy was a success.

18. See "Informe Final de la Observación de las Elecciones Presidenciales" (1994).

19. The amount was almost outrageous. The explanation for this was that the country should avoid the interference of narcomoney in Mexican politics.

20. See the discussion later in the chapter.

21. The Convención Nacional Democrática was a sort of permanent directing commission that evolved from a convention solicited by the Zapatista movement in mid-1994.

BIBLIOGRAPHY

Aguayo, Sergio. 1998. "Electoral Observation and Democracy in México." In Kevin J. Middlebrook, coord., *Electoral Observation and Democratic Transitions in Latin America.* San Diego: Center for U.S.-Mexican Studies, UCSD.

Aguayo, Sergio, and María Luisa Tarrés. 1995a. *Las Enigmáticas ONG Mexicanas: Una Caracterización.* Unpublished ms.

———. 1995b. *Los Organismos No Gubernamentales de Derechos Humanos en México.* Unpublished ms.

Becerra, José. 1998. "La Reforma Electoral de 1996." In César Cancino, coord., *Después del PRI: Las Elecciones de 1997 y los Escenarios de la Transición en México.* Mexico: CEPCOM.

Calderón, E., and D. Cazés. 1994. *Tecnología Ciudadana para la Democracia.* Mexico: La Jornada Ediciones-CIIH-UNAM.

Chávez Sevilla, Alberto. 1998. *Ciudadanía y Cultura Política: Alianza Cívica Guadalajara.* Guadalajara: CIESAS-Occidente, Tesis de Maestría en Antropología Social.

Cohen, Jean L., and Andrew Arato. 1992. *Civil Society and Political Theory.* Cambridge: MIT Press.

Concha Malo, Miguel. 1995. *Los Derechos Políticos como Derechos Humanos.* Mexico: IIS-UNAM/La Jornada/Siglo XXI.

Crespo, José Antonio. 1988. *Los Riesgos de la Sucesión Presidencial.* Mexico: CEPCOM.

Flores Lúa, G., L. Paré, and S. Sarmiento. 1988. *Las Voces del Campo: Movimiento Campesino y Política Agraria, 1976–1984.* Mexico: Siglo XXI.

Foweraker, J., and A. Craig, eds. 1990. *Popular Movements and Political Change in Mexico.* Boulder: Lynne Rienner Press.

García, Sergio, coord. 1997. *Organizaciones No Gubernamentales: Definición, Presencia y Perspectivas.* Mexico: Demos/FAM/IAP.

Harvey, N. 1990. *The New Agrarian Movement in Mexico, 1979–1990.* London: University of London, Research Papers.

Hernández, L. 1995. *Chiapas: La Guerra y la Paz.* Mexico: ADN Editores.

Lean McConnell, Sharon. 1996. *Alianza Cívica: Un Nuevo Actor No Gubernamental en el Ámbito Político Mexicano.* México: FLACSO, Tesis de Maestría en Ciencias Sociales.

Loaeza, Soledad. 1990. *Clases Medias y Política en México.* Mexico: El Colegio de México.

López Aspeitia, Luis Ernesto. 1998. *Imaginarios Sociales y Creación de Ciudadanía: Las Transformaciones Identitarias en Dos Organizaciones Sociales: Asamblea de Barrios de la Ciudad de México y Alianza Cívica.* Mexico: Instituto Mora, Tesis de Maestría en Sociología Política.

Melucci, Alberto. 1996a. *Challenging Codes.* Cambridge: Cambridge University Press.

———. 1996b. *The Playing Self.* Cambridge: Cambridge University Press.

Middlebrook, Kevin J., coord. 1998. *Electoral Observation and Democratic Transitions in Latin America.* San Diego: Center for U.S.-Mexican Studies, UCSD.

Monsiváis, Carlos. 1987. *Entrada Libre: Crónicas de una Sociedad Que Se Organiza.* Mexico: Era.

Morales, Rodrigo. 1995. "La Sociedad Civil y las Elecciones en México: Observadores e Interventores." In *La Voz de los Votos: Un Análisis Crítico de las Elecciones de 1994.* Mexico: FLACSO.

Olvera, Alberto, coord. 1999. *La Sociedad Civil: De la Teoría a la Realidad.* Mexico: El Colegio de México.

———. 2003. "Las Tendencias Generales de Desarrollo de la Sociedad Civil en México." In Alberto Olvera, coord., *Sociedad Civil, Esfera Pública y Democratización en América Latina.: México.* Mexico: FCE.

Olvera, Alberto, and L. Avritzer. 1992. "El Concepto de Sociedad Civil en el Estudio de la Transición Democrática." *Revista Mexicana de Sociología* 4.

Olvera, Alberto, and Cristina Millán. 1994. "Neocorporativismo y Democracia en la Transformación Institucional de la Cafeticultura." *Cuadernos Agrarios,* no. 10.

Olvera, Alberto, Cristina Millán, and Odile Hoffmann. 1997. "Identidades Fragmentadas: Formas, Actores y Espacios de la Modernización en el Campo. El Caso de la Cafeticultura Veracruzana." In Sergio Zermeño, ed., *Movimientos Sociales e Identidades Colectivas.* Mexico: Siglo XXI/CIIH/UNAM.

Ramírez Sáiz, Juan Manuel. 1998. *Y Usted: ¿Ya es Ciudadano? El Modelo Nacional de la Alianza Cívica y Su Aplicación en el Área Metropolitana de Guadalajara.* Guadalajara: Colección La Torre de Babel 13, UdeG.

———. N.d. "El Asociativismo Político en México: El Caso de Alianza Cívica. Guadalajara: DESMOS.

———. N.d. "La Política de y Desde la Sociedad: El Movimiento Mexicano por la Democracia (MMD)." Guadalajara: DESMOS.

Rivera, Liliana. 1998. *Dinámica Sociopolítica Local: Entre Redes y Actores. El Caso de Xico, Veracuz.* Jalapa, Mexico: Universidad Veracruzana.

Sánchez Ruiz, Enrique. 1981. *Los Medios Masivos y el Poder en México.* Guadalajara: ITESO.

Smulovitz, Catalina, and Enrique Peruzzotti. 2000. "Societal Accountability in Latin America." *Journal of Democracy* 11, no. 4.

Tarrés, María Luisa. 1992. *La Voluntad de Ser: Mujeres en los 90.* Mexico: El Colegio de México.

Torres, Gabriel, and Guadalupe Rodríguez. 1994. "El Barzón: Un Nuevo Movimiento Social." *Cuadernos Agrarios,* no. 10.

Zermeño, Sergio. 1974. *El Movimiento Estudiantil de 1968.* Mexico: Siglo XXI.

———. 1996. *La Sociedad Derrotada.* Mexico: Siglo XXI, México.

Documents

Alianza Cívica. 1994. "Organizaciones Que Conforman la Alianza Cívica Nacional." Mimeograph.

Alianza Cívica de Tabasco. 1994. "Informe de la Coordinación de la Alianza Cívica en el Estado de Tabasco." Mimeograph.

Alianza Cívica Nacional. 1994a. "Asamblea Nacional (30 de septiembre–1 de octubre de 1994) Acuerdos." Mimeograph.

———. 1994b. "La Calidad de la Jornada Electoral del 21 de Agosto de 1994: Informe de Alianza Cívica/Observación 1994." Mimeograph, September 19.

———. 1994c. "Criterios y Lineamientos para la Utilización del Financiamiento de la ONU para los Estados." Mimeograph.

———. 1994d. "Las Elecciones Presidenciales de Agosto de 1994: Entre el Escepticismo y la Esperanza: Un Informe sobre las Condiciones Previas." Ed. Sergio Aguayo and Mony de Swaan. Mimeograph, August 19.

———. 1994e. "Informe Narrativo: Proyecto de Observación del Proceso Electoral Presidencial de México de 1994." Mimeograph.

———. 1994f. "Informe sobre la Observación Ciudadana del Proceso Electoral de Agosto de 1994." Mimeograph.

———. 1995a. "Consulta Nacional por la Paz y la Democracia: Resultados Nacionales." Mimeograph, September 4.

———. 1995b. "Presentación." Mimeograph.

———. 1995c. "Referéndum de la Libertad: Manual para Coordinaciones Estatales y Coordinaciones Locales." Mimeograph.

———. 1995d. "Taller Nacional de Educación Cívica: Memoria." Mimeograph, June 23–24.

———. 1995e. "Las Violaciones al Derecho a la Información de los Mexicanos: La Demanda de Amparo de Alianza Cívica contra la Presidencia de la República."

———. 1996. *Alianza Cívica* 1, nos. 2–4.

———. 1998a. "Diagnóstico Alianzas Estatales 1998." Mimeograph, April 21.

———. 1998b. "Documento a discusión en la asamblea nacional." Mimeograph, March.

———. N.d. "Alianza Cívica." Pamphlet.

———. N.d. "Calendario Electoral de 1995 y Participación de Alianza Cívica en la Observación del Proceso Electoral." Mimeograph.

———. N.d. "Consulta Ciudadana, Domingo 26 de Febrero: Informe de Resultados." Mimeograph.

———. N.d. "Orígenes-Historia de Alianza Cívica." Mimeograph.

———. N.d. "Referéndum de la Libertad: Resultados Nacionales." Mimeograph.

Alianza Cívica Veracruzana. 1996. "Encuesta de Opinión sobre Alianza Cívica Veracruzana." *Boletín Alianza Cívica* 1, no. 2.

Alianza Cívica y Academia Mexicana de Derechos Humanos. N.d. "Adopte un Funcionario." Pamphlet.

Coordinación de Alianza Cívica Coahuila. 1997a. "Alianza Cívica Gana Denuncia ante el CEE: El PRI Obligado a Modificar Su Propaganda Electoral" *Boletín Alianza Cívica* 1, no. 3.

———. 1997b. "Presentación ante el IFE de la Investigación de Compra y Coacción del Voto." *Boletín Alianza Cívica* 1, no. 6.

Coordinación de Alianza Cívica de Tabasco. 1996. "Transparencia en la Gestión Pública." *Boletín Alianza Cívica* 1, no. 2.

Coordinación de Alianza Cívica Yucatán. 1997. "Denuncia contra el Sistema Estatal de Noticias de Yucatán." *Boletín Alianza Cívica* 1, no. 6.

Herrera, Nelly. 1996. "Demanda de Amparo contra el Incremento del IVA." *Boletín Alianza Cívica* 1, no. 1.

———. 1997. "Monitoreo de Medios Impresos en Siete Estados." *Boletín Alianza Cívica* 1, no. 5.

Newspaper and Periodical Articles

Becerril, Andrea. 1996. "Confuso, el Código Electoral en Coahuila." *La Jornada*, November 19, 1996.

Becerril, Andrea, and David Brondo. 1996. "Coahuila: Pelea Cerrada entre PRI y PAN." *La Jornada*, November .

Bocanegra, Cecilia. 1997. "Aunque Lenta, la Ciudadanía Está Respondiendo para Actuar como Observadores Electorales." *Diario del Istmo Coatzacoalcos*, April 28.

Camargo, Jorge, and Víctor Martínez. 1997. "Prevalece Acarreo y Compra de Votos." *Reforma*, October 20.

Coordinación Nacional de Alianza Cívica. Carta al Editor. 1997. "Alianza Cívica Pide Aclaraciones sobre Carteles que le Atribuyeron en Villahermosa." *La Jornada*, February 8.

Jiménez, Raymundo. 1997. "En Veracruz, Limitaciones en Normas y Organismos Electorales: Alianza Cívica." *La Jornada*, October 19.

Marí, Carlos. 1997. "Impugnará Oposición Resultados por Vía Legal." *Reforma*, October 21.

Marí, Carlos, and Daniel Moreno. 1997. "Tabasco: Un Estado Polarizado." *Reforma,* October 19.

Medina, Heriberto. 1997. "Señalan 'Fallas' en Coahuila." *Reforma,* July 13.

Rosado Sosa, Azucena. 1997. "Reconocen Sus Miembros la Integración Plural de Ese Organsmo." *Diario del Istmo Coatzacoalcos,* January 27.

Saldierna, Georgina, and Rene Alberto López. 1997. "No Hay Condiciones para Comicios Limpios en Tabasco: Oposición." *La Jornada,* October 18.

Sánchez, Ma. Elena. 1996. "Pide Rogelio Montemayor Atender Pacto de Civilidad." *Reforma,* October 30.

———. 1997a. "Advierten sobre 'Sospechosa' Alza de Votantes: El Aumento en Municipios de 'Elevada' Competencia." *El Diario,* May 14.

——— 1997b. "Compra del Voto y Acarreos, Denuncia la Oposición en Veracruz." *La Jornada,* October 20.

———. 1997c. "Gobierno Veracruzano y PRI Buscan el Fraud: Alianza Cívica." *La Jornada,* October 19.

———. 1997d. "1,725 Casillas Funcionarán el 6 de Julio en Yucatán, Informa el IFE." *El Diario,* May 15.

———. 1997e. "Tibieza de al CEE de Veracruz ante Irregularidades: ONG." *La Jornada,* October 17.

———. 1997f. "Los Usuarios del Transporte Urbano Presentan Problema de Inseguridad." *El Siglo de Torreøn,* September 5.

Interviews

Arrigunaga, Juan M., and Patricia McCarthy Caballero. Fax. June 28, 1994.

Hernandez, Jose Luis. President of IFE's local council in the state of Coahuila, Saltillo, Coahuila. May 29, 1997.

Herrera Rodriguez, Nelli. State coordinator of Civic Alliance. Letter to Jose Luis Hernandez. Coahuila, Saltillo, Coahuila. May 29, 1997.

8

Mobilization and Accountability

A STUDY OF SOCIAL CONTROL IN THE "CABEZAS" CASE IN ARGENTINA

Jacqueline Behrend

In January 1997, only eight months before midterm elections in which Argentine president Carlos Menem's party lost its absolute majority in the Lower House, the charred body of press photographer José Luis Cabezas was found in what remained of his car outside the coastal city of Pinamar. The murder shocked press workers and media executives alike and sparked a mobilization and social response that was to keep the case at the center of society's and politicians' attention over the next few years. The visibility of the protests against Cabezas's murder led politicians and institutions to respond to the claims of civil society organizations. Similarly, a few years earlier, the protests following the murder of conscript Omar Carrasco in the province of Neuquén had managed to attract the attention of national media and sparked outrage among the population. As a result of the scandal that arose, the army acknowledged the violence that existed against conscripts in the force and the government put an end to the compulsory military service that had existed for decades in Argentina. These two cases reflect a new trend of citizens' actions aimed at overseeing those in power that has recently been observed by researchers in Latin America.[1]

With the establishment and consolidation of the institutional requirements considered by the political science literature as necessary for the definition of many Latin American regimes as polyarchies, attention has shifted to the quality of the new democracies. The actual functioning of democratic regimes, as well as the institutional and social conditions that favor the deepening of democracy, has become the new focus of attention. Research has turned its attention to problems of accountability, that is, how to control those who govern and sanction them for their policy outcomes.[2] In this context, civil society, which in countries like Brazil and Argentina had been considered the "celebrity" of the transition to democracy, was once again brought into the limelight.[3]

In recent years, researchers have identified new associative strategies implemented by civil society organizations in Latin America that aim at overseeing political authorities and exercising control over governments.[4] The concept of social accountability thus links two spheres: institutional accountability and civil society initiatives. Social accountability refers to actions carried out by actors with different levels of organization that recognize themselves as legitimate claimants of rights.[5] The politics of social accountability are accompanied by a rights-based discourse and aim at monitoring institutions' response to rights-based claims. The strategies used by civil society and their success also vary depending on the agent that is to be held accountable. That is, social accountability initiatives may aim at eliciting accountability from elected politicians, designated officials, government agencies and institutions such as the police, or independent institutions such as the judiciary. The strategies and threats used to elicit accountability from an elected politician are probably very different from those that may be used to elicit accountability from a judge. The success of these initiatives also depends on the institutional situation of the agent to be held accountable. That is, social accountability initiatives may have greater possibilities of succeeding when the institutions or agents to be held accountable are in a more vulnerable position. The question that then arises is: can social accountability initiatives succeed on their own if the agent to be held accountable is not in a position of vulnerability?

This chapter aims at identifying new associative strategies in Latin American democracies and analyzing how civil society organizations use legal, media, and mobilization strategies to elicit accountability from political authorities. It focuses primarily on two case studies. The first, the "Cabezas case," concerns the mobilization sparked by the 1997 murder of press photographer José Luis Cabezas. The second, the "Carrasco case," focuses on the mobilization that arose after the 1994 murder of the young conscript Omar Carrasco. The latter, although less successful in its legal strategy than the Cabezas case, should be considered highly successful, given the obstacles it faced. The murder occurred in a southern province far away from Buenos Aires, the center of political life, and the victim belonged to a poor working-class family from a small town. The Carrasco case succeeded in achieving national attention, while scores of similar cases in the previous decade had not. Furthermore, the case had a very important policy outcome, as it led to the elimination of compulsory military service in Argentina. In both cases, the main strategy used by civil society organizations was mobilization. However, mobilization was seen as a strategy to accompany claims filed before the judiciary. It was initially used in both cases to signal problems and to set off alarms within both society and institutions. The strategy was then used to maintain the issues on the public agenda and ensure media attention as a form of oversight of institutional actions. In both cases, civil society associations mobilized and became "watchdogs" in the judicial investigations and trials.

Social mobilization may play an important role in controlling and overseeing the performance of democratic institutions and ensuring that they are accountable to citizens. However, this form of control has its limitations and does not gain the same results in every case. Certain conditions influence the effectiveness of social strategies aimed at eliciting governmental accountability.

The Cabezas Case

José Luis Cabezas worked as a photographer for the weekly magazine *Noticias*. At the time of his murder, in January 1997, he was covering the summer season in the coastal city of Pinamar, where politicians and members of the Argentine elite spend their holidays. Cabezas had photographed a powerful businessman, Alfredo Yabrán, who had up to then succeeded in maintaining a low profile. Cabezas's murder was discovered by police investigators and the judiciary to be linked to this businessman and was widely seen as an attack against the press and against press workers' freedom. It immediately caused a commotion within society and sparked a response from media companies and press workers.

The fact that the victim was a member of the press who worked for a large organization meant that the case was able to achieve greater attention and visibility than most human rights violations. Shortly after the case began to be investigated by a lower court, the political links and their implications in the case began to be revealed. An intricate maze of Buenos Aires province police officers, top government politicians, and powerful business interests appeared to be behind the murder. From the beginning of the investigation, it also became evident that each of these sectors would mobilize the resources it had available to prevent the judiciary from getting to the bottom of the case. It is in this context of opacity and secrecy that the mobilization of two associations grouping press workers (UTPBA, the Buenos Aires Press Workers' Union) and press photographers (ARGRA, the Argentine Press Photographers' Association) gained relevance in maintaining the case on the agenda in the years leading to the trial.[6] The two associations mobilized because they believed that making noise and achieving media attention was the only way they could ensure that the investigation would not be filed and that political authorities would find it more difficult to tamper with the investigation.[7]

The social initiatives aimed at holding several agents accountable: the national government and cabinet ministers for their links to Yabrán; the Buenos Aires province government and the provincial police force for their participation in the crime; and finally, the judiciary, whose performance came under close scrutiny throughout the investigation and trial. But apart from holding these agents accountable, the civil society organizations that mobilized in the Cabezas case also aimed at ensuring that criminal responsibility for the murder was established. It is thus important to note the difference between political accountability and criminal responsibility.

As a result of the scandals that surfaced with the Cabezas case, a justice minister was forced to resign; the Buenos Aires provincial police was purged; obscure relations between businessman Alfredo Yabrán and the government were revealed; and the political career of then–Buenos Aires governor and presidential candidate Eduardo Duhalde, one of the Peronist Party's strongest men, was severely damaged.

This section will analyze how the mobilization was organized, what its objectives were, how and with what resources the two civil society groups that acted as watchdog organizations controlled the investigation and the judicial process, what sanctions they were able to impose, and to what extent they were able to exercise control and elicit accountability from the democratic institutions. Since the leaders of both organizations stated their conviction that the constant mobilization prevented the investigation from being mishandled or dropped, I will also seek to assess to what extent mobilization succeeded in drawing public attention to the case and putting authorities in the spotlight.[8] I argue that mobilization in the Cabezas case operated on two levels: the social level and the institutional level, which includes the judiciary and the government. On the one hand, the mobilization of the association grouping press photographers (ARGRA) and its judicial strategy allowed it to be incorporated as a party in the judicial investigation. This enabled ARGRA to participate in the judicial investigation and elicit judicial responses. On the other hand, the mobilization of ARGRA, UTPBA, and the Cabezas family put the case in the limelight and meant that most government actions aimed at interfering in the case came under close press and public scrutiny, and many faced social sanctions. This close attention to anything related to the Cabezas investigation forced government ministers to publicly clarify any relations they had to Yabrán and to account for their involvement and interest in the judicial investigation. Thus, I will analyze the responses that the mobilization strategy elicited from the judiciary, the government, and the public sphere, because it is within the public sphere that social sanctions operate.

The Organization of Mobilization

Cabezas's incinerated body was found on a Saturday morning in January, in the middle of the Argentine summer. Although the first mobilizations were spontaneous and involved the participation of people who were in Pinamar at the time, ARGRA and UTPBA joined efforts over the next months and years to organize regular mobilizations, most of which were attended by a core group of press workers who were able to make noise and achieve visibility. A strategy began to be outlined by the two organizations, which also sought alliances with other civil society organizations with rights-based claims, to maintain the mobilizations over time, after concluding that mobilization was the most effective instrument available to ensure that the Cabezas case remained on the public and political agendas.[9]

The mobilization strategy could only have succeeded with the help of the mass media, which gave the case greater visibility. Although both ARGRA and UTPBA saw mobilization as a central strategy to achieve visibility in the case, their objectives were different.[10] UTPBA adopted a maximalist position in which it mobilized to call attention to the case and to indirectly influence policy making, but it did not seek any institutional participation in the case and discredited the judicial investigation in the charge of a federal court in the

Buenos Aires province city of Dolores.[11] UTPBA's action focused on eliciting social sanctions by denouncing what it saw as corrupt practices and the impossibility of achieving effective justice. It did not directly seek accountability from the authorities. Although in its rhetoric it claimed that it was pursuing justice in the case, its actions throughout the four years between the murder of the journalist and the end of the trial indicate that UTPBA only sought an impact within society that would call attention to the case and provoke social sanctions.[12] However, as I argue here, social sanctions and increased social attention can also force institutions to be more responsive to rights-based claims.

ARGRA, on the other hand, was very critical of the judicial investigation, but its strategy from the start aimed at ARGRA being incorporated into the case as one of the claimants. Its mobilization strategy was thus linked from the beginning to a legal strategy. It sought not only to set off alarms and provoke social sanctions but also to elicit a specific response from the judiciary. It is ARGRA's initiative in the Cabezas case that is most relevant to the concept of social accountability outlined in this book, because although Argentina has seen a great deal of mobilization throughout its history, the mobilization of citizen associations in pursuit of legal claims is more of a novelty that may be attributed to the institutional development and social learning processes that have taken place since the democratization of the 1980s.[13] Furthermore, in most cases, mobilization was used by civil society merely to set off alarms and signal cases of human rights violations; only with the development of the human rights movement as a result of the dictatorship did civil society initiatives begin to make full use of the legal resources and tools available to them.

Union leaders from both ARGRA and UTPBA agree that although the mobilizations were spontaneous immediately following Cabezas's murder, a clear strategy began to be outlined after a few days to make the most of the visibility that mobilizations allowed. The legacy of the human rights movement in Argentina meant that the organizations did not hold back their response and maximized the visibility that the press gave them. However, the Cabezas case marked a precedent in rights-based claims in that for the first time a collective organization was allowed to present itself as a claimant in a case of human rights violations. Up until then, only relatives of victims had been accepted as claimants in Argentine jurisprudence.

Setting off alarms proved relatively easy for UTPBA and ARGRA, not only because Cabezas was a press worker who had been murdered precisely because of his work as a journalist but also because he worked for one of Argentina's large media companies, *Noticias.*[14] *Noticias,* a popular weekly magazine that deals with national politics and current affairs, viewed the crime not only as a violation of human rights but as an attack on press freedom, specifically on the magazine's freedom to investigate and probe the hidden crevices of Argentine politics. The fact that Cabezas worked for *Noticias* is not an insignificant detail, because one of the difficulties that citizens' initiatives face in their actions aimed at eliciting accountability from institutions is lack of visibility. Civil society often lacks appropriate forums and public spaces that allow visibility at a national level. This can become particularly important in cases of initiatives outside Buenos Aires, as will be shown later in this chapter in the analysis of the Carrasco case. Cabezas's murder was not the first crime against a journalist since the return to democracy in the early 1980s, but in this case, the demands for justice had the weight of an important media company behind them.[15]

Thus, the impact that Cabezas's murder had on both press workers and media companies was very significant. The interests of a large publishing group were clearly at stake in this case, although its support for ARGRA and UTPBA's struggle was neither straightforward nor unswerving in the years that followed Cabezas's murder.[16]

Civil society initiatives must often create horizontal alliances with other societal groups in order to succeed in the arena of national politics and achieve visibility. These alliances are not always deliberate or based on equal terms, and in many cases, they merely manifest a momentary convergence of interests. As leaders from both ARGRA and UTPBA pointed out, large media companies contributed to giving the Cabezas case visibility when it was in their own interests to do so.[17] However, their support was not unconditional, and some companies sought to play down coverage of the case after some time.[18]

The Cabezas case benefited from the initial convergence of the interests of most media companies, which sympathized with *Noticias*'s situation; associations grouping press workers; and the victim's family. This meant that the shocking images of the charred car where his body was found, as well as images of the suspects and of political figures who saw the case as an opportunity to reap electoral benefits, were projected on national television and print media. The case was also discussed on most national radio programs. Thus, as soon as ARGRA and UTPBA began to organize mobilizations in Pinamar and Buenos Aires, and later in front of the courthouse in Dolores, the images spread throughout the country and for a long time were a regular feature on most television news programs.

The Political Context

The alarms that the mobilizations over the Cabezas murder set off had a direct impact on the government and on political sectors in general. Cabezas was murdered in January 1997, when Carlos Menem's second government was in a phase of decline and had lost much of the initial appeal that had enabled Menem to be reelected in 1995. During Menem's last three years in office, mobilizations, protests, and citizen initiatives against the government increased as voters appeared to signal the need for a change in representation.[19] In August 1997, the opposition Radical Party and the Frepaso joined forces to form the Alliance, and in the October 1997 midterm congressional elections, the ruling Justicialist Party lost its majority in the Lower House and had to rely on the opposition for quorum. These elections were seen as forerunners to the 1999 presidential elections, in which the opposition hoped to break the Justicialist Party's ten-year grip on power.[20] Thus, Cabezas's murder came right at the beginning of an electoral year, when much seemed to be at stake for both the government and the opposition.

From early on, there was suspicion that Cabezas's murder was linked to his photographs of businessman Alfredo Yabrán, a man who had a vast business empire but practically no public exposure. When newspaper editorials and news reports began to link the businessman to the murder, high-ranking government figures began to defend Yabrán, demonstrating the close links he had to the echelons of power in Argentina.

Cabezas's murder also sparked an immediate reaction from the Justicialist Party governor of Buenos Aires province, Eduardo Duhalde, who had his hopes set on winning the 1999 presidential election. The press photographer's murder occurred right in the middle of Duhalde's district, precisely in the coastal city where he usually went on holiday. The precision and planning surrounding Cabezas's murder evidenced from early on that the crime could not have been carried out without the complicity of the Buenos Aires provincial police force, which was in a vulnerable position at the time, as it had already been seriously questioned for criminal behavior.[21] Thus, responsibility for the crime was also thrown at Duhalde's feet and threatened to put a dramatic end to his political aspirations.[22]

Finally, opposition politicians saw that they could reap political benefits from their support of investigations related to the Cabezas case. This was a low-cost initiative that involved more declamation than action, since it was up to judicial and government institutions to ensure that the murder was solved, giving opposition politicians easy political targets at which to aim their darts. Candidates began to attend the rallies and protests organized by ARGRA and UTPBA and make statements related to the case.

The mobilization set off alarms within society, the government, and political circles and installed Cabezas's murder as an issue on the public, the media, and the government agendas. The convergence of these specific situations (i.e., the role of the media and the fact that it was an electoral year) helped the civil society initiatives achieve visibility and political relevance.

Controlling Politicians through the Use of Social Sanctions

One of the difficulties that citizens' actions aimed at overseeing the performance of institutions face is that, in order to effectively control those in power, citizens must be able to keep their claims on the relevant agendas and must also have a credible threat against politicians. In cases of social accountability, these two issues often go hand in hand. The most credible threat that citizens can use against politicians, apart from withdrawing their vote in the following elections, is the threat of social sanctions. Social sanctions refer to reputation costs and to the possibility of a scandal that could be propagated in the national media, perhaps dramatically ending or damaging a politician's career.[23] But in order for social sanctions to be a threat, the issue at stake has to be considered relevant for a significant portion of the public. Politicians have to feel that an issue is important to their voters in order to take it seriously. Elected politicians greatly depend on their reputations to be reelected; no matter how efficient a politician's career has been, a single scandal or bad publicity can profoundly affect his or her reputation. As John Thompson points out, scandals tell us something about the fragility of power and the ways in which it is exercised in our societies.[24] Political scandals are social struggles that are fought in the symbolic realm, the same realm where civil society tends to act and where citizens' initiatives aimed at eliciting accountability have their greatest strength. In an era of mass media, where politics and politicians' discourses are mediated, scandals acquire great significance. A politician's image may be greatly enhanced by favorable press coverage. Similarly, bad press may severely damage a politician's reputation and dramatically end his or her career. However, it is also true that not all public officials and political negotiators depend on their reputations to reproduce themselves. This is especially true of politicians who are not in the limelight but who, nonetheless, may have a great deal of power and political influence.[25] In these cases, social accountability initiatives may not be as effective.

Reputation costs may be higher, however, when election time is near and candidates know their positions are at stake. And in this sense, reputation costs are more than symbolic punishments, because they directly affect politicians' possibilities for maintaining their jobs.[26]

The media play a central role in pinpointing the issues that are considered to be at the center of the public agenda at a particular moment. Thus, civil society associations often find that they have to operate successfully in the media arena to ensure that the ephemeral attention of the cameras is maintained over an extended period of time. This often proves more difficult than merely signaling and calling attention to their claims at the first moment. Not only do citizens have to provide images that can be effectively transmitted on television, but they also have to face the possibility of resistance from media companies, which often have their own news agendas. However, such companies also have to take into account issues that are considered relevant by society if they want to maintain their audience. Thus, the media and public agendas feed on each other in the creation of news items.[27]

In the Cabezas case, the political scandals that arose and the information that was disclosed through the investigation helped maintain the case in the news after the initial mobilization period. UTPBA and ARGRA had an initial advantage over most civil society associations that seek accountability from government institutions. They were part of the press, so initially they were able to ensure the attention of press workers and media companies. However, judicial investigations in Argentina tend to be long, and this meant that if press workers wanted to make sure that horizontal agencies of accountability would respond to their claims, they had to continue operating on the different agendas over an extended period of time. At this point, each of the associations developed its own strategy in pursuit of its objectives.

ARGRA and UTPBA cooperated to organize mobilizations and rallies in the center of Buenos Aires, in the city of Dolores—where the judge in charge of the investigation was based—and in Pinamar, where Cabezas had been murdered. But ARGRA soon set up a legal strategy and clear objectives in the case. Up to this point, ARGRA had not had a very high public profile and, as a professional organization, had limited its work to setting up training courses for press photographers and representing them at a nonunion level. At a union level, press photographers are represented by UTPBA. Cabezas's murder forced ARGRA to redefine the purpose of its existence and decide what its representative duties should be.[28] About a year after the murder, a members' assembly voted that ARGRA should become legally involved in the case because Cabezas's murder not only personally affected him and his family but threatened press photographers' freedom to work and their personal safety while carrying out their work.[29]

One of the characteristics of ARGRA's initiative was that, from early on in the case, it sought to combine both civil society mobilization and legal action. Mobilization was used to call the attention of society and elected authorities to the case, but the decision to seek an institutional response to the crime led the association to accompany this strategy with legal action.[30] This differs greatly from the strategy pursued by UTPBA, which aimed principally at keeping Cabezas's murder on the agenda and calling attention to human rights violations in contemporary Argentina but did not seek to participate directly in any judicial action.[31] In this sense, UTPBA's action is more typical of the role that unions and social movements have played over the last few decades in Argentine history, whereas ARGRA's initiative corresponds to the social accountability framework precisely because of its use of mobilization to achieve institutional responses.

The difference in ARGRA's and UTPBA's strategies may be attributed to issues of power and representation in two organizations that were competing for representation of the same group. As a state-recognized union, UTPBA officially represented press photographers at a union level, whether they were affiliated and paid union dues or not. In fact, all press workers at the time by law had to belong to the health insurance system provided by UTPBA. Thus, the union had no motivation to compete for the representation of press photographers. But as a professional association, ARGRA most likely would have had to differentiate itself to attract new members and convince photographers that membership was worth the annual one hundred pesos (at the time one hundred dollars) in membership fees. Furthermore, at the time of Cabezas's murder, ARGRA was a very small association that did not even have its own offices.

One of the questions that logically follows is: why do politicians and institutions respond to societal demands based on mobilizations? That is, why is mobilization able to elicit accountability from those who exercise power? The broad answer is that civil society has a powerful threat it can use against politi cians: the threat of social sanctions. Mobilization places certain issues and certain politicians in the spotlight. Media attention and coverage of mobilizations reflect this visibility and propagate it throughout the country. Thus, politicians become more exposed when civil society is able to impose its agenda on the mass media.

In order to understand the strength of the mobilizations following Cabezas's murder, we must bear in mind the importance of symbolic politics in contemporary politics and the intricate maze of power relations in the political and business world that the Cabezas case touched upon and uncovered.

Cabezas's murder occurred in Buenos Aires province territory, a few blocks away from the place where Governor Eduardo Duhalde was spending his summer holidays. The crime took place under his jurisdiction and that of the controversial Buenos Aires provincial police force, and the first and most immediate political victim appeared to be Duhalde, who had hopes of winning the presidency in 1999. Duhalde interpreted the murder as a direct attack on his campaign and on the care he had put into becoming the "natural" successor of President Carlos Menem.[32] It soon became evident to Duhalde and his aides that the governor had no hopes of becoming president if the murder was not solved.[33] His response was immediate. Duhalde sent one of the best-trained men in the provincial police force to head the police investigation and assist Judge José Luis Macchi. This was especially important, since shortly after the investigation began, it was discovered that police had cleared the area of the murder and facilitated the escape of those involved.[34] When police inspector Víctor Fogelman arrived in Pinamar in January 1997 to begin the investigation, he encountered serious irregularities in the collection of evidence at the site of the murder.[35] The media attention that the case provoked from the start meant that television cameras had recorded the carelessness with which police handled evidence at the site. Investigators also discovered that the wife of a former member of the provincial police force, Gustavo Prellezo, had asked for Cabezas's record at a local police precinct. Furthermore, the fact that Cabezas's hands were bound in the way police bind those of suspects led investigators to recognize that members of their own force could be involved in the murder. Prellezo's arrest was the first piece in the puzzle that linked the Buenos Aires provincial police force to the murder. The drawings made from witnesses' descriptions of the men who were seen hanging suspiciously around the site where Cabezas was last seen bore a striking resemblance to members of the police force in the area.[36]

The Buenos Aires provincial police had come under fire repeatedly since the transition to democracy for police brutality and arbitrary violence, and the force had also been linked to shocking crimes such as the 1994 bombing of the AMIA Jewish community center in downtown Buenos Aires. This was not the first time that Duhalde was forced to confront the serious problems that existed within the police force under his control. But whereas on previous occasions Duhalde had defended the police, claiming that it was "the best police force in the world," on this occasion it became evident that his inability to control the force was viewed by society with concern and could seriously damage his political career.[37] Any attack on the Buenos Aires police would inevitably hit Duhalde, and media reports after the Cabezas murder insistently pointed to its link with the provincial police force. Furthermore, the national government immediately pointed out that responsibility for the murder fell on Duhalde's shoulders, since the death had occurred in his jurisdiction.[38]

In this context, the impact of the reputation costs for Duhalde began to be evidenced, and the governor put his weight behind the investigation in an attempt to minimize these costs. One of Duhalde's first steps was to put the police investigators he trusted the most at the helm of the investigation. Duhalde then offered rewards of between one hundred thousand and three hundred thousand pesos to anyone who could provide information on the case. He went personally on several occasions to the city of Dolores, where the judge in charge of the investigation was based, to keep up to date on the progress of the investigation. He also undertook a complete restructuring of the police force and put one of his most trusted and prestigious men, León Arslanian, in charge of the task of reforming the force.[39] As a result, dozens of high-ranking members of the force were suspended. The murder forced Duhalde to be accountable for the crimes committed by the police force under his control.

Duhalde also decided to invest in technology to ensure that progress was made in the case. After initial speculation in the press about the links that the Cabezas murder could have to businessman Alfredo Yabrán, Duhalde acquired state-of-the-art technology from the U.S. Federal Bureau of Investigation to enable investigators to trace and link phone calls (the Excalibur computer program). Duhalde's personal involvement in the case suggests that he perceived that if the provincial government did not put its weight behind the investigation, the reputation costs would fall on the discredited Buenos Aires police force and on him, as the ultimate responsible authority for its performance and for what occurred in the territory under his administration. Duhalde thus took a plunge and risked the animosity of the national government and political and business groups that were later implicated in the crime by the Excalibur computer program, in order to convey an image of accountability and responsiveness.

The Excalibur program proved to be a key piece in the investigation, its "technological objectivity" giving credibility to its findings. Police investigators began to work with the phone numbers found in Prellezo's personal phone book, which had been confiscated upon his arrest. The Excalibur program revealed that on the night of the murder, there had been phone calls from Prellezo to the chief of Yabrán's personal security and to other police officers in the area near Pinamar, who were later accused of clearing the area. The program also revealed extensive communication between Yabrán's security chief, Gregorio Ríos, and top government authorities, particularly then–justice minister Elías Jassan. When the phone calls of Yabrán's entourage began to be traced, suspicious phone calls to officials at the Ministry of the Interior and politicians close to the government were revealed, adding to the reputation costs that had already begun to be evidenced.[40]

The visibility that the case had acquired, due to press workers' mobilization and the intense media coverage, meant that the results of the computer program could not be hidden from the press. Press attention in Dolores was expectant, and every time the Excalibur program revealed new links among national government authorities, members of Yabrán's entourage, and Buenos Aires provincial police officers under suspicion, the results were disclosed to the press by Fogelman and his team. Fogelman gave daily press conferences to update reporters in Dolores on the day's findings.[41] Interior Minister Carlos Corach, meanwhile, decried the use of the Excalibur system as an alleged "witch hunt."[42]

Arguably, the judge and the police could have imposed a veil of secrecy around the investigation; this could have been justified on legal grounds. However, Duhalde had made the decision that in order to save his reputation, he had to allow the results of the police investigation to be completely open to the press, which was already hostile to him because of Cabezas's murder. Duhalde was quoted as saying, "Do they expect me, the government, or the investigators to cover up these calls?"[43] Nonetheless, there were reportedly attempts by the Menem government to ensure that the Excalibur findings remained confidential.[44]

The first victim of the Excalibur program was Justice Minister Elías Jassan. The intense communication between Yabrán's entourage and the minister immediately caught media attention and severely tarnished the minister's public image. This led to his resignation and replacement in the middle of the storm caused by the program's findings. Yet although the government responded to societal pressure by sacrificing Jassan, Cabinet Chief Jorge Rodríguez still openly met with Yabrán in his Government House office to discuss the implications of the case, and Interior Minister Carlos Corach, who was also discovered to have links to Yabrán, remained in his powerful position until the end of Menem's term in office. Thus, although Jassan's resignation shows a clear government response and may be interpreted as social accountability, there were limits to the pressure civil society was able to exert and to the effects that its pursuit of accountability was able to achieve.

The national government, nonetheless, also sought to reap benefits from the case once it became evident that the reputation costs would not just fall on Duhalde but would also touch very closely on members of Menem's entourage. Despite saying that the crime was under provincial jurisdiction, when the weapon that investigators claimed was used to shoot Cabezas was found, Corach went to Dolores and announced the finding to reporters during a press conference.[45] The national government thus sought to take credit for advances in the investigation in an attempt to demonstrate its responsiveness to societal demands.

One direct consequence of the Cabezas case was that Yabrán's business empire became visible, and from that point onward, he could no longer hope to conduct his business in secrecy. Up to the murder, Yabrán had been relatively unknown to the public, and his dealings with the government had been kept secret. Unlike most rich businessmen in Argentina, Yabrán kept his personal life and his business well sheltered from the press and from the covers of glossy magazines. He also operated with a certain contempt for societal institutions and boasted of his close relations with the government.[46] But once Cabezas's murder put Yabrán's business empire under public scrutiny, he could no longer hope to operate with secrecy and contempt for the law.[47] The mobilization and increased public attention surrounding the Cabezas case placed Yabrán and his business dealings under greater visibility and forced the businessman to publicly explain his behavior and his business. Yabrán went on television and discussed his assets and firms on widely viewed programs as a result of the notoriety he gained through the case.[48]

The government was also forced to explain its links to Yabrán and to justify cabinet members' meetings with him. And despite Duhalde's attempts to place himself at the helm of the investigation, once the implications of Buenos

Aires provincial police involvement in the murder became evident, his reputation suffered a severe blow.

Viewed from this perspective, the mobilization surrounding the Cabezas case brought public attention to the murder and the investigation. This attention made it difficult for national and provincial government authorities to ignore the issues that were being raised by the case (i.e., corruption and violence in the provincial police force and Yabrán's links to the government). The threat of social sanctions had an effect on government authorities. As a result, politicians sought to appease public opinion by responding to the claims and demands raised by civil society.

Operating in the Legal Arena

Mobilization as a strategy to elicit accountability from government officials and politicians was used during the initial period of the Cabezas case, when the investigation was carried out by Judge José Luis Macchi in the Buenos Aires province city of Dolores, with the assistance of the team of police experts headed by Víctor Fogelman. By the time the trial began in December 1999, mobilizations had stopped, and the two groups seeking justice in the case (the Cabezas family and ARGRA) concentrated on their legal strategy. The Cabezas case involved two dimensions. On the one hand, political will and decisions were needed to enable the investigation to move forward, because of the connections that the case had to the political and business world. Mobilization and societal pressure had an impact on this dimension, as we have seen. However, there can be no effective accountability in a democracy if judicial institutions are not allowed to work independently, without the interference of political power, business, or civil society. Furthermore, if social accountability is to be democratic, it must operate in the institutional arena and seek a judicial response. Social sanctions and political response are not sufficient for an effective pursuit of justice. Thus, if citizens seek accountability from institutions, they must operate not only in the symbolic realm but also on legal terrain. If civil society mobilization were seen to influence judicial outcomes, the result would be not accountability, but rather pressure on institutions that should, in principle, be able to act with independence from the social actors involved in the cases they investigate.

The Cabezas case showed an important divergence from previous experiences in human rights litigation. The fact that a collective organization was accepted as a legitimate claimant in the case in itself implies the recognition that authorities should be accountable not only to a victim's family but also to all other citizens threatened by a crime's implications.

When ARGRA's members voted to pursue a legal strategy, lawyer Miguel Gaya drew up a legal strategy that was approved by the leadership, headed by Osvaldo Barattuci. ARGRA's strategy combined mobilization and legal resources. The association set itself two objectives in the case: the indictment of those responsible for the crime and the removal of the conditions that made the crime possible.[49]

The first point directly refers to the performance of the judiciary and its capacity to establish criminal responsibility. The second point, however, refers to issues of accountability and deals with other broader societal issues that ARGRA was unlikely to resolve but that implied a certain degree of organization within civil society and the use of symbolic politics. This combination of objectives and strategies is one of the characteristics of social accountability. Citizens' initiatives grouped under the social accountability framework operate in two arenas at the same time: the political and the social. The second point is the one that distinguishes these initiatives from previous mobilization strategies in Argentina and other Latin American countries. Whereas in its legal strategy, social accountability is quite similar to the human rights movement, the way it operates within the public sphere links it more to the new social movements and the politics of identity. This is what Enrique Peruzzotti has described as the second wave of rights-oriented movements and organizations that have civil society as their major terrain of politics.[50] The second objective stated by ARGRA involved staging mobilizations and seeking to maintain the case on the public agenda to call attention to the government's and the judiciary's performance and to make sure they came under public scrutiny if they failed to respond adequately.

Gaya's strategy contained many elements drawn from the human rights movement in Argentina in the late 1970s and early 1980s. But it also showed some fundamental differences. ARGRA decided that Cabezas's murder was not simply a violation of his personal rights but a threat to press workers in general, particularly to photographers. In its view, this meant that all press photographers had legal rights as claimants in the case, because Cabezas's murder affected their freedom to work and was a threat that would continue hanging over them.[51] The murder was seen by ARGRA as a violation of the collective rights of press photographers. For this reason, ARGRA decided that its legal strategy would be centered on the acceptance of the photographers' professional association as a claimant in the judicial investigation. If the court accepted ARGRA as a party in the case, it would be able to incorporate evidence, control the investigation closely, and have a legitimate voice in the investigation.[52]

Initially, only the parents and children of José Luis Cabezas were accepted by the court as legitimate claimants affected by the murder. The lawyer of the magazine where Cabezas had been working at the time of his death, *Noticias*, did not represent the company, but rather Cabezas's youngest daughter. Another lawyer represented the photographer's parents and his two children from his first marriage, in addition to the federal prosecutor from the Public Ministry.[53] It was only after the end of the initial stage of the collection of evidence that the Federal Appeals Court accepted ARGRA as a legal claimant.

The decision to seek ARGRA's incorporation into the case as a legal claimant broke with the strategy normally used by the human rights movement. In human rights trials, lawsuits had usually been filed by individuals' families, making reference to the violation of personal rights. By seeking its incorporation into the case, ARGRA was appealing to the notion of collective rights, which tends to be used more by consumers' associations, but rarely by human rights groups. For this reason, there were few legal precedents to back this claim, and ARGRA was aware of the likelihood that the court would not accept its request.[54] Indeed, the court rejected ARGRA's request twice, but in September 1998, the criminal appeals court in Dolores issued a ruling accepting ARGRA as a claimant in the case. This ruling implied the court's acknowledgment that Cabezas had been murdered because of his professional activity. The ruling came when the initial period of investigation was almost over. This meant that ARGRA was unable to ask for new lines of investigation and had to work with what had been carried out up to then.[55] However, being a party enabled ARGRA to reject the use of certain evidence, to call witnesses, to contest the arguments and methods of the different parties, and to participate in the trial.

Shortly after its acceptance as a claimant in the case, ARGRA signed a technical cooperation agreement with the human rights organization CELS (Centre for Legal and Social Studies). ARGRA had virtually no experience in trials of this sort; its lawyer was a specialist in constitutional issues, with little experience in penal cases.[56] CELS is an NGO founded during the military dictatorship that aims at promoting and protecting human rights and strengthening the democratic system and the rule of law in Argentina.[57] After the transition to democracy, it continued its work in the area of human rights, particularly regarding violations of fundamental rights by security forces, and has provided legal-technical assistance in cases of human rights violations. Through the agreement with ARGRA, CELS provided technical assistance in coordinating the legal strategy. A CELS lawyer, Alberto Bovino, represented ARGRA along with lawyer Miguel Gaya.

ARGRA questioned the way the police had handled the investigation, in which they were basically investigating themselves. However, ARGRA chose to accept those portions of the investigation that had been carried out until then, denouncing what it saw as illegal, rather than adopting a maximalist position and denouncing the whole trial as invalid.[58] There were several elements in the investigation that were doubtful from a legal point of view, such as the fact that it was never clearly explained how the weapon used to murder Cabezas was found. The federal prosecutor and ARGRA also rejected the testimony of two psychiatrists who had illegally extracted a confession from Gustavo Prellezo, the former police officer accused of carrying out the murder.[59]

Eight people were condemned in the trial, three of them members of the Buenos Aires provincial police force at the time of the murder. Although the role of businessman Alfredo Yabrán was never completely clarified, since he committed suicide before the trial even started, the trial condemned those responsible for carrying out the murder and sentenced Yabrán's chief of security as the instigator of the crime. To a great extent, the trial sentenced those responsible for the murder, but it was unable to clarify the intricate maze of interests and relations underlying the crime. However, one interesting element of the court's sentence was the conclusion that Cabezas had been murdered because of his professional activity. The court also stated that the crime had been carried out with the participation of members of the Buenos Aires provincial police force and that the institution's structure had been used to facilitate the crime.[60] In terms of the pursuit of justice, the trial was effective, sentencing those immediately responsible for the crime. The issue that is of interest now is what effect the trial had on the pursuit of accountability and to what extent accountability was achieved.

Was the Outcome Social Accountability?

The mobilization surrounding the Cabezas case led to important social sanctions for the government, provincial authorities, and politicians in general. The trial that took place a few years later produced a judicial sentence and con demned those immediately responsible for the crime. However, what about this case may be characterized as accountability? Did these actions have any impact on the performance of the institutions and the responsiveness of political authorities to civil society? Also, as there were several agents to be held accountable (the government, the police, Yabrán, Duhalde, the judiciary), to what extent was each of them held accountable?

Mobilization was used by ARGRA and UTPBA as a strategy to call attention to the Cabezas case and to achieve visibility in the media. However, increased public attention does not necessarily imply responsiveness from political authorities. And even if social sanctions are in place and politicians are forced to respond, their response might not necessarily imply an improvement in the performance of the democratic institutions and might well be short-lived. That is, social accountability does not refer merely to civil society's ability to make politicians respond to its claims or follow electoral platforms but also to strengthening the institutions that must deliver justice in a democracy. For this reason, mobilization as a strategy in pursuit of social accountability must be combined with strategies that operate in the institutional arena in order to be effective.

One key concept in understanding the role that social accountability may play in a democracy is that of "watchdog" organizations. Watchdog organizations are societal groups that pay particular attention to certain issues and follow their development in the hopes of pinpointing illegal procedures or calling attention to issues that have been left aside or covered up. ARGRA's and UTPBA's roles in the Cabezas case may be better understood through the notion of watchdog associations. As this chapter shows, both organizations demonstrated a remarkable capacity to call attention to the case and keep the Cabezas murder on different agendas. Although ARGRA chose to operate in the institutional arena and become directly involved in the trial, while UTPBA did not, both organizations played a watchdog role in the case.

UTPBA became a watchdog in the case by continuously denouncing what it saw as actions to cover up suspects and alleged irregularities in the investigation and by publicly scrutinizing anything related to the photographer's murder. This watchdog role was carried out in the symbolic realm, and its direct corollaries were the social sanctions UTPBA and ARGRA were able to provoke.

ARGRA also became a watchdog in the Cabezas case, but of a different kind: it became a watchdog both in the symbolic realm and at an institutional level. ARGRA's participation in the trial enabled it to closely scrutinize the court's procedures and to dispute the use of certain evidence (e.g., the alleged murder weapon, which was found in dubious circumstances).

As the earlier analysis shows, the mobilization surrounding the Cabezas case had important consequences and was able to elicit accountability from public officials. To begin with, the Cabezas murder exposed the dealings of one of the most obscure businessmen in Argentina. Furthermore, it revealed the close links that this businessman had with the government. Although his business empire was not dismantled, the case forced the Menem government to clarify its relations with Yabrán and imposed greater scrutiny on this relationship.[61] It also had more immediate consequences, such as the resignation of Justice Minister Elías Jassan. However, it is yet to be seen whether this case will imply a process of social learning, that is, whether this means that, in the future, governments will be more careful about their relations with the business sector or will simply pay closer attention when they believe there are chances of being exposed by the media.

One second point at which social accountability was evidenced was in the purge carried out in the Buenos Aires provincial police force. The Cabezas case forced Governor Duhalde to be accountable for the crimes committed by the police force under his jurisdiction and was the last straw that led to a purge and reform of the force. As will be shown in the example of the Carrasco case, a paradigmatic case often has to arise in order for flawed institutions to fulfill their purpose and be reformed. Yet despite these purges, the reform of the provincial police force was by no means thorough and turned out to be short-lived. In fact, it was suspended, and the government official in charge of the reforms was removed in the heat of the 1999 electoral campaign. This points to one of the problems of social accountability: when public attention is perceived by the government to have shifted to other issues, reforms may be stalled or reversed altogether.

But the effect of the social accountability initiative may also be seen in the judicial outcome. By being incorporated into the case, ARGRA set a judicial precedent that would be used by other civil society associations in the future. Most important, its participation in the trial enabled it to control the judicial investigation from within and to voice its opposition when doubtful evidence was incorporated into the case. From a legal point of view, the Cabezas case had a relatively positive outcome, as the perpetrators of the crime were found and sentenced to prison. However, the network of complicities behind the crime was never fully clarified.

It is difficult to assess whether the mobilization in the case produced any definite changes in the functioning of institutions. Perhaps it is more accurate to say that it signaled the high reputation costs that may result from the government's interference in a judicial investigation when media attention is focused on a case. It also made it difficult for the government to sustain its relations with the Yabrán group. However, ARGRA and UTPBA were only able to achieve this because they had media attention. At a judicial level, the institutional implications are clearer, since ARGRA's incorporation into the case as a legitimate claimant means that, in the future, other civil society organizations will be able to participate in a similar way.

An important conclusion that stands out in this case is that social accountability and mobilization greatly depend on media attention to achieve their objectives and draw attention to their claims. It is unlikely that the government would have responded to the case or that Duhalde would have launched a reform of the provincial police force if both had not perceived the danger of a bad publicity campaign on national media. Scandals are propagated on television, on radio, and through print media. Thus, if the media doesn't pay attention to a case, it is unlikely that civil society organizations will be able to exert pressure on institutions, except through litigation. To further illustrate this point, I will now look at the Carrasco case, which had an important policy and social outcome, although its achievements in the judicial realm were more superficial.[62] The Carrasco case will be analyzed in lesser detail and only with the purpose of drawing a comparison with the Cabezas case and identifying the conditions under which social accountability initiatives are possible and may be effective.

The Carrasco Case

The Carrasco case shows some similarities to the Cabezas case, but what is remarkable about this case is how it succeeded in attracting attention at a national level despite the limitations it faced. Conscript Omar Carrasco's murder took place in a province several kilometers away from Buenos Aires, and the conscript came from a poor family and a small town. Carrasco's murder during his military service was the last straw that finally succeeded in putting an end to compulsory military service in Argentina. In this sense, it had an important policy outcome. Authorities were forced to respond to Carrasco's death, but they were not held fully accountable for it. From a justice perspective, the case was, however, unable to dig deeper than the primary level of responsibility. But at this point, it is important to bear in mind that most judicial outcomes can never fully unearth the networks embedded in society that enable such crimes to be committed.

Omar Carrasco was an eighteen-year-old conscript from a poor family in the city of Cutral Co, Neuquén, who was murdered at a military barracks in the city of Zapala shortly after beginning his compulsory military service in March 1994. His murder was covered up by a network of military officials, including some of higher rank, and his body was hidden for almost a month inside the barracks before being deliberately placed outside military grounds. The judicial investigation showed severe limitations from the start, as the judge handling the case had close links to the military and limited experience.[63] Had it not been for media attention and the fact that human rights organizations decided to sponsor the case, the details of Carrasco's death would most likely have remained in the dark, another unsolved murder.[64]

Carrasco's parents had scant resources available to them to make their case known and call public attention to it. Shortly after the conscript's disappearance, his father went to the press and the judiciary to report it. A journalist from *El Río Negro,* a newspaper from the neighboring province of Río Negro, was interested in the case and published a story on it. This led to a series of articles related to the case, which eventually ended with articles in the national media.[65] *El Río Negro* reproduced a press conference held by Francisco Carrasco, the conscript's father, at the local auditorium of the Asociación de Trabajadores del Estado (ATE), the state workers' union. This initial media attention alerted local human rights organizations to the disappearance of the conscript, and Carlos Segovia and Gustavo Olivera, two lawyers and activists from the Río Negro and Neuquén Current of Human Rights Activists, decided to take the case to the Defense Ministry and Congress. Carrasco's parents were basically alone in their struggle until the umbrella of human rights organizations decided to sponsor the case.[66]

Even before Carrasco's body was found, the army claimed that the conscript had deserted the force and attempted to cover up the brutal beating he had received in the barracks, which led to his death.[67] However, the state in which Carrasco's body was found and the rumors that circulated among other conscripts led parents from Cutral Co to fear the return of their sons to the barracks. Around one thousand people walked behind Carrasco's funeral car in silence until it reached the cemetery, in what would be the first of several silent marches demanding justice in the case and guarantees of safety for conscripts in the Zapala barracks.

Parents' opposition to their sons' return to the barracks forced the army to respond to their demands for reassurance about the conscripts' safety in the barracks. The army was concerned that parents from other parts of the country might also refuse to send their sons to the barracks, which could have serious implications for the force.[68] This eventually did happen in Cutral Co, whose mayor joined the committee formed by the parents and pledged to intercede to persuade the army to extend the Cutral Co conscripts' leave of absence. The mayor informed the provincial governor, who spoke with army chief Martín Balza to notify him of the upheaval.[69]

This coincided with a period of renovation within the force, which began when Balza apologized for the gross human rights violations carried out by the military during the 1976–83 military dictatorship. If Balza wanted to show that the army really meant to democratize itself and become a different institution from the one that had been so tarnished during the military dictatorship, he had to respond to parents' demands for security and justice. The army was being forced to be accountable for the violence against conscripts that had existed for decades but had been systematically covered up. In this context, Balza decided to travel to Zapala and meet with the parents who refused to send their sons back to the barracks.[70] Journalists were allowed into the meeting, which over two hundred parents attended. Members of the Mothers of Plaza de Mayo human rights organization traveled from Buenos Aires to attend the meeting, at which parents denounced other cases of violence and brutality against conscripts, and in an unprecedented sign of accountability, Balza assumed personal responsibility for conscripts' safety.[71]

In the meantime, marches began to be organized in Cutral Co and Zapala. Human rights activists organized marches of silence that initially included around five hundred people but then grew to around three thousand and, finally, ten thousand.[72] Local politicians joined the marches, which attracted the attention of national media.

Gradually, the case began to reach national newspapers, and Defense Minister Oscar Camilión and President Carlos Menem were both forced to comment on the crime. National deputies presented two projects—one of which was approved unanimously by Congress—to discharge the conscripts from the GA 161, where Carrasco had been murdered. In mid-April 1994, Carrasco's parents met with President Menem in Buenos Aires and joined the Mothers of Plaza de Mayo in its weekly march.

The increased attention to the case and the action of independent forensic experts forced Judge Rubén Caro to admit the possibility that Carrasco could have been murdered inside the barracks and to change the designation of the investigation to a "homicide." The prosecutor general sent a federal prosecutor to investigate the case, and the governor of Neuquén also began to complain about the slowness of the investigation headed by Caro.[73]

The Outcome

In order to assess whether citizens' initiatives in pursuit of accountability were successful in the Carrasco case, I will divide the case into three stages: an initial stage of mobilization in which the case achieved public attention, a second stage that was marked by the trial and in which a judicial outcome was produced, and a third stage in which there was a policy outcome that produced enduring changes. In the first stage, social accountability initiatives were greatly successful, managing to draw both local and national attention to the case and turn it into an issue that neither politicians, the army, nor the judiciary could ignore. In the second stage, the civil society initiatives achieved accountability at a primary level of responsibility. However, it was in the third stage that the case showed its overwhelming success as a social accountability initiative.

The Carrasco case achieved public attention once experienced human rights organizations became aware of and adopted it. It is unlikely that the Carrasco family would have been able to call the attention of the national media to the case or even afford a lawyer if the two lawyers from the Río Negro and Neuquén Current of Human Rights Activists had not decided to sponsor them and closely follow the investigation headed by Caro. The Front of Opposition to the Compulsory Military Service (FOSMO), founded in 1982, also joined the protests after Carrasco's death. The Permanent Assembly for Human Rights and the Mothers of Plaza de Mayo, two prominent national-level human rights organizations, also decided to adopt the cause as their own. This gave the Carrasco case greater national visibility and allowed it to benefit from the process of social learning that the human rights groups had undergone with the experience of their struggle during the military dictatorship. Furthermore, these organizations knew how to draw the attention of the press and had established networks of journalists who tended to follow human rights cases.

The marches of silence, similar to the ones carried out in Catamarca after the murder of schoolgirl María Soledad Morales in the late 1980s, signaled the concern of parents and attracted the participation of politicians. But most important, the threat that parents could refuse to send their sons back to the Zapala barracks persuaded the army chief to face up to the crime and assume personal responsibility for conscripts' safety. The case also achieved an important policy outcome: the end of the compulsory military service.

The mobilizations set off alarms throughout society and signaled the existence of a serious problem. In this sense, the Carrasco case was similar to the Cabezas case. Mobilization as a strategy, in addition to media coverage, ensured that both cases achieved prominence and became part of the public, media, and political agendas. The mobilizations forced the judge to pay greater attention to some evidence that he had neglected. However, the mobilizations did not succeed in forcing him to incorporate the testimony of one witness, a conscript named Juan Sebastián Castro, who had seen military officials beat Carrasco on several occasions. They were also unable to prevent the military from tampering with evidence and influencing the judge's actions.[74]

The military officials who were directly responsible for Carrasco's beating and death were tried and sentenced to prison. However, the network of complicity that allowed Carrasco's death and covered it up for almost a month was never uncovered. A second trial to investigate the crime's cover-up, in which around ten military officials were charged, was endlessly postponed until a court finally ruled in June 2005 that the case had become invalid. Judge Caro investigated only the homicide, leaving the cover-up aside. There were also serious irregularities in the testimonies used in the initial stage of the judicial investigation and in the way they were taken.[75] This shows an important difference from the Cabezas case. In the Cabezas case, ARGRA was able to act as a watchdog not only in the initial stage of the investigation but also during the trial, as it became a claimant in the case. However, in the Carrasco case, civil society groups were unable to exert much influence during the judicial investigation.

Measuring Success

The two case studies analyzed here show how civil society initiatives in pursuit of rights-based claims may lead to greater transparency and force public officials and institutions to be more accountable. However, some questions remain.

To what extent are civil society initiatives able to elicit accountability, and under what conditions is this possible? How do we measure success? Furthermore, what are the implications for democracy of this form of control, and what are its limitations?

Success may be measured by creating a scale, with the minimum end being the achievement of the specific objectives that the civil society group in question set itself and the maximum end being the resolution of not just one case in particular but a policy or institutional outcome that affects other cases and addresses the issue in general. Some of the points in the middle could include issues such as agenda setting.

In these two cases, civil society mobilization succeeded in calling attention to the crimes and in increasing public awareness. In the Cabezas case, the groups that organized the mobilizations were able to become watchdogs in the case and control the investigation, as well as participate in the trial. In the Carrasco case, the groups that mobilized in pursuit of justice were less organized and homogeneous and were unable to exercise such a degree of influence. Paradoxically, in the Cabezas case, the objectives of the civil society groups that mobilized were achieved, but there was no enduring policy outcome. Although the Buenos Aires provincial police began to be reformed, and this case was, to an extent, seen as the last straw in the ongoing problem of police corruption and violence, up to this day, the police maintain many practices and have not undergone a deep restructuring.[76] In the Carrasco case, the objectives of the civil society groups that mobilized were perhaps not achieved to the extent that they were in the Cabezas case—perceptions reflected in the media at the time showed that there was a sense that only "the small fish" had been punished for their participation in the crime—but the elimination of compulsory military service as a result of the case was an important policy outcome.

Although both cases were able to provoke a response from the relevant authorities and to prevent the investigations from stagnating, they show divergences and point to certain conditions that must be present if civil society initiatives are to achieve national attention or the attention of political authorities. One of these conditions is media attention. The media is, on the one hand, a reflection of what is perceived as important by society, but on the other hand, it can also call attention to certain issues ignored by society and signal problems in the functioning of political institutions. If Cabezas's murder had not had ample press coverage, it is unlikely that authorities would have been so compelled to respond to social claims for justice and accountability. Likewise, in the Carrasco case, the conscript's murder would never have reached the national arena had it not been for press coverage of the marches of silence in Cutral Co and Zapala. Yet it is also dangerous to rely on the press for actions aimed at eliciting accountability, as media companies have their own agendas and can choose to give more space to certain actions of social accountability than others, depending on their political preferences, commercial interests, viewpoints, and countless other criteria. Therefore, their coverage does not necessarily follow criteria of justice. It is also clear from these case studies that civil society initiatives in the provinces and regions more distant from Buenos Aires must go to greater efforts to achieve government attention, as they are more removed from the center of power. The fact that civil society initiatives in the Carrasco case succeeded in attracting national attention despite being in a small town very far from Buenos Aires must be viewed as another indicator of their success.

Mobilization strategies must also in many cases be accompanied by a legal strategy in order to have an institutional impact. Mobilization is effective for signaling the existence of certain issues and of rights violations. However, rights-based claims demand a political and judicial outcome, and this may only be achieved by a combination of strategies. It is difficult to assess whether these initiatives may have a permanent impact on democracy; it is perhaps more accurate to state that this depends on each individual case. In the Carrasco case, there was a clear policy outcome, the end of compulsory military service, which contributed to strengthening democracy and enhancing citizens' freedom. The case put an end to a strong institution that had lost all social consensus and support. In the Cabezas case, there was no policy outcome, but a judicial precedent was set for civil society when ARGRA was allowed to be a party in the trial. But it is also important to point out that two of the institutions that were held accountable in these cases, the Buenos Aires provincial police force and the army, were already in a weak position and had lost public credibility and prestige. Moreover, a long-term view of the outcomes shows that the reform of the Buenos Aires provincial police was not long lasting and that the deeper responsibilities of the army's command structure in the Carrasco case were never investigated, as the case was allowed to become invalid.

There are some questions that remain unanswered. For example, what are the possibilities of success for civil society initiatives in contexts of low institutionalization and the persistence of traditional forms of domination? Can civil society initiatives contribute to democratizing power relations in what Guillermo O'Donnell calls "brown areas"? Can such initiatives succeed without the attention of the media? These are questions that must be explored in order to fully understand the implications that social accountability can have for Latin American democracies.

NOTES

1. See Smulovitz and Peruzzotti 1999.

2. See Manin, Przeworski, and Stokes 1999.

3. See Stepan 1989.

4. See Smulovitz and Peruzzotti 1999.

5. See Smulovitz and Peruzzotti 2000.

6. The trial began in December 1999 and ended in February 2000, three years after Cabezas's murder.

7. Interview, Osvaldo Barattuci, ARGRA secretary general, and Miguel Gaya, ARGRA lawyer, Feb. 22, 2001; interview, Ana María Cariaga, UTPBA human rights secretary, Mar. 30, 2001.

8. Interviews, Barattuci, Gaya, and Cariaga.

9. Interviews, Cariaga and Barattuci.

10. Interviews, Cariaga and Barattuci.

11. Interview, Cariaga.

12. Interview, Cariaga. Cariaga stated that UTPBA's objective was to place the issue in the media and in society, "to give a response to something that was affecting all press workers and the whole of Argentine society. . . . We didn't direct our demand to the government or the judiciary."

13. For an analysis of processes of social learning in relation to the development of an autonomous civil society, see Peruzzotti 2000.

14. That Cabezas was murdered for setting off alarms was one of the tribunal's conclusions when it issued its ruling. This was also what press workers argued. See CELS and ARGRA n.d.; interviews, Cariaga, Barattuci, and Gaya.

15. Only a few years before, a union leader from UTPBA who was no longer working in a media company had been murdered. Despite various attempts by UTPBA to publicize the crime and stage protests, the murder of Mario Bonino never became an issue that interested the general public, media conglomerates, or press workers themselves. The struggle for justice and accountability in Bonino's murder didn't have the weight of a media company's support behind it and was not perceived as involving a threat against press freedom or the work of journalists. It was only after Bonino's murder was linked to the Cabezas crime in mobilizations and protest marches that people began to be aware of it. Bonino's murder was seen as a crime against a union leader, and this was not as shocking for press workers as a crime against a photographer. Thus, the response was limited to the union where Bonino had worked for the last few years before his murder (interview, Cariaga).

16. Interviews, Baratucci, Gaya, and Cariaga.

17. Interviews, Baratucci, Gaya, and Cariaga.

18. For example, anchorpersons on the daily news program on channel 11 were not allowed to wear the black mourning pin on their lapels that most television journalists began to use as a sign of protest shortly after Cabezas's murder. Although the indepen-

dent organization Periodistas, formed by a group of prestigious Argentine journalists, initially called for news on the Cabezas investigation to be published in all newspapers every single day until the murder was solved, this idea eventually fell along the wayside.

19. In April 1997, schoolteachers grouped in the union CTERA (Confederación de Trabajadores de la Educación de la Repúblic Argentina) began what would become the most visible protest of the 1990s when they set up a tent in front of Congress to demand alternative funding for public education. Teachers rotated on a hunger strike for almost three years. Thus, Cabezas's murder came at a time when social organizations were increasing their demands on the state and expressing their discontent with politicians in innovative and visible ways.

20. The 1999 presidential elections were won by the Radical Party–Frepaso Alliance.

21. The Buenos Aires provincial police force had come under fire in recent years for a string of unresolved cases of police brutality and torture. Duhalde, who as governor was responsible for the police in his district, had come out in defense of the force on several occasions, even calling it "the best police force in the world."

22. The Cabezas case has been interpreted as one of the reasons contributing to Duhalde's defeat in the 1999 presidential elections. However, this did not prevent him from making a political comeback in 2002, when he was appointed president by Congress after the political upheaval of Dec. 2001 and President Fernando de la Rúa's resignation.

23. For an analysis of political scandals, see Thompson 2000.

24. Again, see Thompson 2000.

25. I am grateful to Marcelo Leiras for raising this point.

26. I am also grateful to Marcelo Leiras for this point.

27. For an analysis of the interaction of the different agendas, see McCarthy, Smith, and Zald 1996.

28. The internal crisis ARGRA faced when it began to question its purpose was such that the leadership at the time of the Cabezas murder resigned five or six months afterward, due to their uncertainty as to what role the association should play (interviews, Barattuci and Gaya).

29. Interviews, Gaya and Barattucci.

30. Interview, Gaya.

31. Interview, Cariaga.

32. Shortly after the murder, Duhalde was widely quoted in the press as having said, "Me tiraron un muerto" [They've thrown a dead body at me]. For excerpts of political statements to the press during the investigation of the murder, see Fernández Llorente and Balmaceda 1997. Fernández Llorente covered the Cabezas case for channel 13, one of the largest and most widely watched television channels in Argentina, until he was forced to return to Buenos Aires due to death threats. Balmaceda covered the case for *La Nación.*

33. Duhalde's wife, Hilda González de Duhalde, clearly stated, "My husband can't be president if the homicide of José Luis Cabezas is not clarified" (Fernández Llorente and Balmaceda 1997, 249).

34. See the judge's reports to journalists covering the murder, cited in Fernández Llorente and Balmaceda 1997.

35. A local television channel recorded images of police officers trampling carelessly around the area where Cabezas's charred body had been found (Fernández Llorente and Balmaceda 1997, 81–82).

36. Fernández Llorente and Balmaceda 1997.

37. His statement was widely quoted in newspaper reports at the time.

38. Interior Minister Carlos Corach, qtd. in Fernández Llorente and Balmaceda 1997, 111.

39. The police force was decentralized, among other reforms. But a few years later, the reforms were stalled, and the provincial police force continues to be one of the most questioned institutions in Argentina.

40. Fernández Llorente and Balmaceda 1997, 92–94.

41. See Fernández Llorente and Balmaceda 1997.

42. Fernández Llorente and Balmaceda 1997, 93.

43. Fernández Llorente and Balmaceda 1997, 97.

44. Confidential meetings between Menem and Duhalde, who by then were political enemies, were widely reported to have taken place around June 1997, with the objective of controlling the impact of the Excalibur findings.

45. Fernández Llorente and Balmaceda 1997.

46. Yabrán's request for a meeting with Cabinet Chief Jorge Rodríguez in the middle of the turmoil over the Cabezas murder and the openness with which he was received may be interpreted as a sign of the ease he felt within government circles and also as a message to society that he could still be received at Government House despite the allegations against him. ARGRA's interpretation of the meeting and of Yabrán's involvement in the crime is that the Cabezas crime was perpetrated to show the impunity Yabrán had and to convey the message that the rule of law did not apply to him (interviews, Gaya and Barattucci; CELS and ARGRA n.d.).

47. Yabrán was involved in many state concessions that were highly questioned from this point onward.

48. Yabrán was on the widely viewed political commentary program anchored by Mariano Grondona on one occasion.

49. Interview, Gaya; CELS and ARGRA n.d.

50. Peruzzotti 2000.

51. Interviews, Barattuci and Gaya.

52. Interviews, Barattuci and Gaya.

53. See CELS and ARGRA n.d.

54. Interview, Gaya; CELS and ARGRA n.d.

55. Interviews, Gaya and Barattuci.

56. Interview, Gaya.

57. CELS and ARGRA n.d.

58. Interviews, Gaya and Barattuci. Barattuci explained ARGRA's position, saying: "We knew from the start that the trial that was going to be carried out in Dolores wasn't the best in the world. We weren't going to reach the truth with this trial or at least the whole truth. . . . There were two options, either to completely reject the trial and place ourselves against it, and not accept it, or to accept it as the lesser of all evils and try to be inside to denounce those things that we thought were wrong. If we had walked out, we would have stayed out of it and the trial would have been carried out anyway and we wouldn't have been able to say what we wanted to say in the trial. So we decided to accept the trial, but from the beginning we said that we knew we wouldn't reach the truth with this trial."

59. ARGRA's argument was that if it accepted evidence that had been collected illegally, there could at some point be a mistrial and everything would be brought back to

the starting point, which would not have helped its pursuit of justice. Thus, although it would have been useful to include Prellezo's confession to the two psychiatrists, it denounced the evidence as illegal and argued that there was nonetheless sufficient evidence to indict Prellezo for the crime (interviews, Gaya and Barattucci; CELS and ARGRA n.d.).

60. See CELS and ARGRA n.d..

61. However, the complete maze of political relations that Yabrán had cultivated over two decades was never fully clarified. Yabrán was not just close to Menem and his entourage; he set up his business empire during the military dictatorship, during which he benefited from state concessions; expanded it during Radical Party rule in the 1980s; and continued along the same lines under Menem. Thus Yabrán had many friends in power who were happy to protect him and give him a hand.

62. At this point it is important to highlight that criminal investigations, in most cases, only succeed in uncovering a superficial level of responsibility, because although they establish a criminal level of responsibility, they are most of the time unable to punish all the actions and omissions that participate in the staging of a crime.

63. Federal judge Caro had not been named a judge when he began to investigate Carrasco's case. He had been named as interim judge due to a vacancy in the Zapala Federal Court.

64. For details on the Carrasco case, see Urien Berri and Marín 1995.

65. Urien Berri and Marín 1995.

66. Urien Berri and Marín 1995, 97.

67. In an interview with a journalist from *La Mañana del Sur*, General Díaz, the head of the Zapala GA 161, said Carrasco had deserted. See Urien Berri and Marín 1995, 160.

68. Urien Berri and Marín 1995, 201.

69. Urien Berri and Marín 1995, 202.

70. Urien Berri and Marín 1995, 203. Balza told parents, "I am here to be accountable to society" and "I will come often and here are the journalists, guaranteeing transparency" (qtd. in Urien Berri and Marín 1995, 206, 218).

71. Urien Berri and Marín 1995, 207–9.

72. Urien Berri and Marín 1995, 274–75, 301.

73. Urien Berri and Marín 1995, 277.

74. See Urien Berri and Marín 1995.

75. Urien Berri and Marín (1995) report that conscripts were taken in a military bus to court to testify and were pressured not to implicate their superiors. Furthermore, court officials with little experience questioned witnesses, and Judge Caro later signed the documents as if he had asked the questions and heard the testimony himself.

76. The restructuring of the provincial police force came to an end for political reasons in 1999 when the candidate running to replace Duhalde as governor of Buenos Aires province, Carlos Ruckauf, accused him of being too lax on criminals and called for a greater use of force by the police.

BIBLIOGRAPHY

CELS (Centro de Estudios Legales y Sociales) and ARGRA. N.d. "Informe sobre el Juicio por el Homicidio del Reportero Gráfico José Luis Cabezas," http://www.derechopenal.com.ar (accessed June 2001).

Fernández Llorente, Antonio, and Oscar Balmaceda. 1997. *El Caso Cabezas.* Buenos Aires: Planeta.

Manin, Bernard, Adam Przeworski, and Susan C. Stokes. 1999. "Introduction." In Adam Przeworksi, Susan C. Stokes, and Bernard Manin, eds., *Democracy, Accountability, and Representation.* Cambridge: Cambridge University Press.

McCarthy, John D., Jackie Smith, and Mayer N. Zald. 1996. "Accessing Public, Media, Electoral, and Governmental Agendas." In Doug McAdam, John D. McCarthy, and Mayer N. Zald, eds., *Comparative Perspectives on Social Movements.* Cambridge: Cambridge University Press.

O'Donnell, Guillermo. 1997a. "Democracia Delegativa." In *Contrapuntos.* Buenos Aires: Piados.

———. 1997b. "Otra Institucionalización." In *Contrapuntos.* Buenos Aires: Piados.

———. 2000. "Acerca de las Varias Accountabilities y Sus Interrelaciones." Paper presented at the conference Políticas de Control Ciudadano en Latinoamérica, Universidad Torcuato Di Tella, Buenos Aires, May 18–19.

Peruzzotti, Enrique. 2000. "Towards a New Politics: Citizenship and Rights in Contemporary Argentina." *Citizenship Studies* 4, no. 4.

Schedler, Andreas. 1999. "Conceptualizing Accountability." In Larry Diamond Schedler and Marc F. Plattner, eds., *The Self-Restraining State: Power and Accountability in New Democracies.* Boulder and London: Lynne Rienner.

Smulovitz, Catalina, and Enrique Peruzotti. 1999. "Societal Accountability: The Other Side of Control." Mimeograph.

———. 2000. "Societal and Horizontal Controls: Two Cases about a Fruitful Relationship." Paper presented at the Conference on Institutions, Accountability, and Democratic Governance in Latin America, Kellogg Institute, University of Notre Dame, May 8–9.

Stepan, Alfred, ed. 1989. *Democratizing Brazil.* Oxford: Oxford University Press.

Thompson, John B. 2000. "The Nature and Consequences of Political Scandal." Paper presented at the conference Políticas de Control Ciudadano en Latinoamérica, Universidad Torcuato Di Tella, Buenos Aires, May 18–19.

Urien Berri, Jorge, and Dante Marin. 1995. *El Último Colimba.* Buenos Aires: Planeta.

PART TWO

Watchdog Journalism and Social Accountability

9

Media Scandals and Social Accountability

ASSESSING THE ROLE OF THE SENATE SCANDAL IN ARGENTINA

Enrique Peruzzotti

THE PUBLIC LIFE of many democracies, old and new, is being shattered by the recurrent breakout of media scandals. From the United States to Australia, from France to Colombia, the behavior of presidents, members of cabinet, legislators, and high-ranking public officials has been the object of intense public scrutiny as the result of the uncovering of questionable acts by the media. The prominence that political scandals are gaining in contemporary democracies has generated an important debate about the role and consequences of such media scandals. The aim of this chapter is to contribute to the ongoing debate by analyzing the link between media scandals and accountability. The analysis will be guided by a central concern: determining the contribution of political scandals to the establishment of more accountable democratic governments in societies like the Latin American ones, where mechanisms for controlling government have been traditionally weak. Through the analysis of a recent scandal that shattered Argentine political life, the role of the media as an informal watchdog of democratic government will be evaluated.

Media Scandals and Accountability

Do media scandals help promote governmental accountability? Or do they rather encourage political disbelief and cynicism? There seem to be major disagreements among analysts on the role that scandals play in democratic life. While some authors see media coverage of corruption and wrongdoing as a paradigmatic example of democratic accountability, others tend to view it as part of a worrisome pattern of negative politics that is increasingly corroding the quality of political life.

A positive evaluation of scandals is to be found in the work of authors like Andrei Markovits and Mark Silverstein. In one of the first volumes dealing with the role of scandals in political life, Markovits and Silverstein establish a direct correlation between political scandals and legal accountability, defining political scandals as the public exposure of unlawful governmental acts. Political scandals, they argue, involve the revelation of "any activity that seeks to increase political power at the expense of process and procedure."[1] Scandals (financial, sexual, etc.) that do not strictly entail a breach of due process or law, even if they involve notorious politicians like Gary Hart or Bill Clinton, cannot be rigorously considered political. By definition, political scandals are narrowed to the denunciation and exposure of political situations that involve an abuse of public power and a breach of process and procedure. This is why, Markovits and Silverstein argue, the phenomena of political scandals fundamentally occur in liberal representative democracies, that is, in a type of regime where power is made accountable through the establishment of constitutional and legal norms that tame its use and exercise. There consequently exists, for Markovits and Silverstein, an elective affinity between democratic regimes and scandals, for only the former provide institutional norms and mechanisms to make power visible and accountable.

Scandals are consequently understood as a by-product of the working of the system of checks and balances that distinguishes liberal democracies from authoritarian regimes. Democratic regimes provide institutional safeguards that lower the costs for either the press or the opposition of denouncing governmental wrongdoing. Whenever there is an opposition and an independent press willing to fulfill an active watchdog role over unscrupulous governmental officials, political scandals will follow. By exposing wrongdoing and activating judicial mechanisms, Markovits and Silverstein argue, political scandals contribute to reinforcing the legitimacy of law and due process. In their view, scandals strengthen social trust in the institutional framework of democracy, reaffirming the citizenry's belief that the institutional safeguards that the mechanisms of legal accountability provide in those exceptional cases in which the trust placed in certain political figures is breached are in place and functioning.[2] The rituals of political scandal make the abstract values of liberal democracy tangible and visible.[3]

Benjamin Ginsberg and Martin Shefter advance a very different evaluation of scandals.[4] According to these authors, the proliferation of scandal politics in political life is only an aspect of a wider phenomenon that has been negatively transforming the dynamics of democracy: the transition from electoral to postelectoral politics: "In recent years elections have become less decisive as mechanisms for resolving conflicts and constituting governments in the United States. . . . Rather than engage in an all-out competition for votes, contending political forces have come to rely upon such weapons of institutional combat as congressional investigations, media revelations, and judicial proceedings to defeat their foes. In contemporary America, electoral success often fails to confer the capacity to govern, and political forces have been able to exercise considerable power even if they lose at the polls or, indeed, do not compete in the electoral arena."[5]

In this view, scandals, far from promoting more transparent and accountable governments, have very harmful consequences for legal and political institutions of accountability. According to Ginsberg and Shefter, media exposés represent a crucial weapon of a form of politicization that makes mechanisms of accountability instrumental in discrediting political opponents. The use of congressional investigations, media exposés, and judicial proceedings, in an overly politicized way, undermines the legitimacy of mechanisms of legal accountability, which are reduced to a partisan weapon in a ruthless struggle for power. The "politics by other means" not only weakens legal mechanisms of accountability but is also contributing to the decay of the quintessential institution of political accountability: elections. If this state of affairs persists, they conclude, the democratic character of the American regime will be at stake.[6]

Still other authors, such as John B. Thompson and Fernando Jiménez, in two very interesting and comprehensive analyses of the subject, have provided a middle-way assessment of media scandals.[7] Thompson, for example, acknowledges that Markovits and Silverstein's definition of political scandal is too narrow and consequently inadequate to properly assess the role that scandals play in contemporary political life. He argues for the need to broaden the concept to include the sort of phenomena highlighted by Ginsberg and Shefter. Thompson thus defines political scandals as any type of transgressions committed by individuals who are situated within the political field, whether they involve a breach of due process or not. Scandals, he argues, are an important weapon of competitive politics, for the public disclosure of certain transgressions committed by a politician might severely damage a crucial resource of electoral politics: the individual's reputation. This is why Thompson claims that even scandals that are apparently nonpolitical, like those dealing with private issues, possess political significance and thus cannot be left outside of the definition of political scandals. In fact, what seem to predominate in many democracies are scandals fueled by narrow-minded intraelite power struggles. Sex scandals, for example, are increasingly becoming a crucial weapon of negative politics since they provide an effective way to destroy the reputation of public figures, even when the issues at stake have no connection to the public interest. The periodic resort to smear campaigns in the media, Thompson warns us, can erode public confidence in politicians and wear away social trust in democratic institutions.[8]

In this rendering of the concept, the elective affinity that exists in Markovits and Silverstein's analysis between scandal and accountability is loosened, yet it does not completely disappear, as is the case in Ginsberg and Shefter's account. The link is now present only in a certain subset of political scandals that Thompson denominates "power scandals." The concept of power scandals returns to Markovits and Silverstein's definition: power scandals are those scandals that expose actions that "contravene or seek to circumvent the rules, laws and established procedures that govern the exercise of political power."[9] By unveiling abuses of power that otherwise would have remained secret, Thompson argues, power scandals might significantly contribute to rendering power visible and accountable. However, even within this subset of scandals, Jiménez warns us, this is not always the case. Scandals do not automatically trigger a process of social control; rather, their effects on governmental accountability depend on the institutional response they generate. If judicial or other institutions of control oblige the questioned agent to respond to the allegations in a satisfactory way or punish the representative for his or her actions, social trust in representative institutions is restored. Failure to do so will extend the questioning not only to the officials involved but also to the representative system.[10]

Is there a way to minimize the negative effects of scandals and to boost their accountability-strengthening role? In the first place, the existence of certain institutional features in a society can help lessen some of the negative effects of media exposés. Democratic regimes that uphold open and clear standards of conduct for public officials and possess robust and effective mechanisms for investigating and punishing wrongdoing are better equipped for counteracting the negative effects of scandals than are regimes in which these features are absent.[11] Second, the social organization of news making and the existence of ethical and professional standards for journalists and media organizations are also fundamental.[12] The existence of a professional code of ethics in regard to issues such as protection of the privacy of individuals, and accuracy of the information and reliability of sources and journalists' investigations, might prevent some of the excesses of a commercially driven media interested in exploiting scandals to increase sales or ratings, or the sort of coverage that is heavily shaped by the disclosures and intentions of elite actors. These two points, the existence of impartial and effective judicial mechanisms and agencies of control and professional practices and standards of journalism, are important variables to be taken into account when analyzing the dynamics of political scandals in Latin America.

Accountability Deficits and Watchdog Journalism in Latin America

It is generally agreed that in Latin America institutional mechanisms of accountability are extremely weak and ineffective.[13] Perhaps the author that has most forcefully advanced such argument is Guillermo O'Donnell. For him, the absence of working mechanisms of "horizontal accountability" is the defining feature of some of the new democracies in the region. In his view, the lack of a network of public agencies willing or able to undertake actions of control or legal sanctions in relation to governmental wrongdoing is what differentiates some of the new democracies from older representative ones. The outcome is a form of polyarchy, which he terms *delegative*, where the legal dimension of accountability is largely absent and the only form of control of governmental actions is ex-post-facto electoral verdicts.

Whether one completely agrees with O'Donnell's diagnosis or not, it is evident that the workings of institutions of legal accountability confront serious challenges and obstacles in many of the new Latin American democracies. Yet it has also been noticed that the last democratizing wave brought significant changes in the patterns of civic engagement in the region.[14] One of the most noteworthy developments is the emergence of a politics of social accountability that is being mobilized by a heterogeneous group of civic- and media-based initiatives.[15] On the one hand, new civic associations, social movements, and NGOs have sprouted throughout the continent, such as human rights organizations, civic networks that monitor elections to prevent fraud, social movements against police abuse and violence, and citizens' organizations that demand clearance of public information. On the other hand, changes within media organizations have given rise to a more inquisitive type of watchdog journalism that in recent years has played a crucial role in the disclosure of numerous cases of governmental wrongdoing.[16]

Three important developments have contributed to the rise of watchdog journalism in Latin America. The first is the democratization wave that affected most of the continent and established a protective legal framework guaranteeing press freedom. Undoubtedly, the workings of critical journalism take place in an institutional setting that is far from resembling that of established democracies: acts of violence against the press are still present in many of these democracies, and the existing legislation imposes some legal obstacles to press denunciations.[17] Yet if compared with the climate of terror and censorship that predated the democratizing wave, the continent has made great progress toward the stabilization of a friendly environment for investigative or watchdog reporting.[18]

The second development that contributed to the emergence of a more critical form of journalism is the shift to market-based media organization. The process of privatization of the media implemented by numerous governments in the region has favorably changed press-government relations, opening up a more critical and distant form of reporting of official activities.[19] While states still possess considerable resources to control or reward certain media organizations, the consolidation of large commercially driven media conglomerates has greatly loosened the financial dependency of the sector on the state.

The third development refers to the cultural changes experienced in the region. The emergence of a more critical and sophisticated citizenry and electorate transformed established notions of representation. Representative institutions are now subjected to a more demanding model of representation that places the issue of legal and political accountability at the forefront of public debates.[20] The appearance of a more exigent civil society created an avid market for the products of watchdog journalism. In the past decade, many books written by renowned investigative journalists dominated the best-seller charts of several countries of the region, and investigative TV programs also obtained high ratings. In brief, the institutional, economic, and cultural developments of the last decades made possible the emergence of a more inquisitive type of journalism in the region.

Watchdog journalism gained political ascendancy in the 1980s and 1990s. Numerous media exposés of governmental wrongdoing began to take a considerable toll on the fate of officials and governments, from top to low-ranking officials. The fact that power scandals have become the predominant form of scandal in contemporary Latin American democracies, largely outnumbering other kinds of scandals, has led many analysts and journalists to conclude that the media is taking seriously its role as a fourth estate. The phenomenon also supports the previously mentioned argument about the existence of a new social environment in which the lines about what constitutes proper or acceptable political behavior have been drastically redrawn: "delegative" or corrupt practices that in the past were socially tolerated (or that at best fell into what Jiménez refers as a "gray zone" of imprecise contours and debatable principles) are now subject to intense scrutiny and generate public outrage.[21]

Watchdog journalism became a central actor in the politics of social accountability, sometimes acting independently, sometimes giving voice and visibility to the denunciation of civic actors. In both roles, watchdog journalism accomplished major victories. On the one hand, media exposés generated major political and institutional crises. In Brazil and Peru, disclosures of corruption brought down the Collor de Mello and Fujimori administrations. In Colombia, press investigations of alleged contributions made by the Cali cartel to the 1994 electoral campaign almost resulted in the impeachment of President Ernesto Samper. In Argentina, a newspaper investigation of an illegal sale of weapons by the Argentine government to Ecuador during its war with Peru led to the house arrest of ex-president Carlos Saúl Menem. On the other hand, watchdog journalism has been a crucial ally of countless social movements and NGOs in denouncing different forms of governmental wrongdoing.

The concept of social accountability introduces a new variable to the debates on media and accountability. In the discussion about scandals, the press and the opposition were considered the main means of disclosure of wrongdoing, given their privileged access to inside information.[22] Political scandals were thus largely seen as intraelite games, the outcome in each case fundamentally depending on the postures and maneuvers adopted by media and political elites.[23] The citizenry and society at large only played a passive role as "public opinion." The societal variable always appears in this literature as loose public opinion that with its outrage or reprobation grants certain disclosures the identity of scandal. As Thompson and Jiménez argue, no social outrage, no scandal. The concept of social accountability, by focusing on the role played by organized civil society in the agenda of accountability, adds a third actor to the game.

In Latin America, many scandals resulted not from elite disclosures but from denunciations by social groups and organizations that reacted against specific cases of wrongdoing or violation of rights.[24] This statement is not meant to underplay the significant role that the press played in many of these public dramas. It has been argued that the press acts as an invaluable ally in the politics of social accountability. In fact, most civic claims for equal treatment under the law, due process, or judicial independence began to exert considerable pressure on the political system only after they had attained significant media coverage and visibility. Thanks to the media, local cases attracted the attention of the whole nation.[25] Without media attention, many of these initiatives of social accountability would have remained invisible to the general public.

The coverage of demonstrations and mobilizations not only provided a channel to make certain voices known and keep certain stories alive but also put moral pressure on those under public scrutiny, as well as on corresponding political and judicial authorities. Media visibility raises the costs of inaction for horizontal agencies of accountability: under close public opinion and media scrutiny, it is very costly for public officials or politicians to turn a blind eye to civic claims for justice. In fact, the most successful cases of social accountability simultaneously combine social mobilizations, media visibility, and the multiple activation of institutional channels.

The political ascendancy of watchdog journalism and the political impact of its activities pose several questions regarding the implications that such journalism has for the agenda of accountability in the region. What are the consequences of political scandals and media exposés? Can the Latin American media be considered independent? Is the image of a fourth estate adequate to describe the workings of journalism in the region? Do media exposés and denunciations help to strengthen democracy and governmental accountability? Or are they an instrument of the "politics by other means" that ultimately feed political cynicism and apathy?

In a context characterized by a peculiar combination of strong social demands for accountability and weak institutions of control, how should the role and consequences of political scandals be evaluated? For many of the authors mentioned in the previous section, political scandals can play a constructive role in societies where there is *both* a culture of accountability *and* an effective system of horizontal mechanisms to control and punish wrongdoing. If one of these prerequisites is lacking, as seems to be the case in many of the new democracies of the region, can scandals still play a positive political role? Under what circumstances? Can political scandals always be considered a privileged tool of the politics of social accountability? Or do media exposés simply provide the stage for intraelite battles of "politics by other means"? While the analysis of a single case will not likely allow us to adequately address all of these questions, it will help us shed some light on the reach and limitations of the media as an agent of accountability. Through the analysis of the paradigmatic case of a "power scandal" in Argentina, it is possible to reflect on the extent to which media scandals contribute to improving the agenda of accountability in the region.

The Senate Scandal in Argentina

The Senate scandal was triggered by an editorial by a prestigious journalist suggesting that the passing of the labor reform law in the Senate had been accomplished through bribes. The scandal had a major impact on Argentine political life and greatly affected the political capital of the Alianza administration. The Senate scandal was not an isolated or exceptional event: in the previous decade, the Argentine public sphere had been bombarded by countless scandals and media exposés of corruption and wrongdoing. In the 1990s, watchdog journalism gained national notoriety by disclosing countless episodes of official corruption. One of the first scandals surfaced in 1991 when the newspaper *Página 12* revealed that the then–U.S. ambassador to Argentina had sent a letter to the government in which he accused high-ranking officials of soliciting bribes from the U.S.-based Swift corporation to allow for the import of machinery. Only months later, the president's sister-in-law, Amira Yoma, was implicated in a drug-money-laundering scandal. Shortly afterward, two close aides of Menem were involved in the sale of rotten milk to a federal nutritional program for poor children. Another prominent member of the administration, the head of the national agency providing social services for senior citizens (PAMI), had to step down due to accusations of receiving bribes from favored providers. An exposé about the building of an oversized airstrip near Menem's private summer residence in Anillaco ended when the TV station concerned decided to cancel the program. In 1995, a major scandal broke out when the newspaper *Clarín* revealed that Argentine weapons had been sold to Ecuador (Argentina was one of the guarantors of the 1942 peace treaty between Ecuador and Peru). Months later, the media revealed a new and much more important sale of weapons, to Croatia in 1991, which violated the United Nations' embargo.[26] The extent and periodicity of media exposés during the Menem administration even led some authors to wonder whether the citizenry was reaching a state of scandal fatigue.[27]

Why then focus on the Senate scandal? Why choose this specific case over the innumerable number of scandals that proliferated throughout the 1990s? What makes this scandal distinctive or particularly relevant for the analysis of media and accountability? This scandal represents the "power scandal" par excellence. This is not merely another case of corruption; it involves a type of affront that goes to the core of representative institutions. The Senate scandal was qualitatively different from other cases of corruption: it did not cast doubt simply on the reputation of some isolated politicians or public officials but on the whole structure of the Argentine representative system.

First, the scandal cast serious doubt on the workings of vertical electoral mechanisms of accountability. The accusation that laws passed by the legislative power had been attained through bribes goes to the heart of the representative contract. If there is a generalized belief in the citizenry that their political representatives respond to the highest bidder, elections lose all meaning as a mechanism of will formation. The vertical bond that unites civil society with representative institutions does not serve to generate responsive governments but is distorted by obscure corrupted practices at the institutional level.

Second, the scandal affects not only the credibility of vertical electoral mechanisms of accountability but also that of horizontal ones, for the alleged wrongdoing points to a perverse form of relationship between legislative and executive powers that, if proved, would also make meaningless the idea of horizontal checks and balances among state powers.

Third, the analysis of the Senate scandal also serves to shed light on the dynamics of certain subset of scandals: those scandals (1) that are largely motorized by the press and (2) in which the process of news gathering is the result neither of the workings of investigative reporting nor of civic movements or societal organizations. Rather, news in such scandals comes from elite sources: the Senate scandal broke into the public scenario as the result of insider information being passed to a certain media outlet. In this sense, this specific scandal helps us evaluate the workings and limitations of the practice of watchdog *denuncismo* as opposed to investigative journalism.

Fourth and finally, the scandal serves to show to what extent the press can fulfill its role as a fourth estate in an environment like that of many of the new democracies, that is, in an institutional and political environment hostile to the idea of public scrutiny. The scandal can consequently illustrate some of the shortcomings or limitations of informal mechanisms of accountability in a setting where most of the institutional actors have mastered the art of "surviving accountability."[28]

What were the main episodes of the scandal? The Senate scandal was initiated at the end of June 2000 by a political editorial in the newspaper *La Nación* denouncing reports that Congress's passage of the Labor Reform Law had been attained through bribes. The editorial, written by respected journalist Joaquín Morales Solá, made public rumors that had been circulating since February. The rumors suggested that a group of Peronist senators had received substantial bribes from members of the executive power in exchange for their favorable vote on the governmental project on labor reform. The political impact of the editorial's disclosure was augmented by the initiatives of two notorious politicians: Senator Antonio Cafiero and then-vice president Carlos Alvarez. As a direct result of Morales Solá's editorial, Cafiero presented a motion in the Senate to investigate the matter a week after the editorial was published. Alvarez, who was chairman of the house, also initiated a judicial cause to investigate the matter and in the month of August read an anonymous pamphlet that had been circulating in the Senate describing how the bribes had been paid in a meeting of a senatorial commission.

The actions of Cafiero and Alvarez helped give the denunciation and rumors a public form, forcing the Senate to take a stand on the issue and activating other horizontal mechanisms of accountability, like the judiciary and the Anticorruption Office. Within the Senate, a debate took place about the course of action to be assumed by the institution in general and, specifically, by the senators directly involved in the scandal. Several members of the house requested the removal of the legislative privilege of immunity for all members of the Senate to allow the judiciary to investigate them. Parallel to the judicial proceedings, the Anticorruption Office initiated its own investigation and demanded that the State Intelligence Agency (SIDE) submit information about all of its accounts, since rumors indicated that the bribe money had come from the secret accounts of that office. Eventually, the Federal Penal Chamber unified all judicial proceedings related to the case in one cause under the responsibility of Judge Carlos Liporaci. Ironically, Liporaci himself was the subject of another corruption scandal: the judge had been accused of illegal enrichment by the media, for he could not justify the purchase of a million-and-a-half-dollar mansion.[29]

When Senator Cafiero testified in front of Judge Liporaci, he incriminated three colleagues of the Upper House. The next day, *La Nación* published an anonymous interview held between a staff journalist of the newspaper and a member of the Senate. In the interview, the senator not only admitted having received a bribe to pass the labor law but also declared that bribing was a regular procedure in the Upper House.[30] When he later publicly denied having been interviewed by *La Nación,* the newspaper revealed his name and confirmed the existence of the meeting.

Public suspicions were further fueled by Judge Liporaci's public statement that in his view there were serious indications of the existence of bribes.[31] Liporaci requested the suspension of the legislative privileges of eight senators, seven from the Peronist opposition and one from the Radical Party. After a heated debate, Congress passed a law that did not annul legislative privileges but simply established certain restrictions. The law allowed the judge to interrogate and process the suspected senators but not to incarcerate them. Simultaneously, the NGO Poder Ciudadano intensified its campaign to demand a public statement of income and patrimony from the members of Congress. Of a total of sixty-nine senators, only forty-seven presented such a statement, although it is worth noting that four of the suspected senators refused to make their patrimony public.[32]

Simultaneously, the Council of Magistrates opened a process to investigate the alleged charges of corruption against Judge Liporaci. Two months later, Liporaci would declare the "lack of merit" of all the suspected senators. In January, the prosecutors appealed Liporaci's ruling. In February, the Council of Magistrates suspended Liporaci from his post and initiated a judicial procedure to remove him. To avoid the trial, Liporaci resigned in March. The cause passed to the hands of two more judges, Gabriel Cavallo and Rodolfo Canicoba Corral.

In the meantime, the scandal generated an earthquake in the governing administration. Vice President Carlos Alvarez had assumed a decisive attitude in the case, which he saw as a crucial test for the governing alliance's electoral promise of greater transparency and accountability in government. The reaction of President Fernando de la Rúa to the episode instead was more cautious. Although he made a conscious effort to appear as not obstructing the judicial proceedings under way, he stated on several occasions that he believed that the alleged charges were unfounded.[33] The different attitudes assumed by the two political heads of the governing coalition generated a tense political climate. The Radical Party closed ranks around the government and the Senate, while Alvarez publicly demanded the resignation of those public officials who were suspected of taking part in the political operation that had generated the scandal: Labor Minister Alberto Flamarique and Fernando de Santibañez, head of SIDE. Flamarique was suspected of having paid the bribes with secret funds from SIDE. Not only were Alvarez's pleas to remove these individuals ignored, but the cabinet change that the president announced in mid-August to relaunch his battered administration promoted Alberto Flamarique to the position of general secretary of the presidency.

Alvarez's response to this presidential announcement was not long in coming: that same day he presented his resignation as vice president in a televised public address in which he confirmed his suspicion of senatorial wrongdoing. Alvarez's unexpected decision opened a gap in the governing coalition that would only broaden with time. After Flamarique and De Santibañez resigned, the first the same day as Alvarez and the second two weeks later, the scandal gradually faded from the public eye. By the month of December, there was little media coverage of the case.[34]

Lessons from the Senate Scandal

What lessons can we draw from the Senate scandal? If viewed from the angle of the scandal's contribution to more accountable government, it left a questionable legacy, for in the eyes of large sectors of Argentine public opinion, the episode evidenced both the malfunctioning of institutional mechanisms of accountability and the reticence of political elites to bring more transparency to public office. I have argued elsewhere that the event marks a turning point in the relationship between civil and political society and provides an indispensable clue for understanding the subsequent electoral and social developments that significantly altered the national political scenario.[35] The Senate scandal also showed the limitations of a certain subset of initiatives of social accountability: those that are largely motorized by media *denuncismo.*

Vertical and Horizontal Deficits

There are several reasons that aid understanding of why this particular scandal helped nourish a generalized feeling of civic skepticism about the actual workings of Argentine representative institutions. In the first place, the scandal cast serious doubt throughout the population about the effectiveness of formal mechanisms of accountability, both legal and electoral. On the one hand, it cast a shadow on the belief that elections could provide an effective mechanism of popular control. First, the fact that the scandal involved a recently elected administration that had campaigned around a strong anticorruption discourse served to confirm to large sectors of the population that the problem of legal unaccountability was not circumscribed to a particular administration but affected all of political society. Therefore, a simple change of government would not eradicate the problem. The electoral road to change had failed, and the expectations of political transparency that the Alianza had raised in the electorate had been quickly betrayed. The way in which the whole Argentine political society had closed lines in defense of its prerogatives and corporate interests and the fact there were no major political figures, with the sole exceptions of Carlos Alvarez and Antonio Cafiero, who acted promptly to dissociate themselves from the alleged transgressors further confirmed for many citizens their belief that representative institutions had detached themselves from the wishes and aspirations of the people. Second, the very nature of the scandal —the accusation that the laws passed by Congress were attained through bribes—openly eroded the belief in elections as an effective mechanism of political accountability. As argued above, this was not simply another corruption case but an event that cast serious doubt on the operation of the Argentine representative system.

On the other hand, the scandal made visible the deficits and malfunctioning of the network of horizontal mechanisms of accountability in Argentina. The way the whole affair unfolded was a tragic display of how many of the institutional safeguards to check governmental actions had been distorted and expropriated by unscrupulous officials who had mastered the art of "surviving accountability." The scandal touched controlling agencies in all three branches of government. At the judicial level, proceedings against nine senators were initiated in August 2000. At the level of the executive power, three different agencies were involved: the Anticorruption Office, Sindicatura General de la Nación (SIGEN), and Administración General de Ingresos Públicos (AFIP). At the legislative level, the scandal involved a senatorial commission of inquiry, the Commission of Constitutional Affairs, and the Comisión Bicameral de Fiscalización de los Organos y Actividades de Seguridad Interior e Inteligencia.

The attitude assumed by those controlling legislative mechanisms that could have played a role in shedding some light on the episode was deceptive, only serving to confirm that the institution had closed ranks in defense of its prerogatives and interests and was hostile to any supervision. Neither the inquiry nor the monitoring commission was ever activated: the senatorial commission of inquiry created by some Peronist members of the Senate to investigate the alleged bribes was dissolved four days later.[36] The other legislative commission, which the Anticorruption Office tried to activate, met a similar fate.[37] The bicameral commission that had been established to control and supervise the activities of state intelligence agencies refused to submit any information to the Anticorruption Office, which had demanded data about the alleged use of SIDE's secret funds to pay Senate bribes.[38]

On the judicial front, the results were no better. Despite the efforts of the prosecutors, the judicial proceedings have remained stagnant since August 2001 and more likely will be closed without any major judicial implication for any of the figures involved in the scandal. The cause has been handled by three different judges: the above-mentioned Liporaci, who resigned to avoid a trial on corruption by the Council of Magistrates; Gabriel Cavallo, who dropped the cause in September 2000 because the Senate was going to vote shortly on his promotion to justice of the Federal Penal Chamber (it is worth noting that many of the incriminated Senators participated in the judge's appointment); and Rodolfo Canicoba Corral.

At the executive level, the Anticorruption Office, an organism that was created to supervise the behavior of executive agencies but had no jurisdiction over the legislative or judicial powers, opened an administrative investigation aimed at determining if any of the executive agencies had made irregular use of public funds. In particular, it attempted to trace the movement of funds during the months preceding the scandal of three agencies that were suspected as possible sources of the bribes: SIDE, the Ministry of the Interior, and the

Ministry of Health. For this purpose, it requested the help of two other executive agencies, SIGEN and AFIP, and of the already mentioned Comisión Bicameral de Fiscalización de los Organos y Actividades de Seguridad Interior e Inteligencia. While it met the resistance of the latter, it received a more positive response from the first two agencies. However, SIGEN faced the refusal of de Santibañez when it attempted to gather information from SIDE. While these agencies were able to document the existence of a nontransparent process of payments and use of public funds, no direct connections could be established with the bribes themselves.[39]

Those horizontal actors that were pushing the investigation, like the prosecutors, Alvarez, and the Anticorruption Office, met the resistance or reluctance of other horizontal agencies that, given the interdependence of the system of checks and balances, could successfully block the investigation. The fact that, despite the press, no external social agents were capable of exerting pressure and/or bringing new evidence to the investigation further contributed to the cause's stagnation.

In conclusion, the operation of horizontal agencies did not generate an institutional closing to the scandal, nor did it result in any type of formal sanctions. At best, what the scandal accomplished was imposing reputation costs on many of its protagonists. As a result of the scandal, certain figures were forced to quit their posts, among them Labor Minister Alberto Flamarique; SIDE director Fernando de Santibañez; the respective presidents of the Radical and Peronist blocs in the Senate, Raúl Galvan and Augusto Alasino; the provisional president of the Senate, José Genoud; and Vice President Carlos Alvarez. Yet despite the shock wave that the scandal sent through the representative system and the political crisis it generated, there was no institutional closing of the episode. In spite of the seriousness of the allegations, the issue simply vanished.

For many authors, it is precisely the closing of the ritual of disclosure, investigation, and discussion with some sort of institutional punishment that serves to ultimately reaffirm belief in the institutional safeguards that representative democracy provides to reduce the risks of electoral delegation.[40] If that institutional closing is missing, a scandal, rather than reaffirming and strengthening public trust in democracy, will simply erode public confidence in representative institutions.[41] The attitude assumed by political society and by some horizontal agencies did not contribute to convincing the citizenry that institutional safeguards were in place and functioning.

Denuncismo

The scandal also serves to illustrate some problematic features of journalist practice that need to be addressed to adequately understand the potential and limitations of the media as an agent of accountability. Specifically, the Senate scandal showed some problematic aspects of media *denuncismo*. The term *denuncismo* refers to the proliferation of media disclosures of alleged wrongdoing that are based not on journalist investigations but on rumors or "off-the-record" leaks. For some authors, the absence of a strong investigative tradition in Latin American journalism and the obstacles newsrooms confront in gaining access to information have resulted in a process of information gathering that is highly dependent on "off-the-record" official sources.[42] Such dependence of reporters and editors on tips and leaks passed along by anonymous sources poses serious constraints on the practice of journalism, and these limitations become visible in episodes like the Senate scandal, where a rumor about alleged inappropriate behavior in the Senate, made public by a press editorial, sparked one of the most serious political and institutional crises of the Argentine representative system since the return to democracy.

The phenomenon of *denuncismo* poses some interesting questions for the assessment of the media as an agent of social accountability. As argued above, the concept of social accountability aims at providing a framework for the analysis of a heterogeneous group of media and civic initiatives. Via this concept, the media is included as an actor that sometimes participates as a crucial ally of social movements and civic organizations and sometimes acts on its own. In brief, the media participates in the politics of social accountability in two different roles. In the first, it gives voice and visibility to civic claims that otherwise would remain invisible to public opinion. Usually, the combination of mobilization strategies by societal actors with the activation of some horizontal agencies and extensive media coverage provides an effective way to exert pressure on public authorities in specific cases of governmental wrongdoing. In these cases, the social actors behave as sensors that provide evidence and information regarding unlawful governmental actions, initiating a story in the press. In the past decade, the Argentine scenario has witnessed many such alliances between social actors and media, as in the cases of María Soledad Morales, José Luis Cabezas, Omar Carrasco, Bulaccio, Ingeniero Budge, Memoria Activa, and so on. In some cases, the actions of the civic claimants gain the supplementary support of formal or informal societal watchdogs that gather and supply information about the monitored agency or official, as is the case, for example, with such organizations as CELS and CORREPI in relation to police violence.

In other cases, denunciation comes from the news-gathering activities of a journalistic investigation that presents specific proof of wrongful actions, as in the cases of the arms-sale scandal in Argentina or the La Cantuta scandal in Peru or of leaks obtained by certain journalists due to their cultivation of contacts within the political system.[43] In such cases, information does not originate in organized sectors of civil society, as in the numerous episodes of human rights violations, nor does it originate in the initiatives of a network of NGOs or mobilized social movements. Rather, information is the product of media disclosure.

A large proportion of the Argentine scandals that have recently proliferated belong in one of these two categories. In this respect, two different situations of information gathering can be distinguished. In the first, the information that leads to a certain exposé is independently obtained, either through a journalistic investigation (as in the arms case) or through the workings of societal watchdogs or social movements (as in the María Soledad Morales case or the numerous cases of police violence). In the second particular subset of exposés, such as the Senate scandal, information is the product of making public leaks obtained from official sources.

In cases like the Senate scandal, where the press neither investigates nor receives information from nonelite social groups regarding the specifics of a case, scandal dynamics remain tied to the willingness of elite informers to provide new or additional leaks or proofs. This type of scandal therefore evolves at the rhythm of interelite conflicts. Such a situation leaves the media at the mercy of the dynamics of "politics by other means," in which press disclosures are used by some sectors to harm the reputation of their enemies. Deep-seated rivalries among governmental factions, or the opposition's interest in weakening the standing of those in power, stimulate this sort of press denunciation of wrongdoing.[44]

There are two implicit dangers in *denuncismo.* The first is that of ventriloquism, that is, the danger that the press is actually speaking for concealed sources using the exposé as a weapon in a battle for power.[45] The role of the press as a ventriloquist for hidden power, although it might appear on the surface to be a paradigmatic case of the fourth estate, is far from promoting accountability and transparency in political and public life. As Silvio Waisbord argues, "the paradox is that while aiming to shed light on political and economic practices, watchdog journalism facilitates the perpetuation of the politics of secrecy by which political wars are waged underhandedly."[46] The media thus takes part in a questionable behind-the-scenes market of leaks that leaves reporters prone to political manipulation.[47]

A second danger of *denuncismo* is the inflation of public expectations for justice, which makes any institutional response to the denunciation insufficient or inadequate.[48] The proliferation of media exposés turns the public sphere into a battleground for ferocious interelite confrontations, where a torrent of cross-accusations, rumors, and innuendos feeds the newsrooms while simultaneously fueling the outrage of public opinion.

Media Scandals and Social Accountability in Latin America

What does the analysis of the Senate scandal teach us about the workings of mechanisms of control? When can media scandals have a greater chance to positively contribute to the goals of the politics of social accountability? To productively contribute to the ongoing debate about the positive or negative effects of media exposés on political life, further empirical studies are needed to shed light on how different variables—the institutional quality of the mechanisms of accountability, the social organization of the media, the different actors and resources that participate in the drama of disclosure, and so on—affect the dynamics and outcomes of certain scandals. This would allow us to elaborate a typology of scandals containing phenomena that might very differently affect the agenda of democratic accountability. While further comparative research on the dynamics and outcomes of political scandals in the region is needed, some tentative conclusions about the workings of media exposés as a mechanism of accountability can be extracted from the analysis of the Senate scandal in Argentina.

The Senate scandal sheds light on the achievements and limitations of a certain subset of media exposés: those that are triggered by denunciations based on leaks provided by official sources. In the Senate scandal, two crucial elements were missing. On the one hand, the exposé relied on information provided by official sources and was thus dependent on the delivery of further leaks or evidence by elites or horizontal agencies. While there was a conscious effort to gather additional information on the part of the media and some horizontal agencies, these initiatives met the many obstacles that political elites pose to any form of independent inquiry that could make visible transgressions or wrongdoings. On the other hand, the societal leg of the controversy was missing due to the reluctance or inability of both Alvarez and the network of NGOs concerned with issues of accountability to build up mobilizational support from civil society, which could have exerted additional moral pressure on the political elites. The scandal generated widespread outrage in public opinion, but this outrage did not lead to a social movement or any other organized form of civic engagement.

In short, the scandal's contribution to the theory of social accountability is that it draws attention to the centrality that the process of information gathering has in determining the dynamics of the multiple conflicts that are taking place in many of the new democracies of the region between civil and political actors over the nature of the rules and mechanisms that constrain and regulate the practice of democratic representation.

NOTES

1. Andrei Markovits and Mark Silverstein, "Introduction: Power and Process in Liberal Democracies," in Andrei Markovits and Mark Silverstein, eds., *The Politics of Scandal: Power and Process in Liberal Democracies* (New York and London: Holmes and Meier, 1988), 6. Also see Theodore J. Lowi, "Foreword," in Markovits and Silverstein, *Politics of Scandal.*

2. Markovits and Silverstein, "Introduction," 9. See also Jeffrey Alexander, "Culture and Political Crisis: 'Watergate' in American Memory," in J. Alexander, ed., *Durkheimian Sociology* (Cambridge: Cambridge University Press, 1988), 187–224.

3. Lowi, "Foreword"; Alexander, "Culture and Political Crisis."

4. Benjamin Ginsberg and Martin Shefter, *Politics by Other Means: Politicians, Prosecutors, and the Press from Watergate to Whitewater* (New York and London: W. W. Norton, 1999).

5. Ginsberg and Shefter, *Politics by Other Means,* 16.

6. Ginsberg and Shefter, *Politics by Other Means,* 184.

7. John B. Thompson, *Political Scandal: Power and Visibility in the Media Age* (Cambridge: Polity Press, 2000); Fernando Jiménez, *Detrás del Escándalo Político: Opinión Pública, Dinero y Poder en la España del Siglo XX* (Barcelona: Tusquets Editores, 2002), and "Possibilities and Limits of Political Scandal as a Form of Social Control," *REIS* (English ed.), no. 96 (1996): 49–76.

8. Thompson, *Political Scandal,* 251.

9. Thompson, *Political Scandal,* 196.

10. Jiménez, "Possibilities and Limits," 54.

11. Thompson, *Political Scandal*, 267–68; Jiménez, "Possibilities and Limits."

12. Thompson, *Political Scandal;* Silvio Waisbord, *Watchdog Journalism in Latin America: News, Accountability, and Democracy* (New York: Columbia University Press, 2000); Fernando Lattman-Weltman, "Medios y Transición Democrática: La (des) Institucionalización del Panóptico en Brasil," paper presented at the conference Estrategias de Accountability Social en América Latina: Acciones Legales, Medios de Comunicación y Movilización (Universidad Torcuato Di Tella, Buenos Aires, Apr. 10, 2003).

13. See Guillermo O'Donnell, "Horizontal Accountability in New Democracies," in Andreas Schedler, Larry Diamond, and Mark F. Plattner, eds., *The Self-Restraining State: Power and Accountability in New Democracies* (Boulder: Lynne Rienner, 1999); and "Delegative Democracy," *Journal of Democracy* 5, no. 1 (1994). For similar arguments, see Francisco Weffort, "What Is a New Democracy?" *International Social Science Journal,* no. 136 (1993); and Laurence Whitehead, "The Alternative to 'Liberal Democracy': A Latin American Perspective," in David Held, ed., *Prospects for Democracy* (Cambridge: Polity Press, 1993). For two different critiques of such a diagnosis, see Adam Przewroski's contribution to this volume; and Enrique Peruzzotti, "The Nature of the New Argentine Democracy: The Delegative Democracy Revisited," *Journal of Latin American Studies* 33, part 1 (Feb. 2001): 140–41.

14. Enrique Peruzzotti, "Towards a New Politics: Citizenship and Rights in Contemporary Argentina," *Citizenship Studies* 6, no. 1 (2002); and "Civic Engagement in Argentina: From the Human Rights Movement to the 'Cacerolazos,'" paper presented at the Woodrow Wilson Center meeting of the Argentine Program (Buenos Aires, July 2002).

15. Enrique Peruzzotti and Catalina Smulovitz, "Accountability Social: La Otra Cara del Control," in Peruzzotti and Smulovitz, *Controlando la Política,* 23–52.

16. See Waisbord, *Watchdog Journalism.*

17. See Silvio Waisbord, "Bad News: Violence against the Press," paper presented at the conference of the Association for the Education in Journalism and Mass Communication (Baltimore, 1998).

18. Waisbord, *Watchdog Journalism,* 63.

19. Waisbord, *Watchdog Journalism,* 65.

20. For an analysis of the changes experienced by the model of representation in Argentina, see Enrique Peruzzotti, "Reshaping Representation: Argentine Civil and Political Society in the 1990s," paper presented at the conference Rethinking Dual Transitions: Argentine Politics in the 1990s in Comparative Perspective (Weatherhead Center for International Affairs and the David Rockefeller Center for Latin American Studies, Harvard University, Mar. 20–22, 2003).

21. Jiménez, "Possibilities and Limits," 60.

22. Lowi, "Foreword"; Silverstein and Markovits, "Introduction"; Jiménez, "Possibilities and Limits"; Thompson, *Political Scandals.*

23. Jiménez, "Possibilities and Limits," 65. Waisbord, *Watchdog Journalism,* is an exception.

24. See, e.g., Silvio Waisbord, "Interpretando los Escándalos: Análisis de su Relación con los Medios y la Ciudadanía en la Argentina Contemporánea," in Peruzzotti and Smulovitz, *Controlando la Política.*

25. See Catalina Smulovitz and Enrique Peruzzotti, "Societal and Horizontal Controls: Notes about a Fruitful Relationship," in Scott Mainwaring and Christopher Welna,

eds., *Democratic Accountability in Latin America* (Oxford: Oxford University Press, 2003); Jacqueline Behrend, "Mobilization and Accountability: A Study of Societal Control in the Cabezas Case in Argentina," paper presented at the Workshop on Societal Accountability (Buenos Aires, Universidad Torcuato Di Tella, Nov. 29–30, 2001).

26. For an analysis of watchdog journalism in Argentina, see Waisbord, "Interpretando los Escándalos"; and Heriberto Muraro, *Políticos, Medios, Periodistas* (Buenos Aires: Fondo de Cultura Económica, 1997).

27. Waisbord, "Interpretando los Escándalos," 315–20.

28. Juan María Maravall, "Accountability and Manipulation," in Adam Przeworski, Susan C. Stokes, and Bernard Manin, eds., *Democracy, Accountability, and Representation* (Cambridge: Cambridge University Press, 1999), chap. 5.

29. For a discussion of *denuncismo,* see Waisbord, *Watchdog Journalism,* 113 ff.; and Lattman-Weltman, "Medios y Transición Democrática."

30. In an off-the-record interview, Senator Cantarero stated: "We are all in these. . . . There were some idiots that spoke out simply because they were left outside of the deal" (*La Nación,* Aug. 30, 2000).

31. "Hay elementos concordantes, graves y precisos que el hecho el cual se califica como soborno, previsto en el codigo penal en su Articulo 256 con la última reforma, ha existido."

32. Those senators were Augusto Alasino, chair of the Peronist *bancada* in the Senate; Ricardo Branda; Ramón Ortega; and Angel Pardo. The final two senators had been implicated by Cafiero's statement to the judge.

33. See *La Nación,* Aug. 27, 2000.

34. For an account of the scandal from the perspective of two of its protagonists, see Joaquín Morales Solá, *El Sueño Eterno: Ascenso y Caída de la Alianza* (Buenos Aires: Editorial Sudamericana–*La Nación,* 2001), chap. 3; and Chacho Alvarez and Joaquín Morales Solá, *Sin Excusas* (Buenos Aires: Editorial Sudamericana–*La Nación,* 2002).

35. See Peruzzotti, "Reshaping Representation," and "Civic Engagement."

36. *La Nación,* Sept. 2, 2000.

37. See Hernán Charosky, "Honestos y Audaces: Realizaciones y Límites de la Política Anticorrupción," in Marcos Novaro, ed., *El Derrumbe Político en el Ocaso de la Convertibilidad* (Buenos Aires: Editorial Norma, 2002), 245–46.

38. A rumor had circulated, confirmed by Senator Cantarero in his "off-the-record" interview with *La Nación,* that the payments had been made by SIDE.

39. For a description of the role of the Anticorruption Office in the Senate scandal, see Charosky, "Honestos y Audaces," 223–51.

40. Markovits and Silverstein, "Introduction," 2.

41. On the links between the Senate scandal and the current crisis of representation, see Peruzzotti, "Reshaping Representation."

42. Waisbord, *Watchdog Journalism,* chap. 4, 93–118. See also Lattman-Weltman, "Medios y Transición Democrática"; and Gerardo Reyes, *Periodismo de Investigación* (Mexico: Editorial Trillas, 1996).

43. For a detailed description of the arms scandal in Argentina, see Daniel Santoro, *Venta de Armas, Hombres del Menem: La Investigación Periodística que Reveló el Escándalo del Tráfico a Ecuador y Croacia* (Buenos Aires: Planeta, 1998). For an analysis of the La Cantuta scandal in Peru, see Efraín Rua, *El Crímen de la Cantura* (Lima: ERS Ediciones, 1996).

44. Waisbord, *Watchdog Journalism,* 113.

45. Waisbord, *Watchdog Journalism,* 108.

46. Waisbord, *Watchdog Journalism,* 108–9.

47. In fact, there were numerous speculations regarding which political group was behind the political operation.

48. Lattman-Weltman, "Medios y Transición Democrática," 29.

10

Reading Scandals

SCANDALS, MEDIA, AND CITIZENSHIP IN CONTEMPORARY ARGENTINA

Silvio R. Waisbord

A FEW WEEKS after a cease-fire was declared in the 1995 Ecuador-Peru war, a scandal broke out in Argentina. Initial revelations that Argentine weapons had been sold to Ecuador flew in the face of what was publicly known about the involvement of the government in the war. Because Argentina was one of the guarantors of the 1942 peace treaty, the government had adopted a neutral position and made efforts to bring both countries to the negotiation table. Revelations suggested, however, that it had armed one of the parties at war. Early denunciations were found to be just the tip of the iceberg. In November 1995, the media revealed that the sale of seventy-five tons of armaments to Ecuador was actually a "minor business" of a larger operation: the sale of sixty-five hundred tons of weapons to Croatia in 1991. If the charges were true, the arms-dealing operations had violated the embargo imposed by the United Nations during the war in the Balkans.[1]

The Ecuadorian and Croatian sagas became part of a complex scandal with plenty of obscure details and topsy-turvy operations. If scandals usually beget other scandals, often rooted in cover-ups of original crimes, the arms scandal has not been the exception. The 1995 blast at an army ammunition site that killed seven people, wounded three hundred others, and destroyed several neighborhoods in the town of Rio Tercero was suspected of being linked to the arms scandal. Opposition representative Horacio Viqueira, one of the most outspoken legislators during the scandal, called it sabotage. It was speculated that the explosion was intended to eliminate traces that might have linked the disappearance of weapons from the site to the sale made to Croatia. The government affirmed that it was an accident. A number of seemingly unrelated deaths of military personnel and civilian professionals who had worked at the army arsenal provided more fodder for rumors about the elimination of witnesses who "knew too much" about the arms dealings. Lastly, revelations that Ecuador had actually paid $6 million for only $1.2 million worth of weapons spun another thread of the arms scandal.[2]

The press, some members of the opposition, and the prosecution accused the Ministries of Defense, the Economy, and Foreign Affairs, along with the armed forces, of having planned the sale of weapons and covering up the operations. The Carlos Menem administration rejected any responsibility. It offered assorted arguments to explain why Argentine weapons wound up on the battlefields of the Amazonian jungle and the Balkans. Originally, the government claimed that it had not sold weapons to either Croatia or Ecuador and ignored the fact that Argentine weapons had been used in the wars. President Menem asserted that the previous administration of Raul Alfonsín had sold the weapons. Then–defense minister Oscar Camilión suggested that the United Kingdom had actually sold weapons that had been taken from Argentine troops that surrendered in the 1982 Malvinas/Falklands war. Cabinet members stated that Fabricaciones Militares, the state-owned arms manufacturing company, had sold weapons to Venezuela and Panama through arms dealers and speculated that if the arms wound up in the wrong hands it was not the government's responsibility but rather the middlemen's. If illegal operations took place, officials argued, it was "behind our backs."

Several revelations, however, undermined the administration's efforts at stonewalling and detaching itself from the operations. The companies Debrol and Hayton Trade, which were mentioned in official documents as the mediators of the Panama and Venezuela deals, were found to be "rubber-stamp" organizations. The Venezuelan government categorically denied having purchased Argentine weapons and even threatened to break diplomatic relations. Judge Jorge Urso later concluded that Venezuela had never received weapons and that, instead, Ecuador had. Critics pointed out that Panama was an unlikely destination for the arms; it has not had an army since the 1989 U.S. invasion, and its police force doesn't need heavy weapons.[3] The newspaper *Clarín* threw a bombshell by publishing a decree signed by President Menem and several ministers approving the sale of weapons to Panama and Venezuela. *Clarín*'s coup was followed by revelations that President Menem and four cabinet members had signed three other secret decrees authorizing the shipments between 1991 and 1995. It was later made public that Federico Bartlett and Arturo Ossorio Arana, then the ambassadors to Croatia and Peru, respectively, had wired several communiqués to the Ministry of Foreign Affairs informing it about the presence of Argentine weapons in the Balkans and in the Amazonian war. These revelations disarmed official explanations and, as would be expected, angered the government, which continued maintaining its innocence.[4]

The arms scandals put in evidence the nature of the new media politics in Argentina, namely, the emergence of scandal news and scandal politics. By analyzing the arms scandals against the background of other domestic scandals, the goal of this chapter is to tease out the new dynamics of political communication. In doing so, this chapter also addresses broader themes that underlie the study of scandals in contemporary democracies: What are media scandals? Are scandals moments for public involvement and moral regeneration, as several studies have argued? What if scandals neither bring citizens into public life nor provoke massive public outrage? Are they scandals? Do scandals require scandalized publics? Are all scandals equal?

Models of Scandals

Answering these questions requires that we distinguish among different types of scandals. Not all scandals are equal. They are about different subjects, trigger different political and media processes, and elicit different public responses. Recent Argentine scandals can be classified into three categories that outline differences as well as elements shared in common.

The arms scandal fits the category of scandals that essentially deal with official corruption. The majority of the scandals that rocked the Menem government during its ten-year tenure, which was dotted with scandals, belong to this category.[5] The first scandal surfaced in 1991 when the newspaper *Página 12* revealed that then–U.S. ambassador Terence Todman had sent a letter to the government in which he accused a high-powered official of having asked the

U.S.-based Swift company for bribes to allow the import of machinery.[6] Months later, Amira Yoma (President Menem's sister-in-law and appointments secretary), her husband, and other associates were implicated in Yomagate, a scandal that involved drug-money laundering.[7] Shortly thereafter, two close aides to President Menem were implicated in the sale of rotten milk to a federal program for poor children. A scandal brought down the former head of the national social program for senior citizens after she was accused of receiving bribes from favored providers. A television exposé about the building of an oversized airstrip near President Menem's private residence triggered a short-lived scandal that was quickly terminated after the owner of the television station decided to cancel the news program. The IBM–Banco Nación scandal embroiled top executives of Argentina's national bank, with close links to government higher-ups, in charges of receiving kickbacks from IBM Argentina for approving a multimillion-dollar contract. Several judges were at the center of many scandals, accused of a host of crimes: protecting smugglers, bribes, extortion, and complicity in police corruption.

A second category of scandals foregrounds the violation of human rights: the murder of schoolgirl María Soledad Morales in the northwestern province of Catamarca; the death of army private Omar Carrasco; the assassination of news photographer José Luis Cabezas, who was investigating shady dealings between a businessman and government officials; and the bombing of the Israeli embassy and the AMIA, the headquarters of the Jewish Social Services Center. If scandals require the revelation of corruption, as political scientist Theodore Lowi states, these cases certainly fit the bill.[8] Authorities were suspected of involvement in murder, cover-ups, and the mishandling of subsequent investigations.

A third category of scandals typically involves tabloid stories featuring celebrities in trouble. A television diva was suspected of rigging her top-ranked game show. Soccer stars were accused of drug use and child molestation. A former boxing idol was found guilty of homicide.

This taxonomy suggests several characteristics of Argentine scandals. The first category includes typical scandals involving official crimes and misdemeanors, scandals that carry the suffix *gate,* such as Swiftgate, Yomagate, Milkgate, PAMIgate, and so on. Human rights scandals, instead, have not been dubbed *gates.* There was no "Catamarcagate," "Carrascogate," "Cabezasgate," or "AMIAgate," although officials were implicated in wrongdoing (murder, cover-ups, the mishandling of investigations) in all these scandals. *Gate* seems to be used to denominate only those scandals that fit the Watergate mold, that is, purely *affaires d'état* that involve government corruption and deceit but not ordinary citizens or human rights violations.

Another striking characteristic is that private companies have not been at the center of the many scandals of the 1990s. Considering that the Argentine economy experienced dramatic changes in that decade, in which dozens of state-owned companies were privatized and corruption was suspected in many cases of privatization, scandals did not break. Even the IBM–Banco Nación affair, which for the first time put a major global company in the scandal spotlight, mostly focused on the practices of government officials, internal rivalries, and connections between officials and IBM executives. News about high-politics battles virtually overshadowed business practices.

Sexual scandals have been almost absent. Rumors about the sexcapades of politicians generate jokes and parodies rather than scandalous news. The scandal involving Judge Norberto Oyarbide might be the exception. It featured the outing of a homosexual judge and his connection to a gay nightclub in an upper-middle-class Buenos Aires neighborhood. The broadcast of a security video showing Oyarbide half naked with another man unleashed a media frenzy that put male prostitutes and a gay bordello at the center of the scandal and led to predictable "sex, lies, and videotapes" headlines. This was not just a sexual affair; confrontations among police departments reportedly spurred the scandal. It was alleged that Oyarbide had protected police corruption and that police chiefs, in complicity with the brothel's owner, had blackmailed Oyarbide by leaking information and the video to the press. The Oyarbide scandal suggests that, in a homophobic society, heterosexual officials are spared sexual scandal, but homosexual officials might not be, especially when unidentified interests make X-rated videos available to ratings-minded television talk shows and voyeuristic audiences.[9]

All Scandals Are Media Scandals

What is distinctive about different types of scandals? Why are certain events unified under the term *scandal*? Scandals originate in the publication of information that contradicts what is publicly known about certain individuals and institutions. Scandals bring out duplicitous behavior. The arms scandal unfolded after it was reported that the government had been involved in actions that breached existing laws. The revelations pointed at Argentina's presumed two-faced position during the Ecuador-Peru war and the military conflict in the Balkans. Although Argentina apparently followed international rules and declared itself to be neutral, the government had violated laws. Scandals raise questions about public reputations, positions, and images that result from the exposure of information about misdeeds that had remained private. Scandals start when information comes out about someone having committed an act that contradicts legal and/or moral standards. Such information is no longer privy to a few individuals but becomes widely disseminated. Transgressions that have been known only to participants and accomplices must cross the threshold of publicity in order to become a scandal. In Argentina, cabinet members were involved in kickbacks and influence peddling, military officers in murder, and sports celebrities in drug use. But these violations only became scandals after the media publicized them.

To put it differently, wrongdoing isn't sufficient for scandals to break out; instead, the revelation of corruption is a necessary condition. Scandals broke even though courts later proved that suspects were innocent. Scandals do not need legal proof of corruption but, mainly, allegations that wrongdoing existed. Making corruption public is the defining element of scandals. In times when publicity is synonymous with mediated publicity, the media wield unmatched power in converting secret acts of wrongdoing into scandalous actions. If it is hard to imagine a scandal without media attention, this is because of the capacity of the media to produce and distribute information that reaches mass audiences.

Sociologist John B. Thompson has made a persuasive argument about the affinity between scandal and the media. Thompson writes, "the rise of mediated scandals is to some extent a product of the transformation wrought by the development of communication media. . . . Mediated scandals are intrinsically connected to the new forms of visibility and publicness created by the media. Mediated scandals arise when activities hitherto concealed are disclosed or made visible through the media: the media become the principal mechanism through which corruption is made visible to others."[10] Thompson offers a first approximation to understand the logic of scandal politics. Media publicity adds the spark that fires the gunpowder of corruption. Scandals presuppose visibility of illegal actions that were invisible, and the media gives visibility in today's large-scale societies. This is why all scandals are, essentially, media scandals.

The Argentine case offers sufficient evidence to support this argument. The rise of scandal politics would have been unthinkable without the growing centrality of the media in Argentine politics. The entering of expressions such as "media politics," "mediated candidates," and "mediated justice" into the country's political vocabulary attests to a process in which publicity has lately become associated with media attention.[11]

The process of mediatization has been partially the result of the explosion in the number of radio and television stations and the nationalization of the media. While most towns and cities had one or two television channels until the late 1970s, the remarkable growth of cable television has ushered in a different media environment. With a penetration rate of over 55 percent of television households, Argentina is the most cabled country in Latin America. Cable systems typically feature twenty-four-hour domestic and regional news services, which have paid relentless attention to different scandals. This has made it possible for Buenos Aires stations to become widely available throughout the Argentine territory, acting as the only truly national media. The multiplication of the number of radio stations has also contributed to a different media environment, one that puts in place an echo chamber for scandal news. Popular morning news shows, a staple of both AM and FM radio stations, offer nonstop news and commentary on daily events. Morning newspapers basically set the agenda for television and radio news. Although newspaper consumption has dropped considerably since the early 1980s, dailies still set the agenda for other media.

Since the return of democracy in the 1980s, the growth and nationalization of the media has overshadowed the role of political organizations that historically occupied the center of public life in Argentina as institutions for participation and involvement of citizens in public affairs. Whereas political parties, unions, and social movements formerly monopolized political life, the media has become the central political stage.[12] It controls access to the fishbowl of public life. It is the network that links together the public actions of different institutions. It offers outlets for going public. If early views hoped that democracy would strengthen traditional political institutions, the process has arguably fallen short of such expectations, instead heightening the centrality of the media as both arena and actor in the waging of political battles.

If arguments about the media having conquered public life in late capitalism have it right, scandals offer evidence of this process. Scandals might be understood along Habermasian lines as a manifestation of the media colonization of the public sphere and a public life that has fallen victim to manufactured publicity. No other institution can compete with the media as arbiters of publicity, deciding what acts of corruption and subsequent developments merit public attention. No public space can successfully compete with the media as the ringmaster of scandals. Societies come to know about the existence of scandals through the media.

Scandals might also illustrate the view that we live in a postmodern world in which mediated signs have replaced (political) reality and that politics has moved from traditional to mediated agoras.[13] Scandals appear to us as media events, as conclusive evidence that politics happens in mediated spaces and that the media, to use Murray Edelman's expression, construct the "political spectacles" of our time.[14] After all, scandals are fundamentally experienced, and become remembered, as media images. For example, John Dean during his congressional deposition and Richard Nixon saluting from the helicopter after resigning *are* Watergate; Oliver North raising his hand before a congressional committee and Ronald Reagan affirming not remembering conversations *are* the Iran-Contra scandals; Clinton wagging his finger denying sexual relations with Monica Lewinsky and their embrace during one of the president's public appearances *are* Zippergate. In Argentina, images of Sister Martha Pelloni (principal of the school María Soledad Morales attended and organizer of the "marches of silence"), Luis Tula and Guillermo Luque (found guilty of the murder), and the marches of silence became symbols of the scandal. Images of Amira Yoma and her fugitive husband turned into the symbol of Yomagate. A photograph of José Luis Cabezas that was plastered everywhere, media appearances by Alfredo Yabrán (the businessman suspected of being the intellectual author of the Cabezas murder), and images of news photographers marching in the streets and raising their cameras in remembrance of their murdered colleague became identifiers of the Cabezas scandal.

Publicity is what counts in scandals. Media inattention is tantamount to symbolic annihilation. Media images forge perceptions about the existence of scandals. Images of prosecutors and judges talking to reporters, witnesses scurrying through throngs of onlookers and camera crews, suspects sitting in congressional chambers, "man-in-the-street" interviews testing public reactions, and nonstop media appearances of commentators and pundits, as semioticians would have it, are signs of scandals. Headlines about the decisions of congressional committees and judges, reports and columns on the positions of the actors involved, and photos of public mobilizations also connote scandals.

Media coverage is the barometer that indicates the existence (or absence) of a scandal. If splashed in headlines, scandals seem present and relevant; if buried inside or ignored, scandals may be considered over. We know that a scandal may be on the verge of extinction when it is no longer front-page news and images of scandals become less frequent or disappear. Media absence determines that scandals may be moving into another phase, becoming a minor footnote in historical records or enshrined in a country's political memory. Media presence suggests that moribund scandals might be resurrecting. Scandals that refuse to die are precisely those that may not only persist in prosecutors' investigations but may be brought back to public attention by the media.

The media gives life to scandals in many ways. Media revelations are often at the genesis of scandals. Although the exact date of birth of the arms scandal is a matter of contention between the two leading Argentine newspapers, it is beyond a doubt that a news story gave the scandal its initial push. *La Nación* claims motherhood because it published a story on February 26, 1995, that revealed that there were suspicions in Peru that Ecuador had received Argentine weapons. The story didn't generate much reaction, and the newspaper abandoned the story in subsequent days.[15] *Clarín*'s version is that the scandal gained momentum only after the paper reported on March 6 that Argentina had sold weapons to Ecuador.[16] Although important, exposés and investigative reports might not be the media's main contribution to fanning the flames of scandals. It is not unusual for muckrakers to rake prosecutors' probes rather than to conduct independent investigations according to the orthodoxy of investigative journalism or to take the back seat after prosecutors and congressional investigations take the lead.[17]

Newspapers also contribute to scandals by setting the political temperature; editorials that exonerate or call authorities to resign indicate the position of influential voices. Although their impact might be limited among general readers, editorials, particularly during political crises, are mandatory reading for elites. It would be hard to conclude that *Clarín*'s call for the resignation of then–defense minister Oscar Camilión was directly responsible for bringing him down a few weeks later, but, coming from Argentina's largest and most influential daily, it should not be ignored as the expression of powerful actors.[18]

Aside from investigations and editorials, the media fundamentally injects life into a scandal by making visible the actions and words of different actors involved in a scandal. All scandals require the media to put the spotlight on individuals and processes. Media inattention unplugs the oxygen tank that scandals need to survive. So when cameras cover prosecutors and judges waving or talking to reporters, congressional hearings are fully televised or short snippets are included in newscasts, morning radio shows discuss and dissect recent developments, and rallies and vigils are broadcast, the media makes scandals real.

Without exposure in the Buenos Aires media, neither the murder of María Soledad Morales in Catamarca nor the death of Omar Carrasco in Neuquén would have become full-fledged scandals. The local media in these provinces have been historically close to local powers involved in the murders and do not have the reach of metropolitan news organizations. It was only after the latter drew attention to the murders, subsequent investigations, and public mobilizations that the dynamics of the scandals deeply changed. The scandal around the murder of news photographer Cabezas was different. The murder was likely to receive a great deal of media attention because it literally hit home for journalists and news organizations. Already sensitive about antipress violence in the aftermath of ninety disappeared reporters during the last military dictatorship and over one hundred registered attacks during the 1990s, journalists came together to condemn the murder and demand justice. For them, the murder was an attack on human rights and press freedom, an indication of the escalation of antipress attacks, and a macabre reminder of the worst years of state repression.

The importance of the media in the life of scandals becomes apparent in the symbolic politics waged to shape public opinion. Scandals, as sociologists Kurt Lang and Gladys Lang have argued, are "battles for public opinion." Symbols are key in the attempt to sway public opinion during scandals.[19] Col. Egberto Gonzalez de la Vega, who was charged in the arms scandal, knew that symbolic politics was at play when he decided to testify without military uniform, leaving the army "out of the scandal," as the press remarked. Symbolic politics was also at play when Gen. Martín Balza opted, instead, to wear his uniform when he gave his testimony to Congress.

Regardless of attire and other elements that communicate institutional belonging and cultural meaning, individuals themselves become symbols of corruption when under the media spotlight. This is why the Menem administration made efforts to dissuade Congress from calling cabinet members to testify in different causes. Media visibility, particularly in settings where scandals unfold (courtrooms, congressional chambers), immediately links individuals (and administrations) to a scandal. Businessman Alfredo Yabrán, no student of Roland Barthes, knew this principle of scandal politics perfectly when he warned journalists, "Taking a picture of me is like shooting me in the forehead."[20] Yabrán's comments correctly recognized that media publicity rapidly bridges the distance between being an anonymous citizen and being the symbol of scandal. An exasperated President Menem made a similar assumption when, in the middle of the Cabezas/Yabrán scandal, he lashed out, "The media have condemned Yabrán."[21] Only after the media relentlessly put attention on Yabrán, especially after he was suspected of having ordered the murder of Cabezas, did he become synonymous with the scandal. Likewise, former members of the Menem administration who had been accused of corruption amid high-profile scandals arguably became enshrined in the government's "hall of shame" even though most of them were never found guilty of any crime.[22]

Aware that media publicity is the surest shortcut between anonymity and scandal, forces interested in keeping a scandal alive fear that a scandal might fall silent in the media. Prosecutors leak information to friendly journalists and news organizations with the hope that their own investigations and decisions will become public. Parties interested in gaining political advantage want adversaries embroiled in wrongdoing to be in the media spotlight as much as possible. Televised hearings and other media events might simultaneously raise the visibility of adversaries as wrongdoers and of the opposition as corruption busters. This is why high-ranking government officials who are summoned to testify, if unsuccessful in invoking immunity, try to persuade prosecutors to accept written depositions and congressional committees to keep cameras out of hearings. President Menem, as a witness, chose to send a written deposition to prosecutor Carlos Stornelli. Even a short trip to prosecutors' offices, regardless of legal consequences, is likely to attract a media frenzy that could indelibly link an individual to a scandal. Television broadcasts of congressional hearings may have a similar effect. Consequently, keeping a low profile, which essentially means avoiding or having sporadic media appearances, might lower the chances of being publicly pegged to scandals.

Even when scandals disappear from the media's radar, and images of prosecutors and accused individuals become few and far between, it is still the media that warns readers that a scandal has not died and survives in judicial investigations. Many scandals do continue even after cameras have stopped hounding prosecutors and witnesses, experts on the case have vanished from television screens, and headlines show no traces of them. But when scandals have an afterlife beyond the media, it's still the media that has to remind citizens that scandals haven't died. We may ignore them, the media tell us, but they aren't gone.

In summary, because all scandals are media scandals, they offer evidence to support scholarly views that the media is the only institution endowed with the power to confer life in media-saturated societies and that the reality of scandals becomes what the media tell us about them.

Publicity and the Institutional Architecture of Scandals

The adoption of a media-centered approach to understanding scandals has important shortcomings, however. It runs the risk of being insufficiently political, of subsuming all scandals to media operations and decisions without addressing the politics that generate events and processes for media coverage. It minimizes the actions of a myriad of institutions that make scandals possible. No question, Congress, the judiciary, and mobilized publics depend on and crave media attention to gain wide presence during scandals, but the media are not self-sufficient in generating scandal stories.

Consider the evolution of the arms scandal. Judging from its media presence, the arms scandal hasn't maintained a regular pace since its beginning. It had a sputtering development, with high- and low-intensity media moments. If we take front-page news about the scandal, the landscape of media attention shows many peaks and prolonged valleys. Intrigued about this seesaw media pattern, I asked journalists, politicians, and the prosecutor who investigated the denunciations what the key moments of the arms scandal were between 1995 and 1998. Invariably, they pointed to the same events. Some were media exposés such as the publication of a telegram in which Ambassador Ossorio Arana told the Ministry of Foreign Affairs about the presence of Argentine weapons in the Ecuador-Peru war. Other events involved coverage of actors investigating the scandal, such as the decision of prosecutor Carlos Stornelli to charge twenty-two officials with illicit association and the public testimony given to Congress by Labor Minister Erman Gonzalez (who was defense minister at the time the weapons were sold to Croatia). These were media frenzies, but they certainly required other actors to be possible.

Here I suggest that scandals are emergent forms of political warfare that, depending on the type of scandal, feature different publics at battle. What the recent succession of scandals suggests is new forms of political action and communication in Argentine democracy. Scandals represent the convergence of different interests and actions rather than the isolated actions of one institution or individual. The figure of the lone scandalmonger who single-handedly puts into motion and sustains a scandal only makes sense in conspiratorial minds and in views that attribute to the media an all-powerful role, ignoring the fact that scandals require a certain institutional architecture.[23] The dynamics of scandals are institutionally located. Consequently, the analysis requires placing a network of institutions at the center. Individuals and individual institutions, as discussed below, do make a difference by spilling information and investigating allegations. In the arms scandal, broken loyalties (military officers who had been snubbed at the time of promotion decisions and civilian personnel of Fabricaciones Militares) seeded the ground for information leaks. But without institutions receptive to indiscretions and legal frameworks that facilitate the publication of secret affairs, the intentions and actions of single individuals and organizations run up against difficult hurdles. This is why scandals express the workings of "scandal machines."[24] For the wheels of scandal to run for a long time, one institution pouring gas into the machine isn't sufficient. A scandal is likely to have a short ride if only one institution or individual pumps the gas.

Which actors use scandals to engage in "politics by other means"?[25] Are elites and ordinary citizens equally active? Who is at the center of scandals? Answers to these questions depend on the type of scandal. The Argentine cases suggest that elites are the protagonists of scandals that deal with official corruption and scandals that deal with civil rights violations featuring elites and citizens. Political elites are at the center of high-politics scandals as information leakers, as well as carriers and targets of investigations: presidential aides, cabinet members, representatives, military commanders, and judges. Citizens rarely, if ever, enter such scandals. None of the stories on the arms scandals analyzed in *Clarín* and *La Nación* since 1995 mentioned "the public," even strategically by quoting or featuring opinion polls that could have legitimized the work of journalists.

Human rights scandals are different. Elites are present, but ordinary citizens are also present as sources of information and subjects of news. These scandals feature ordinary people as victims at the center of the story (a schoolgirl, an army private, a news photographer, and employees who died in bombings) and as witnesses, sufferers, and participants in public mobilizations.

Officials do not appear as involved in influence peddling and kickbacks, but as perpetrators of human rights violations and orchestrators of cover-ups.

In contrast to gatelike scandals, human rights scandals have generated intense and prolonged public mobilizations. They were the catalysts for the emergence of budding social movements concerned with the defense of civil rights. Heirs to the discourse of human rights organizations during the antidictatorial struggles in the 1970s and 1980s (such as the Mothers of Plaza de Mayo), these movements similarly raised issues of truth and justice. Their forms of public mobilization and display, "marches of silence" and candlelight vigils to demand investigation and justice, also showed the influence of earlier human rights organizations. The latter's legacy was also visible in the central place that the issue of memory had during the scandals. The place at the roadside where the body of María Soledad was found became a makeshift memorial where citizens congregated in remembrance of the murder. (It was reported that it had more visitors than the sanctuary of the local Virgin.) "Don't forget Cabezas" became the rallying cry of journalists after the Cabezas murder. In the aftermath of the bombings of Jewish institutions, the organization "Memoria Activa" (Active Memory) was formed to remember the attacks.[26] And, as in earlier human rights struggles, women played a central role in the organization of citizens, and families and young people participated in mobilization efforts.

Scandals that deal with official corruption, like the arms scandal, almost inevitably originate in elite machinations. Only elites are likely to have sensitive information about state secrets and illegal operations. Only elites have fluid access to newsrooms and are capable of attracting reporters' curiosity. Ordinary citizens are unlikely to be responsible for setting high-politics scandals in motion. The power of elites lies in their power as newsmakers; citizens, in contrast, are mostly powerless in getting media attention.[27] Presidents, cabinet members, judges, prosecutors, and members of Congress not only are the subject of news but also provide raw information to newsrooms that manufacture news. The arms scandal shows not only that newsmakers attract media attention but that they might also direct it to specific transgressions in which they are interested.

Reporters observe that because neither Congress nor the judiciary was particularly active during 1996 and 1997, there was less news about the arms scandal. The decision of prosecutor Carlos Stornelli to launch an all-out investigation in March 1998, along with the decision of some members of the opposition to carry out further investigations, put the wind behind the sails of the scandal, and consequently, more news became available. A sample of two front pages a week in *Clarín* and *La Nación,* Argentina's most influential dailies, shows evidence in support of this conclusion. After having received a great deal of media attention in late 1995 and early 1996, particularly during the events that led to the resignation of then–defense minister Oscar Camilión, the scandal as news story virtually vanished. The arms scandal was in the headlines only once during 1997. The Cabezas/Yabrán scandal, and to a lesser degree the AMIA investigation, the María Soledad Morales trial, and other minor affairs, were regular scandalous news. The arms scandal found new media life in mid-1998.

What sustained the arms scandal during its four-year life was the conformation of a three-legged institutional structure formed by the judiciary, Congress, and the media. Scandals might not necessarily need to enter the public conversation to have a long life, as media scholar Elizabeth Bird has suggested.[28] Except for a few sporadic moments, the arms scandal did not dominate public discussions, but different powerful actors remained interested enough to keep it alive. Whereas prosecutors did not aggressively pursue charges and were suspected of mishandling investigations and protecting suspects in other scandals, prosecutor Carlos Stornelli carried the investigation forward and openly confronted General Balza and the government. Stornelli was the target of the president's ire and of attempts to isolate and/or remove him, particularly after he charged several officials with illicit association in October 1998. Journalists, some legislators, most federal prosecutors, and the three members of the Second Federal Chamber, where the case was located, strongly supported him.

The work of a few representatives of the Unión Cívica Radical and the Frepaso, the two leading opposition parties in Congress, was important, too. These parties repeatedly called attention to the scandals and made calls for wide-ranging hearings. Their efforts ran against the Peronist-dominated Congress, which stonewalled proposals for hearings. The opposition did not solidly rally behind the petition for investigations, however. Some observers speculate that members of the opposition, convinced that they would win in the 1999 presidential election, were disinclined to wage an all-out investigation and instead opted to keep the issue on the political back burner. One was quoted as saying that "it's easier that everything remains the same. . . . Nobody wants to make a decision about such a sensitive matter as who will succeed [army chief] Balza in an election year."[29] The calls made by some representatives demanding that the charges be fully investigated met with lukewarm support or indifference from prominent fellow party members. Whereas some representatives raised suspicions about the role of army commander General Balza in the operations, others rushed to his defense and supported him during his deposition in Congress. Former president Raul Alfonsín advised fellow party representatives: "He's the best thing the government has. Take care of him."[30] The timing of intra-Peronist battles also dictated the tempo of the investigations. Open confrontations between President Menem and Governor Eduardo Duhalde over the nomination of candidates for the 1999 presidential ticket trickled down to Congress. Duhalde loyalists repeatedly sent threatening signals, warning Menemistas that if their leader was not at the top of the ticket, they would push for wide congressional hearings (which would certainly embarrass Menem's cabinet members).[31]

A Journalist's "Hell of a Story"

The combined efforts of members of Congress and the judiciary were key to prolonging the life of a scandal that, many times, seemed like it would go away. Most of their efforts were devoted not just to investigations but to media publicity of alleged crimes. Prosecutor Stornelli and Representative Viqueira have both observed that without the press, the scandal would have died long ago.[32]

Why did media organizations chase the story? In Argentina, where publishers have been inseparable from larger political battles and exercised unmistakable influence, editorial politics are always suspected of prompting news companies to cover specific stories about wrongdoing.[33] But understanding the actual motives that prompt newspapers and newscasts to follow or ignore scandals is not easy. The political and journalistic grapevines are full of speculations about why certain news organizations stress or downplay scandals. From personal vendettas to business dealings, from political sympathies to arm-twisting politics, the range of speculations is huge. It is almost impossible to find solid evidence to account for dissimilar interests and positions among news organizations, however.

What is remarkable about the arms scandal is that, unlike previous scandals in which one newspaper "owned" a story and carried out much of the investigation, the three most influential Buenos Aires newspapers have all covered the story. Moreover, they have maintained attention to the scandal for a long period of time. *Clarín* turned into the flag bearer of the scandal by throwing several punches at the government and giving the story ample space. After having extensively covered the murder of Omar Carrasco, a scandal that also shook military hierarchies, *La Nación* devoted substantial coverage to the arms scandal. *La Nación* editor Jorge Urien Berri observes that the story was of great interest to military personnel and lawyers, who are some of the paper's core readers.[34] *Página 12* also covered the scandal, although it confronted several problems. Working for a newspaper that had repeatedly pounded on the government, the armed forces, and the judiciary, its reporters lacked fluid contacts with sources in those institutions who would have offered exclusive information.[35] Moreover, by the time *Página 12* found its niche, *Clarín* and *La Nación* had already crowded the field of news coverage. The arms scandal was unlike previous scandals in which *Página 12* was the leading and, often, the solitary newspaper in search of sensitive information.

Editorial agendas, however, don't entirely explain why news organizations cover news scandals. Scandal stories also need to be journalistically appealing. They need to have elements that fit the conventions of newsrooms and appeal to the culture of journalism. If a scandal is a "hell of a story," as has been observed, it is, above all, a journalist's "hell of a story."[36]

News about official wrongdoing enjoys a substantial advantage over other news about wrongdoing because it fits standard journalistic principles about the newsworthiness of official actions. The arms scandal involved a coterie of officials who fit the cast of characters from *All the President's Men.* If cabinet members, ambassadors and foreign attachés, military chiefs, and members of the judiciary and Congress are typically the subjects of news, they are more so when they are in trouble, fire accusations, offer justifications, contradict themselves, are caught red-handed, and so on.

Scandal news is not like any other news. Few other types of news have a similar capacity to induce an adrenaline rush in the newsroom and send journalists into a frenzy. Reporters frantically anticipate the possibility of finding juicy tidbits, and editors reshuffle resources and newsholes. The pulse of newsrooms goes faster, particularly on days when what newsrooms deem to be explosive revelations are publicized. Scandals offer plenty of opportunities to drop bombshells as testimony of good reporting. Scandal news offers the opportunity to achieve professional notoriety. For a journalistic culture that prizes knocking down cabinet members and presidents as measures of professional achievement, the arms scandal was obviously attractive. It embroiled several ministers and high-ranking military officers in a web of corruption and offered the latent possibility of high-impact journalistic coups.

Scandal news is, like war coverage or investigative stories, a kind of news that offers an opportunity for a reporter to make a name for him- or herself.

Professional credentials may be determined by how colleagues evaluate an individual's performance in a high-profile scandal story. Professional names can be made (or unmade) with the coverage of scandal news. The arms scandals were to *Clarín*'s Daniel Santoro what Watergate was for Bob Woodward and Carl Bernstein. His coverage earned him the Rey de España award, one of the most prestigious awards for journalists in the Spanish-speaking world, granted annually by the king of Spain, Juan Carlos I. This definitely catapulted him higher in the world of Argentine journalism. What fellow colleagues consider a job well-done might become the aura that follows a reporter wherever he or she goes. A reporter might become forever associated with coverage of one scandal.

Scandals not only stroke professional egos but also certify credentials. Among journalists, such concerns are more present than whether scandal stories reap higher sales and ratings for their employers. In Argentine newsrooms, which are increasingly governed by the culture of professional journalism, prestige and monetary incentives have recently become more important.[37] Still, journalists need to be mindful of editorial lines and reactions to stories among the upper brass. Reporters who covered the arms scandal often had to balance their interest in the story with editorial positions, carving out spaces and pushing boundaries to get stories through, knowing that their organizations were under continuous pressure from identified and unidentified interests to kill the stories.

The arms scandal offered sufficient elements to be a journalist's dream story, particularly for those immersed in military topics. It was about intrigue, backstabbing, double-crossing, and wrongdoing in high places. It featured a cast lifted out of a John Le Carre potboiler: high government officials, military officials, intelligence agents, and arms dealers involved in a complex operation in which tons of arms and millions of dollars changed hands. It was a circuitous story that left an extensive paper trail including contracts; presidential decrees; documents about ghost companies; and reports by intelligence services in Argentina, Croatia, Ecuador, and Peru. As a thriller without a known finale, the scandal had unexpected twists that made it journalistically irresistible. What started as an investigation about an apparently small arms-dealing operation turned into a far-reaching scandal.

The publication of a smoking gun, a presidential decree authorizing the sale of weapons, also stimulated journalistic interest. Secret documents that peg President Menem to the arms dealings, even though he ducked any responsibility, gave the scandal a unique twist. No hard evidence linking him to the alleged crimes of members of his administration had been published in previous scandals. Instead, the availability of documents with his signature fed the rumor mill and speculations about—to paraphrase one of Watergate's for-the-history-books phrases—what the president knew and when he knew it.

The fact that the scandal was peppered with high-noon political drama provided even more attractive elements. Resignations and congressional hearings are not just news events; they offer attractive news hooks. Former defense minister Oscar Camilión and air force commander Juan Paulik resigned in 1996 after Judge Urso charged them with malfeasance. Former Fabricaciones Militares executives Luis Sarlenga and Edberto González de la Vega were criminally processed. Prosecutor Stornelli called two other ministers to testify, Foreign Affairs Minister Guido Di Tella and Labor Minister Erman Gonzalez (defense minister at the time the weapons were sold to Croatia). Army commander Martín Balza was also in the eye of the scandal's hurricane. Stornelli charged him with illicit association, misappropriation of weapons, and altering public documents. The prosecutor concluded that Balza couldn't have ignored the fact that army weapons were missing and had wound up in countries at war. Col. Diego Palleros, the head of the arms-dealing company Hayton Trade, was charged, then fled to South Africa. After a two-year silence, his declaration to a *Clarín* reporter that "the government knew about the sale [of weapons]" not only reverberated in political circles but also found newsrooms salivating for more shocking statements.[38]

If all these elements weren't sufficient to make the Pavlovian newsrooms drool, persistent rumors about the linkages between several deaths and the scandal were the cherry on top of a mouthwatering story. Foul play was suspected in the explosion of the Rio Tercero ammunition site in November 1995.[39] The October 1996 crash of the helicopter carrying former Fabricaciones Militares director Gen. Juan Carlos Andreoli and the former military attaché in Lima (who had notified military authorities about the existence of Argentine weapons in the Ecuador-Peru war) spurred rumors.[40] The heart attacks that killed Vicente Bruzza and Francisco Callejas, both of whom were civilian technicians at the army arsenal that exploded, also fueled speculations. And in the context of previous and subsequent suicides that the press had skeptically received, the death of navy captain Horacio Estrada in August 1998 was also followed by a flurry of gossip and conspiracy theories.[41] Fugitive arms dealer Col. Diego Palleros had mentioned Estrada as someone who was familiar with the operations. Although the death was officially declared a suicide, the press smelled a rat and second-guessed the coroner. It reported that the gun had been in his right hand (Estrada was left-handed) and that, according to the testimonies of several relatives and friends, Estrada hadn't seemed particularly distressed or shown suicidal tendencies. Pornographic videos and a bottle of champagne found in Estrada's apartment added yellow color to a story made in tabloidland.

So Many Denunciations, So Little Outrage

The arms scandal was a great story for journalism. A journalist's "hell of a story" might be the public's yawn, however. Argentine scandals suggest a similar scenario; what gets journalists rubbing their hands together with anticipation might not excite citizens. What for journalists might be significant moments in the life of the republic and high peaks in the history of the press might be media static for citizens.

Journalists admit that the arms story was not a best-seller or a subject of intense public conversation.[42] Although the scandal made evident inner dynamics in the functioning of political power and brought along plenty of sensational elements to satisfy diverse media appetites, it did not elicit wide attention, let alone electrify the public. It basically remained, as journalists have observed, a story for reporters, too much of an insider's story. Readers have not gathered around newsstands anxiously waiting for breaking news, nor has the scandal made ratings go through the roof.

Several indicators of public opinion confirm such impressions. The arms scandal held a different priority in the minds of journalists than it did in the public mind. Opinion polls show that citizens did not seem particularly interested in the scandal. Public mobilizations, a traditional form of the expression of public opinion in Argentine politics, did not take place. Unlike human rights scandals, in which rallies and vigils were organized and deeply affected the course of the scandals, citizens did not take to the streets to petition for investigation and resignations. Neither political parties nor other political and civic associations urged citizens to mobilize. Nor did citizens inundate their representatives with letters and phone calls to demand specific actions. Granted, such forms of public action are still rare in Argentine politics, but even minimal changes could have suggested growing public interest. In sum, there were no visible signs to suggest that the arms scandals struck a chord that would prompt public interest and actions. If citizens were outraged at the revelations, they kept their discontent private.

Is the seeming lack of public interest in the arms scandal a sign of political apathy, of citizens absorbed in private pursuits rather than in public life? The fact that the arms scandal did not visibly irritate the public can hardly be considered conclusive evidence of an apathetic public. By the same measure, the mobilizations of thousands of citizens during the scandals that unfolded after the murders of María Soledad Morales, Omar Carrasco, and José Luis Cabezas, and the bombings of the Israeli embassy and the headquarters of the Jewish Social Services Center, suggest the opposite, a highly active and participatory citizenry that takes action and manifests opinions through different forms of public display.

Neither set of cases offers grounds to conclude that "citizens are passive" or "citizens are active." Instead of reaching for blanket conclusions, it is necessary to analyze why specific scandals spark (or fail to spark) public interest and action and what public chords they strike. Scandals need to be analyzed on two levels: as occasions for citizenship (audiences-as-citizens) and as media events (citizens-as-audiences). Let me turn to considering these levels.

Scandal Fatigue

As a news story that reflects aspects of the state of Argentine democracy, the arms scandal did not evince much excitement among audiences-as-citizens. Prosecutor Stornelli rhetorically asked, "Where's the public reaction? When the Supreme Court tried to take away the case [from Judge Urso], there was no indignation, no scandal."[43] The scandal covered the same ground already tilled by a long list of scandals about government corruption: officials abuse public positions for private gain. What was new about the arms scandal that Argentines had not heard before? In the aftermath of scandals that hammered home the idea that officials line their pockets with public monies, it is possible that the public grew jaded and lost enthusiasm for scandalous news. Considering that large segments of the public seem convinced that politicians are corrupt, as opinion polls reflect, should it be surprising that scandals about newly discovered webs of corruption hardly scandalize anyone?[44] Scandals require the publicity of information that contradicts widely held ideas about individuals; the clash between previous and new opinions breeds scandalous reactions. So unless stories are about someone who was widely perceived to be honest and reputable, should citizens be scandalized when media stories confirm what they already suspect?

In Argentina, mediated corruption has become so ubiquitous that it hardly scandalizes large segments of the public. Its effect, or lack thereof, can be understood along the lines of Keith Tester's argument about the incapacity of the media to build a sense of moral solidarity, because terrible events are so visible on television screens and in newspapers that audiences are desensitized.[45] Tester finds philosopher Richard Rorty's position that the media can successfully operate as a channel for the transmission of moral solidarity to be improbable. Through the media, millions of citizens are familiar with the calamities that affect fellow humans but are seemingly unsusceptible to so much suffering. The repetition of images of human tragedies and the spectacularization of people's suffering strip them of any moral significance. What is apparently morally important becomes debased of any moral power. More visibility makes such images less likely to elicit compassionate feelings. Inundated by images of famine, devastation, and war, citizens do not make a leap to develop moral bonds with other human beings. The media does not motivate people to act; instead, it has an anesthetic effect. The result is "compassion fatigue," a permanent sense of dèjá vu among overstimulated and bored audiences inattentive to new images of suffering.[46]

Tester provides elements to understand the inability of scandals to stir citizens' blood. The silence during the arms scandal suggests "scandal fatigue" among Argentines. It did not visibly enrage vast numbers of the public partially because previous scandals might have been too successful at instilling the sentiment that corruption is widespread. How can new scandals shake citizens seemingly numbed by ceaseless revelations? The sedimentation of scandals telling similar stories and raising identical morality tales results in the banalization of corruption. Because it is so common, according to the media, it has become banal, hardly a matter of public outrage.

A scenario of "scandal fatigue" raises questions about the place of morality in scandals. Scandals, we are told, are basically about morality, about moral lapses, about individuals who cross expected ethical boundaries and violate shared moral standards.[47] Political scientist Carolyn Funk writes, "scandal is the shorthand for publicized behaviors by a politician that are in conflict with society's moral standards."[48] Scandals feature outraged publics that find certain behaviors morally offensive. Read through a Durkheimian glass, they are moments of social cohesion and regeneration. By outing and stigmatizing deviant behavior and purging corrupt individuals from the political system, scandals reinforce social mores and reaffirm the social order. Scholars Andrei Markovits and Mark Silverstein offer a clear example of this view: "Invariably, scandals serve to strengthen the community's *collective conscience* [italics in the original]. In addition to reaffirming and ultimately strengthening the bonds of a common morality, scandals help to create the scapegoats, enemies and pariahs needed by all communities. . . . The ritual of scandal and punishment provides social systems with a means for self-legitimization and purification. Scandals, in short, constitute an important opportunity for reaffirming the social order."[49]

If citizens are not always revolted (or do not always express such feelings publicly), can scandals be interpreted as moments for social integration? A proposition central to media audience studies offers an alternate way to deal with this question: the meaning of the text is not identical with the meaning that audiences draw from texts. Because audience reception is selective and multiple interpretations are possible, meaning lies in the unique engagement between audiences and texts. Considered as media events, scandals also offer separate textual and audience levels. The texts of scandals might outline moral boundaries, but audiences might get a quite different message. Newspaper exposés or speeches lambasting corruption do offer neat lessons in morality, drawing clear boundaries between right and wrong. The language of outrage that permeates media exposés does not invariably translate into outraged publics, however.[50] The lessons that different publics draw from scandals might be completely different. They might not draw any at all or become deeply involved. They might be mostly inattentive to stories and only pay perfunctory attention to developments. They might be unmoved by loud expressions of outrage. They might find reported behaviors morally reprehensible but decide to keep their feelings private.

So, particularly in the context of "scandal fatigue," if diverse publics react differently to scandals, should scandals necessarily be interpreted as civic teachings in morality and engines of social integration? If citizens seem desensitized to the arms scandal, does scandal news effectively outline moral boundaries and reaffirm ethical standards? Perched on Durkheim's theory, we might conclude that the cascade of scandals in contemporary Argentina, scandals that gobble each other up and rarely find closure, is the expression of a society deeply concerned about morality and in the midst of a process of moral regeneration. But the silence of citizens during "gate" scandals (such as the arms scandal), widespread feelings of nihilism, and the lack of legitimacy of political institutions hardly indicate moral regeneration in progress. Such scandals suggest, instead, the inclination among political elites to resort to media politics to battle each other out, rather than a society deeply concerned with morality. And politics, rather than moral crusading and ethical cleansing, drives elites to push and sustain scandals.

It would be mistaken, however, to draw the opposite conclusion: moral laxitude dominates, and a state of postmorality is pervasive. Human rights scandals offer evidence that citizens do find certain acts morally objectionable and make their outrage public by mobilizing in demand of truth and justice. Citizens seem to recover from "scandal fatigue" when they feel that certain acts affect them. This is why different publics responded so passionately to news about the violation of human rights and, at best, paid casual attention to the arms scandal. Human rights–related scandals created and/or directly touched existing constituencies and featured many "participatory moments."[51]

The murder of María Soledad Morales initially touched relatives and schoolmates but later evolved into an issue that galvanized large sectors of the population, who marched in the thousands. María Soledad, as she became nationally known, could have been anyone's daughter, dreaming of becoming a model and involved with a married man. In a country where the abuse of army privates is legendary, the death of Omar Carrasco was followed by demonstrations near the military garrison where his body was found and in the rest of the country. He could have been anyone's son or friend abused by army authorities. News about the cold-blooded murder of news photographer José Luis Cabezas spread like a brushfire in newsrooms sensitive to endless episodes of antipress violence and ignited massive demonstrations and actions by journalists. For journalists, the brutal murder of a colleague meant that all were targets; banners in rallies read "We are all Cabezas." And against the background of a long history of anti-Semitic acts, the bombings of the Israeli embassy and the Jewish Social Services Center were one-two punches that went directly to the heart of the Jewish community. The bombings left no doubt that the Jewish community was (and remained) the intended victim. Barricades cordoning off Jewish institutions (schools, yeshivas, temples) to minimize the possibility of car bombs became ominous reminders of a community under siege.

The arms scandal neither directly affected a community of citizens nor generated a constituency. The murders of María Soledad Morales, Omar Carrasco, José Luis Cabezas, and hundreds of people at the bombings, instead, were both personal tragedies for relatives, friends, colleagues, and schoolmates and issues of significance, proximity, and currency to citizens who mobilized to demand justice. The murders were not old stories but current events that resonated with the lives of ordinary people and citizens concerned about power abuses. Doubtless, the arms scandal is an issue of relevance to all Argentines as members of a national political community. It is about the administration of public resources. Public monies were assigned to a state-owned company to produce armaments, and supposedly, profits were made out of the sale of weapons. It is also about the legal and ethical dimensions of the behavior of public officials who, apparently, took advantage of public office for private gain and violated national and international laws. If confirmed to be true, the intentional explosion of an army ammunition depot and the murder of several individuals glaringly violate fundamental laws and basic ethical principles. The question is not whether Argentina sold weapons, which some citizens might repudiate, but what the transactions reflect about the workings of Argentine democracy. Citizens, however, might not perceive that any of these issues affect their lives or, if they do, might opt not to publicly mobilize to express their opinions.

A Boys-with-Toys Story

Scandals affect not only audiences-as-citizens but also citizens-as-audiences. Do citizens avidly follow scandals because they are concerned about the health of the republic? Or are they interested in being amused by peeking into the antics and lives of the rich and famous? Some scandals might be the best show in town for media audiences; others touch off public mobilization because they affect people as citizens.

When the boundaries between news and entertainment are continuously blurred, scandals as media events are news and entertainment. We lose sight of important dimensions of scandals if we presume that those that have citizens glued to their television sets are of immediate concern to them only (or mainly) as members of a political community. This might be true, but why not contemplate the possibility that attention-grabbing scandals are good, entertaining stories that captivate audiences? In media narratives, the subject, the characters, the plot, the action, and other dramatic elements are greatly important in determining the kind of audience attention scandals receive. What is the story about? Whose story is it? Who tells the story? What dramatic elements are presented? What audiences might find the story interesting?

Except for fans of high-politics news, the arms scandal hasn't been a terribly interesting story. Who but military personnel and specialists can find stories packed with details about rifles, cannons, and mortars to be pleasurable reading? Who but news junkies can follow a Russian-doll news story that holds scandals inside scandals and multilayered sagas? Who but legal connoisseurs can keep track of three judicial causes and understand stories full of legalese?[52]

If the subject was not of tremendous interest to most audiences, neither were the individuals at the center of the scandal. All scandals tend to focus on individuals rather than on institutions.[53] Affairs involving political (and other) celebrities are likely to attract more attention than those implicating ordinary citizens. The cast of characters in the arms scandal lacked political personalities, populated by peripheral politicos and military officers. Even the cabinet members involved hardly fit the mold of political celebrities, lacking what journalists call "sellable" angles. It was a heavily masculine narrative centered on boys-with-toys in trouble.

Low entertainment value sets the arms scandal apart from previous high-politics scandals that featured individuals who straddled the boundary between hard and soft news, made front-page news in political and entertainment magazines, and had a weakness for appearing in all media. Former interior minister Jose Luis Manzano, who resigned amid revelations of corruption, was the target of political reporters and paparazzi. Maria Julia Alsogaray, the presidential appointee who spearheaded the privatization of the telephone company and was caught in a scandal, was featured on the cover of a newsweekly scantily dressed and frolicking with show-biz divas. President Menem's telegenic and attractive sister-in-law was at the center of Yomagate. President Menem has often been both applauded and criticized for being a media "crossover" politician. Equally at ease at cabinet meetings and discotheques, rallies and resorts, official ceremonies and offshore competitions, Menem himself has been a typical subject of serious news and tabloid news. His low profile during the arms scandal, one journalist observed, took away an element that could have made the scandal more interesting to various audiences.[54]

The narrative of the arms scandal can be understood by setting it against the dominant narratives of human rights scandals. The latter had melodramatic structures with stock characters who stood for moral polarities. There were heroes and villains representing virtue and vice, right and wrong, power and powerlessness. Do-gooder María Soledad, her lower-middle-class family, and humble Sister Pelloni were pitted against María Soledad's cheating lover Luis Tula; rogue Guillermo Luque (the son of a local representative); and the Saadis, a political dynasty that had ruled the province for four decades (some of its members were suspected of a cover-up). Mild-mannered private Omar Carrasco and his poverty-stricken family were pitted against contemptuous military officers and immoral judges. Big-hearted and well-intentioned news photographer José Luis Cabezas was pitted against corrupt police officers, corrupt politicians, and a corrupt all-powerful businessman. The victims of the bombings at Jewish institutions and their families were pitted against a two-faced government and questionable investigators, police, and intelligence services.

Instead, the arms scandal was a drama of the court, not of commoners. The plights of unknown court members hardly resonate with audiences. There are no ordinary victims as protagonists with whom audiences could identify. The blast at the army arsenal had many ordinary victims, but they were not at the center of the scandal, nor did they receive extensive coverage.[55] The absence of victims (except for the seldom invoked figure of the abstract citizen victimized by corrupt officials) lessened the potential emotional appeal of a scandal full of imperturbable, straight-faced officials. The María Soledad scandal, in contrast, featured quite a different cast. María Soledad was Laura Palmer to the local Twin Peaks. The fact that the tabloid newsweekly *Gente* devoted plenty of attention to the scandal indicates that it was not just hard political news. The story "That Night It Was Me or María Soledad" featured one of her schoolmates spilling details about the orgies that the sons of the powerful organized, in which they drugged and abused girls from poor families. Another story provided morbid details about María Soledad's corpse. In an interview, Sister Maria Pelloni accused the local elite of murder and the bishop of hiding the truth. The high expectations generated by the trial in 1996 suggested that this was not just another scandal involving stuffy and obscure officials but one that had an audience-grabbing plot and characters who could perfectly compete with afternoon soap operas and bring in new audiences.

The arms scandal did not unleash wide reaction either as a public issue or as a media story. As a public issue, it did not tap into the typical concerns of most citizens. It was situated far from most people's lives in comparison with other "gate" scandals, such as the one that involved the head of the national program for senior citizens in kickbacks and influence peddling. The latter tapped into the preoccupations of a large number of citizens, who either personally or through relatives depend on that program for health care and other basic needs. The arms scandal, instead, is a quintessential *cause d'état* that, although it competed for the public interest, did not attract public interest.

As a media story, it was a magnet for journalists but lacked narrative elements that could have attracted large audiences. It squarely fit the frames and format of "serious news" consumed by the "attentive public." It did not offer any angles that might have pushed it to straddle "quality journalism" and "other news."[56] Nor was it part of an "audience-building strategy" by the tabloid media, a strategy that has turned business news into scandals in the British media.[57] No riveting courtroom drama, no ordinary victims who touched citizens-as-audiences, no female protagonists, no melodrama that crystallizes moral polarities. Scandals that deal with matters of public interest (such as the abuse of public office and the cover-up of crimes) might not have wide repercussions without human-interest storylines. Scandals that feature staple themes of tabloids (such as dramas of political celebrities, the plights of ordinary citizens in extraordinary situations) have added value that appeals to citizens-as-audiences uninterested in hard news about political elites.[58]

The different reactions to the arms scandal, excitement in political circles and newsrooms and indifference among citizens, indicate that different publics experience scandals differently. If we only look at media hype, we might get a distorted view of scandals. "Gate" scandals are typically cause celebres of political elites and journalists. They do not require either citizens to burst out or to be long-lasting events; instead, they need powerful actors with media access to fan the flames. Citizens-as-audiences might follow them and even express outrage at revelations, but unless they become audiences-as-citizens they often remain "phantom publics." In contrast, scandals that directly affect ordinary citizens as members of small and large political communities engender different political dynamics. When they cross media boundaries, straddling "quality" and "tabloid" news, they are able to engage a diversity of publics removed from and uninterested in high politics. They also show that, at least momentarily and around specific issues, even "scandal-fatigued" audiences recover and become citizens mobilized to demand accountability and justice. The contrast between these two categories tells us that scandals neither are made equal nor are similarly linked to questions of citizenship and morality. "Gate" scandals have been the subject of media frenzies and triggered high-politics action and gossip but have largely remained the white noise of contemporary Argentine democracy. Instead, nothing has lately sounded more powerfully than mobilized publics outraged at violations of civil rights and at official responsibility and duplicity in the murders of ordinary citizens.

NOTES

1. It was reported that the first shipment, aboard a Croatian ship, one of a total of four transporting two hundred containers with weapons, left Buenos Aires in Sept. 1991. An unconditional ally of the United States, the Argentine government had supported Croatia in the conflict and its struggle for independence and participated in peace-keeping activities. Argentina was the first Latin American country to recognize Croatia's independence. Whether Argentina equipped Croatia with the green light of the U.S. government is not clear. Many observers concluded that such a large-scale and sensitive operation would have been impossible without knowledge and consent from the State Department, which at the time was interested in strengthening Croatia to prevent Serbia from becoming the region's dominant power. See Matilde Sanchez and Ana Barón, "El Arsenal que Bendijo Clinton," *Clarín,* Oct. 4, 1990.

2. A detailed account of the scandal is presented in Daniel Santoro's *Venta de Armas: Hombres del Gobierno* (Buenos Aires: Planeta, 1998).

3. Eduardo van der Kooy, "Nafta sobre Fuego," *Clarín,* Apr. 5, 1996.

4. The government brought a lawsuit against *Clarín.*

5. See Silvio Waisbord, "Knocking on Newsroom Doors: The Press and Political Scandals in Argentina," *Political Communication* 1 (1994): 19–34.

6. See Horacio Verbitsky, *Robo para la Corona* (Buenos Aires: Planeta, 1991).

7. See Roman Lejtman, *Narcogate* (Buenos Aires: Sudamericana, 1993).

8. Theodore Lowi, "Foreword," in Andrei S. Markovits and Mark Silverstein, eds., *The Politics of Scandal: Power and Process in Liberal Democracies* (New York: Holmes and Meier, 1988).

9. Why political affairs are more typical than sexual affairs in Argentina deserves close attention, but this question goes beyond the goal of this chapter. Latin American politics are virtually exempt from sexual scandals. If Puritanism is commonly indicated as responsible for sex scandals in the United Kingdom and the United States, the absence of a Puritan culture in Catholic countries could have the opposite effect. Such an explanation, however, runs the risk of attributing all differences to "culture" without addressing how culture is incorporated into the complex dynamics of scandals. Scandals do not just happen because the religious values of citizens clash with publicized acts. An alternative is to consider arguments that see the post-1960s sex scandals in the United States as the outgrowth of the cultural wars. If such wars inspired the latest batch of sex scandals, the absence of cultural wars in Argentina probably helps explain why such scandals are rare unless, as in Judge Oyarbide's case, they bring elements of voyeurism and "deviant" sexual practices.

10. John B. Thompson, "Scandal and Social Theory," in James Lull and Stephen Hinerman, eds., *Media Scandals* (New York: Columbia University Press, 1996), 154.

11. Sibila Camps and Luis Pazos, *Justicia y Televisión: La Sociedad Dicta Sentencia* (Buenos Aires: Perfil, 1999).

12. Silvio Waisbord, *El Gran Desfile: Campañas Electorales y Medios de Comunicación en Argentina* (Buenos Aires: Editorial Sudamericana, 1995).

13. This position brings together strange scholarly bedfellows. For some examples, see Jean Baudrillard, *In the Shadow of Silent Majorities . . . Or the End of the Social* (New York: Semiotext(e), 1983); Pierre Bourdieu, *On Television* (New York: New Press, 1998); and Giovanni Sartori, "Video-Power," *Government and Opposition* (1989): 39–61.

14. Murray Edelman, *Constructing the Political Spectacle* (Chicago: University of Chicago Press, 1988).

15. The exposé prompted the cancellation of the fourth shipment of weapons to Ecuador.

16. Attorney Ricardo Monner Sans states that *Clarín*'s story prompted him to bring a lawsuit against the government (interview, Buenos Aires, Mar. 1999). Neither journalists nor the plaintiff expected early denunciations and the lawsuit to trigger a full-fledged scandal, however. They didn't anticipate that alleged crimes would involve powerful cabinet members and army hierarchies. They had little idea about the dimensions of the operation and did not suspect that initial revelations were sitting on top of a complex operation. Nor was this the first denunciation that affected the government. A record of numerous denunciations involving government officials that had previously run into dead ends dissuaded journalists from hoping that the arms case would be different. Nor did Congress swiftly react to the revelations and order wide-ranging investigations. Against the background of previous scandals, that prosecutors failed to investigate, that judges threw out and manipulated causes, that the government had stacked the Supreme Court, and that the Peronist-controlled Comisión de Juicio Político in Congress rejected petitions for investigations and hearings, there were no grounds for thinking that a scandal would unfold.

17. Access to prosecutor's investigations violates judicial secrecy, but it barely raises eyebrows in Argentina. In the arms scandal, the Menem administration threatened to reveal conversations between a journalist and prosecutor Stornelli and between Stornelli and Representative Horacio Viqueira, a member of the opposition. Viqueira was quoted as saying, "My relation with Stornelli is one of total collaboration" (Jorge Urien Berri, "El Contrabando a Ecuador y Croacia," *La Nación*, Nov. 4, 1998). The regular collaboration between reporters and judges is a public secret in political circles. Regardless of individual motives for pursuing an investigation, both parties take advantage of this relation: reporters lack legal protection to get information and talk to witnesses and prosecutors, and judges need regular access to the media to raise the public profile of their investigations.

18. *Clarín*'s position was particularly telling considering that Camilión had been formerly linked to the newspaper as a member of the Movimiento de Integración y Desarrollo (MID), the party that had a powerful influence on the paper for decades.

19. Gladys Engel Lang and Kurt Lang, *The Battle for Public Opinion: The President, the Press, and the Polls during Watergate* (New York: Columbia University Press, 1983). Also see Amy Fried, *Muffled Echoes: Oliver North and the Politics of Public Opinion* (New York: Columbia University Press, 1997); and Robin Andersen, "Oliver North and the News," in Peter Dahlgren and Colin Sparks, eds., *Journalism and Popular Culture* (London: Sage, 1992).

20. Qtd. in "Yabrán y Noticias: Una relación llena de conflictos," *Noticias*, May 25, 1997, 26–29.

21. The Menem administration was battered by speculations that Yabrán kept close contacts with many of its members.

22. See "1989–1999: El Libro Negro de la Corrupción," *XXI*, Dec. 23, 1998.

23. An example of the latter view is offered in Gene Lyons, *Fools for Scandal: How the Media Invented Whitewater* (New York: Franklin Square Press, 1996).

24. Suzanne Garment, *Scandal: The Crisis of Mistrust in American Politics* (New York: Random House, 1991).

25. Ben Ginsberg and Martin Shefter, *Politics by Other Means: The Declining Importance of Elections in America* (New York: Basic Books, 1990).

26. On memory and scandal, see Michael Schudson, *Watergate in American Memory: How We Remember, Forget and Reconstruct the Past* (New York: Basic Books, 1992).

27. For an early treatment of this question, see Stanley Cohen and Jock Young, *The Manufacture of News* (London: Constable, 1973). For a recent analysis, see W. Lance Bennett, "An Introduction to Journalism News and Representation of Politics," *Political Communication* 13 (1986): 373–84.

28. Elizabeth Bird, "What a Story: Understanding the Audience for Scandal," in Lull and Hinerman, *Media Scandals*, 99–121.

29. "La Herencia del Gral. Balza," *Trespuntos*, Sept. 16, 1998.

30. Qtd. in "El General en Su Laberinto," *XXI*, Sept. 3, 1998, 39–42.

31. The Comisión de Juicio Político had twenty-seven members: eight are Menemistas, six are Duhaldistas, and eleven belong to the opposition. The other two are independents. The government only had a majority with the support of Duhalde's bloc.

32. Interviews, Carlos Stornelli and Horacio Viqueira, Buenos Aires, Mar. 1999.

33. See Silvio Waisbord, "Investigative Journalism and Political Accountability in South American Democracies," *Critical Studies in Mass Communication* 13 (1996): 343–63; and *Watchdog Journalism in South America: News, Democracy and Accountability* (New York: Columbia University Press, 2000).

34. Interview, Jorge Urien Berri, Buenos Aires, Mar. 1999.

35. Interview, Susana Viau, Buenos Aires, Mar. 1999.

36. Bird, "What a Story."

37. See Silvio Waisbord, "Barks and Bites: Watchdog Journalism in South America" (unpublished ms.).

38. The government reacted by calling Palleros "a delinquent" and the charges "ridiculous" and "an infamy."

39. Walter Goobar, "Rio Tercero: El Atentado," *XXI*, Oct. 8, 1998, 36–38; Raul Kollman, "Donde se Fueron las Bombas," *Página 12*, Oct. 4, 1998.

40. See Olga Wornat, "Ultimos Días de la Víctima," *XXI*, Sept. 9, 1998, 40–41.

41. Other suicides that were skeptically received by the press were those of Alfredo Yabrán and Marcelo Cattaneo, an executive linked to the IBM–Banco Nación affair. See Alberto Amato, "Suicidios Argentinos S.A.," *Clarín*, Oct. 11, 1998; and Marisa Grinstein, "El Triángulo del Horror," *Noticias*, Sept. 12, 1998, 100–102.

42. Interviews, Viau and Urien Berri.

43. Interview, Stornelli.

44. See "Encuesta de Gallup: El 96% de los Argentinos Cree Que la Corrupcion Es 'Elevada,'" *Clarín*, Jan. 3, 1997.

45. Keith Tester, *Media, Culture and Morality* (London: Routledge, 1994).

46. The expression paraphrases Susan D. Moeller's idea of "compassion fatigue." See her *Compassion Fatigue: How the Media Sell Disease, Famine and War* (New York: Routledge, 1999).

47. See Thompson, "Scandal and Social Theory"; and Andrei S. Markovits and Mark Silverstein, "Introduction," in Markovits and Silverstein, *The Politics of Scandal*, 1–12.

48. Carolyn Funks, "The Impact of Scandal on Candidate Evaluations: An Experimental Test of the Role of Candidate Traits," *Political Behavior* (1996): 1–24.

49. Markovits and Silverstein, "Introduction," 4–5.

50. David Protess et al., *The Journalism of Outrage* (New York, Guilford Press, 1991).

51. The expression is historian David Thelen's in his study on the Iran-Contra scandal. See his *Becoming Citizens in the Age of Television* (Chicago and London: University of Chicago Press, 1996).

52. Three judges investigated three separate cases: conspiracy, fraud, misappropriation of weapons, and the alteration of public documents (Jorge Urso); the trafficking of gunpowder (Julio Speroni); and the trafficking of cannons and rifles (Marcelo Aguinsky).

53. See John Tomlinson, "'And Besides, the Wench is Dead': Media Scandals and the Globalization of Communication," in Lull and Hinerman, *Media Scandals*, 65–84.

54. Interview, Viau.

55. See "Memorias del infierno," *Clarín*, Apr. 25, 1999.

56. See John Langer, *Tabloid Television: Popular Journalism and the "Other News"* (London: Routledge, 1998).

57. Howard Tumber, "'Selling Scandal': Business and the Media," *Media, Culture and Society* 15 (1993): 345–61.

58. On tabloid news, see Ian Connel, "Personalities in the Popular Media," in Dahlgren and Sparks, *Popular Culture*, 64–83.

PART THREE

Some Theoretical Issues

11

Accountability and Civil Society

Andrew Arato

Representation, Popular Sovereignty, and Accountability

REPRESENTATIVE GOVERNMENT is a medieval, Western invention. Whether we agree with Rousseau's condemnation or Hegel's applause concerning the meaning of feudal origins, we should certainly notice that medieval representation faced no legitimation problems. Estate assemblies simply made present to the prince, directly or through the imperative mandate, social orders that were already powerful and that retained or increased their power through representation. All who counted as parts of the political nation were included, and there was no division between represented and representatives. But when the heirs of the estates, Parliament in the seventeenth century and the Constitutional Convention and the Assemblee Constituante in the eighteenth, claimed to exercise constituent and legislative powers on the basis of representing the sovereign people, a legitimation problem opened up that was not solved then and has not been since, and will never be fully solved. Many of the struggles around revolutionary constitution making in the French Revolution involved the problem of representing the popular sovereign, and since none of the institutional (royal veto, appeal to popular assemblies) or extrainstitutional (popular insurrection, popular presence in the galleries) devices could solve the problem, the results were disastrous for both representation and popular government (Baker). The point is not simply, as Bernard Manin would have it, that the new representative assemblies created aristocratic rule in the name of democratic legitimacy. As he himself mentions, eighteenth-century normative theory (Rousseau, Kant, or Madison) distinguished between form of sovereignty and form of government.[1] Popular sovereignty could work in this conception with (generally: "only with") nondemocratic government, and it was easy enough to extend (as against Rousseau) the concept of government to include the legislature. With this said, moreover, with respect to what came before (pace Manin), namely the society of orders and absolutism, modern representative government indeed represented the cause of democratization, even if elections are rightly considered aristocratic by the then irrelevant criteria of ancient democracy.

More serious (as Edmund Morgan has shown) was the reversal involved in representing popular sovereignty: the representatives who appealed to the people's authority actually constituted the people and its meaning (as electorates with specific qualifications, as assemblies of ratification elected in specific ways, as amending powers under demanding rules). Thus they seemed to claim authority stemming ultimately from themselves alone, the very meaning of autocracy. This tension (between democratic claims and autocratic authorization) led to attempts to continually expand the meaning of "the people" postulated by legislatures in a self-serving manner and thus to the logic of inclusion that Manin too recognizes as the democratic dimension of modern representative government. If we claim that authority comes from the people as a whole and not from the legally constituted, obviously partial people, then democratic legitimacy requires that the gap between the people in the two senses be continually reduced. From the constitution of 1793, the Jacksonian Revolution, and the English reform bills, to women's and young persons' suffrage, and to the establishment of the electoral rights of excluded ethnic groups and long-term residents, representative democracy has been a story of political inclusion.

Inclusion, however, opens up another gap: the larger the number of socially and economically weak individuals included in elections, the greater the difference of power between the electorate and the representative body, between the "people's two bodies" as it were. The point is not simply that election as such is a principle of distinction, but rather that an uneducated, relatively poor, hard-working electorate has much greater difficulty observing, criticizing, and controlling elected officials than did the more privileged social strata of predemocratic representative regimes. Mass political parties, the major institutions of representative democracies, cannot mediate the gap between electors and representatives without internally reproducing the identical duality. In other words, only if the distance between representatives and represented can be relativized can mass parties play their mediating role, which would in addition depend on their internal solution of the problem of representation.

Here I focus only on the gap between citizen and government. In general, I see five normative sets of claim complexes that have a chance of reducing the immense gap between represented and representative in modern democracy. Accountability, one of these sets, is best understood in relation to them.

Rights and Constitutionalism

Perhaps the most important reason that the gap under modern democracies between representative and represented does not constitute a new form of autocracy is because rule itself has become a weaker and more limited relationship than under most previously existing regimes (Sartori). The modern citizen replaces the potential officeholder of past republics not only as a source of legitimacy but as a carrier of equal rights.[2] Granted, these rights empower the citizen and limit the rulers only if they are enforceable, generally through judicial procedures. Thus constitutionalism, along with its major instruments, written constitutions formulated as legally applicable rules, amendment rules of some difficulty, and constitutional review, helps legitimate representative democracy by reserving powers to the citizens and by making sure that the rules of the game are not at the disposal of elected officials. Constitutionalism is the major modern mechanism guaranteeing popular sovereignty in the sense of including beyond the representatives an expanding circle of participants who are responsible for fundamental law making and revision.

Nevertheless, constitutionalism does not solve all the relevant problems. Primarily, even if not all powers are assigned to the legislature, the powers that are could always be used in an unjust manner and could turn oppressive. No constitutionalism can preemptively anticipate all sources of injustice. Second, amendment rules could be bypassed by legislation, which often is constitutional law making, at best thinly disguised. Third, constitutional review that can guard against the first two types of abuses must be particularly strong and active, and precisely this type of review itself has serious legitimation problems. When one type of aristocracy (the legislative one) is battled by another (the judiciary), democratic legitimacy is hardly increased. Indeed, an elected legislature has better democratic claims than do unelected judges (especially with lifetime appointments).

Deliberation versus Identity

As against Carl Schmitt's view, modern democracy in large-scale, complex societies cannot be based on identity between rulers and ruled, even in Aristotle's sense of taking turns at ruling and being ruled. Referendum democracy and the imperative mandate could establish the electorate as the real legislature, but only at the cost of incoherent and irrational decision making and, even worse, the impossibility of decision makers having the opportunity and ability to interact with and persuade one another. To be sure, identity in modern society could in principle be seen in ultimately Hobbesian terms: the people are constituted and gain their corporate existence only through the emergence and continued existence of a sovereign, legislative power. The will of this person or body *is* therefore the will of the people, by definition. While in the United States, since before the Revolution, this view, reappearing as the claim of parliamentary sovereignty, was considered an opening to legislative tyranny, it took a while for it to be fully discredited in France (in Sieyes's version) and has by now a shadow existence in its historical home, Great Britain, as the narrowly legal but not the political form of sovereignty.[3] The concept of deliberation represents a more open, admittedly incomplete version of this second effort to secure identity. It is the idea that a genuinely common will can be achieved only through deliberation and mutual persuasion that lead to "free representation" and the rejection of the rigidities of direct democracy. When, however, the legislative body offers itself as the sole site of public deliberation, the objections remain the same as in the case of the doctrinaire version of parliamentary sovereignty: in the name of the people, the legislature may generate through discussion only its own corporate will and possibly only the partial will of the strongest faction. Even if legislative deliberation is monitored and influenced by societal processes of deliberation, there are no institutional guarantees within a purely deliberative model of democracy that can make sure that public-regarding reasons are not used in a merely rhetorical manner and that the inputs of public opinion will be seriously considered by a legislature.

Identification and Trust

Trust in representatives means that we believe that the use of public-regarding reasons and the consideration of available public inputs are authentic. But why would or should we trust people whom we never met and do not personally know? The normal condition of modern representative democracy is distrust rather than trust. Yet it is an empirical truism that charismatic and plebiscitary leaders of parties and governments are indeed trusted. What Carl Schmitt refers to as identity, but is better understood as identification, is indeed a process by which elected leaders overcome the feeling of distance between the representative regime and the represented. Identification works because in contexts of mobilization the motives of people are influenced by the leaders and because the desire to be led itself becomes an important motive. Nevertheless, as everyone since Weber knows, under modern conditions charismatic leadership and popular mobilization are both limited in time. The justified suspicion that the leader is other than he appears is always present, along with identification, and populist democracy almost always turns authoritarian because under modern conditions a part of the population does not readily identify. As has often been the case in Argentina, authoritarian measures against a part inevitably affect the rest, with increasing political alienation as the result. Democracy as identification can remain democratic only as a road to more democracy, as under some examples of populist politics in the name of inclusion, but never as a longer-term substitute for institutionalized democracy.

Similitude and Descriptive Representation

It would be hard to deny that it is easier to trust representatives if they resemble us, in a plural society all the various meanings of "us." Descriptive or pictorial representation of groups can perhaps be seen as our replacement of direct participation, with the assembly as the microcosm of the societal macrocosm.[4] Manin's claim that election is based on the principle of distinction, and therefore resemblance is impossible, does not in itself carry the day against advocates of descriptive representation.[5] Each group can and should choose its own best to represent it, and yet these "betters" can nevertheless resemble their groups in everything but assumed ability. Moreover, a descriptively representative body need not be as inimical to deliberation as an assembly of bound delegates, precisely because here representatives are trusted to deliberate in the place of the represented. However, pictorial representation strictly speaking has a strong democratic deficit. If deputies are to represent society's groups in a strict manner, this would have to be prearranged in the tradition of the supreme soviets of old, hardly paragons of democratic representation. If groups are to vote for their own representatives (and who is to choose what groups are allowed to do so?), the result is pictorial representation only if electors are required to vote for one of their kind—a rule incompatible with the freedom to become a candidate or with voting freely. If groups both large and small receive guaranteed representation, the principle of one person–one vote would probably be abandoned. Finally, proportional representation, the one method compatible with electoral freedom that *can* produce representation even for relatively small constellations of identity or interest, *cannot guarantee* descriptive representation.

Accountability and Retrospective Judgment

Deliberation, identification, and similitude provide only *sociologically* plausible links between representatives and represented. There is nothing in descriptive or pictorial representation per se to *legally* stop representatives chosen from among the members of a group from violating the interests of that group. The same can be said for a deliberative parliament and for a leader with whom the masses identify. Undoubtedly, the only such link that positive (i.e., sanctionable) law can provide is accountability, based on the ability of voters, individuals or groups, to hold representatives to account for (to answer for, to be responsible for, and to be punished or rewarded for) what they do.[6] Manin is right: accountability is *retrospective judgment* especially with respect to elected representatives who cannot be forced to adhere to promises or programs while in office, but who can be punished for their omissions and commissions at subsequent elections.

If voters cannot (and ought not) compel representatives to implement specific policies, they can nevertheless make it in their interest to do so, especially if they (as empirical studies suggest) take the records of incumbents into account during elections.[7] Accountability does not make mandates unfree, as Hanna Fenichel Pitkin seems to imply,[8] but does limit and restrict the behavior of incumbents *if* they are interested in reelection. Representatives, unlike delegates or ambassadors, have no strict instructions and may indeed violate promises and programs and still be reelected. It is their whole performance that will be judged, and if departure from the views of constituents leads to success it will be easily forgiven. But regular elections do mean that there will be popular judgment on past actions and that representatives cannot without serious consequences emancipate themselves from the interests and opinions of those who constitute the supposed sovereign of democracies. Accountability is not a merely formal matter for this reason, as Pitkin argues, but she is right that it is not in itself a norm or a normative justification of anything. At its basis, however, is a "hypothetical imperative" in Kant's sense. *If* we value the connection between representatives and represented, *then* accountability is an important means for advancing this *democratic* norm. Whether or not, therefore, we are convinced of the democratic potentials of deliberation, identification, and/or similitude, it would be absurd to deny that political accountability would have to be, at the very least, a crucial dimension of any modern democracy where the identity of rulers and ruled is a thing of the past.

Note that I am speaking here only of *political* accountability, which alone has direct relevance to the link between the representatives and the represented. Undoubtedly, elements of what I depict above as constitutionalism, or more generally the rule of (public) law, could be presented in a parallel fashion as *legal* accountability of officials, who if they break the law are expected to give a full account of and take responsibility for their actions. This form of accountability is, however, not to the people and does not bridge the gap between rulers and the ruled except to the extent that it is one of the tools of *constitutionalism.*

Institutional Design

Can political accountability alone account for a democratic relationship of representatives and represented, the reality of popular sovereignty in a modern representative regime? Should constitution makers everywhere design regimes seeking to maximize the accountability of political officials? Can accountability be stabilized without other (in themselves not accountable) democratic linkages? In order to answer these questions, I will present the ideal type of a regime of pure accountability, one that in principle could be the aim of all efforts of institutional design. Not surprisingly, perhaps, the abstract model will turn out to be, with a few "improvements," the Westminster model of parliamentary democracy.

First, a regime of pure political accountability would have to be (as Juan Linz argues) a parliamentary one and, I add, one based on a single legislative chamber. Accountability assumes "identifiability" (Linz) or "assignability" (Manin), and separation of powers under presidentialism (and even bicameralism) allows in principle the attribution of blame to another power with whom one must compromise to achieve anything. Note that along with bicameralism we would be rejecting a strong version of federalism where the units are present in national legislation through an upper chamber.

Second, and similarly, such a regime is inimical to coalition government, where the blame game can be played out among the partners. Since not only proportional representation but even single-member first-past-the-post elections leave the door open to coalitions, the electoral rule would have to be even more strongly majoritarian than the English first-past-the-post system. Since, for reasons explained later, a regime of accountability needs a vocal parliamentary opposition, and would not need supermajorities, as provided for by the famous Argentinean Saenz Peña Law, for example, it would be enough if the first-place party in list voting would receive, say, 51 percent of the seats. The internal discipline of such a party could then be further enhanced by the requirement that after deliberations caucuses must vote as a block. By adopting accountability as our only goal, with the adoption of majoritarian electoral rules, we would be of course abandoning any emphasis on the similitude of representatives to the represented, which would be enhanced by parliamentary representation (PR) and at least permitted (assuming geographical nonhomogeneity) by first-past-the-post single-member elections.

Third, a regime of pure political accountability would need short electoral terms and relatively easy dissolution of the legislature and could not allow term limits of any kind. Accountability is a function of time, because given enough time, actions for which one would be held responsible can be forgotten or compensated for. The time of office holding should probably be kept at two or three years. A parliamentary regime of course makes the head of the executive more accountable than a president because votes of no confidence (and removal for political reasons) can occur at any time and not only at the end of a rigidly defined term. Thus it is a regime of double accountability: the executive is accountable to parliament, and parliament is accountable to the voters. We might reason that the latter form of accountability could also, in principle, be enhanced if there was an institutional possibility of the recall of deputies. This possibility must be rejected, but only because it is incompatible with the control of parliamentary government, which could not function if the members could be constantly drawn into reelection campaigns. In my scheme, recall is also potentially incompatible with majoritarianism (a government could lose its majority and be forced into coalition through recall) and would make individual deputies accountable at the possible cost of making parties less so. But the next best thing to recall, namely *relatively* frequent parliamentary elections and *relatively* easy dissolution by the executive or the parliamentary majority, would certainly enhance accountability. While incumbents cannot be made to run (or to live forever), there is no way to make sure that everyone will be accountable. Evidently, however, term limits of any kind would have to be strictly forbidden for members of the executive and the legislature. An official who is not around to run again becomes politically (though not legally) unaccountable in his or her last term.

Fourth, the banning of private electoral contributions and the public financing of elections would be required. A person or a party cannot be genuinely accountable to the voters if first and foremost accountable to special sources of financing. It might not be enough, as in the United Kingdom, to control only campaign expenditures. The input side too should be limited, perhaps to very small private contributions.

Fifth, it is easy to show that a regime of pure political accountability is incompatible with constitutionalism as we know it. Constitutional designers seeking to maximize accountability could not permit constitutional amendments passable only by supermajorities or, even more important, countermajoritarian constitutional review by courts. Of course supermajorities would be no problem if the winning party would be awarded enough seats. But any supermajority that requires the participation of any minority in passing constitutional amendments would diminish the accountability of the majority party, which could blame the opposition for not passing amendments it does not want; such a system would even allow playacting on the part of this majority in voting for constitutional changes that would lose anyway. The same could be done in the case of legislation that would not be offered or would be offered in a purely rhetorical manner because of the feigned or real expectation that a constitutional court would declare it unconstitutional. Even the possibility of delay by the courts interferes with pure accountability, especially if the judges themselves are not accountable to the electorate. Accordingly, judges of the highest courts would have to be electable, for short but renewable terms. Note therefore that the ideal type would have to exclude the two major, legally defined guarantees of modern constitutionalism, though it is quite compatible with a written constitution.

So much for what a regime of pure political accountability would look like. It would be different from Westminster parliamentarism only in having only a single chamber, an even more majoritarian electoral rule, perhaps a written constitution, shorter terms, and even stricter rules of party finance. Critics who could take their ammunition from the long history of both the functioning and the criticisms of the British parliament could immediately point to the obvious deficiencies of the model. But its defenders too could insist on the Westminster model as proof of the strong possibility of democratic stability and a tradition of informal constitutionalism under a regime of pure accountability. For me, the Westminster model points to an important precondition of a workable regime based on accountability: the existence of a loyal opposition in parliament. This highly desirable, though unfortunately not designable, feature of the British polity is important, because without the critical monitoring, thematization, and publicization of the proposals, actions, and omissions of a governmental majority, accountability cannot work: the voters must know what it is for which they should hold the majority party to account in light of policy alternatives that could have been followed. The existence of a loyal opposition throws light on both the words and the deeds of the government and embodies the existence of alternatives. But of course a loyal parliamentary opposition can do this, as all major nineteenth-century theorists and even critics of parliamentary democracy realized, only if free debate, discussion, and criticism extend beyond the walls of parliament to the civil public sphere.[9] A regime of accountability can work only in tandem with civil society and the public sphere.

Civil Society and the Public Sphere

The inevitable turn to the public sphere to complete the model already implies that a regime of accountability cannot be pure and that it needs (at the very least) a dimension of deliberative democracy to function at all. In my conception, public sphere and civil society belong together: the former concept points to the partially institutionalized processes of communication so important for democratic politics, the latter to the organizational substratum of groups, associations, and movements required for the generalization of the experience of communication, as well as for its political influence. While the public plays the all-important role of monitoring actions that are later to be rewarded or sanctioned, civil associations prepare voters for collective participation and response that can actually make a difference in the electoral fate of representatives. Everyone today knows that it is organized groups whose retrospective judgment elected officials must above all fear.

Both public sphere and civil society go beyond a model of pure accountability. Although accountability cannot work without them, it is no longer pure with them. And this is not only because of the normative role of deliberative democracy. We are right to regard the public sphere and civil society as mediations between the represented and their representatives, as it were reducing the gap and the tension between them. This mediation is not one-directional, in the sense of informing the represented and preparing them for retrospective acts of judgment. Discussion and criticism also monitor the state of mind of the electorate for the representatives. They are therefore able to respond to public opinion early, test the consequences of departures from programs and promises, reverse course if need be, and try to persuade the public through words and action. In this interaction concerned sectors of the electorate gain anticipatory and prospective influence over policy. Through civil society and the public sphere democracy recovers something of its lost, participatory character. When the *influence* of civil society and its movements, however, reaches the threshold of civil disobedience, we reach the limit beyond which representative democracy would be itself under threat by an illegitimate form of *power*.[10] As organs of representation, the associations and movements of civil society can refer to a far narrower world of citizens than representative assemblies can. Any attempt to exercise power on such bases would reverse the work of inclusion, without which no politics today can have the stamp of democratic legitimacy. The public sphere and civil society must complete and complement rather than replace the accountability of representation.

Unlike the structures of democratic government, the highly *desirable* practices of a vibrant and influential public sphere and civil society are only in part *designable* and in an important part depend on self-constitution, self-organization, and self-activity.[11] Here my concern is what can be designed. We can and should legally establish the frameworks within which civil and public interaction are possible, and we can do a great deal by enacting the fundamental freedoms of association and communication (thought, press, assembly, and even privacy—the freedom to withdraw from communication and publicity, without which the others are not possible). In the age of electronic media, a still scarce resource, regulation can and should extend its work to achieving access and visibility for the full plurality of groups and opinion, something that would be best accomplished by a variety of institutional forms (state, private, and public), as well as rules that guarantee the equality of political opportunity.

Finally, given that the organizations and initiatives of civil society play a societal role, it may be possible and desirable to guarantee them societal resources. Since a democratic society need not increase the influence of undemocratic organizations, internal democracy should be perhaps a precondition of public financing. There is little question that constitutionally enacted rights of communication, media democracy, and public financing can make an important contribution to the development of a culture within which civil society and the public sphere can reinforce a regime of accountability. And yet many historical examples indicate that neither genuine accountability nor a strong public sphere may exist in societies where all of these desiderata are formally provided for.[12]

Returning to Institutional Design

Two things should be noted. First, it is not enough to enact the relevant rules: in order to be institutionalized, they must also be enforced. And second, assuming that the relevant rights are institutionalized, and thus enforced, it is nevertheless obvious that no institutional design can guarantee that actors and speakers will actually organize themselves, participate in public discussion, and become concerned about politics. Both factors point to additional ways in which a regime of accountability is in itself incomplete.

Adding Constitutionalism (without Guardianship)

The ideal typical regime described here as one of pure political accountability is perhaps the most powerful imaginable type of democratic regime. The very factors that make its actions unambiguously identifiable and assignable, and therefore open to retrospective judgment, are the factors that make government under this regime so unified, powerful, and capable of decisive, even unilateral action. Such a government may use its power to continually reinforce the possibility of an electorally accountable regime. To an important extent, this is what happened in the twentieth-century United Kingdom even before the appearance of European institutions on the scene. But this type of government may also use this power to reinforce incumbency and to make the functioning of oppositions, especially those outside of parliament, impossible. This is evidently what the Westminster Parliament repeatedly did in the seventeenth and eighteenth centuries. The self-serving powers of incumbents are very well symbolized by some of the terms that are benchmarks in the history of the Westminster regime: the Long Parliament and the Septennial Law. It is beside the point that today Parliament would not and could not extend its own term in office by simple statute. The reasons for such an outcome are specific to British history and have little relevance in general. Evidently it is the negative lessons of the earlier period of the formation of parliamentary government that are instructive for new democracies, at least where we do not want to wait a hundred years or more for the coming of a desirable form of democratic regime. In the United Kingdom, it is the power of civil society that would stop Parliament from passing a modern version of the Septennial Law, which would not be illegal or unconstitutional even today. In many new democracies legal powers of this type would gravely inhibit civil and public initiatives that in the UK would control the abuse of these powers. Thus we need to make the abuse of power illegal: legal accountability is almost everywhere a sine qua non of political accountability.

Everywhere with a recent history of dictatorship, aside from minorities, most people have bad memories indeed of opposing or even criticizing governments. Aside from periods of high mobilization, only a regime of formal enforcement of the constitutional rights and statutory regulations of civil society and the public sphere can give people (and not only heroes) confidence in exercising their relevant rights. Enforcement must mean that officials who interfere are themselves open to legal sanctions: that they are accountable legally whether or not they will stand for reelection. Such formal enforcement entails an independent, nonpolitical judiciary and a constitutional court. Of course there is always the danger that such a court removes too much from the agenda of accountable decision makers, while itself becoming unaccountable. In my view, a more precise formulation of rights and of the jurisdiction and membership of the court may help somewhat to avoid the outcome of constitutional court "guardianship,"[13] but what would really help would be the formulation of amendment rules that, unlike the U.S. and British extremes, would avoid both extreme difficulty and a purely parliamentary procedure. When there is a reasonable chance to enact a constitutional amendment that reverses judicial decisions, the Constitutional Court is no longer fully unaccountable—a judge being overruled on appeal represents an important sanction. As in political accountability, the possibility of being overruled by the people (here as amending rather than electoral power) is part of the political accountability of judges who may also be open to legal accountability through impeachment. While both forms of accountability enter into the structure of the judicial decisions of unelected judges, in their case only the political judgment that may reverse their ruling carries the element of true deterrence.

Adding Similitude (without Pictorial Representation)

No one wants to participate and pressure without the chance of having an influence. A government of pure accountability may be too powerful to listen. The retrospective judgment of the people can be faced later, when the past perhaps can be reinterpreted and justified. Given their political and financial advantages, it would be hard to devise any media structure that would completely neutralize the advantages of incumbents, who may nevertheless pursue their advantages in a fully legal manner. It is therefore unlikely that, again with the exception of contexts of high mobilization, people will organize and speak out if they have no chance of being heard. Or: they are likely to organize anti-systemic movements that may destabilize both civil society and democratic government. But if citizens do not speak out and organize in self-limiting political initiatives and forums, the monitoring and informational role of public opinion can be damaged, making accountability itself an empty promise. Because today, especially in the United States, access is guaranteed to important lobbies and above all to the sources of political funds, the political structure of influence of civil society is highly inequitable and deformed. Evidently, the whole lobbying system should be reformed by a new system of campaign finance, including not only the public financing of parties but also civil associations and initiatives that play a public, monitoring role.

In *Civil Society and Political Theory,* following a suggestion by Habermas, Jean Cohen and I speak of sensors in the political system open to the influence of civil society. In particular we argue that the parliamentary public represents this sensitivity to discussions in the civil public sphere. This claim, true as far as it goes, would itself require that many of today's parliaments take decisive action to restore the integrity of deliberation. Of course it must always be an open question which clusters of interest, identity, or opinion are salient enough to gain a measure of descriptive representation. Self-organization, acting through proportional representation and putting pressure on the parties that nominate, can hopefully resolve the issue in most cases. Today I would further develop this conception, originally too much under the influence of an idea of rational discourse, by arguing that parliamentary discussants will be especially sensitive to societal speakers if at least some of them can identify with the particular life conditions that give their speech its particular meaning. And conversely, societal speakers will have the confidence of being heard if representatives that share their life experiences are there to understand, relay, and amplify the message.

There are two undesirable and even dangerous versions of this idea. People may very well believe that plebiscitarian leaders hear them, and it is worthwhile to mobilize behind them. But such a project does not complement accountability but replaces it, does not complete democracy but exposes it to authoritarian manipulation. Instead of the people controlling their leaders, the latter gain undemocratic forms of control over the former. While the leader is like the people only in their mistaken belief, pictorial or descriptive representation can in principle produce even the statistical resemblance of society as a whole. But aside from the undemocratic form of choosing such representatives (or the danger of choosing incompetents if it were done by lot or scientific sampling), exact representation of identities would violate the modern principle of representation. Representatives would become the stand-ins for particular identities and would be expected to use particular rather than "public-regarding" reasons in their deliberation. While there would still be no imperative mandate, and deputies could be persuaded if it could be shown that their constituencies would gain from a policy they originally opposed, genuine deliberation, which must be based on having at least some public project in common, could not take place.

Plebiscitary leadership, generally involving the direct elections of presidents, cannot be made compatible with a regime of accountability. The same is not true of at least elements of descriptive representation. Proportional representation is a fully competitive democratic method of elections, and it has the logically and empirically demonstrable tendency to produce at least some descriptive representation. In order to maximize the accountability of *individual* deputies to voters, a proportional system can be designed consisting only of deputies with mandates in electoral districts.[14] In such a system, there will be some representatives representing at least discrete and insular minorities, and of course women. If this does not occur spontaneously, legislation (as recently in France) can make it worthwhile for parties to represent those systematically excluded previously.

Of course it must always be an open question whether clusters of interest, identity, or opinion are salient enough to gain a measure of descriptive representation. Self-organization, acting through proportional representation and putting pressure on the parties that nominate, can hopefully resolve the issue in most cases. Only in the most striking cases of exclusion, as in the case of women in France, should legislative intervention select targets for more descriptive representation. However it is done, it is all-important to avoid demographic essentialism, in other words, quotas and guarantees. Thus restricted, descriptive representation can play an important role within an overall framework of democratic accountability.

Political accountability is an important principle that helps to make sense of popular sovereignty, under representative democracy. But if we make it the only such principle, we endanger accountability itself. On the level of institutional design, accountability should be complemented by institutions of deliberation, constitutionalism, and descriptive representation. But for accountability to really work, the self-activity of citizens in democratic publics and civil society remains the most important precondition.

NOTES

1. Bernard Manin, *The Principles of Representative Government* (Cambridge: Cambridge University Press, 1997).

2. Manin, *The Principles of Representative Government.*

3. See A. V. Dicey, *Introduction to the Study of the Law of the Constitution* (New York: St. Martin's, 1961).

4. Hanna Fenichel Pitkin, *The Concept of Representation* (Berkeley: University of California Press, 1967).

5. See Anne Philips, *The Politics of Presence* (Oxford: Oxford University Press, 1995).

6. See Pitkin, *The Concept of Representation,* 55.

7. Manin, *The Principles of Representative Government,* 179–80.

8. Pitkin, *The Concept of Representation,* 55.

9. See Karl Marx, *The Eighteenth Brumaire of Louis Bonaparte* (Moscow: Progress Publishers, 1977).

10. See Jean Cohen and Andrew Arato, *Civil Society and Political Theory* (Cambridge: MIT Press, 1992).

11. Cohen and Arato, *Civil Society and Political Theory.*

12. Contemporary Hungary, ten years into a new democracy, is a case in point.

13. Carl Schmitt, *Der Hüter der Verfassung* (Tübingen: J.C.B. Mohr, 1931).

14. See Andrew Arato, "The New Democracies and American Constitutional Design," *Constellations: An International Journal of Critical and Democratic Theory* 7, no. 3 (2000).

12

Social Accountability in Latin America and Beyond

Adam Przeworski

The Problem of Social Accountability

HERE IS HOW I understand the problem to which this volume is addressed. Suppose that you live in a situation where teachers do not appear in school, mail is delivered irregularly, police extort bribes, people languish in jails without being judged, social security checks fail to arrive, perhaps even salaries of public employees are not paid on time. What can you do about it?

You can vote in the next election for a party that offers a program for correcting this situation. You will be exercising prospective electoral control.

You can vote in the next election against the incumbent government. You will be exercising retrospective electoral control by using the institutional mechanism of electoral accountability.

You can direct yourself to the judicial system or in some countries to an ombudsman, demanding that the government does not violate and does fulfill its legal obligations. In some countries, you can wait for a public authority (say, the Ministerio Público in Brazil) to take the initiative. In either case, you will be relying on an institutional mechanism of checks and balances, what Guillermo O'Donnell calls "horizontal accountability."

You can join a movement, or what these days is called an NGO, and publicly demand that these problems be solved.

Finally, you can recount the situation to a journalist, hoping that he or she will make a stink. But, at least according to Silvio Waisbord, the journalist will have heard so many similar stories that yours will not attract much attention.

You can do one more thing, but I will keep it for later.

In the end, there is little you can do. Electoral mechanisms, whether prospective or retrospective, are a weak instrument of popular control (see Przeworski, Stokes, and Manin 1999). Mechanisms for direct control of citizens over public bureaucracies have existed only in very rare democracies and have never functioned well. So you are left with the alternatives of protesting publicly, which does work from time to time, or waiting for the horizontal mechanisms of accountability to kick in.

The Culture of Lament

Is this situation specific to Latin America? This is a question with implications both for research and for political strategies. Let me thus define it carefully.

One can think that democracy is a form of government that permits effective control of governments by citizens. Indeed, for some authors (Dahl 1971; Riker 1965), the ability of citizens to control governments is almost a definitional feature of democracy. Democracy, in this view, can function well and does in the majority of European countries where Democratic institutions are highly consolidated. According to Nuria Cunill Grau, effective citizen control over governments is possible, but this is not the case in Latin America. For these authors, something about Latin America, in other words, is distinctively deficient.

But one can also think that the weakness of popular control over governments is generic to democracies. Certainly, there are differences among particular democratic systems. But in this view, institutions of democracy, or more precisely of "representative government" (Manin 1997), are just generically insufficient to enable popular control over governments. People do elect governments and express their views and demands during electoral terms, and particular organs of the state can check and balance one another (Manin 1994), but elections are not an effective instrument of popular control, separation of powers does not generate checks and balances when different powers are controlled by the same parties (or collude for other reasons), and citizens cannot exercise direct control over public bureaucracies. Democracy may be the best form of government that was ever invented, but it is congenitally, structurally weak as a mechanism of popular control over governments. This is just the way life is.

The first view is widely shared, both in Latin America and among scholars living in the "consolidated" democracies. The idea that a president of Brazil may be subject to tighter horizontal control than a prime minister of the United Kingdom unleashes a fury of protests. It is treated as inconceivable and even as offensive: somehow many Latin Americans see it as taking something away from them, while others are bewildered that one "dares" compare an old democracy to a Latin upstart. And since for me this fact is just self-evident, I am puzzled by these reactions. I attribute them to a "culture of lament."

Horizontal Accountability

The most prominent exponent of the view that Latin American democracies are distinctly deficient is O'Donnell (1991, 1997). According to him, contemporary Latin American democratic institutions do not contain sufficient checks and balances, or what he terms "horizontal accountability." As a consequence, people elect presidents, who then govern unconstrained by the institutional framework. Instead of being "representative," as in the developed countries, Latin American democracies are thus "delegative."

Now, since I several times heard Margaret Thatcher say, "You had your chance, you elected me, now I govern and you shut up," and I never heard Fernando Henrique Cardoso say the same, I immediately wonder which of these two democracies is "delegative." All I can do is look for some systematic data. Since the conceptualization of "horizontal accountability" is not obvious and the data are far from perfect, I do not want to claim that my evidence is conclusive. But it will make you wonder.

One way to think about "horizontal accountability" is to follow George Tsebelis (1995) and just count the number of institutional actors (excluding or including political parties) that must cooperate, or at least consent, for the government as a whole to undertake a particular action. To imprison someone, for example, the legislature must pass laws allowing the state to imprison someone for a particular offense, in some countries the chief executive must

12.1 Institutional and Political Indicators of Chief Executive Accountability				
	ALLHOUSE	COALITION	GOVFRAC	BICAM
Latin America	0.1250	0.56	0.29	0.56
OECD	0.2000	0.55	0.28	0.35

sign the law, courts must sentence the particular person, and the bureaucracy must put him or her in prison. If we count political parties, then it must also be true that enough parties must favor the particular piece of criminal legislation to obtain a legislative majority. I constructed a variable, VETO1, that adds presidents who are chief executives, the number of legislative chambers, and autonomous subnational governments. In turn, the variable VETO2 adds to VETO1 the number of effective government parties. On the average, as of 1995, in an average of the fifteen Latin American democracies there were 2.93 VETO1 players; in twenty-two Organization for Economic Cooperation and Development (OECD) democracies there were 2.27. If the number of government parties is added, the numbers are 4.88 VETO2 players in Latin America and 4.35 in the OECD countries.

This way of thinking about horizontal accountability does not distinguish, however, whose accountability is being considered. The number of veto players is the same for every political actor, thus obfuscating the differences among them (Gandhi and Przeworski 2000). Yet the idea of separating powers, and more specifically of institutionalizing checks and balances, seems to have had different origins in different countries. In revolutionary France, the danger was parliamentary sovereignty: since Parliament was the highest expression of popular will, there would be nothing to prevent it from exercising its legislative function in an absolutist manner (on these issues, see Kelsen 1929). Hence, royal veto over legislation, short terms of office, or other moderating devices were needed to temper parliamentary zeal. In many other countries, particularly those that adopted presidential institutions, the power to be tempered was that of the executive. Simon Bolivar's *Discurso de Angostura* (1818) made the threat of executive dictatorship apparent. Hence, "horizontal accountability" may mean constraints on the legislature or constraints on the executive. I will follow O'Donnell in analyzing it as a source of constraints on the chief executive.

A chief executive is more accountable if he or she does not control the relevant houses of the legislature (ALLHOUSE = 1 if controls, from Beck et al.

12.2 Central Bank and Lower-Level Governmental Autonomy Indicators of Chief Executive Accountability

	BANKS	STATE	MUNI
Latin America	0.35	0.78	1.66
OECD	0.36	1.48	1.93

2000), if the government is a coalition (COALITION = 1 if it is constructed, from Beck et al. 2000), if government parties are highly fractionalized (GOVFRAC, from Beck et al. 2000), and if the legislature is bicameral (BICAM = 1 if it is constructed, from Henisz 2000). Table 12.1 presents the averages of these indicators for sixteen Latin American and twenty OECD democracies in 1995.[1]

These are rough indicators, but they offer no basis to think that chief executives are any less accountable in Latin America. The chief executive controls the legislature somewhat more frequently in the OECD countries, coalition governments are equally frequent, and the number of effective parties composing these coalitions is identical, while bicameralism is more frequent in Latin America. Note, moreover, that chief executives have powers of legislative initiative in all realms of policy in all the OECD countries except the United States and that they have such powers in some realms, most importantly budgets, in all Latin American countries. True, some Latin American presidents have decree powers, but as long as members of government coalitions fear that the government will fall, so, de facto, do all prime ministers in the OECD democracies.[2]

Yet another way of thinking about horizontal accountability of the executive is to consider sources of power that are not controlled by him or her: independent central banks and the autonomy of lower levels of government from the central government both limit the realm of freedom of the chief executive.[3] Consider, therefore, BANKS (from Cukierman and Web 1995 for the decade of the 1980s) and two variables that indicate whether state/province governments (STATE, from Beck et al. 2000) and municipal governments (MUNI, from Beck et al. 2000) are locally elected.[4]

Central banks are identically independent in the two regions. In turn, subnational units are more likely to be governed by elected authorities in the OECD countries. Yet considering all these indicators together, there is absolutely no reason to think that horizontal accountability of the executive is less tight in Latin America than in the "consolidated" democracies.

These numbers may or may not be convincing. Let me return, therefore, to the comparison of Brazil and the United Kingdom. The Brazilian president has extensive powers (Figuereido and Limongi 1999), more extensive than his Argentine and Bolivian counterparts, although not as wide-ranging as the Chilean presidency (Anastasia 1999). Brazilian presidents can initiate ordinary legislation, require that a bill be processed as urgent, propose amendments to the constitution, issue decrees in some areas, veto legislation, name ministers, and appoint one-third of the Tribunal de Contas.[5] But a British prime minister can do the same, de jure or de facto: he or she can initiate legislation, control the legislative agenda, name ministers, and appoint heads of various control bodies. Between 1989 and 1998, the strong Brazilian presidents succeeded in having 68.0 percent of their bills passed within the same year in which they were proposed. Moreover, 83.8 percent of all legislation that was passed was initiated by the executive. But British prime ministers had 93.2 percent of their bills passed, while 83.1 percent of all bills passed were initiated by the executive (Figuereido 2000). Indeed, the rate of legislative success of the Brazilian presidents was lower than in any of the eleven OECD countries listed by Figuereido, and the rate of the Argentine presidents between 1984 and 1997 was even lower than in Brazil, 64.1 percent (Jones et al. 2000). Where, then, is democracy "delegative": in a country in which the executive gets his or her way 68 percent of the time or in one where the executive gets his or her way 93.2 percent of the time?

Perhaps Latin American chief executives are less accountable than their OECD counterparts in some important ways that were not captured by these comparisons. But I hope to have at least shifted the burden of proof. Lament is not enough.

Political Parties and Social Accountability

Why is the theme of social accountability so important in many Latin American democracies? The answer, I think, is that the political institution that once was the quintessential instrument of social accountability no longer performs this role. Obviously, I am speaking of political parties, and perhaps less obviously but again, this transformation of political parties is not limited to Latin America.

If we were discussing the topic of social accountability in 1913 or still in 1950, it would have been obvious how it is exercised. Recourse to parties is what I skipped in my introductory list of "what you can do." In 1913 or 1950, you would have stood up at the weekly or monthly party meeting; you would have exhorted the party to do something about teacher absenteeism, the mail, or government checks; the local party organization would have resolved to transmit the demand to higher party authorities or directly to the relevant government bureaucracy. If your party was in the opposition, you would perhaps have not gotten much action from the government, but your demands would have entered the platform of your party in the next electoral campaign. If your party controlled the relevant bureaucracy, you would have gotten satisfaction or at least the promise of such.

The role of political parties requires a clarification. According to democratic theory, or at least the parts of this theory that recognize the existence of political parties at all, parties are supposed to be vehicles by which citizens are represented in the public realm. But public bureaucracy is supposed to be nonpartisan, in the sense of not favoring supporters of one or another party. Parties are supposed to advocate and implement different policies, but partisan governments are supposed to treat all citizens equally. In fact, in many countries, from India to Italy, or even more subnational units, governing parties developed clientelistic institutions that in the United States bear the name of "party machines."[6] As the anecdote in the footnote suggests, party machines are a mechanism of social accountability, but only for those citizens who are willing to sell their vote, in one form or another, for the services offered by the party.

But even machines are these days at best vestiges of the past. For reasons into which I will not delve, mass political parties became over time purely electoral organizations that function intermittently at the time of elections. They lost their socially integrative function: no one could say today, with Ostrogorsky: "Do not convince them, take them in socially." Parties try to convince individuals to vote for their members by relying mainly on mass media. Any kind of a daily, permanent connection is gone.

None of the above is specific to Latin America. I need not document the decline of party membership, readership of party newspapers, or party activities in Western Europe. I do not have comparable numbers for Latin America, but it is difficult to imagine that political parties could be weaker than among the OECD countries. One repeated claim is that citizens' confidence in political parties is exceptionally low in Latin America. This is yet another lament. I know of no country where political parties (or politicians) do not occupy last place among the institutions with regard to which people are asked to express their confidence. Parties everywhere are no longer instruments of social accountability, and people everywhere seem to hold them in low esteem.

NGOs and Social Accountability

The search for social accountability is not devoid of fashions. "Communes," associations of direct producers, were Pierre Prudhon's way of solving the problem: simply bypassing the existing state institutions. But state institutions can coerce, so they cannot be ignored, and only a political party can achieve control over the state: this was Marx's message to the First International in 1867. A century later, parties had already been discredited: since all parties did was compete in elections, social movements became the only way in which popular demands could be promoted. But social movement were either violently repressed or died quietly, and now social accountability can be exercised only through nongovernmental organizations.[7]

There are three reasons one should not be blinded by this recent fashion. The first one concerns the incentives of the NGOs. Not only do they represent particularistic interests, but, like all organizations, they are populated by people who may not be devoid of self-interest. Particularistic interests lead to corporatist arrangements that exclude those who are not organized and not included. Self-interest leads to "capture": collusion between those who are supposed to take accounts and those who are supposed to render them. This is an old theme in Western Europe, excellently analyzed by Cunill Grau (1997), so I will not continue.

A related danger, also highlighted by Cunill Grau (1997), is that mechanisms of social accountability can have a highly nonegalitarian effect. They offer access to the political system to those who have resources to organize and promote their interests. One should not forget that the most influential nongovernmental organizations in our societies are business lobbies. It is seductive to speak of "watchdog" organizations. But perhaps the "watchdog" organization that affects the welfare of Argentines most is Moody's risk-rating service. If this watchdog organization declassifies Argentina from A- to B++, the country loses hundreds of millions of dollars. In the end, elections are the most egalitarian mechanism of access to politics. They may not be effective, but they are egalitarian.

Finally, as emphasized again by Cunill Grau, one must consider the effect of new mechanisms of accountability on the existing ones. Public supervision of government bureaucracies may enhance participation but may also paralyze it. Referenda, imperative mandates, and recall, a new trend in Latin America, do enhance popular control over governments, but one must examine the dangers they may create for the coherence of public policy and for individual rights.

Do not get me wrong. There is something to lament about Latin America: the inequality of incomes. It would be redundant to cite the numbers (but see Przeworski 1998). The fact is that income distribution in Latin American countries is much more unequal than in either Western or Eastern Europe and that, if anything, the inequality is increasing. Although the distribution of income in the least unequal Latin American country is more unequal than in the most unequal Western European one, and Western European countries redistribute a sizeable part of market-earned incomes (Milanovic 1999), redistribution of income through transfers is minimal in Latin America. I should note that this assertion is not based on a systematic comparison of numbers. But one does not even need numbers: it is sufficient to look at the categories in the national accounts to find that many items that represent transfers in Western Europe are just absent in Latin American countries. Transfers to households, other than retirement pensions, are not even mentioned in the euphemistically entitled *Economic and Social Progress in Latin America,* a publication of the Inter-American Development Bank (1996). Redistribution through social policies fares no better. As of 1990, public educational expenditures constituted 4.3 percent of GNP in Latin America and the Caribbean and 5.7 percent in the industrial countries, and they were highly regressive. Public health expenditures made up 3.55 percent of GNP in Latin America and the Caribbean and 5.88 percent in the industrial economies, while private health expenditures amounted to 1.9 percent in industrial countries and 2.7 percent in Latin America and the Caribbean. Some people earn high incomes and consume and purchase educational and health services. Others struggle to survive. And governments do little to alter this situation.

But is this because democratic institutions are distinctly deficient in Latin America? I do not think so, and I hope to have shown that this cannot be the reason. Hence, I am skeptical that the high degree of inequality and prevalence of poverty in Latin America are due to the weakness of mechanisms of accountability, electoral, horizontal, or social. What they are due to, I do not know.

NOTES

1. Since only democracies are considered, Mexico (as of 1995), Paraguay, and Peru are not included.

2. Note that veto powers are a constraint not on the chief executive but on the legislature.

3. Ideally, one would also want to include some measures of judicial independence, but no reliable data comparing countries seem to be available.

4. These two variables are coded 2 if both the legislature and the executive are elected, 1 if only one is elected, and 0 if neither is elected. Numbers of observations vary for each column.

5. The Chilean president can also call for a plebiscite and appoint a regional administration.

6. Having lived in Chicago, I know how these worked. Once my car was frozen in a thick layer of ice; I called the city government and waited fruitlessly. After a couple of days (in Chicago, ice does not melt), I called the local precinct captain. He was at my door in one hour, pointing out that I had not voted in the last local election. But I answered that I am a registered Democrat and promised to vote next time. My car was free a few hours later.

7. Putnam's (2000) observation is that many people prefer to pay others to promote their values rather than spending the time doing so themselves.

BIBLIOGRAPHY

Anastasia, Fatima. 1999. "Responsibilazação por Controle Parlamentar." Working paper prepared for CLAD, Caracas.

Beck, Thorsten, George Clark, Alberto Groff, Philip Keefer, and Patrick Walsh. 2000. "New Tools and New Tests in Comparative Political Economy: The Database of Political Institutions." Washington, D.C.: World Bank.

Cukierman, Alex, and Steven Web. 1995. "Political Influence on the Central Bank: International Evidence." *World Bank Review*, September 9, 1995, 397–423.

Cunill Grau, Nuria. 1997. *Repensando lo Público a Través de la Sociedad.* Caracas: Nueva Sociedad.

Dahl, Robert. 1971. *Polyarchy: Participation and Opposition.* New Haven: Yale University Press.

Figuereido, Argelina Cheibub. 2000. "Institutional Power and the Role of Congress as a Mechanism of Horizontal Accountability: Lessons from the Brazilian Experience." Paper presented at the Conference on Institutions, Accountability, and Democratic Governance in Latin America, Kellogg Institute, University of Notre Dame, May 8–9.

Figuereido, Argelina Cheibub, and Fernando Limongi. 1999. *Ejecutivo e Legislativo na Nova Ordem Constitucional.* Rio de Janeiro: Fundação Getúlio Vargas.

Gandhi, Jennifer, and Adam Przeworski. 2000. "Political Institutions and Redistribution of Income." Paper presented at the annual meeting of the American Political Science Association, Washington, D.C., September.

Henisz, Witold. 2000. "The Institutional Environment for Economic Growth." *Economics and Politics* 12, no. 1: 1–31.

Inter-American Development Bank. 1996. *Economic and Social Progress in Latin America.* Washington, D.C.: The Johns Hopkins University Press.

Jones, Mark, Sebastian Saiegh, Pablo Spiller, and Mariano Tommasi. 2000. "Amateur Legislators, Professional Politicians." Buenos Aires: Universidad San Andres.

Kelsen, Hans. 1929. *Vom Wesen und Wert der Demokratie.* Aalen: Scientia Verlag.

Manin, Bernard. 1994. "Checks, Balances, and Boundaries: The Separation of Powers in the Constitutional Debate of 1787." In Biancamaria Fontana, ed., *The Invention of the Modern Republic.* Cambridge: Cambridge University Press.

———. 1997. *Principles of Representative Government.* Cambridge: Cambridge University Press.

Milanovic, Branko. 1999. "Do More Unequal Countries Redistribute More? Does the Median Voter Hypothesis Hold?" Washington, D.C.: World Bank.

O'Donnell, Guillermo. 1991. "Delegative Democracy?" East-South System Transformations Working Paper 21. University of Chicago.

———. 1997. "Horizontal Accountability and New Polyarchies." Paper presented at the conference Institutionalizing Horizontal Accountability, Institute for Advanced Studies of Vienna and International Forum for Democratic Studies, Vienna, June 1997.

Przeworski, Adam. 1998. "O Estado e o Cidadão." Paper presented at the conference Sociedade e Rerforma do Estado, São Paulo, March 26–28.

Przeworski, Adam, Susan C. Stokes, and Bernard Manin, eds. 1999. *Democracy, Accountability, and Representation.* New York: Cambridge University Press.

Putnam, Robert. 2000. *Bowling Alone: The Collapse and Revival of American Community.* New York: Simon and Schuster.

Riker, William. 1965. *Democracy in America.* 2d ed. New York: Macmillan.

Tsebelis, George. 1995. "Decision-Making in Political Systems: Veto Players in Presidentialism, Multicameralism, and Pluripartism." *British Journal of Political Science* 25: 289–325.

13

Notes on Various Accountabilities and Their Interrelations

Guillermo O'Donnell

I HAVE FOR some time been involved in, and concerned about, a subject that I call "horizontal accountability." The definition I have offered of this term is as follows: "The existence of state agencies that are legally enabled and empowered, and factually willing and able, to undertake actions that span from routine oversight to criminal sanctions or impeachment, in relation to actions or omissions, by other state agents or agencies, that may be qualified as unlawful."[1]

I differentiate this type of accountability from vertical accountability, which I define as the mechanism of elections. I also notice, among the good news that the contemporary picture offers, that

> in many new democracies various organizations have emerged (some of them human rights organizations that have broadened the initial definition of their mission) that vigorously demand that state officials respect the basic *liberal* freedoms and guarantees of (mostly) the weak and the poor. Other organizations supervise elections and undertake other *democratic* tasks, such as trying to educate the population in the knowledge and

> exercise of their political rights. Still others act as *republican* watchdogs of the lawfulness of state actions in terms both of their possible encroachment over other state agencies and of appropriate ethical conduct by public officials.[2]

In the above I underscore the words *liberal, democratic,* and *republican* because, as I argue elsewhere, they are the three major currents, partially concurrent and partially conflictive, that combine in contemporary democracies.[3] Based on this, I also make two other arguments: one, that the weight of each of these currents varies quite substantially in different democracies; and two, that in a good portion of them, the case of Latin America included, the relative weight of the liberal and republican currents is markedly weaker than the democratic one. I also argue that the weakness of the liberal and republican dimensions is expressed, among other ways, in serious horizontal accountability deficits.

On the other hand, in listing the "good news" earlier, I drew on data generated by research on social movements, human rights, civil society, social capital, and other issues. Catalina Smulovitz and Enrique Peruzzotti take two important steps concerning these phenomena.[4] First, they band these phenomena under the concept of (vertical) social accountability, differentiating such mechanisms from the traditional mechanism of vertical electoral accountability. Second, they present a number of arguments and hypotheses about the characteristics and consequences of social accountability.

Obviously, like the concept of horizontal accountability, social accountability includes phenomena that, even though they share characteristics allowing them to be considered part of the same concept, have distinguishing features. This makes it advisable to engage in what this volume advances: an analytical and empirical exploration of some of these characteristics, not only in themselves but also comparatively as they appear in different national and subnational contexts. For such an exploration to be possible, I argue, it would be convenient to build typologies of various kinds of social accountability phenomena; otherwise we risk getting lost in the wide variety of situations empirically included in this concept.

The following observations are intended to contribute to the issues addressed in this volume. However, since lately I have been interested in horizontal accountability, my comments will mainly explore its interrelationship with social accountability.

Horizontal Accountability and the Rule of Law

I argue elsewhere that for horizontal accountability to work reasonably well, it is useful, although not sufficient, for at least one state agency to be seriously committed to acting in the direction of making it effective. For horizontal accountability to work, in particular over powerful segments of the state and government, the convergent and coordinated work of an entire network of institutions with legal authority, decision-making autonomy, and determination has to exist. With the exemption of some rare cases of impeachment, the effectiveness of this network leads very often to courts, especially higher courts, where final rulings are handed down against individuals situated in other state agencies. It is likely that the existence of a network of agencies (including courts) seriously determined to make horizontal accountability work acts as an invisible, albeit important, factor against wrongdoing and corruption. When horizontal accountability is effective and perceived as such, it becomes important not only for what it does but also for what it prevents.

For horizontal accountability to work, there must be a democratic state of law, especially in relation to the upper echelons of the state—the executive—where historically it has been more difficult to control and eventually sanction the respective officials. This effectiveness is the republican dimension of democracy. It entails the obligation of rulers and in general of state agents to accept and respect the legal and constitutional limitations of their respective jurisdictions, both in relation to other public jurisdictions (which I call the obligation of no trespassing) and insofar as they should not put private interests above the public ones they are supposed to serve (the obligation not to be corrupt).

As Argentina's recent history shows, the weakness of horizontal accountability can coexist with at least some liberal, or civil, rights, including those that are especially relevant for social accountability such as freedom of expression (including freedom of the press), freedom of assembly, and freedom of movement and association.[5] On the other hand, if a certain executive power—it matters very little whether it is delegative or not at this point, but certainly one very similar to Argentina's a short while ago—dauntlessly sets out to eliminate or neutralize horizontal accountability's mechanisms and, in so doing, exhibits intentions to trespass the legally established boundaries of its authority, then one ought to be skeptical about the willingness of that executive to honor the civil rights of those who undoubtedly have challenged him or her while exercising social accountability.

If despite this situation social accountability still exists, manifesting itself in a variety of ways, it will certainly not be because there is full democratic rule of law or a government that accepts it. As Smulovitz and Peruzzotti point out, it will be because there are people and organizations in society who feel with enough intensity that they find it worthwhile to engage in initiatives of social accountability and have the individual and collective capabilities to do so. That these rights exist under governments that are not liberal or republican can only be explained by the fact that, as Smulovitz and Peruzzotti also notice, those exercising social accountability would impose prohibitive costs in any attempt to eliminate these rights. In addition, if these rights were eliminated, such a government would no longer be able to enjoy the benefit of international legitimacy that a reasonable degree of respect for these rights generates. What this means is that in the contemporary world, democratically elected governments can, to a certain extent, get away with violating horizontal accountability (especially when not too much corruption is involved) but cannot seriously and systematically violate rights such as expression, assembly, movement, and association. To a great extent this is true because these rights must exist for the sake of the democratic dimension of electoral accountability (vertical) implied in competitive elections. Without a reasonable degree of enforcement of civil rights, that is, without the possibility of holding competitive elections in which the opposition could truly challenge the ruling party, the existing regime would no longer be democratic.[6] Thus, though analytically and empirically different, accountability's three dimensions, electoral, societal, and horizontal, are closely related. What are the implications of this?

Interrelationships

Elsewhere I mention two types of horizontal accountability.[7] The first, which I label "balancing" institutions, refers to the three traditional powers—executive, legislative, and judicial—that constitutions, starting with the U.S. and now practically all over the world, try to balance.[8] Throughout history, these institutions have been supplemented, at different sequences and with different characteristics depending on the country, by agencies that I term "appointed" (*asignadas*)—for example, the offices of prosecutors, auditors, *conseils d'état,* and ombudsmen. The creation of these institutions was a consequence of the deficits of balancing institutions as instruments of horizontal accountability.

These deficits are several. First, they are reactive and, therefore, intermittent; they only react when a wrongdoing has been committed by another power or is about to be. Second, they frequently involve dramatic and politically costly conflicts among the supreme state powers, a situation that worsens because actors are often suspected of acting for partisan reasons.[9] Last, since the attention of those that hold the respective powers is focused on carrying out their own constitutional duties, and given the growing complexity and specialization of state bureaucracies and policies, balancing institutions turn out to be blunt instruments for the exercise of horizontal accountability.

In the face of these deficits, appointed agencies have some advantages. Rather than exercising control in a reactive and intermittent manner, many of these agencies are proactive and permanent. In addition, their actions invoke professional, apolitical criteria that tend to diminish the hype and conflicts usually involved when balancing institutions intervene. Finally, appointed agencies can specialize in digging through some of the complex and often arcane terrains of state bureaucracy and policies.

Ideally, the workings of both types of horizontal accountability agencies should complement each other. As I mention earlier, their effectiveness depends on their having the legal authority, the will, and the information to undertake the pertinent actions. I will not elaborate here on the implications of these observations. However, given the topic of this volume, my observations up to this point may help to imagine a map of state institutions. In this map we can find, first, the great balancing institutions, which we can evaluate in terms of their effectiveness as elements of horizontal accountability. We can also observe, with important variations from country to country, a series of appointed agencies. Some have broad jurisdiction over several types of issues, while others are quite specialized, and still others can be found at the subnational level, and any might relate exclusively to state bureaucracies or to elected officials, or to both. After having drawn this surely complex map, the really important question is which of these agencies effectively fulfill their responsibilities as horizontal accountability institutions.

From a social accountability perspective, this map can be rather discouraging. In Latin American countries it may well be the case, and often is, that practically none of these agencies, whether balancing or appointed, are willing or able to perform their specific horizontal responsibilities. Yet to those engaged in social accountability such a map may signal some strategic opportunities.

The existence of at least some horizontal accountability agencies that are willing and able to carry out their responsibilities (although let us say that due to an ineffective judiciary they are prevented from closing the cycle of their respective processes) is an important element of social accountability *induction.* In general, the chances for the success of a given social accountability action, or at least for its receiving a serious hearing, are strongly influenced by the disposition to consequently act on the part of some relevant horizontal accountability agencies. But the same holds true in the opposite direction. The existence of certain social accountability demands, especially if they are well organized, continuous, and present in the media, is surely an important source of *stimulation* for some horizontal accountability agencies to assume their responsibilities.

No doubt each dimension of accountability (the two verticals, electoral and societal, and the two horizontals, balancing and appointed) is in itself important. But I am convinced that a good part of the more interesting and politically relevant phenomena (as well as of those that need further research) may be found in the interactions among these dimensions. This seems to me especially relevant for those cases in which, as is usually true of Latin America, several of these dimensions malfunction. It is in these interactions, both of induction and stimulation, where chances to move forward in the much-needed democratization of these countries can be found.

Finally, horizontal accountability has a lateral effect on the exercise of vertical accountability, both electoral and societal. Both balancing and appointed institutions are not generally designed to generate information that may be accessed by the public or the media. But if these agencies work more or less effectively, they generate information that can be appropriated for the exercise of electoral and social accountability. Though rarely mentioned, this is a very important contribution that horizontal accountability can make to strengthening democracy, even in relation to its vertical electoral and social dimensions.

About Social Accountability

After this journey through the interactions between vertical and horizontal accountability mechanisms, I return to the valuable concept of social accountability, which term has been coined by the editors of this volume. It is important to recall the origins of this concept. The idea that an active, well-organized society invigorates a representative regime and promotes accountability of public officials is as old, at least, as Locke. In the twentieth century, the Anglo-Saxon pluralists (Bentley, Truman, and the first Dahl) emphasized, often to the extreme, the role played by organized social groups in a democracy. More recently, the work (supposedly neo-Tocquevillean) of Robert Putnam and the literature about social capital have resurrected interest in the political inputs of society. Smulovitz and Peruzzotti have contributed productively to this question. The novelty of their contribution lies, I think, in two aspects that their predecessors overlooked. One is the notion that the main orientation of the actions embraced by the concept of social accountability is not—at least directly—the satisfaction of material interests. Rather, the actions focus on demands that certain matters of general interest are "adequately" considered by the government and/or that a given state agency adjust its actions according to what is legally prescribed to it. Although I suspect that sometimes it will not be easy to distinguish among them, social accountability agents and movements are not "pressure groups," "interest groups," or "neocorporatist" institutions, about all of which, as we know, there is abundant literature.[10] The second original aspect of the concept of social accountability that is worth highlighting, not only because of its importance but also because it is a new phenomenon in Latin America since the transitions from authoritarian rule, is that, as these authors have insisted, social accountability demands are usually formulated in the language of rights and legality.[11]

The concept of social accountability seems useful, among other reasons, because it bands together a series of diverse activities that share some common features. Furthermore, Smulovitz and Peruzzotti convincingly argue that social accountability is an important component of democratic life. Once the analytically convenient step has been taken of grouping under one concept a diverse series of activities with some important common characteristics, the next step is to disaggregate the concept into subtypes, in order to examine certain specific, uncommon characteristics and consequences of these activities. Although this step is of course not atheoretical, its principal implication is empirical and comparative. Prudently, the initial Smulovitz and Peruzzotti work does not venture much in this direction, in anticipation of later empirical and comparative contributions (of which the present volume is the first manifestation).

Toward a Research Agenda

I have suggested the convenience of creating social accountability typologies. Of course, the usefulness of a typology depends on the questions asked. Typologies can be based on the characteristics of the agent of social accountability: whether individuals, social movements, formal organizations, and so on. Or they can be based on the repertoire and strategies of the agents. Or, of course, these typologies can intersect. This said, I would suggest a few more possibilities that, given my central interest in horizontal accountability, will not be surprising. The concept of social accountability relies, as Smulovitz and Peruzzotti suggest, on the Hirschmanian idea of voice.[12] This is a voice that, as suggested by the vertical metaphor, is aimed "upward," from society toward the government. I am tempted to say that the "verticality" of social accountability has a tendential destiny. It is a voice that expects and demands to be heard by some state agencies so they in turn act over other state agencies.

Some empirical questions derive from this. Which social accountability actions are heard, and which are not? What role do balancing and appointed agencies play? Which social accountability actions lead to some sort of state response activity but finally fail because they do not follow a complete institutional and decisional path? A fine-tuning of these questions, combined with types of horizontal accountability agencies, may function as a first road map for studies across cases or along time, at the national or subnational level.

This perspective also seems pertinent in view of some useful points raised by Smulovitz.[13] Exercising social accountability requires not only a high degree of subjective intensity concerning the issue in question but also sufficient personal and organizational resources (some combination of time, information, media access, capacity of public and/or interpersonal communication, and at times money). The absence of any combination of these resources condemns many questions to the silent cemetery of nonissues. This is especially serious in Latin American countries, where resources are distributed in an extremely unequal fashion. Since, as we know, research on nonissues is a methodological hell, if we are not willing to confront this question directly, we could ask what the eventual effectiveness of social accountability entails for socially weak or excluded sectors. What resources or strategies may such sectors employ? What points of access and/or occlusion do they find in the state and government? What kinds of actions have been successful in certain cases? How decisive and lasting are their achievements, if any? To what degree do these actions tend to generate public goods, or goods for the sectors mobilized, or individual benefits for some of them? How and when does the media (and what type of media) cover these actions?

Obviously with the preceding questions I do not intend to be rigorous or exhaustive. But I should add that the type of research that may emerge from these questions would be especially interesting if compared with data related to similar actions of relatively privileged sectors. Likewise, it would be interesting to compare cases in which popular sectors act alone with instances in which their demands are assumed or supported by relatively privileged sectors or associations.

I now add a note of caution for the future development of this promising line of study about social accountability. Be aware that the definition of social accountability almost inexorably leads to questions concerning the echo that the voice exercised in this way finds in the state and the government.[14] This matter pertains to one of the traditional topics of political science: that of social demands, or inputs, on the state and government, and this line of thinking leads us to ask about the type of actors, the ways in which they formulate their demands, the resources they mobilize, and the constraints that limit their actions and their chances of success. The advantage of the definition of social accountability advanced by Smulovitz and Peruzzotti is, as I already mention, that it restricts the topic to a subset of inputs: actions that do not invoke, at least directly, material interests and that are expressed mainly in a language of rights and legality. However, the variety and complexity of the phenomena that still remain in this subset are enormous. For this reason, I suggest that the theoretical and empirical development of a novel and interesting concept such as social accountability requires, as has often been the case in the social sciences, a careful appropriation of its lineage and experimentation with subtypes to be tested in their usefulness by means of comparative and longitudinal research.

NOTES

1. Guillermo O'Donnell, "Horizontal Accountabilities in New Democracies," in Andreas Schedler, Larry Diamond, and Marc F. Plattner, eds., *The Self-Restraining State: Power and Accountability in New Democracies* (Boulder and London: Lynne Rienner Publishers, 1999), 38. See also Guillermo O'Donnell, "Horizontal Accountability: The Legal Institutionalization of Mistrust," in Scott Mainwaring and Christopher Welna, eds., *Democratic Accountability in Latin America* (New York: Oxford University Press, 2003).
2. O'Donnell, "Horizontal Accountabilities in New Democracies," 43.

3. To keep this chapter from being too long, I will also refer to my "Horizontal Accountabilities in New Democracies" as it applies to these three terms.

4. See Catalina Smulovitz and Enrique Peruzzotti; "Societal Accountability in Latin America," *Journal of Democracy* 11, no. 4 (2000): 147–58; and "Societal and Horizontal Controls: Two Cases about a Fruitful Relationship," in Mainwaring and Welna, *Democratic Accountability in Latin America.*

5. For a discussion of these rights and their relationship to political democracy, see Guillermo O'Donnell, "Democracy, Law, and Comparative Politics," *Studies in International Comparative Development* 36, no. 1 (2001): 5–36. In this text I argue that a democratic state of law (*estado democrático de derecho*) not only establishes and supports rules and laws inherent in a definition of political democracy (or polyarchy). It is also a legal system that "closes," since no one, even though he or she may try, is exempt from these rules. I also point out that the subsequent *de legibus solutus* prohibition constitutes one of the characteristics that differentiates political democracy from authoritarian regimes or states.

6. The basis for these statements can be found in O'Donnell, "Teoria Democratica y Politica Comparada," *Desarrollo Economico* 39, no. 56 (2000): 519–70.

7. Guillermo O'Donnell, "Horizontal Accountability."

8. This is even the case of European parliamentary regimes that since the Second World War have adopted several types of judicial review of the constitutionality of acts by other branches.

9. It needs to be remembered that my definition of horizontal accountability does not include any type of interaction among government institutions, even if they imply mutual control. It refers exclusively to actions initiated by a state agency on the basis of a claim that another agency has committed or is about to commit an illegal act.

10. Since all of these groups, including social accountability groups, have in common the fact that they make demands on the state, it is likely that this literature will offer analytical and empirical points that could prove useful for the study of social accountability.

11. See n. 5. Also see Catalina Smulovitz, "Constitucion y Poder Judicial en la Nueva Democracia Argentina: La Experiencia de las Instituciones," in Carlos Acuña, ed., *La Nueva Matriz Politica Argentina* (Buenos Aires: Nueva Vision, 1995), 71–114; and Enrique Peruzzotti, "Modernization and Juridification in Latin America: A Reassessment of the Latin American Development Path," *Thesis Eleven* 58 (1999): 59–82.

12. Albert Hirschman, *Exit, Voice and Loyalty: Responses to Decline in Firms, Organizations and States* (Cambridge: Harvard University Press, 1970). I suspect that the abundant literature this book originated could also be useful for the analytical and empirical study of social accountability.

13. Catalina Smulovitz, "How Can the Rule of Law Rule: Cost Imposition through Decentralized Mechanisms," in José María Maravall and Adam Przeworski, eds., *Democracy and the Rule of Law* (Cambridge: Cambridge University Press, 2003).

14. It should be noted that sometimes a neglected voice can have important consequences. For example, demands that repeatedly never end in punishment of an act of corruption or wrongdoing can heavily influence public opinion and help defeat the ruling government at the polls. In other words, there could also be an important connection between the societal and electoral dimensions of vertical accountability.

14

Concluding Remarks

Enrique Peruzzotti and Catalina Smulovitz

Social Accountability and Redrawing the Frontiers of Citizenship

What can be learned from the different initiatives of social accountability that have been analyzed in this volume? Can they help us to shed new light on prevailing diagnoses of the state of democracy in Latin America? Are social accountability mechanisms changing the ways in which democracies operate in the region? Do they represent a voice strong enough to improve the quality of representative arrangements in Latin America? While the set of experiences that are the focus of previous chapters might be too limited for challenging long-standing and deep-rooted institutional and political practices, they nevertheless serve as an index of a number of important developments that have taken place in many of the region's civil societies, adding an optimistic note to what has so far been a predominantly somber diagnosis about the state of democracy in the region.

A common thread links most of the experiences of societal accountability analyzed in this volume. They show that previously socially tolerated or unquestioned practices are now not only being perceived as injurious but are also being readdressed in the form of rights-oriented claims. Police abuse, governmental corruption, electoral fraud, unequal enforcement of the rule of law, and human rights violations have not been uncommon practices in the region. However, only recently have they become the object of social claims and the rallying point of rights demands oriented toward political authorities. The transformation of these ingrained practices into rights claims, which led to the organization of different sorts of civic movements and initiatives to address them, reveals that the notion of citizenship is undergoing important transformations, as are the inherited notions of what constitutes the most adequate institutional environment for the effective exercise of citizenship rights. The different experiences analyzed here, where previously neglected issues are suddenly converted into vociferous rights controversies, show that in many of the new democracies inherited notions of citizenship are being contested, expanded, or redefined. Insofar as the extension and scope of citizenship are not given, but contingent on the actions and discourses that social actors exercise in the public sphere, the analyzed experiences provide a space to observe how the frontiers and content of citizenship in the region are the object of political contestation.

The cases also illustrate that once injuries and demands are understood in the language of rights and accountability, the linkage between citizens and political authorities changes. A more demanding and critical attitude of the citizenry toward their representatives results in the emergence of a politics of social accountability and introduces a healthy element of distrust into the representative bond.[1] When the relationship between citizens and political authorities becomes mediated by a discourse of rights and accountability, the entitlements and obligations of citizens and of political authorities are redefined. From the point of view of the citizens, such a transformation implies that they can now demand that, and eventually force, political authorities to respond to and intervene in disputes that could be avoided or ignored before, when they were not seen as problematic. By putting into the spotlight questionable institutional practices of public officials, the politics of social accountability has established accountability issues as one of the dominant topics on the region's public agenda in the past decade. Furthermore, as claims and initiatives have grown in number and scope, the accountability agenda has been substantially broadened. In the past years, the number of matters, as well as the number of governmental agencies, that are under public scrutiny has expanded well beyond what was considered the classic repertoire of accountability issues to include a broad set of questions that range from the meeting of sound environmental standards to the transparency of the public bidding process.

The politics of social accountability is guided by a general concern about legal and procedural questions: a central goal of this form of politics is to improve the procedures that regulate the behavior of public officials and strengthen the devices to control and punish any deviation from due process. In these novel struggles, in which sectors of the citizenry monitor the behavior of political elites and evaluate the performance of existing institutional safeguards against unscrupulous public officials, a new link between citizens and politicians is being forged. Representative institutions are now under the close scrutiny of different social actors willing to mold existing practices and arrangements to the novel cry for governmental accountability. Yet the questions remain: Does this form of politicization necessarily increase the accountability of political authorities? What consequences does it have for the representative relationship?

Social Accountability and Representative Institutions

Assessments of the effects of accountability mechanisms have usually focused on the existence of institutional sanctions. Some authors argue that unless institutional and mandatory sanctions, such as judicial sentences or adverse electoral results, take place, there are no conclusive indicators of the performance of these mechanisms.[2] Without some form of enforcement or formal sanction, political actors lack any "real" incentive to change their behavior. Does this mean that the reviewed initiatives of social accountability are consequently irrelevant for assessing changes in the working of governmental agencies and actors? The cases analyzed here show that even when they possess not mandatory but largely symbolic effects, the mechanisms of social accountability cannot be easily disregarded. As most of the cases illustrate, the combination of social pressure and media exposure is usually not only an effective way to force political authorities to give public explanations for their actions but in many cases has also had an institutional impact: on some occasions, this combination has motivated legislative shifts (e.g., police reforms, reform of oversight procedures for judicial nominations, an end to compulsory military service); in other situations, they have forced the activation of an otherwise reluctant network of horizontal agencies (e.g., parliamentary investigative commissions) or the resignation of public servants who were implicated in or suspected of acts of wrongdoing (e.g., the resignation of *prefectos* in Brazil and of governors in Argentina). Even though these outcomes are not the result of the imposition of formal sanctions by a mandatory institution, social accountability mechanisms have been able to successfully restrict the abilities of political authorities to act in discretionary or unresponsive ways.

Consider, for example, the case of police abuse. Even though judicial sanctions of abusive policemen have been scarce, the analysis shows that social accountability mechanisms have been able to transform an old and relatively hidden phenomenon into a highly visible and relevant question on the public and electoral agenda. As a result of the emergence of social initiatives against police violence, multiple and diverse actors have become involved in a public debate about existing institutional practices and the need to address a process of reform of the police, facilitated legislative changes and administrative purges, and led establishment of social watchdog agencies. All these outcomes show that the ability of civil society actors to hold public officials accountable for their behavior has increased, even if these initiatives have resulted in only a limited number of judicial sanctions of wrongdoers.

Assessment of the existence of accountability cannot be restricted to the presence of institutional tools and sanctions. In spite of the difficulties involved in its evaluation, these results show that accountability can be achieved through informal means. Social demonstrations, media scandals, and civic actions might be successful in mobilizing public opinion and, in turn, generating important reputation costs for the officials or agencies under the spotlight. In contrast to formal sanctions, symbolic ones do not automatically produce compulsory outcomes. Their diffuse character prevents both controlling and controlled actors from knowing whether negative reputation costs will actually activate institutional and compulsory mechanisms. There is no certainty, for example, that reputation sanctions will necessarily change voting behavior. Paradoxically, such uncertainty might serve to enlarge the threat capacity of symbolic sanctions. Since their actual extent or effects cannot be anticipated, public officials eager to avoid their potential indeterminate effects are encouraged to attempt preemptive defensive behaviors. Thus, even though public authorities do not know whether reputation sanctions will actually end up generating institutional sanctions, they know these sanctions can affect them and, consequently, adjust their behavior accordingly.

Evaluation of the impact of symbolic or reputation sanctions is always a difficult task, for it inevitably has to rely on indirect indicators such as changes in the array of issues on the political agenda, the occurrence of legislative changes, administrative purges, or evidence about the creation of social watchdogs. Although these indicators regarding the effectiveness of social sanctions are not unrelated, they cannot be considered as categories of an ordinal scale. While in certain cases (e.g., police abuse in Argentina), social accountability follows a path that includes all types of outcomes (agenda setting, response to the specific case, legislative change, administrative purges, and the creation of social watchdogs), in others, such as certain media scandals, the results include public exposure and administrative purges, although not necessarily the other outcomes.

Let us turn now to some of the consequences of the politics of social accountability for representative institutions. As mentioned, the expansion of the frontiers of citizenship entails the expansion of the number of issues that merit rights and accountability claims. Such expansion improves citizens' ability to realize their interests, to protect themselves from arbitrary political powers, and to control the way in which public authorities behave on public matters. This virtuous scenario assumes that the existence of multiple and decentralized external eyes overseeing political authorities' behavior results in the constitution of limited governments because it increases the costs of violating norms, as well as the number of individuals interested in law abidance. The uncontrolled proliferation of a diffuse, yet highly vocal mass of claims and actions acts as an effective and continuous surveillance mechanism of public behavior that reinforces virtuous behavior and thus democratic rule. However, is the cycle always virtuous? What happens when societal accountability mechanisms fail to produce results? That is, what happens when demands for the accountability of political authorities or public servants are mobilized and yet positive outcomes do not follow?

As the different chapters here show, the emergence of citizen claims and the organization of citizen movements have placed the demand for the "quality" of democratic institutions at the center of the debates about democracy in the region. These demands and activities have introduced procedural questions and due-process worries as a crucial yardstick to evaluate the performance of political representatives. The emergence of citizen and civil society organizations organized around demands for governmental accountability introduces a form of politicization that differs from party politics or special-interest representation. In contrast with the former, the movements and associations engaged in initiatives of control of public authorities do not fund their interventions through the representative character of their demand or the extended nature of their voice. Their legitimacy derives from procedural or countermajoritarian claims. The irruption of this sort of demand might introduce some noise and tension into relations of representation that in certain cases might adversely affect the link of citizens with their political representatives. While this form of citizenship politicization aims at improving the quality and performance of political institutions, under certain circumstances it might inadvertently weaken the ability of the representatives to exercise their authority by introducing a permanent state of malaise regarding the behavior of representatives. In other words, the distrust necessary for the exercise of citizen surveillance might create, at the same time, citizen disaffection and distance from the political community, potentially weakening the political and social integration of a community.[3]

In its virtuous face, social accountability demands trigger a commendable cycle that results in the establishment of better and more effective mechanisms of accountability that help to build and reinforce social trust in representative arrangements. Yet this is not always the case. Under certain circumstances, such a continuous exercise of distrust may not trigger any political or institutional response. In those cases where the "healthy" exercise of distrust does not render the expected outcomes but encounters the refusal of politicians to abide by the civic cry for accountability, the outcome might be the generalization of cynical and destructive forms of civic distrust.

Relations of accountability rest on a delicate equilibrium between trust and distrust. Accountability cannot take place unless citizens show a certain amount of distrust about what political authorities might do. Citizens accept delegating authority to their representatives because the exercise of "institutionalized distrust," as Guillermo O'Donnell has labeled it, protects the trust involved in the delegation that takes place in the representative relationship.[4] Citizens can only trust their representatives if the tools for the exercise of distrust reassure them that it is sensible to trust. And is only sensible to trust if the exercise of "institutionalized distrust" is possible and if it has empirical consequences. "Institutionalized distrust" is then a necessary condition for the sustainability of the trust required in representation.[5] Thus, when accountability and rights claims take place but political authorities are able to block, elude, or prevent the imposition of any type of sanction, the multiplication of experiences of social accountability may result in the implosion of the representative linkage rather than in its reinforcement. In these cases, the continuous and persistent exercise of distrust ends up putting into question rather than reinforcing the representative linkage. Peruzzotti's analyses of the recent Argentine crisis eloquently show the deleterious effects social accountability mechanisms may have when continuous and persistent claims are repeatedly disregarded.[6] We can conclude, then, that the long-run effects of social accountability experiences on democratic rule are contingent on the outcomes they achieve and that both implosion and reinforcement of the representative link are likely outcomes of its exercise.

Under what conditions do social accountability mechanisms produce positive accountability outcomes? In other words, what conditions facilitate their success or failure? The case studies presented here indicate that the effectiveness of social accountability mechanisms appears to be related (1) to the mobilization and organization of uncoordinated public opinions, (2) to the interaction among different strategies and mechanisms of accountability, and (3) to the existence of institutions with the ability to enforce sanctions. As we have mentioned, from the citizens' point of view, one of the advantages of social accountability mechanisms is that to pursue accountability claims they do not have to fulfill majoritarian requirements. Intensity and noise are necessary conditions for claimants to be heard, but they do not warrant their success. Uncoordinated and isolated voices can only be successful in achieving accountability outcomes if they are able to show some threatening potential—that is, if the initially lonely and vocal claims can become or are perceived as a threat that might jeopardize a politician's career or the prestige of an agency or administration. While intensity and noncoordination allow isolated actors to introduce accountability claims and topics into the public agenda, achievement of accountability outcomes depends on their transformation into massive and likely threatening opinions. Thus, while at the outset citizens advancing social accountability claims can elude the difficulties involved in the collective organization of noncoordinated and isolated actors, in the end their success is tied to their ability to mobilize the support of a considerable sector of public opinion. For voice to become a threat, it has to become organized and massive, and unless it does, it cannot threaten the imposition of reputation costs, nor can it activate preemptive or defensive behaviors by public officials. Thus, even though the initiation of social accountability processes can bypass the representative difficulties imposed by horizontal and vertical mechanisms, their success depends in the end on the collective organization of the claimants.[7]

The cases also show that achievement of outcomes through social mechanisms depends on the interaction among different accountability strategies and different types of accountability.[8] For success to take place, interactions must occur not only among different social accountability strategies (mobilizational, mediatic, and judicial) but also among the different types of accountability. Mobilizational strategies, for example, feed media-based ones, which in turn help activate or oversee judicial ones. This process of "multiple activation" and interaction among strategies is critical for the achievement of accountability outcomes.[9] Unless social accountability mechanisms activate "fire alarms" and make claims visible, the threat of reputation sanctions cannot be established. In the absence of a symbolic threat, the incentives for public authorities to consider the possible costs of their actions are lacking. Once mediatic and mobilizational strategies are able to establish reputation threats, it is likely that electoral preference, and in turn electoral results, may change. It follows, then, that the success of social mechanisms is critical for the imposition of electoral accountability and for the breakdown of the stalemates that paralyze or prevent the workings of horizontal mechanisms. Thus, even if we were to concentrate the analysis on the performance of electoral or horizontal mechanisms, their relationships and interactions with social mechanisms cannot be disregarded insofar as their activation is, to a certain extent, subordinate to their impact on the organization of electoral preferences.

A final condition needs to be considered. The success of social accountability mechanisms requires the existence of institutions with the ability to impose sanctions. At least in the Latin American region, the emergence of social accountability mechanisms is related to the existence of institutional deficits. Given the arguments advanced in this volume, where the emergence of social accountability mechanisms is sometimes analyzed as an alternative tool for confronting institutional deficits, the existence of institutions with sanctioning abilities can be read as an inconsistent requirement. Furthermore, social accountability mechanisms have been analyzed as processes that not only could lead to the control of public policies but could also contribute to the reconstruction of weak and questioned institutions. Is this, then, a contradictory and inconsistent requirement? Does it make sense to assert that the success of social accountability mechanisms requires institutions when what is being denounced is the lack of the required institutions? In our view, this apparent contradiction rests on a mistaken diagnosis about the ways institutions operate. In this regard, it should be noted that actors exercising social accountability mechanisms might acknowledge institutional deficits in certain arenas, while at the same time they recognize and resort to existing institutional capacities in other scenarios. Indeed, their social accountability strategies are usually oriented toward the mobilization and activation of certain institutions with the goal of addressing institutional deficits or wrongdoings in some other arenas. For example, local movements in "brown areas" might resort to national institutional arenas to denounce the faulty operation of local institutions. Actors and citizens' organizations realize this, and they organize their social accountability strategies in ways that allow them to use the opportunities found in a complex and heterogeneous institutional arena to achieve their results. They use the diverse opportunities found in different internal institutional arenas (the strategy of multiple activation), and when no internal arena is available, they call for the intervention of international institutions. In some cases, this has meant strategies in which operating actors with claims regarding provincial situations call for the intervention of national institutions in order to readdress their local claims.[10] In others, when civic actors face a hostile domestic institutional environment, they resort to international allies in order to influence domestic politics.[11] Although no success is guaranteed, the actors exercising social accountability mechanisms know that the threat of some sort of institutional sanction is an important complement to a reputation threat. They know that while they lack the ability to directly impose institutional sanctions, their actions can nevertheless activate domestic or international institutions "with teeth" or with considerable political influence. Once we understand that institutions operate in separate yet interconnected arenas, the inconsistency of the assertion regarding institutions' need for the success of social accountability mechanisms is defused, and the specific relationship social mechanisms have with institutions is revealed.

While more research is needed to fully understand how these innovative forms of control operate and how they might contribute to the development of more accountable governments, the case studies presented in this volume clearly show that the notion of social accountability provides democratization theory with a useful conceptual tool that can help us rethink established assumptions about the problem of political accountability and shed new light on the complex and continuous task of re-creating and perfecting representative arrangements.

NOTES

1. Enrique Peruzzotti, "Demanding Accountable Government: Citizens, Politicians and the Perils of Representative Democracy in Argentina," in Steve Levitsky and Victoria Murillo, eds., *Argentine Democracy: The Politics of Institutional Weakness* (University Park: Pennsylvania State University Press, 2005).

2. Andreas Schedler, "Conceptualizing Accountability," in Andreas Schedler, Larry Diamond, and Marc Plattner, eds., *The Self-Restraining State: Power and Accountability in New Democracies* (Boulder: Lynne Rienner, 1999).

3. The question about how much trust and distrust a society can bear has been addressed by authors such as Albert Hirschman, "Los Conflictos Sociales como Pilares de la Sociedad de Mercado Democrática," *Agora* 4 (1996); Gabriel Almond and Sydney Verba, *The Civic Culture* (Princeton: Princeton University Press, 1963); and Margaret Levy, "A State of Trust" (European University Institute, working paper 96/23, 1996).

4. See Guillermo O'Donnell, "Horizontal Accountability: The Legal Institutionalization of Mistrust," in Scott Mainwaring and Christopher Welna, eds., *Democratic Accountability in Latin America* (Oxford: Oxford University Press, 2003).

5. See Piotr Sztompka, *Trust: A Sociological Theory* (Cambridge: Cambridge University Press, 1999); Enrique Peruzzotti, "Demanding Accountable Government."

6. See Peruzzotti's contribution to this volume and "Demanding Accountable Government."

7. See Mark Irving Lichbach, *The Rebel's Dilemma* (Ann Arbor: University of Michigan Press, 1998).

8. See O'Donnell, "Horizontal Accountability," 49.

9. See the chapter by Ana Tereza Lemos-Nelson and Jorge Zaverucha in this volume.

10. See, e.g., the Carrasco case analyzed here by Jacqueline Behrend or the María Soledad case analyzed in Catalina Smulovitz and Enrique Peruzzotti, "Societal and Horizontal Controls: Notes about a Fruitful Relationship" in Mainwaring and Welna, *Democratic Accountability in Latin America.*

11. See in this regard Margaret Keck and Kathryn Sikkink, *Activists beyond Borders: Advocacy Networks in International Politics* (Ithaca: Cornell University Press, 1998).

CONTRIBUTORS

Andrew Arato is professor of sociology at the New School for Social Research. He is the author of *Civil Society, Constitution, and Legitimacy* (Rowman and Littlefield, 2000) and *From Marxism to Democratic Politics* (M. E. Sharpe, 1993) and coauthor (with Jean Cohen) of *Civil Society and Political Theory* (MIT Press, 1992). He also serves as editor of *Constellations: An International Journal of Critical and Democratic Theory.*

Jacqueline Behrend is a D.Phil. candidate in politics at the University of Oxford and a CONICET scholar. She received her first degree in political science from the University of Buenos Aires and holds an M.Phil. in Latin American studies from the University of Oxford. She has taught at the University of Buenos Aires and is currently writing a thesis on social protest and provincial politics in Argentina. Her past research has focused on social protest and mobilization, and she has also published articles on provincial politics in Argentina.

Rosangela Batista Calvancanti is a researcher at the Instituto de Estudos Economicos, Sociaes e Politicos de São Paulo, Brazil. She is the author of *Ciudadania e acesso à justiça* (IDESP, 1999).

Claudio A. Fuentes has earned a Ph.D. in political science (University of North Carolina at Chapel Hill) and one in history (Universidad Católica de Chile). He is currently director of the Latin American Faculty of Social Science (FLACSO-Chile). Among his most recent publications are the edited volume *Promesas de Cambio: Izquierda y Derecha en el Chile Contemporáneo* (Editorial Universitaria, FLACSO, 2003) and "After Pinochet: Civilian Policies toward the Military in the 1990s Chilean Democracy," *Journal of Interamerican Studies and World Affairs* 42, no. 3 (2000).

Nuria Cunill Grau is the director of the Program for Documentation, Information, and Editorial Production at the Latin American Centre for Development Administration (CLAD), Caracas, Venezuela. She is the author of *Repensando lo Público a Través de la Sociedad: Nuevas Formas de Gestión Pública y Representación Social* (Nueva Sociedad, 1997) and *Participación Ciudadana: Dilemas y Perspectivas para la Democratización en los Estados Latinoamericanos* (CLAD, 1991).

Ana Tereza Lemos-Nelson received her Ph.D. in government and international studies from the University of Notre Dame. She is currently an adjunct professor in the Department of Social Sciences at the Federal University of Rio Grande do Norte, Brazil, where she is also coordinator of the Interdisciplinary Research Center for International Human Rights. She is the author of several articles on human rights and public security in national and international journals.

Guillermo O'Donnell is Helen Kellogg Professor of Government and International Studies at the University of Notre Dame and a Fellow of the American Academy of Arts and Letters. He is the author of *Modernization and Bureaucratic Authoritarianism* (Institute of International Studies, University of California, 1972), *Estado Burocrático Autoritario* (Editorial de Belgrano, 1982), and *Contrapuntos: Ensayos Escogidos sobre Autoritarismo y Democratización* (Paidos, 1997); coauthor (with Phillippe C. Schmitter and Lawrence Whitehead) of *Transitions from Authoritarian Rule* (The Johns Hopkins University Press, 1986); and coeditor (with, respectively, Juan E. Méndez and Paulo Sérgio Pinheiro, and Víktor E. Tokman) of *The (Un)Rule of Law and the Underprivileged in Latin America* (University of Notre Dame Press, 1999) and *Poverty and Inequality in Latin America* (University of Notre Dame Press, 1998).

Alberto J. Olvera Rivera is a researcher at the Social Research Institute of Universidad Veracruzana, Mexico. He is the editor of *La Sociedad Civil: De la Teoría a la Realidad* (Colegio de Mexico, 1999) and a member of the editorial committee of *Metapolítica.*

Enrique Peruzzotti is a professor in the Department of Political Science and International Studies, Torcuato Di Tella University, Buenos Aires. He has published articles on democratic theory, civil society, and democratization in Latin America in the *Journal of Democracy,* the *Journal of Latin American Studies, Constellations: An International Journal of Critical and Democratic Theory, Thesis Eleven, Citizenship Studies, Lua Nova,* the *Journal of Third World Studies, Politica y Gobierno, Rex Publica,* and *Revista Mexicana de Sociología.*

Adam Przeworski is a professor of politics at New York University and a Fellow of the American Academy of Arts and Sciences. He is the author of *Democracy and the Market: Political and Economic Reforms in Eastern Europe and Latin America* (Cambridge University Press, 1995) and *Sustainable Democracy* (Cambridge University Press, 1995); coauthor (with Luiz Carlos Bresser Pereira and José María Maravall) of *Economic Reforms in New Democracies: A Social Democratic Approach* (Cambridge University Press, 1993); and coeditor (with Susan C. Stokes and Bernard Manin) of *Democracy, Accountability and Representation* (Cambridge University Press, 1999).

Catalina Smulovitz is director of the Department of Political Science and International Studies, Torcuato Di Tella University, Buenos Aires. She is the author of

Oposición y Gobierno: Los Años de Frondizi (CEAL, 1987) and of articles on judicial power, constitutionalism, and citizenship in Latin America that have appeared in *La Nueva Matriz Política Argentina* (ed. Carlos Acuña; Nueva Visión, 1995) and in the *Journal of Democracy, Desarrollo Económico,* and *Agora.*

Silvio R. Waisbord is Senior Program Officer at the Academy for Educational Development. He is the author of *Watchdog Journalism in South America: News, Accountability, and Democracy* (Columbia University Press, 2000) and *El Gran Desfile: Campañas Electorales y Medios de Comunicación* (Editorial Sudamericana, 1995).

Jorge Zaverucha received his Ph.D. in political science from the University of Chicago. He was a visiting professor at the Department of Government at the University of Texas, Austin. He has received grants from the MacArthur Foundation, the Ford Foundation, and the Mellon Foundation and a Fulbright. He presently teaches at the Federal University of Pernambuco (UFPE), heads the Center for Study of Coercive Institutions at UFPE, and is a senior researcher at the Conselho Nacional de Desenvolvimento Científico e Teconológico. He has published the following books: *Rumor de Sabres: Control Civil ou Tutela Militar? Estudo Comparativo das Transições Democráticas no Brasil, na Argentina e na Espanha* (Editora Atica, 1994), *Frágil Democracia: Collor, Itamar, FHC e os Militares (1990–1998)* (Civilização Brasileira, 2000), *Polícia Civil de Pernambuco: O Desafio da Reforma* (Editora da Universidade Federal de Pernambuco, 2003), and *FHC, Forças Armadas e Polícia: Entre o Autoritarismo e a Democracia* (Civilização Brasileira, forthcoming). He also edited the books *Democracia e Instituições Políticas Brasileiras no Final do Século XX* (Edições Bagaço, 1998) and (with Maria Rosário Barros) *Política de Segurança Pública* (Massangana, 2002).

INDEX